Entrepreneurship
IN ACTION

Entrepreneurship
IN ACTION

MARY COULTER
SOUTHWEST MISSOURI STATE UNIVERSITY

Prentice
Hall

Upper Saddle River, New Jersey 07458

Library of Congress Cataloging-in-Publication Data

Coulter, Mary K.

    Entrepreneurship in action / Mary K. Coulter.

      p.   cm.

    Includes index.

    ISBN 0–13–946088–8 (pbk.)

    1. New business enterprises.   2. Entrepreneurship.   I. Title.

HD62.5.C65   2000

658.1′1—dc21   00-055780

Executive Editor: David Shafer
Managing Editor (Editorial): Jennifer Glennon
Editorial Assistant: Kim Marsden
Assistant Editor: Michele Foresta
Media Project Manager: Michele Faranda
Senior Marketing Manager: Michael Campbell
Managing Editor (Production): Judy Leale
Production Editor: Emma Moore
Permissions Coordinator: Suzanne Grappi
Production Assistant: Keri Jean
Associate Director, Manufacturing: Vincent Scelta
Production Manager: Arnold Vila
Manufacturing Buyer: Diane Peirano
Senior Designer: Steve Frim
Design Manager: Patricia Smythe
Interior Design: SettingPace
Cover Design: Steve Frim
Cover Art/Photo: Tony Stone Images
Associate Director, Multimedia Production: Karen Goldsmith
Manager, Print Production: Christina Mahon
Composition: Rainbow Graphics

10 9 8 7 6 5 4 3 2 1
ISBN 0-13-946088-8

To Jan Strube and the late Curt Strube—
the two best entrepreneurs I know!

Brief Contents

Contents

CHAPTER 2: THE CONTEXT OF ENTREPRENEURSHIP   32

Issues Affecting Entrepreneurship in Action   33

The new economy   33

Legal environment   45

Changing world of work   48

Social responsibility and ethics   50

Identifying Environmental Opportunities   53

Understanding Competitive Advantage   56

Chapter Summary   57

Key Terms   58

Sweat Equity   60

Entrepreneurship in Action Cases   61

Pedagogical Material

SECTION 2   ENTREPRENEURIAL VENTURES— START-UP ISSUES   66

CHAPTER 3: RESEARCHING THE VENTURE'S FEASIBILITY   66

Pedagogical Material

CHAPTER 4: PLANNING THE VENTURE   104

CHAPTER 5: ORGANIZING THE VENTURE   134

Pedagogical Material

CHAPTER 6: LAUNCHING THE VENTURE   166

Pedagogical Material

SECTION 3   MANAGING THE ENTREPRENEURIAL VENTURE   200

CHAPTER 7: MANAGING PROCESSES   200

Pedagogical Material

CHAPTER 8: MANAGING PEOPLE 242

Pedagogical Material

CHAPTER 9: MANAGING GROWTH AND OTHER ENTREPRENEURIAL CHALLENGES   282

Pedagogical Material

Preface

Welcome to the first edition of *Entrepreneurship in Action*! I'm very excited about bringing you this book. I believe it's unlike any other entrepreneurship textbook available on the market. Why? Because it emphasizes, explains, and celebrates the realities of being an entrepreneur—it shows entrepreneurship *in action*. I wrote this book because I felt there was a definite need for a book that conveyed the exciting realities of entrepreneurship. Entrepreneurship is such a fascinating topic—why not have a book that brings that excitement to students studying entrepreneurship? How does *Entrepreneurship in Action* do this? I think my book's unique features do just that and I'd like to describe these features for you.

Chapter-Opening Entrepreneurship in Action Case

Every chapter opens with a description of a real entrepreneur in action, facing the challenges that entrepreneurs must deal with, and making good and even some not-so-good decisions. The entrepreneurs profiled include Dineh Mohajer of Hard Candy (Chapter 1), Jeff Bezos of Amazon.com (Chapter 2), Brenda Laurel of Purple Moon (Chapter 3), Liisa Joronen of SOL Cleaning Service (Chapter 4), Bill Gross of idealab! (Chapter 5), Nicholas Graham of Joe Boxer Company (Chapter 6), John Healy of *Vintage Bike* magazine and Coventry Spares (Chapter 7), Ted Castle of Rhino Foods (Chapter 8), and William Williams of Glory Foods (Chapter 9). Each case ties in to the chapter material and is referenced at various points throughout the chapter. These fun stories relate the excitement of the entrepreneurial adventure. It certainly *is* an adventure that you're embarking on!

Entrepreneurs in Action

This chapter box theme provides examples of entrepreneurs from different types and sizes of entrepreneurial ventures. You'll discover what's involved with being an entrepreneur, and you'll read about different entrepreneurial approaches and philosophies. Again, it's another way to see entrepreneurship *in action*.

Rapid Review

I've also used this innovation in my other textbooks (*Management* by Stephen P. Robbins and Mary Coulter; and *Strategic Management in Action*). In multiple places throughout each chapter, you'll find a box that lists review questions addressing the material that you've just read. These questions will help you review and assess whether you understand the material you've just read. I believe that you'll find this feature to be a convenient and useful way to review and reinforce key chapter information.

FYI (For Your Information)

This chapter box theme provides information about a particularly interesting entrepreneurial topic or idea. Some of the FYIs include male versus female entrepreneurs, e-commerce, trend spotting, building a healthy culture, the ABCs of trademarks and patents, speed counts, delegating like a pro, combating sexual harassment, and when success is failure. There are many other interesting and fascinating entrepreneurial topics covered as well.

The Grey Zone

Ethical and social responsibility issues challenge entrepreneurs in their entrepreneurial pursuits. This chapter box theme describes some of these issues. You don't just read about the issues; you're also asked to think critically about what you would do in this situation. As you'll find out, there are no easy answers when it comes to these grey zone dilemmas.

Global Perspectives

This chapter box theme describes entrepreneurs *in action*, with the focus on global entrepreneurs and entrepreneurship. From a movie theater chain in Mexico to a spice empire in South Africa, you'll discover that entrepreneurship is a global phenomenon.

Sweat Equity

You may have heard the term *sweat equity* before. It refers to the hard work and effort—the sweat—an entrepreneur puts into an entrepreneurial venture in order to build equity value. This end-of-chapter feature presents five assignments that you must "sweat" to complete. These sweat equity assignments cover a broad spectrum of entrepreneurial topics. Many involve writing brief research papers or researching a topic on the Web. I tried to design these assignments to show you the reality of entrepreneurship—again, entrepreneurship *in action*.

Entrepreneurship in Action Cases

These *Entrepreneurship in Action* cases provide descriptions of entrepreneurs and the challenges and issues they're facing. Discussion questions at the end of each case get you "into" the case and ask for your input on the challenges, issues, and dilemmas that are presented. Three of these cases are in every chapter—one is the chapter-opening *Entrepreneurship in Action* case—and they cover a broad spectrum of entrepreneurial businesses. Some examples of the entrepreneurial ventures described include a wine importer, a manufacturer of foam advertising structures, and a CPA firm. These cases are fun to read and provide another dose of entrepreneurship *in action*.

Video Cases

In addition to the written *Entrepreneurship in Action* cases, there are two video cases presented at the end of every chapter. The actual videos are segments from the *Small Business 2000* television series. The written cases include discussion questions for you to answer. These video cases are also an excellent way to really see entrepreneurship *in action*. You'll hear the voices and see these real-life entrepreneurs as they deal with current issues and challenges.

Killer Apps Appendix

The Killer Apps Appendix provides some additional information to help you in your journey to being a successful entrepreneur. There are four major parts included in the Appendix. First, some additional information about business plans is provided. Then, a section is devoted to explaining the essentials of the evolution of e-business and the implications of e-business design for entrepreneurial organizations. Next, a section provides an annotated list of entrepreneurship Web sites. Finally, additional cases describe entrepreneurs in action that you can read for your own enjoyment and learning or that your professor may assign you to read and analyze.

As you can see by the descriptions of all the unique features in *Entrepreneurship in Action*, I've tried to provide you as close an experience to what it's like to be an *entrepreneur in action*, other than actually being one. I truly hope that the excitement and exhilaration of being an entrepreneur comes through and motivates you to pursue the fun, but demanding, journey of becoming one.

I need to thank a number of people for their contributions to this book. Without them, *Entrepreneurship in Action* wouldn't be here. First and foremost, I'd like to thank my students, past and present, who always challenge me to think about how I present information to them in class. They have made me a better communicator because I then try to write in such a way that topics and concepts are explained clearly—and, in an interesting and fun fashion! I'd also like to thank my department head, Barry Wisdom, and my college dean, Ron Bottin. Your support and encouragement mean a lot to me. Of course, there are my departmental secretaries, Carole Hale and Anita Looney. You ladies are *super* to work with. And, Anita, a special "thank you" for all those wonderful figures and tables you created for me! You are truly a word processing wizard!

Then, I'd like to recognize the individuals who provided me with intelligent and thorough reviews. They are as follows: Sol Ahiarah, Buffalo State University; Susan J. Fox-Wolfgramm, San Francisco State University; Harriet Stephenson, Seattle University; and Richard L. McCline, San Francisco State University. I sincerely appreciate your insights into my proposed book. I know the final product is better because of your suggestions! Thank you!

Supplements

- **Instructor's Manual with Test Item File**
  The Instructor's Manual contains Learning Objectives, Expanding Chapter Outlines with teaching tips and highlighted text features, and teaching notes to end-of-chapter material for each chapter in the text. Each Test Item File chapter contains true/false, multiple choice, chapter essay, and case essay questions. Together, the questions cover the content of each chapter in a variety of ways providing flexibility in testing the students' knowledge of the text.
- **Companion Web site**
  The Prentice Hall Companion Web site features an interactive and exciting online student study guide. Students can access multiple choice, true/false, and Internet-based essay questions that accompany each chapter in the text. Objective

questions are scored online, and incorrect answers are keyed to the text for student review. For more information, contact your local sales representative.
- **Small Business 2000 video**
  Small Business 2000 segments feature inside perspectives on real entrepreneurs and their experiences both creating and maintaining small businesses. Two SB2000 segments are provided for each chapter in the text for a total of eighteen segments.
- **Instructor's Resource CD-ROM containing electronic Instructor's Manual, computerized Win/PH Test Manager, and PowerPoint Electronic Transparencies**
  Containing all of the questions in the printed Test Item File, Test Manager is a comprehensive suite of tools for testing and assessment. Test Manager allows educators to easily create and distribute tests for their courses, either by printing and distributing through traditional methods, or by online delivery via a Local Area Network (LAN) server. The PowerPoint Electronic Transparencies contain a comprehensive package of text outlines and figures corresponding to the text and are designed to aid the educator and supplement in-class lectures.

Acknowledgments

I'd also like to thank the wonderful people at Prentice Hall, my publisher. As usual, all of you have been just super to work with! First off, there's my local sales representative, Shawna Kelly, who encouraged me to write this book. Shawna, thanks for believing in me and being such a good friend. Then, a big THANK YOU to my senior editor/ acquisitions editor, David Shafer. David, you were great (as usual)! Thanks for being my sounding board and helping me make this book what it is! A special thank-you to Natalie Anderson for her unwavering support and . . . well, just for being a friend! Thanks Natalie! Then, there's the rest of the management team at the home office. Thank you Kim Marsden for always sending me what I needed on a moment's notice! Thanks Michele Foresta for your support and follow-up on the all-important supplements. Thanks to Jennifer Glennon for helping bring this book to reality! And, of course, I must give a big THANKS to Michael Campbell, my marketing manager. Michael, you are so knowledgeable and so good to work with! Thanks for all your great ideas! Then, of course, I cannot forget the incredibly talented and competent production people. Thank you, Judy Leale. You were great to work with (as always!)! Then, thanks to Emma Moore and Suzanne Grappi and the other members of the production team. You helped make this book a reality! I'd also like to thank the individuals involved with creating the excellent supplements that accompany this book. These people include Len Nass, Monmouth University for creating the Instructor's Manual and Tom Kaplan, Fairleigh Dickinson University–Madison for creating the Test Item file, Companion Web site, and the PowerPoint transparencies. Thank you for your hard work!

Finally, I'd like to say THANKS to my family—my wonderful and truly supportive husband, Ron, and my bright, beautiful, and remarkably well-adjusted daughters Sarah and Katie. Sarah and Katie, through junior high basketball season, cheerleading, pom squad practices and performances, Sarah getting her driver's license, and all the other fun times of being teenagers, you two have been very patient with me and my hectic schedule. Thanks for everything that you do to help. All three of you provide that much-needed balance to my life. What I've been able to do, I couldn't have done without the three of you! I love you all very much!

Mary Coulter
Southwest Missouri State University

Entrepreneurship
IN ACTION

1

ENTREPRENEURS AND ENTREPRENEURSHIP

LEARNING OBJECTIVES

After reading this chapter, you should be able to:

1. Define entrepreneurship.
2. Describe the historical perspectives of entrepreneurship.
3. Distinguish between entrepreneurship and intrapreneurship.
4. Explain what entrepreneurial ventures are and how they're different from small businesses.
5. Explain why entrepreneurship is important.
6. Outline the steps in the entrepreneurial process.
7. Describe who entrepreneurs are and what they do.
8. Discuss the rewards and challenges of being an entrepreneur.

ENTREPRENEURSHIP IN ACTION CASE #1

Nailing Down Success

She's been called a fashion renegade, but that hasn't stopped this Generation Xer from achieving success as CEO of her own company in a tough and competitive industry.[1] Dineh Mohajer runs her business her way and thumbs her nose at convention. With product names such as Dog, Dork, Sissy, and Trailer Trash, Mohajer's company, Hard Candy, has carved out a niche in the staid and conservative nail polish industry. What's her story?

As a fashion-conscious 22-year-old, Mohajer hated the brilliant red nail polishes that were for sale in stores. The bright colors clashed with her trendy pastel-colored clothing. Instead, she wanted pastel nail colors that would match what she was wearing. When she couldn't find the nail polish colors she was looking for, Mohajer decided to mix up her own. She did just that in her kitchen, mixing a bit of white polish with blue dye and painting

Maybe you've had an experience like Dineh Mohajer did—wanting a product or service that simply did not exist. Did you do something about it? Did you attempt to create or locate the product? Or maybe *your* personal dream is to be your own boss and not have to answer to someone else at work; to have control over what you do, how you do it, and how much you earn. Whatever your personal reason is for taking this course and reading this book, there's no doubt that entrepreneurs and entrepreneurship are playing important roles in today's global business environment. What *is* entrepreneurship and who *are* entrepreneurs? These are the main topics that we're going to look at in this chapter. So whether you want to be the next Michael Dell, Bill Gates, Ted Turner, or Dineh Mohajer, or whether you just want to pursue your own personal dreams, understanding entrepreneurship in action is an important first step!

WHAT IS ENTREPRENEURSHIP?

Practically everywhere you turn these days, you'll read or hear about entrepreneurs. Go pick up a current newspaper or general newsmagazine. Or log on to one of the World Wide Web's news sites. Chances are you'll find at least one story (and probably many more) about an entrepreneur or an entrepreneurial business. Entrepreneurship is a popular topic these days! But exactly what is it? Let's see if we can answer this by looking at how entrepreneurship is defined.

Definition of Entrepreneurship

If someone asked you right now to describe what you think entrepreneurship is, what would you say? How would you go about describing it? Defining entrepreneurship may seem a simple and easy task. But it isn't! There are about as many definitions of entrepreneurship as there are people who have written about the subject! Everyone seems to have his or her own ideas about what it is and how best to describe it. Let's explore some of these myriad ways that entrepreneurship has been defined.

Entrepreneurship has long been described by researchers and writers with terms such as *new, innovative, flexible, dynamic, creative,* and *risk-taking.* Many authors have said that identifying and pursuing opportunities is an important part of entrepreneurship.[2] Other authors have said that entrepreneurship involves the creation of value, the process of

her own creation on her nails. The colors Mohajer created caught the eyes of her friends and they all wanted to know where they could get some. Sensing that she might have a "hot" product on her hands, Mohajer brought samples of her homemade nail polishes to Fred Segal, a chain of trendy shops in Los Angeles. As soon as Mohajer's nail polishes hit the store shelves, customers were snapping them up at $18 a bottle. Immediately, Segal's owner called Mohajer and told her to deliver 200 more bottles. Working frantically for two days almost around-the-clock, Mohajer delivered the 200 bottles of pale yellow, violet, and blue polish. Evidently, Mohajer's nail polishes had captured the attention of customers as these bottles also flew out the door. And Dineh Mohajer, entrepreneur, was on her way to nailing down success!

starting or growing a new profit-making business, the process of providing a new product or service, and the intentional creation of value through organization by an individual contributor or small group of partners.[3] Another definition of entrepreneurship that's been used is "the process of creating something different with value by devoting the necessary time and effort, assuming the accompanying financial, psychological, and social risks, and receiving the resulting rewards of monetary and personal satisfaction."[4] Even the professional association for the management academic discipline (the Academy of Management) has come up with its own broad definition of entrepreneurship: "the creation and management of new businesses, small businesses, and family businesses."[5] We could also cite numerous other definitions. But even given this wide variety of definitions of entrepreneurship, we can observe some common themes running through them.[6] (See Figure 1-1.) Let's look closer at each of these common themes so we can get a better understanding of what entrepreneurship is.

One of the common themes found in the definitions of entrepreneurship recognizes the important role that the entrepreneur plays. There's no doubt that without a person who's willing to do what an entrepreneur does, there would be no entrepreneurship! Because the entrepreneur is a critical element in entrepreneurship in action, we're going to wait and discuss more completely later in the chapter who entrepreneurs are and what they do. But keep in mind that entrepreneurship isn't possible without an entrepreneur! Any definition should recognize that.

Another common definitional theme of entrepreneurship is innovation. Entrepreneurship involves changing, revolutionizing, transforming, and introducing new approaches. Think back to what Dineh Mohajer did with her pastel-

Figure 1-1

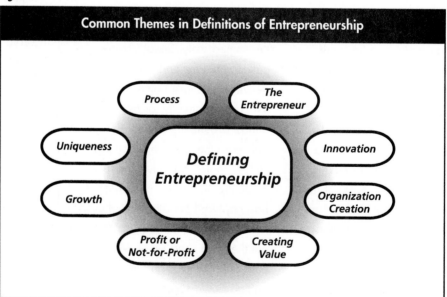

Common Themes in Definitions of Entrepreneurship

- Process
- The Entrepreneur
- Uniqueness
- Innovation
- **Defining Entrepreneurship**
- Growth
- Organization Creation
- Profit or Not-for-Profit
- Creating Value

Source: Based on W. B. Gartner, "What Are We Talking About When We Talk About Entrepreneurship?" *Journal of Business Venturing,* Vol. 5, 1990, pp. 15–28.

colored nail polishes. These products were not available in the marketplace—this particular customer need was not being met. So she innovated, created a new product, and in the process, revolutionized the nail polish industry. Entrepreneurship involves innovation.

The third common theme that we see in definitions of entrepreneurship is organization creation. What is this and what does it have to do with entrepreneurship? In order to pursue the opportunities for innovation and creating value, there must be some organized and planned efforts and actions. Without the creation of some type of organized effort—whether as an individual or as a group of individuals—the ability to marshall resources to pursue the entrepreneurial opportunity will be limited, if not completely shut off. So any definition of entrepreneurship must recognize that some organized approach is necessary.

Next, we find that the process of creating value is a common theme in describing entrepreneurship. What does it mean to "create value"? One interpretation is that through entrepreneurship, new products, services, transactions, approaches, resources, technologies, and markets are created that contribute some value to some community or marketplace.[7] Through entrepreneurship, resources are transformed into outputs such as products or services. During this transformation process, value is created because the entrepreneur is fashioning something worthwhile and useful. Another way to view this is that value is also created through the financial exchange as customers purchase the entrepreneurial organization's products and services.

Another theme often found in definitions of entrepreneurship is a recognition that entrepreneurship can take place in both profit and not-for-profit environments. Although we tend to assume that entrepreneurial activity is geared at making a profit (and much of it is), entrepreneurship can occur in social service agencies, in community arts organizations, or in any other type of not-for-profit setting. For example, Susana Valadez, an anthropologist by training but now an avid entrepreneur, established an enterprise to help revitalize the Huichol Indian tribe's jewelry-making tradition. Jewelry pieces created by artisans at the Huichol Center for Cultural Survival and Traditional Arts are big hits in the United States, Europe, and Japan. Even film stars have been seen wearing the intricately beaded jewelry. The revenues from the jewelry sales go to help Huichol Indian families and to preserve the ancient culture and arts of this tribe.[8]

The next common theme in entrepreneurship definitions is growth. One major difference between entrepreneurial ventures and other small businesses is the emphasis on growth. Entrepreneurship is about growing a business and pursuing opportunities as they arise. It's not about standing still or being content to stay in one market or with one product. Entrepreneurship involves growth.

Another theme commonly found in definitions of entrepreneurship is that of uniqueness. Entrepreneurship is fundamentally concerned with variation—the new combinations and new approaches that entrepreneurs bring to life. Therefore, the very nature of entrepreneurship infers differences, not the norm.[9] Through entrepreneurship, unique products are created and unique ways of doing things are pursued. Entrepreneurship isn't merely copying or imitating what others have done. It's doing something new, something untested and untried, something unique.

The final theme commonly found in definitions of entrepreneurship is the recognition that it *is* a process. A process very simply is a set of ongoing decisions and actions. Entrepreneurship is not a one-time phenomenon; it occurs over time. It involves a series of decisions and actions from initial start-up to managing the entrepreneurial venture to even exiting it. Later in this chapter, we're going to look at the specific steps involved in the entrepreneurial process.

Now that we've looked at the common themes found in definitions of entrepreneurship, how are *we* going to define it in this book? Here's our definition of **entrepreneurship**: the process whereby an individual or a group of individuals use organized efforts and means to pursue opportunities to create value and grow by fulfilling wants and needs through innovation and uniqueness, no matter what resources are currently controlled. This definition encompasses the complex and multifaceted elements of entrepreneurship. It also alludes to many of the common themes that we just looked at.

Now that we have a good grasp of *how* entrepreneurship is defined, let's look at how it has evolved. Why look at the past? Examining the past can give us a deeper appreciation and understanding of how we view entrepreneurship today. When and how did entrepreneurship theory evolve? Figure 1-2 provides a summary time line of the development of entrepreneurship theory.

Historical Perspectives on Entrepreneurship

Entrepreneurship is not a twentieth- or twenty-first-century phenomenon, although the current high level and prevalence of interest in all things entrepreneurial would tend to make you think that it was! Early in the eighteenth century the French term *entrepreneur* was first used to describe a "go-between" or a "between-taker."

Richard Cantillon, a noted economist and author in the 1700s, is regarded by many as the originator of the term *entrepreneur*.[10] Cantillon used the term to

Figure 1-2

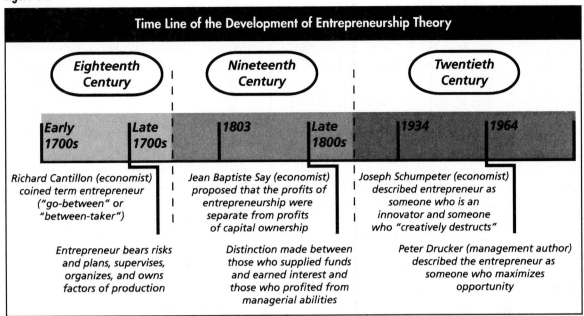

Time Line of the Development of Entrepreneurship Theory

Eighteenth Century | **Nineteenth Century** | **Twentieth Century**

Early 1700s | Late 1700s | 1803 | Late 1800s | 1934 | 1964

Richard Cantillon (economist) coined term entrepreneur ("go-between" or "between-taker")

Jean Baptiste Say (economist) proposed that the profits of entrepreneurship were separate from profits of capital ownership

Joseph Schumpeter (economist) described entrepreneur as someone who is an innovator and someone who "creatively destructs"

Entrepreneur bears risks and plans, supervises, organizes, and owns factors of production

Distinction made between those who supplied funds and earned interest and those who profited from managerial abilities

Peter Drucker (management author) described the entrepreneur as someone who maximizes opportunity

refer to a person who took an active risk-bearing role in pursuing opportunities. This individual—the entrepreneur—served as the bridge between someone who had the capital, or money, but who chose not to personally pursue those opportunities. Instead an individual (or group of individuals) financed the pursuit of opportunities and the entrepreneur served as the go-between—the active (actively involved) risk-taker. Late in the eighteenth century, the concept of entrepreneurship was expanded to include not only the bearing of risks but also the planning, supervising, organizing, and even owning the factors of production.

The nineteenth century was a fertile time for entrepreneurial activity as technological advances during the industrial revolution provided the impetus for continued inventions and innovations. Early in this century, the view that the entrepreneurial process was a unique set of actions became even more pronounced when noted economist Jean Baptiste Say proposed that the profits of entrepreneurship were distinct and separate from the profits arising from the ownership of capital. (This distinction can still be seen today if you consider the role that venture capitalists play—that is, in owning and providing capital—in supporting entrepreneurial activities.) Then, toward the end of the nineteenth century, the concept of entrepreneurship changed slightly again to distinguish between those who supplied funds and earned interest and those who profited from entrepreneurial abilities.

During the early part of the twentieth century, there wasn't much change in how the role of entrepreneurship was viewed. Entrepreneurship was still believed to be distinct and different from management. However, it wasn't until the mid-1930s that the concept of entrepreneurship added another dimension. That's when economist Joseph Schumpeter proposed that entrepreneurship involved innovations and untried technologies. He explained that what entrepreneurship involved was **creative destruction**, which is defined as the process whereby existing products, processes, ideas, and businesses are replaced with better ones.

The Grey Zone Continuing changes in technology have cut the shelf life of most employees' work skills. As wave after wave of technological innovations appear (Schumpeter's creative destruction process at work), what ethical obligations do entrepreneurs have toward worker skill obsolescence? Should an entrepreneur be concerned with the fact that his or her innovations and unique ideas might eliminate the need for certain work skills? What do you think?

Schumpeter believed that through the process of creative destruction, old, inefficient, and ineffective approaches and products were replaced with better ones. Through the destruction of the old came the creation of the new. Schumpeter proposed that entrepreneurial ventures were the driving force behind this process of creative destruction. Schumpeter's description of the process of creative destruction served to highlight further the important role that innovation plays in entrepreneurship. As our earlier definition of entrepreneurship pointed out, the concepts of innovation and uniqueness are (and have always been) integral parts of entrepreneurial activity.

The final development from the twentieth century that we want to discuss in the evolution of how we view entrepreneurship is Peter Drucker's contention that entrepreneurship involves maximizing opportunities. Drucker is a well-known, well-respected, and prolific authority on management issues. What his perspective added to the concept of entrepreneurship is that entrepreneurs recognize and act on opportunities. Drucker says that entrepreneurship doesn't just happen out of the blue but arises in response to what the entrepreneur sees as untapped and undeveloped opportunities.

Although we've looked at only a few small pieces from entrepreneurship's long and colorful past, keep in mind that the history of entrepreneurship continues to unfold. Its history is still being written today! Through ongoing research and studies of entrepreneurs and entrepreneurship, what we know about entrepreneurship continues to evolve and improve. We'll highlight many of these important research findings as we cover material throughout the rest of the text.

As we continue our search into exploring what entrepreneurship is, it may help to clarify the concept by explaining what it *isn't*. Although entrepreneurs and entrepreneurial activities have been studied for well over three centuries, there are some misconceptions about it.[11]

Misconceptions About Entrepreneurship

1. *Successful entrepreneurship takes only a great idea.* Having a great idea is only part of the equation for successful entrepreneurship. Understanding the demands of the different phases of the entrepreneurial process, taking an organized approach to developing the entrepreneurial venture, and coping with the challenges of managing the entrepreneurial venture are also key ingredients to successful entrepreneurship.

2. *Entrepreneurship is easy.* You may think that because you're pursuing your passion and you have an intense desire to succeed that it's going to be easy. However, be forewarned that entrepreneurship is *not* easy! It takes commitment, determination, effort, and hard work. Even with these qualities, it *still* isn't effortless! Entrepreneurs often encounter difficulties, but successful ones are those who can thrive in spite of the difficulties.

> ### *Entrepreneurs in Action*
>
> Eloise Blackmon of F&B Transportation in Gary, Indiana, knows how difficult being a successful entrepreneur is. As a former welfare recipient, Blackmon was well aware of the transportation problems faced by individuals who are trying to move off of public assistance to self-sufficiency. She herself faced this situation as she struggled during her one-hour lunch break to get her son from his morning kindergarten class to his afternoon day care setting. With no alternative transportation available, Blackmon had no choice but to go on welfare. However, during the time she was on welfare, Blackmon was on the phone with day care centers and elementary schools asking if other people faced the same dilemma. The response—a resounding yes! So she has made it her business to get children and people where they need to be. Every week, her vans deliver adults and children to jobs and day care centers around the city. Eloise Blackmon has worked hard to get her successful business up and running.
>
> *Source:* A. Walmac, "Reality Check," *Working Woman*, July–August, 1998, p. 32.

3. *Entrepreneurship is a risky gamble.* Because entrepreneurship involves pursuing new, untested approaches and ideas, it must be a gamble. Right? Not really. Although entrepreneurs aren't afraid to take risks, entrepreneurship involves carefully calculated risks, not unnecessary risks. In fact, there are times when successful entrepreneurship means avoiding or minimizing risks.
4. *Entrepreneurship is found only in small businesses.* Many people have the mistaken idea that entrepreneurship is associated only with small organizations. The truth is that entrepreneurship can be found in any size organization. On the other hand, just because an organization is small doesn't automatically make it entrepreneurial.
5. *Entrepreneurial ventures and small businesses are the same thing.* This misconception is so widespread that we're going to address it more completely in the next section.

Entrepreneurial Ventures and Small Business—The Differences

Many people think that entrepreneurial ventures and small businesses are one and the same. However, there are some important differences between the two. Let's look first at what a small business is.

What constitutes a "small" business? Although there is no universally accepted definition of a small business, most definitions use some quantitative measure of the number of employees or annual sales. In addition, the Small

Entrepreneurship Versus Intrapreneurship

How can a large organization be entrepreneurial in nature? Well, given an environment characterized by turbulent and chaotic markets, technological complexity, and global opportunities and threats, being entrepreneurial just may be the key to long-term success and survival! In large organizations, the process of using organized efforts and means to pursue opportunities to create value and grow by fulfilling wants and needs through innovation and uniqueness is called **intrapreneurship**. It's the pursuit of entrepreneurship within the confines of a large organization. Intrapreneurship provides large organizations the opportunities to adapt quickly to changes in the marketplace, to go in new directions without having to acquire or merge with an existing business, and to try out new products and processes. For example, at Texas Instruments Inc., its IDEA program, in which individual employees are encouraged to pursue new ideas in areas that might not be related to their assigned job responsibilities, has contributed an estimated $500 million in profits and cost savings to the company's bottom line during its almost 25-year existence. Other large organizations that are well-known for their emphasis on intrapreneurship include AT&T, DuPont, 3M, and Hewlett-Packard.

Sources: T. D. Schellhardt, "David in Goliath," *Wall Street Journal*, May 23, 1996, p. R14; C. Carrier, "Intrapreneurship in Small Business: An Exploratory Study," *Entrepreneurship Theory and Practice*, fall 1996, pp. 5–20; and T. Stevens, "Idea Dollars," *IW*, February 16, 1998, pp. 47–49.

Business Administration (SBA), a federal agency of the U.S. government that provides loans, advice, and assistance to small businesses, has different definitions for a small business depending on what industry it's in. For instance, the cutoff point for a small business in the metal can fabrication industry is 1,000 employees, whereas in the wholesale hardware industry, it's 100 employees.[12] In this book, we're going to define a **small business** as one that is independently owned, operated, and financed; has fewer than 100 employees; doesn't engage in any new or innovative practices; and has relatively little impact on its industry.[13]

Now, what constitutes an entrepreneurial venture? As we discussed previously, entrepreneurship involves using organized efforts to pursue opportunities to create value and grow by fulfilling wants and needs through innovation and uniqueness, no matter the resources currently controlled. Therefore, we're going to define an **entrepreneurial venture** as an organization that is pursuing opportunities, is characterized by innovative practices, and has profitability and growth as its main goals.

Obviously, although there are some definitional and actual overlaps between small businesses and entrepreneurial ventures, we are going to view them as different. A small business isn't necessarily entrepreneurial in nature just because it's small. To be entrepreneurial means being innovative and seeking out new opportunities. Even though entrepreneurial ventures may start small, they do pursue growth. Some new small firms may grow, but many will remain small businesses, by choice or by default.

Yes, there are some distinct differences between small businesses and entrepreneurial ventures. These differences are summarized in Table 1-1.

TABLE 1-1   Differences Between Small Businesses and Entrepreneurial Ventures

Small Business	Entrepreneurial Venture
■ Independently owned, operated, and financed	■ Innovative practices
■ Fewer than 100 employees	■ Goals are profitability and growth
■ Doesn't emphasize new or innovative practices	■ Seeks out new opportunities
■ Little impact on industry	■ Willingness to take risks

Rapid Review ◀◀|

✓ What are some of the ways that entrepreneurship has been defined by various researchers?

✓ List the common themes found in the definitions of entrepreneurship. (Hint: There are eight of them!)

✓ How are we defining entrepreneurship?

✓ What are some of the key developments in the historical development of entrepreneurship?

✓ What role does creative destruction play in entrepreneurship?

✓ List the misconceptions about entrepreneurship and address why these are misconceptions.

✓ How is entrepreneurship different from intrapreneurship? How are they the same?

✓ What is an entrepreneurial venture? How is it different from a small business?

The Current Importance of Entrepreneurship

Using any number of various information and media sources, you can access and read statistics about how many small businesses there are, how many workers they employ, and how much of the gross national economic output they're responsible for. The headlines scream the facts: Small businesses "represent over 99% of all employers, employ 52% of the private workers, provide virtually all of the net new jobs, and provide 51% of the private sector output."[14] These statistics, as collected by various research firms and government agencies, reflect the economic activity of all *small* businesses, not just that of entrepreneurial ventures. Because we've made a point of distinguishing between small businesses and entrepreneurial ventures, these statistics don't tell the entire story we want to know. Instead, let's try to look at what entrepreneurship contributes. Then the questions become: How can we measure the importance of entrepreneurship? Does entrepreneurship contribute to economic vitality? and How does it do so?

Entrepreneurship is, and continues to be, important to every industry sector in the United States and in other global economies. Its importance can be shown in three areas: innovation, number of new start-ups, and job creation.

Innovation. Innovating—a process of changing, experimenting, transforming, and revolutionizing. As we know from our earlier definition, innovation is one of the key distinguishing characteristics of entrepreneurial activity. The "creative destruction" process that's inherent in innovating leads to technological changes and employment growth.[15] Entrepreneurial firms act as these "agents of change" by providing an essential source of new and unique ideas that might otherwise go untapped.[16] Statistics back this assertion up. New small organizations generate 24 times more innovations per research and development dollar spent than do *Fortune* 500 organizations, and they account for over 95 percent of new and "radical" product developments.[17]

Global Perspectives

Is the popularity of entrepreneurship just a U.S. phenomenon? If we look at the data from other countries around the world, our answer to that question would have to be a resounding *no*! In Europe, a number of dynamic entrepreneurial companies are emerging, creating jobs, and spurring economic development even as that continent's industrial giants are laying off workers. (Sounds a lot like the United States, doesn't it?) Even in China, Japan, and Korea, entrepreneurship is flourishing! Entrepreneurs are pursuing market opportunities in spite of the difficulties of dealing with often stifling governmental policies. In Latin America, entrepreneurship is beginning to play a more important role. Given the importance of economic development to the overall long-term health of a region, it's no wonder that the number of entrepreneurial ventures is on the increase!

Sources: J. Case, "Is America Really Different?" *Inc.: The State of Small Business Special Issue*, 1996, pp. 108–9; S. Kishkovsky and E. Williamson, "Second-Class Comrades No More: Women Stoke Russia's Start-Up Boom," *Wall Street Journal*, January 30, 1997, p. A12; M. Schuman, "Korea's Grads Reject Stuffy Chaebols to Try Their Own Hand at Business," *Wall Street Journal*, June 11, 1997, p. A18; S. WuDunn, "Incubators of Creativity," *New York Times*, October 9, 1997, p. C1; J. Flynn et al., "Startups to the Rescue," *Business Week*, March 28, 1998, pp. 50–52; J. H. Christy, "Growth Comes in Small Packages," *Forbes*, June 1, 1998, pp. 166–68; and I. Johnson, "Entrepreneurs in China Hope for Relief from Stifling Policies," *Wall Street Journal*, March 11, 1999, p. A18.

The passionate drive and intense hunger of entrepreneurs to forge new directions in products and processes and to take risks set in motion a series of decisions and actions that lead to the innovations that are important for economic vitality. Without these new ideas, economic, technological, and social progress would be slow indeed.

Number of New Start-Ups. Because all businesses—whether they fit the definition of entrepreneurial or not—at one point in time were new start-ups, the most convenient measure we have of the role that entrepreneurship plays in this economic factor is to look at the number of new firms over a period of time. The assumption that we have to make, then, is that some of these new firms engage in decisions and activities that would characterize them as entrepreneurial in nature.

The latest data available on the number of new businesses are shown in Table 1-2. Looking at the data in the table, we see that since 1990 the number of new businesses has continually increased. Again, under the assumption that some of these new businesses engage in innovative practices and pursue profitability and growth as main goals—that is, they're entrepreneurial ventures—we propose that the pursuit of entrepreneurship contributed to the overall creation of new firms. Why is the creation of new firms so important? It's important because these new firms contribute to economic development through such benefits as product–process innovations, increased tax revenues, societal betterment, and job creation.

Job Creation. We know that job creation is important to the overall long-term economic health of communities, regions, and nations. Just how important are entrepreneurial ventures to job creation? Once again, the only data we have to answer that question cover all small businesses. (But presumably some of these small businesses would be considered entrepreneurial ventures.) Those data paint

TABLE 1-2 Number of New Businesses, 1990–1997*

	1990	1995	1996	1997
New Employer Firms	769,124	819,477	842,357	885,416
New Incorporations	647,675	768,180	786,482	798,917
Total	1,416,799	1,587,657	1,628,839	1,684,333
% Increase		↑2.5%	↑3.4%	

* Latest data available

Source: Based on "Small Business Answer Card 1998," *SBA Online*, **www.sba.gov/advo/stats**, September 18, 1998.

an eye-opening picture! The latest available numbers show that during the time period from 1992 to 1996, virtually *all* net new jobs were generated by small firms with fewer than 500 employees. Very small businesses (those with fewer than 20 employees) accounted for a whopping 77.2 percent of this growth![18] As you can see, new organizations were creating jobs at a torrid pace even as many of the world's largest and well-known global mega-corporations continued to downsize! Obviously, these numbers reflect the continuing importance of entrepreneurial firms as job creators.

Now that we've established how important entrepreneurship is to the rate of product and process innovations, to the number of new start-ups, and to new job creation, we need to look at how entrepreneurship takes place. Does it consist of

Entrepreneurs in Action

Si Wai Lai is making waves in Niagara Falls, New York. A native of Guanghzou, China, Lai spent $56 million to buy property in and around Niagara-on-the-Lake, Ontario, Canada. (She gets her funds from her twin brother, Jimmy Lai, who is one of Hong Kong's most successful entrepreneurs.) Although Jimmy may be putting up the dough, his sister is running the show. Her goal is to make this sleepy little hamlet a year-round tourist destination—something along the lines of Orlando, Florida. According to Lai, the natural wonder (the Falls) that brings people to this location is underleveraged. Through her innovative efforts, new businesses are sprouting and jobs are being created. What a good example of the economic miracle that can happen when entrepreneurship flourishes!

Source: J. Doebele and A. Tanzer, "Hong Kong Comes to Niagara Falls," *Forbes*, November 17, 1997, pp. 116–21.

simple, unconnected, and random acts, or is there some method and continuity to creating a new venture? Are there specific and identifiable steps that entrepreneurs follow as they start and proceed through the entrepreneurial experience? Although each entrepreneurial experience is going to be different because of differing situations and circumstances, there do appear to be common decisions and actions that entrepreneurs engage in as they get their entrepreneurial ventures up and running.

The Entrepreneurial Process

What's involved in the entrepreneurial process? Figure 1-3 illustrates the main decisions and actions that entrepreneurs deal with as they pursue their entrepreneurial ventures. From exploring the various aspects of the entrepreneurial context to identifying opportunities and possible competitive advantage(s) to starting and managing the entrepreneurial venture, entrepreneurs make decisions and engage in activities that are part and parcel of entrepreneurship in action. Let's take a closer look at each of these decisions and activities.

Exploring the Entrepreneurial Context. Why is it important to look at the entrepreneurial context? Because the context determines the "rules" of the game

Figure 1-3

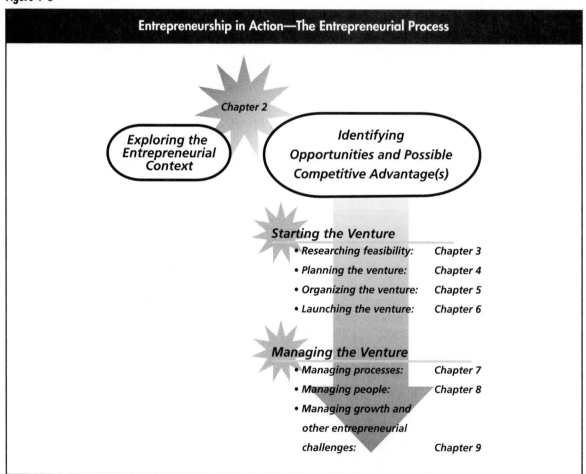

and what decisions and actions are likely to meet with success. For instance, the coach of a baseball team analyzes its specific context (factors such as the condition of the playing field, the cohesiveness of the team's players, player injuries, or maybe even the team's current rankings in its division) in contemplating what decisions and actions might work best. So, too, must entrepreneurs be aware of the external environmental context within which entrepreneurial decisions are made and actions taken. Also, it's through exploring the context that entrepreneurs confront that critically important decision—that is, identifying opportunities and possible competitive advantages. (Refer again to Figure 1-3.) Only through exploring the context can entrepreneurs uncover those untapped opportunities and potential competitive advantage(s) that may lead to the development of a potentially successful entrepreneurial venture.

Identifying Opportunities and Possible Competitive Advantage. A crucial aspect of entrepreneurship is the pursuit of perceived opportunities. What are **opportunities**? They're positive external environmental trends or changes that provide unique and distinct possibilities for innovating and creating value. Think back to our chapter-opening *Entrepreneurship in Action* case. Dineh Mohajer recognized the fashion trend of pastel colors as an opportunity to create nail polishes in those colors. However, just identifying an opportunity isn't enough. The entrepreneurial process also involves pinpointing a possible competitive advantage. A **competitive advantage** is what sets an organization apart; it's an organization's competitive edge. Having a competitive advantage is crucial for an organization's long-term success and survival. Even not-for-profit organizations (such as governmental agencies, community arts organizations, or social service groups) need something that sets them apart—something unique that they offer in order to stay in business. We'll cover the related aspects of exploring the entrepreneurial context and identifying opportunities and competitive advantage in Chapter 2.

Starting the Venture. Once entrepreneurs have explored the external environmental context and identified opportunities and possible competitive advantages, they must look at the issues involved with actually bringing their entrepreneurial venture to life. Included in this phase of the entrepreneurial process are the following activities: researching the feasibility of the venture (Chapter 3), planning the venture (Chapter 4), organizing the venture (Chapter 5), and launching the venture (Chapter 6). Each of these activities is important to being an entrepreneur in action, and we'll cover each more thoroughly in the chapter indicated.

Managing the Venture. Once the entrepreneur has the entrepreneurial venture up and running, then what? We have to recognize and understand that there's more to entrepreneurship in action than just starting the venture. An entrepreneur also must effectively manage the venture by managing processes (Chapter 7), managing people (Chapter 8), and managing growth (Chapter 9). We'll cover the intricacies of managing the entrepreneurial venture in the chapters indicated.

In addition, we need to look at some special issues facing entrepreneurs. Given the dynamic nature of the external environment and the volatility of market opportunities, entrepreneurs constantly need to keep on top of the changing landscape. One way to do this is by being a **world-class organization**, which very simply is an organization that is the best in its world at what it does. We'll cover what it means to be a world-class organization in Chapter 7. Finally, in Chapter 9,

Rapid Review ◀◀|

- ✓ What role does entrepreneurship play in innovation?
- ✓ Why is entrepreneurship important in the number of new start-ups?
- ✓ How does entrepreneurship contribute to job creation?
- ✓ Is the pursuit of entrepreneurship important only in the United States? Explain.
- ✓ Draw the entrepreneurial process model and explain it.
- ✓ What are opportunities and competitive advantage, and why are they important in entrepreneurship?
- ✓ What is a world-class organization? Why might this concept be important to entrepreneurship?

we'll look at some unique entrepreneurial situations such as minority and women-owned entrepreneurial ventures, family businesses, co-preneurs, and the challenges in the entrepreneur's personal life.

Although you may think it odd that we look at the person—the entrepreneur—in a textbook on entrepreneurship in action, actually it's that person who makes it all happen. Without that individual who's willing to take the risk to pursue an opportunity, entrepreneurship wouldn't occur! In the next section, we want to focus more closely on the person by looking at who entrepreneurs are and what they do.

WHO ARE ENTREPRENEURS AND WHAT DO THEY DO?

Describing *who* entrepreneurs are has been (and continues to be) a favorite pursuit of academic researchers and other popular business press writers, as well. One thing we need to get straight first as we look at the entrepreneur as an individual is our definition of **entrepreneur**. We're going to define an entrepreneur as someone who initiates and actively operates the entrepreneurial venture.[19] Inherent in this definition is the idea that the entrepreneur is not just the person who identifies the opportunity(ies) that are the basis for pursuing and initiating the entrepreneurial venture, but is also that person who operates the entrepreneurial venture. The entrepreneur "does" the venture as well as "dreams" it up. Now that you know how we define an entrepreneur, you might be asking yourself, Am I (or could I be) an entrepreneur? Well, maybe we can better answer that question by looking at the characteristics of entrepreneurs.

Characteristics of Entrepreneurs

How would you describe well-known entrepreneurs such as Bill Gates (of Microsoft fame), Michael Dell (founder of Dell Computer), or Dineh Mohajer (founder of Hard Candy, as described in our chapter-opening case)? Would you be apt to describe their background (demographic) profile or their personality characteristics? Or might you focus more on what made them want to be entrepreneurs—that is, what preceded their intentions to become entrepreneurs? Each of these approaches can be (and has been) used to describe entrepreneurs.[20] Let's look closer to help us get a better understanding of who entrepreneurs are.

Demographic Profile of Entrepreneurs. If we wanted to use the demographic approach to describe who entrepreneurs are, we would look at the characteristics of the individual's personal background and environment. Some of the more popular demographic factors that have been examined in various research studies of entrepreneurs include the following:

1. *Family birth order.* Studies have shown that firstborn children tend to seek out more responsibility and be high achievers, which researchers say is likely to correlate with being an entrepreneur.[21]

Male Versus Female Entrepreneurs

Just how different are male and female entrepreneurs in the way they run their businesses? One study looked at the differences between male and female entrepreneurs in the areas of planning, controlling, internal communication, human resources management, work-related tasks, customer service, networking, and on-the-job personal time. The results showed that women tended to engage in the following behaviors more often than their male counterparts:

- Controlling behavior
- Internal communication
- Human resources management
- General work-related tasks

The most surprising result? That of controlling behavior, which has long been thought to be predominantly a male trait. In this study, women actually reported more instances of assertive and controlling behavior than did the men. Another interesting result was that male entrepreneurs tended to use more on-the-job time for personal matters such as reading the newspaper, talking with drop-in visitors, and so forth.

Source: C. Mulhern, "A Different World," *Entrepreneur*, July 1998, p. 36.

2. *Gender.* Overall, studies have shown that men are much more likely to start a business than are women.[22]

3. *Work experience.* There's some evidence that having worked in a small business or having had prior entrepreneurial experience is positively related to being an entrepreneur.[23]

4. *Education.* Studies have shown that having a high school diploma sharply raises a person's odds of trying to start a business.[24]

5. *Entrepreneurial family.* Various studies have found that entrepreneurs tend to have parents who were entrepreneurial.[25]

Other demographic traits that have been studied by researchers looking at entrepreneurs include marital status, age, education level of parents, and socioeconomic status.[26]

Although it's fun to look at these demographic characteristics (and perhaps to measure how your own personal background matches up), the problem with trying to create a demographic profile of a typical entrepreneur is that these models aren't widely applicable and don't account for every situation. Just because people may have these demographic characteristics doesn't automatically mean that they will be entrepreneurs. Likewise, just because people don't have these characteristics doesn't mean that they won't be entrepreneurs. Because using demographic characteristics to describe entrepreneurs hasn't exactly provided the perfect approach, perhaps we can learn something about who entrepreneurs are by looking instead at their personality characteristics.

Personality Profile of Entrepreneurs. What type of personality traits do entrepreneurs have that might distinguish them from nonentrepreneurs and what traits do they have that might predict who will be a successful entrepreneur? Is there a classic "entrepreneurial personality"? Those are the questions that the personality approach to describing entrepreneurs has attempted to answer. Even as far back as 1848 when Mill characterized an entrepreneur as "riskbearing," researchers and writers have tried to pinpoint entrepreneurial personality characteristics.[27] Although the personality approach suffers from the same types of descriptive concerns as the demographic approach—that is, being able to pinpoint specific personality characteristics that all entrepreneurs share—this hasn't halted attempts by writers to list common traits.[28] For instance, one list of personality characteristics included the following: high level of motivation, abundance of self-confidence, ability to be involved for the long term, high energy level, persistent problem solver, high degree of initiative, ability to set goals, and moderate risk-taker.[29] Another list of characteristics of "successful" entrepreneurs included high energy level, great persistence, resourcefulness, the desire and ability to be self-directed, and relatively high need for autonomy. Another recent development in this area was the proposed use of a proactive personality scale to predict an individual's likelihood of pursuing entrepreneurial ventures. What is a proactive personality? Very simply, it describes those who are more prone to take actions to influence their environment—that is, they're more proactive. Obviously an entrepreneur is likely to exhibit proactivity as he or she searches for opportunities and acts to take advantage of these opportunities.[30] Various items on the proactive personality scale were found to be good indicators of a person's likelihood of becoming an entrepreneur, including gender, education, having an entrepreneurial parent, and possessing a proactive personality.

Even though the personality approach to describing entrepreneurs, like the

FYI

Type E's

Is there a Type E (entrepreneurial) personality? A recent study suggests that entrepreneurs tend to share certain characteristics that set them apart from their corporate counterparts. According to this study, these common traits included the following:

1. Aggressively pursues goals; pushes both self and others
2. Seeks autonomy, independence, and freedom from boundaries; very individualistic
3. Sends consistent messages; very focused and doesn't deviate from purpose
4. Acts quickly, often without deliberating
5. Keeps distance and maintains objectivity; expects others to be self-sufficient and tough-minded
6. Pursues simple, practical solutions; able to cut through complexity and find the essential and important issues
7. Is willing to take risks, comfortable with uncertainty
8. Exhibits clear opinions and values; makes quick judgments, often finding fault and having high expectations
9. Impatient regarding results and with others; "just do it" mentality
10. Positive, upbeat, optimistic; communicates confidence

What do you think of this list? Does *your* personality fit this profile?

Source: J. Chun, "Type E Personality," *Entrepreneur,* January 1997, p. 10.

demographic approach, isn't flawless from a methodological viewpoint, it has provided us with a better understanding of who entrepreneurs are. However, perhaps we could get an even clearer picture by looking at entrepreneurs from the perspective of their behavioral tendencies (intentions) toward creating and starting an entrepreneurial venture.

Intentions Profile of Entrepreneurs. Given the limitations of both demographic and personality profiles for describing entrepreneurs, the current focus of entrepreneurship researchers has been on attempting to understand the decision (intention) to become an entrepreneur. How do studies of entrepreneurial intentions relate to understanding who entrepreneurs are? They do so by helping us better understand the situational context, the person, *and* the process the individual goes through as he or she contemplates being an entrepreneur.

An underlying anchor behind the entrepreneurial intention approach is that being an entrepreneur clearly represents planned, intentional behavior.[31] This means that proponents of this approach believe that the decision to be an entrepreneur isn't accidental, but instead is the result of a combination of personal and contextual factors. Figure 1-4 shows these relationships in an early model of entrepreneurial intentionality. As you can see, the entrepreneurial action (decision) by an individual is preceded by the intention to do so, which in turn is influenced by both contextual factors (social, political, economic opportunities) and personal factors (history, personality, abilities).

Does this approach make sense for understanding who entrepreneurs are? Well, one important thing it does is help us recognize the interplay of personal *and* contextual factors in being an entrepreneur. Continuing research into understanding entrepreneurial intentions is helping refine our knowledge of entrepreneurs and the factors that influence the entrepreneurial decision.[32]

By now, you should have a fairly good grasp of who entrepreneurs are and the various ways to describe them. But knowing who entrepreneurs are doesn't tell us anything about what they do. That's the next topic we need to explore.

Figure 1-4

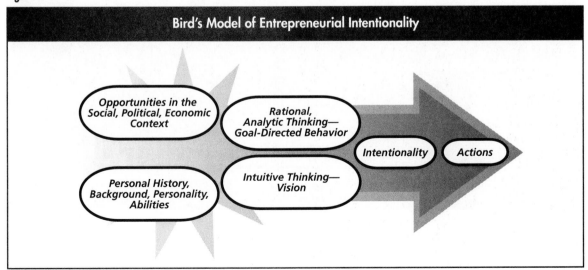

Bird's Model of Entrepreneurial Intentionality

Source: Republished with permission of *Academy of Management Review*, from "Implementing Entrepreneurial Ideas: The Case for Intention," Vol. 13, No. 3, 1988, p. 444.

FYI

Have You Got What It Takes?

Do you think you've got what it takes to be an entrepreneur? Take the following quiz!

Answer these questions to see if you're cut out to run your own show.

1. Can you look at an inkblot that clearly represents a ship and see a horse or a lamppost as well?
- Yes
- No

A Rorschach test may be the best way to spot an entrepreneur. Management gurus cite a tolerance for ambiguity as one of the crucial intellectual assets needed to run a company.

2. You're in the front row at a comedy club. The headliner beckons you onstage to be part of the act. What do you do?
- Plead laryngitis.
- Step up to the mike.

Being able to think on your feet is a must for a business owner (and having a sense of humor doesn't hurt). Entrepreneurs have to constantly sell themselves and their company—to employees, customers, investors, the media, and the general public.

3. You are considering taking a cycling vacation. Which would you prefer?
- Mountain biking on rugged terrain.
- A gentle cruise on a smooth road.

When you own a business, there's no such thing as coasting. The path to success is filled with massive potholes, bumps, hills, hazards—and competitors who are pedaling just as furiously.

4. Can you take no for an answer?
- Yes
- No

If you can, forget it. Venture capitalists may turn down your proposals 25 times before you strike pay dirt. Skepticism should not leave you feeling rejected—it should motivate you to learn from the experience, change your pitch, and try again.

5. You're ready to buy a new home. Which do you do?
- Find an existing house you're happy with.
- Find a vacant lot and supervise the construction of your dream house.

Entrepreneurs are, at root, builders. In fact, creating a business from scratch is a lot like building a house. You've got to carve out your territory, plan a structure that will withstand the elements, and hire specialists to do the labor, all the while staying within your budget.

6. Your neighbor's daughter shows up at your door in full Girl Scout regalia, selling cookies. You already have a cabinet full of Thin Mints. Can you resist?
- Yes
- No

If you can, that's a big plus. Running a company means saying no just as often as saying yes—to friends, neighbors, and even kids asking for money.

7. Can you simultaneously watch—and absorb—the nightly news, edit a presentation, and conduct a three-way conference call with your brother and sister?
- Yes
- No

Start-up companies are not distinguished by a division of executive labor. One minute you're the CFO, the next you're handling a marketing issue, then you're dealing with a personnel problem. And, more often than not, you're doing them all at once.

8. You've planned a long-weekend getaway for months. The night before departure, your plumbing explodes. Now you've got to stay

home and bail out the basement. What do you do?

● **Go into a deep funk.**

● **Roll up your sleeves and take it in stride.**

If nothing else, entrepreneurs must be flexible. When you're the boss, owner, and chief investor, no problem is too small for your attention. "If you're rigid about what you want to do, it's not going to work," says Ralph Subbiondo, a partner in Ernst & Young's entrepreneurial services group. "That doesn't mean you can't be rigid in your ideals and goals, but you have to be flexible on a day-to-day basis."

Entrepreneurial Aptitude

If you answered all eight correctly, what are you waiting for?

Say goodbye to your boss, fire up your business, and don't look back.

Half right? Start up in your spare time but keep a paycheck coming in. Or find a co-conspirator to help you kick-start your company.

Fewer than four? Keep your day job. Some of us just aren't cut out to be our own boss.

Source: Working Woman, July–August 1998, p. 46. Reprinted with permission of MacDonald Communication Corporation. Copyright © 1999 by MacDonald Communication Corporation.

What Entrepreneurs Do

Describing what entrepreneurs do isn't an easy or simple task! No two entrepreneurs' specific work activities are exactly alike. In a general sense, entrepreneurs are creating something new, something different. They're searching for change, responding to it, and exploiting it.[33] Yet, maybe we can get a better picture if we look at what entrepreneurs do in terms of broad categories of entrepreneurial activities. We can also find some similarities by re-examining what happens in the entrepreneurial process. (Refer back to Figure 1-3.) Those activities are pretty apt descriptions of what entrepreneurs do.

Initially, an entrepreneur is engaged in assessing the potential for the entrepreneurial venture and then dealing with start-up issues. In exploring the entrepreneurial context, entrepreneurs are gathering information, identifying potential opportunities, and pinpointing possible competitive advantage(s). Then, armed with this information, the entrepreneur begins researching the venture's feasibility—uncovering business ideas, looking at competitors, and exploring financing options. After looking at the potential of the proposed venture and assessing the likelihood of a successful pursuit, the entrepreneur proceeds to planning the venture. What's involved here? It includes such activities as developing a viable organizational vision and mission, exploring organizational culture issues, and very importantly, creating a strong and effective business plan. Once the entrepreneur has resolved these planning issues, then he or she must look at organizing the venture, which involves choosing a legal form of business organization, addressing other legal issues such as patent or copyright searches, and coming up with an appropriate organization design for structuring how work is going to be done. After these start-up activities have been completed, the entrepreneur is ready to actually launch the venture. What happens during this phase? It includes setting goals and strategies and establishing the technology–operations methods, marketing plans, information systems, financial–accounting systems, and cash flow management systems.

Once the entrepreneurial venture is up and running, the entrepreneur's attention switches to managing it. (Remember what we said earlier: Entrepreneurs

> ## Entrepreneurs in Action ▶
>
> Have you ever been on one of those tour boats where you could view the fish and other fascinating aquatic life underneath you? Many of these semisubmersible boats are made by Sub Sea Systems, Inc. of Sacramento, California. Co-owners Jim Mayfield and Patrick and Michael Stafford (who are brothers) decided in 1989 that building these boats for the tourism industry was a pretty good bet. However, launching the idea was anything but smooth sailing. They built their first semisubmersible boat on speculation and mortgaged their homes to pay the design expenses. In addition, they had the formidable task of getting approval from the U.S. Coast Guard for the boat's design specifications. That process alone took 18 months. However, before the first boat was completed, the company had signed contracts to design and build two more. Finding a niche in this industry has required the owners to adjust to the changing demands of the tourism industry. But through it all, the owners maintained their sense of humor. Mayfield says laughingly, "We like to say we're going under every day and loving it."
>
> *Source:* C. Goodman, "The View from Below," *Nation's Business,* September 1998, p. 79.

"do" as well as "create.") What's involved with managing the entrepreneurial venture? One important activity involves managing the various processes that are part and parcel of running a business: doing things such as making decisions, establishing action plans, analyzing the venture's internal and external environments, measuring and evaluating performance, and stimulating and making needed changes. The entrepreneur also engages in important activities associated with managing people such as selecting and hiring, appraising and training, motivating, managing conflict, delegating tasks, and being an effective leader. Finally, the entrepreneur engages in activities associated with managing growth: developing and designing strategies for growth, dealing with crises, exploring various avenues for financing growth, valuing the venture, and perhaps even eventually harvesting or exiting the venture.

As you can tell from the above descriptions, being an entrepreneur is an exciting proposition! Entrepreneurs do a variety of things and deal with a multitude of issues. In fact, one writer concluded that entrepreneurial behavior was complex, intentional, and passionate.[34] Yet, it's primarily because of these characteristics, that it's prudent for you to know from the start the rewards and challenges of being an entrepreneur.

The Rewards and Challenges of Being an Entrepreneur

Would you enjoy being an entrepreneur? Are you prepared to deal with the rewards and challenges? Although many entrepreneurs "fell into" their roles, the fact that you're reading this book indicates that you're putting concentrated time

| **TABLE 1-3** | **The Rewards and Challenges of Being an Entrepreneur** |

Rewards	Challenges
▲ High degree of independence—freedom from constraints	▼ Must be comfortable with change and uncertainty
▲ Get to use a variety of skills and talents	▼ Must make a bewildering number of decisions
▲ Freedom to make decisions	▼ May face tough economic choices
▲ Accountable to only yourself	▼ Must be comfortable with taking risks
▲ Opportunity to tackle challenges	▼ Need many different skills and talents
▲ Feeling of achievement and pride	▼ Must be comfortable with the potential of failure
▲ Potential for greater financial rewards	

and effort into studying the field and trying to learn all that you can about it. Part of that education needs to be making sure that you understand the upside and downside of entrepreneurship. Table 1-3 provides a list of the major rewards and challenges of being an entrepreneur.

The rewards associated with being an entrepreneur are numerous! Many individuals pursue it primarily because of the high degree of independence that it allows them. In fact, researchers have found that the freedom from others' constraints—that is, the ability to be independent—is the dominant attraction for entrepreneurs.[35] Also, the facts that as an entrepreneur, you have the freedom to make decisions, you can experience feelings of achievement and pride, you are accountable to only yourself, and you have the opportunity to tackle a wide variety of challenges using a wide variety of skills and talents are other positive aspects. The possibility of achieving greater financial rewards, although an important factor, doesn't appear to be a primary reason why individuals pursue entrepreneurship. Yes, the potential to make loads of money can be intoxicating. However, the financial rewards, which for most entrepreneurs are a nice secondary benefit, are not their primary reason for being an entrepreneur.

What about the challenges associated with being an entrepreneur? Successful entrepreneurs will tell you that it's an all-consuming passion, that it's hard work, that it involves sacrifices (personally and professionally), and that it's never the same one day as it was the previous day. To be an entrepreneur means that you must be comfortable with change and uncertainty. In fact, the very essence of entrepreneurship (an abbreviated version of our earlier definition: using organized efforts to pursue opportunities through innovation and uniqueness)

Rapid Review ◀◀|

✓ Who is an entrepreneur?

✓ What focus does each of the three approaches to describing entrepreneurs have?

✓ How do male and female entrepreneurs differ?

✓ Describe the characteristics of the Type E personality.

✓ What are the drawbacks of the demographic and personality approaches to describing entrepreneurs?

✓ How does the entrepreneurial intentions approach contribute to describing entrepreneurs?

✓ Describe what entrepreneurs do.

✓ List the major rewards and challenges of being an entrepreneur.

implies that change is the normal state of affairs for entrepreneurs. With change comes uncertainty and risk. Entrepreneurs must be comfortable with taking risks. In addition, many of the challenges associated with being an entrepreneur involve making choices. Entrepreneurs face a bewildering array of decisions, which may, at times, mean making tough economic choices and dealing with the potential of failure.

As we said at the beginning of the chapter, entrepreneurship is attracting a lot of attention these days. After reading this chapter, you should now have a better understanding of this strong interest in entrepreneurs and entrepreneurship. You should also be able to describe both what entrepreneurship is and who entrepreneurs are.

CHAPTER SUMMARY

Entrepreneurs and entrepreneurship are playing important roles in today's global business environment. Entrepreneurship is defined as the process whereby an individual or a group of individuals uses organized efforts and means to pursue opportunities to create value and grow by fulfilling wants and needs through innovation and uniqueness, no matter what resources are currently controlled. There's a lot of history behind entrepreneurship. From Cantillon's coining of the term *entrepreneur* in the eighteenth century to Schumpeter's explanation early in the twentieth century of the process of creative destruction, entrepreneurial activity has been an important part of the economic scene. Even though entrepreneurship has been an important part of society for many years, there are still many misconceptions about it. One of the major ones is that entrepreneurial ventures and small businesses are one and the same. However, an entrepreneurial venture is an organization that is pursuing opportunities, is characterized by innovative practices, and has profitability and growth as its main goals. The pursuit of entrepreneurship plays an important role in innovation, in the number of new start-ups, and in job creation.

Another important aspect introduced in this chapter is what happens in the entrepreneurial process. The main decisions and actions that entrepreneurs deal with as they pursue entrepreneurial activities include exploring the various aspects of the entrepreneurial context, identifying opportunities and possible competitive advantage(s), starting the entrepreneurial venture, and managing the venture. An important thing to realize about the entrepreneurial process is that without an entrepreneur, it wouldn't happen!

An entrepreneur is defined as someone who initiates and actively operates the entrepreneurial venture. Entrepreneurs have been studied from different aspects—their background (demographic) profile, their personality characteristics, and their intentions to be an entrepreneur. But in addition to understanding who entrepreneurs are, it's also important to understand what entrepreneurs do. Keep in mind that no two entrepreneurs' work activities are exactly alike. However, if we use the activities involved in the entrepreneurial process (assessing the entrepreneurial context, dealing with start-up issues, and managing the entrepreneurial venture), we get a good description of what entrepreneurs do. Do these activities sound interesting? Before you decide to be an entrepreneur, you need to be aware of the rewards and challenges of being one.

KEY TERMS

➠ *Entrepreneurship:* The process whereby an individual or a group of individuals uses organized efforts and means to pursue opportunities to create value and grow by fulfilling wants and needs through innovation and uniqueness, no matter what resources are currently controlled.

➠ *Creative destruction:* The process described by economist Joseph Schumpeter whereby existing products, processes, ideas, and businesses are replaced with better ones.

➠ *Intrapreneurship:* The pursuit of entrepreneurship within the confines of a large organization.

➠ *Small business:* A business that is independently owned, operated, and financed; has fewer than 100 employees; doesn't engage in any new or innovative practices; and has relatively little impact on its industry.

➠ *Entrepreneurial venture:* An organization that is pursuing opportunities, is characterized by innovative practices, and has profitability and growth as its main goals.

➠ *Opportunities:* Positive external environmental trends or changes that provide unique and distinct possibilities for innovating and creating value.

➠ *Competitive advantage:* What sets an organization apart; its competitive edge.

➠ *World-class organization:* An organization that is the best in its world at what it does.

➠ *Entrepreneur:* Someone who initiates and actively operates the entrepreneurial venture.

SWEAT EQUITY

1. The participation of women in the workforce during the latter part of the twentieth century has had a profound impact on the general economy. Between 1987 and 1996, the number of women-owned businesses increased by 78 percent nationwide. Although many of these businesses are small, each, in its own way contributes to the economy. Using the library or Internet, find three examples of women-owned entrepreneurial ventures. Describe their businesses, and, if enough information is given, describe the challenges they have faced. Be sure to cite your sources!

2. You've been asked to make a presentation before the local chapter of the Young Entrepreneur's Organization (**www.yeo.org**) about the advantages and drawbacks of the Internet and World Wide Web for entrepreneurial ventures. After doing some research on this topic, draw up a detailed outline of the key points you want to make. Again, be sure to cite your sources.

3. How has the role of an entrepreneur changed? According to Tom Richman (see "The Evolution of the Professional Entrepreneur," in *Inc.'s The State of Small Business Special Issue,* 1997, pp. 50–53), today's entrepreneur is more of a *professional* entrepreneur who relies more on intellect, not gut instincts. Here are some other comparisons Richman provided of the "then" entrepreneur versus the "now" entrepreneur:

Then:	**Now:**
Boss	Leader
Secretive	Open
Self-reliant	Inquisitive
Lone ranger	Networker
Quick decisions	Takes time to build consensus

Based on what we discussed in this chapter, do you agree with these characterizations? Why or why not? How do you think these "new" characteristics might change our description of what entrepreneurs do?

4. If entrepreneurship and stories about entrepreneurs are such hot topics, just how popular is entrepreneurship education? Research how and where entrepreneurship is being taught today. (Your focus might be on the elementary, secondary, or college level.) Write a report (at least two pages in length) on your findings. Be sure to include at least two visual representations of data in the form of tables, graphs, charts, or maps.

5. Statistics gathered as part of the *National Panel Study of U.S. Business Start-Ups* found that 7 out of 10 start-ups are begun by people aged 25 to 34 (*Entrepreneur*, November 1997, p. 60). What do you think the implications might be for the young adults starting these businesses; individuals and organizations financing these ventures; and government agencies that provide assistance to new ventures?

ENTREPRENEURSHIP IN ACTION CASES

CASE #1: Nailing Down Success

Entrepreneurship in Action case #1 can be found at the beginning of Chapter 1.

Discussion Questions

1. Is entrepreneurship evident in Dineh Mohajer's story? Explain.

2. Is Hard Candy an example of Schumpeter's creative destruction? Why or why not?

3. Put yourself in Mohajer's shoes, and describe what you initially had to do as an entrepreneur and what you do now in your role as an entrepreneur.

CASE #2: Fine Wine

Todd Alexander, founder of Vendemmia, Inc. (which means "harvest" in Italian), decided in college that he wanted to get paid for something that he would otherwise do for free. That "something" was going to Italy a lot, drinking good wine, and eating good food!

As a high school exchange student, Alexander traveled to Italy for the first time. His wonderful experiences there ignited a passion for all things Italian. During college, he returned to study the language. This would prove to be extremely useful as he pursued his passion for the Italian culture. After graduating from college, Alexander got a job working as a management trainee for a New Jersey–based wine distributor. After a short time there, he went to work for a retail wine company. The experience and knowledge about different aspects of the wine business gained while working for others would also prove valuable. But Alexander was ready to try something else. Having long had the dream of writing a book on wines, he decided to return to Italy to do his research. It was during this six-month trip and visits with local wine makers that he decided he was going to become a distributor and import Italian wine because the vintners were dissatisfied with their U.S. distributors.

Alexander returned home to Atlanta, borrowed money from his family to start the business, and Vendemmia, Inc. was born. During his first year of operation, he did it all—everything from mopping floors to making wine deliveries in his own vehicle. But after the first year, he was able to repay his family in full. Today, he employs a sales team and delivery personnel. Alexander is able to concentrate on building the venture and nurturing the important relationships with wine makers in both Europe and California. He says the goal for his business, in keeping with his personality, is "ambitious, but not greedy." After all, he still wants to have fun at it and to be able to enjoy what he's doing!

Discussion Questions

1. Would you classify Todd Alexander as an entrepreneur? Explain.
2. How have Alexander's background experiences and personality contributed to his pursuit of this business? Do you think that this is a good approach for other potential entrepreneurs? Why or why not?
3. Todd Alexander keeps alluding to his "passion" for all things Italian. Is passion an important factor in entrepreneurship? Explain.

(*Sources:* R. Lieber, "Lessons from America's New Entrepreneurs," *USA Weekend,* August 21–23, 1998, pp. 4–5; M. Whigham-Desir, "Ship It!" *Black Enterprise,* May 1997, pp. 62–66; and C. V. Clark, "Drinking in Profits," *Black Enterprise,* September 1997, p. 33.)

CASE #3: Cashing In

If "an entrepreneur is someone who knows how to turn a setback into an opportunity," then Jeffrey Jetton and Steven Wright would definitely be entrepreneurs! As partners in Card Capture Services Inc. (CCS), they've faced significant challenges in getting their now-successful venture up and running.

Back in 1993, CCS sold credit card processing machines to restaurants, grocery stores, and department stores around Portland, Oregon. Many of these merchants would accommodate customers by advancing cash against credit cards. However, credit card issuers didn't like this practice because they were being deprived of that revenue. If the issuer caught a merchant doing this, it would drop them. Needless to say, this practice was highly risky both for the merchants and for CCS! Wright and Jetton figured there had to be a better solution. What these merchants needed was an inexpensive machine that would dispense cash just like an ATM. Out of a potential crisis came an opportunity!

Wright and Jetton helped found a new industry of independent ATMs. There are more than 50,000 of these machines dispensing cash at locations such as convenience stores, casinos, bars, and bowling alleys. Wright and Jetton's CCS is the nation's largest supplier of these machines. During 1997, their private company realized approximately $3 million profits on revenues of $27.5 million. Sensing another opportunity, the company's ATM machines do other things than just spit out cash. The ATMs' video screens tout in-store specials and customers can also get stamps and phone cards.

You might be asking yourself about now, just how CCS and the merchant make money off of these machines. Users of these "independent" ATMs pay a fee for the convenience. First, they pay a "foreign" fee, which goes to their card-issuing bank as a penalty for not using one of its ATMs. The other fee is a surcharge—the price a customer pays for the convenience of having an ATM handy. CCS keeps 20 percent of this surcharge, the merchant gets 80 percent, and they both get a cut of the foreign fee. Counting it up, CCS gets up to $.55 in fee income per transaction and the merchant gets as much as $1.45.

All in all, the initial crisis faced by Wright and Jetton, although risky, seemed pretty mild. But it wasn't quite as easy to get this entrepreneurial venture up and running as it sounds. To make their idea work, they had to find an inexpensive machine. Every manufacturer they went to said that there was no

market for low-end ATMs. But finally, they located a small company in Mississippi that made a strange-looking terminal (tall, narrow, tacky beige color), but the price was right! Another crisis resolved! But the popularity of the machines with merchants precipitated the next crises—managing rapid growth and the surge of new competitors coming into the market. Wright and Jetton knew that this was a pivotal point for their venture. Their solution? Bringing in professional help. They hired an old college pal, David Grano, who was in management at Nextel Communications. Grano brought his marketing background and fresh ideas to the table. With Wright, Jetton, and Grano running CCS, the company appears to be well-positioned to address whatever new crises may happen to pop up!

Discussion Questions

1. Do you agree with the description of an entrepreneur as someone who knows how to turn a setback into an opportunity? How does this fit in with our chapter definitions of entrepreneur and entrepreneurship?

2. Using the model of the entrepreneurial process (Figure 1-3), describe the evolution of CCS.

3. Would you classify CCS as a small business or an entrepreneurial venture? Support your choice.

(*Source:* C. Hawn, "The Soul of a New Machine," *Forbes*, April 20, 1998, pp. 74–76.)

 VIDEO CASE #1: Wizards of Wheels

Bicycling is a booming industry! Enthusiasts point to its appeal as a great family sport that can be enjoyed at low cost and that can be done in a variety of locations particularly

because bicycles are easily transported from one place to another. Easily transported, that is, *if* the bicyclists have a reliable, safe, and easy-to-use bicycle rack on their vehicle. Some of the world's best bicycle racks are made by Sara and Chris Fortune's company, Graber Products of Madison, Wisconsin.

Chris Fortune says that consumers, and dealers, want products that are user friendly. Graber Products is striving to supply that product. He says that whenever Graber develops a new product, three very simple and very basic "musts" need to be met: (1) The bicycle racks *must* stay on the car, (2) the bikes *must* stay on the rack, and (3) the racks *must* not scratch or mar the owner's vehicle. These three musts guide product innovation and development at Graber.

Innovation is one of the top business issues that face Graber Products. Through its product innovation process, Graber wants to go beyond what's already on the market. It doesn't merely want to copy what other industry competitors have already done because that would make it extremely difficult for the company to gain market recognition. It isn't just Chris and Sara who recognize the importance of innovation to Graber's long-term success. Everyone at Graber talks about innovation. For instance, the company's talented toolmakers who bend and mold the pieces of steel into the simple yet functional bicycle racks are constantly innovating. They have to, and they have the freedom to do so. In the

company's cellular manufacturing system—which is similar to an assembly line but instead of using some parts that are made elsewhere outside the assembly line, cellular manufacturing relies on all parts being processed right in the plant—employees can design tools or processes that make them more efficient and help them achieve higher product quality levels. The cellular manufacturing system has led to two important results at Graber. First, it's improved the quality of parts because employees are now dealing with a much smaller production run. In addition, efficiency has improved by almost 25 percent.

Discussion Questions

1. What role do you think innovation plays at Graber Products?
2. Do you think there's a connection between innovativeness in *producing* a product and in *developing* a product? Explain.
3. How do you think the three product development "musts" that Chris Fortune describes might impact the innovation process at Graber Products?
4. What aspects of the entrepreneurial process do you see in this video clip? Explain.

(*Source:* Based on *Small Business 2000,* Show 410.)

VIDEO CASE #2: 24 Hours

Marc Katz founded his eating and entertainment spot, Katz Deli, in Austin, Texas. Located on Austin's famous 6th Street, Katz Deli is open 24 hours a day, seven days a week. Live bands play in the bar above the deli every night. The club employs around 100 people and has annual sales of approximately $5 million.

Marc, a third-generation deli and restaurant owner, learned his skills growing up in the family deli in New York City. His bright yellow vintage Cadillac convertible says a lot about the type of person he is—outgoing and showy. Austin appears to be a city that accepts this kind of energy. Katz also has very specific ideas about running a business and the image he wishes to convey for himself and his business. He values all his employees and does not segregate by skill, role, or anything else. This attention to his operation and his way of treating his employees seems to be a fundamental principle that he lives by.

Discussion Questions

1. Is Marc Katz an entrepreneur? How does his personality fit in with profiles of entrepreneurs? Explain.

2. How has Marc's background contributed to his entrepreneurial venture? Think of the obvious and not-so-obvious factors.

3. Marc says that, in a way, the dishwasher is the most important person in his business. What did you think about the role of a dishwasher or others in a business like this one before you heard this? What do you think of his discussion of how he feels about his staff?

4. What can you learn about entrepreneurship in action from Katz? Be specific.

(*Source:* Based on *Small Business 2000, Show 507.*)

ENDNOTES

1. S. Sansoni, "Fashion Renegade," *Forbes*, March 10, 1997, p. 72; M. Hornblower, "Great Xpectations," *Time*, June 9, 1997, pp. 60–61; and A. Mulrine, "For the Truly Polished Man," *U.S. News & World Report*, June 9, 1997, p. 13.

2. W. A. Sahlman and H. H. Stevenson (eds.), *The Entrepreneurial Venture* (Boston, MA: Harvard Business School Publications, 1992), p. 1; J. R. Van Slyke, H. H. Stevenson, and M. J. Roberts, "The Start-Up Process," in Sahlman and Stevenson (eds.), *The Entrepreneurial Venture*, p. 81; W. D. Bygrave, "Theory Building in the Entrepreneurship Paradigm," *Journal of Business Venturing*, Vol. 8, No. 3, 1993, pp. 255–80; J. C. Huefner and H. K. Hunt, "Broadening the Concept of Entrepreneurship: Comparing Business and Consumer Entrepreneurs," *Entrepreneurship Theory and Practice*, Vol. 18, No. 3, spring 1994, pp. 61–75; N. F. Krueger Jr. and D.V. Brazeal, "Entrepreneurial Potential and Potential Entrepreneurs," *Entrepreneurship Theory and Practice*, Vol. 18, No. 3, spring 1994, pp. 91–104; M. Warshaw, "The Entrepreneurial Mind: An Interview with Jeffry A. Timmons," *Success*, April 1994, pp. 48–51; D. Krackhardt, "Entrepreneurial Opportunities in an Entrepreneurial Firm: A Structural Approach," *Entrepreneurship Theory and Practice*, Vol. 19, No. 3, spring 1995, pp. 53–69; and L. W. Busenitz, "Research on Entrepreneurial Alertness," *Journal of Small Business Management*, Vol. 34, No. 4, October 1996, pp. 35–44.

3. B. J. Bird, *Entrepreneurial Behavior* (Glenview, IL: Scott, Foresman and Company, 1989).

4. R. D. Hisrich, "Entrepreneurship and Intrapreneurship: Methods for Creating New Companies That Have an Impact on the Economic Renaissance of an Area," in R. D. Hisrich (ed.), *Entrepreneurship, Intrapreneurship, and Venture Capital* (Lexington, MA: Lexington Books, 1986), p. 89.

5. S. A. Shane, "Who Is Publishing the Entrepreneurship Research?" *Journal of Management*, Vol. 23, 1997, pp. 83–95.

6. W. B. Gartner, "What Are We Talking About When We Talk About Entrepreneurship?" *Journal of Business Venturing*, Vol. 5, 1990, pp. 15–28.

7. Bird, *Entrepreneurial Behavior*, p. 3.

8. L. Taylor, "Accidental Entrepreneur," *Working Woman*, April 1999, p. 17.

9. W. B. Gartner, "Words Lead to Deeds: Towards an Organizational Emergence Vocabulary," *Journal of Business Venturing*, Vol. 8, 1993, pp. 231–40.

10. R. D. Hisrich and M. P. Peters, *Entrepreneurship* (Boston, MA: Irwin McGraw-Hill, 1998), p. 7.

11. D. Kansas, "Don't Believe It," *Wall Street Journal*, October 15, 1993, p. R8; and J. Chun, "To Tell the Truth," *Entrepreneur*, April 1998, pp. 106–13.

12. Code of Federal Regulations 13:121 (Washington, DC: U.S. Government Printing Office, January 1, 1994), pp. 354–67.

13. J. W. Carland, F. Hoy, W. R. Boulton, and J. C. Carland, "Differentiating Entrepreneurs from Small Business Owners: A Conceptualization," *Academy of Management Review*, Vol. 9, No. 2, 1984, pp. 354–59; and T. L. Hatten, *Small Business: Entrepreneurship and Beyond* (Upper Saddle River, NJ: Prentice Hall, 1997), p. 5.

14. "Small Business Answer Card 1998," a report prepared by the SBA Office of Advocacy, *SBAOnline*, **www.sbaonline.sba.gov/ADVO/stats/answer.html**, September 18, 1998.

15. "The New American Evolution: The Role and Impact of Small Firms," a report prepared by the Office of Economic Research of the U.S. Small Business Administration's Office of Advocacy, June 1998, *SBAOnline*, **www.sbaonline.sba.gov/ADVO/stats/evol_pap.html**, September 18, 1998.

16. P. Almeida and B. Kogut, "The Exploration of Technological Diversity and Geographic Localization in Innovation: Start-Up Firms in the Semiconductor Industry," *Small Business Economics*, Vol. 9, No. 1, 1997, pp. 21–31.

17. R. J. Arend, "Emergence of Entrepreneurs Following Exogenous Technological Change," *Strategic Management Journal*, Vol. 20, No. 1, 1999, pp. 31–47.

18. "The Facts About Small Business, 1997," a report prepared by the Office of Advocacy of the U.S. Small Business Administration, September 1997, *SBAOnline*, **www.sbaonline.sba.gov/ADVO/stats/fact1.html**, September 18, 1998.

19. J. Cunningham and J. Lischeron, "Defining Entrepreneurship," *Journal of Small Business Management*, January 1991, pp. 45–61.

20. P. B. Robinson, D. V. Simpson, J. C. Huefner, and H. K. Hunt, "An Attitude Approach to the Prediction of Entrepreneurship," *Entrepreneurship Theory and Practice*, summer 1991, pp. 13–31.

21. Ibid.

22. M. Selz, "Study Scrutinizes People Who Would Be Entrepreneurs," *Wall Street Journal*, December 14, 1995, p. B2; and L. Kolvereid, "Prediction of Employment Status Choice Intentions," *Entrepreneurship Theory and Practice*, fall 1996, pp. 47–56.

23. Ibid.

24. Selz, "Study Scrutinizes People Who Would Be Entrepreneurs," p. B2.

25. Kolvereid, "Prediction of Employment Status Choice Intentions," p. 47.

26. Robinson et al., "An Attitude Approach to the Prediction of Entrepreneurship," p. 15.

27. G. d'Amboise and M. Muldowney, "Management Theory for Small Business: Attempts and Requirements," *Academy of Management Review*, Vol. 13, No. 2, 1988, p. 230.

28. Robinson et al., "An Attitude Approach to the Prediction of Entrepreneurship," p. 13.

29. B. M. Davis, "Role of Venture Capital in the Economic Renaissance of an Area," in Hisrich (ed.), *Entrepreneurship, Intrapreneurship, and Venture Capital*, pp. 107–118.

30. J. M. Crant, "The Proactive Personality Scale as a Predictor of Entrepreneurial Intentions," *Journal of Small Business Management*, July 1996, pp. 42–49.

31. N. F. Krueger Jr. and D.V. Brazeal, "Entrepreneurial Potential and Potential Entrepreneurs," *Entrepreneurship Theory and Practice*, spring 1994, pp. 91–104.

32. Ibid.

33. P. F. Drucker, *Innovation and Entrepreneurship: Practice and Principles* (New York: Harper & Row), 1985.

34. Bird, *Entrepreneurial Behavior*, pp. 7–8.

35. M. Jamal, "Job Stress, Satisfaction, and Mental Health: An Empirical Examination of Self-Employed and Non-Self-Employed Canadians," *Journal of Small Business Management*, October 1997, pp. 48–57.

THE CONTEXT OF ENTREPRENEURSHIP

ENTREPRENEURSHIP IN ACTION CASE #1

King of the Online Jungle

2,300 percent. That was the impressive number that caught Jeff Bezos's attention in 1994.[1] It reflected the explosive growth in the use of the Internet—a rate of about 2,300 percent a month. What would you have done if you had seen that number somewhere? Ignored it? Wrote it off as a fluke? Well, Bezos decided that something dramatic was happening and he was going to get in on it!

At the time, Bezos was a successful stock market researcher and hedge fund manager on Wall Street, but that monthly 2,300 percent growth rate kept nagging at him. "I hadn't seen growth that fast outside of a petri dish," Bezos recalls. He decided to quit his job and pursue his vision for online retailing. He narrowed a long list of products he believed could be sold over the Internet down to two: books and music. He finally settled on books for two simple reasons: More products to sell

Staking his claim in the rapidly exploding world of the Internet and online commerce obviously turned out to be a wise decision for Jeff Bezos. His story offers an appropriate illustration of the importance of considering, interpreting, and understanding the context in which entrepreneurship takes place. It's a story of recognizing how the "rules of the game" were changing and then jumping in to take advantage of those changes. In this chapter, that's what we want to look at: how the "rules" are changing and the various factors that influence when, where, how, and why entrepreneurs pursue their vision. We'll be discussing some important contextual topics (including the characteristics of the new economy, legal issues, the changing world of work, and social responsibility and ethics) that are affecting entrepreneurial organizations. In addition, we're going to examine the important concepts of opportunity and competitive advantage. Just as Jeff Bezos did, you need to understand the context that entrepreneurs face as they pursue their entrepreneurial dreams.

ISSUES AFFECTING ENTREPRENEURSHIP IN ACTION

It's an exciting world out there! No one could argue that fact! To be a successful entrepreneur in action, it's important to understand what "that exciting world" consists of. What's happening out there that could impact (positively or negatively) your entrepreneurial venture? What changes and trends are evident or not so evident? Contextual factors are so important to recognize and understand that entrepreneurship researchers have studied them in relation to the overall development of entrepreneurial activity and found that, generally, environmental conditions do impact the emergence and growth of entrepreneurial enterprises in a country.[2]

What are these contextual issues that have the potential to affect entrepreneurship in action? The main ones we're going to look at in this section include the new economy, legal factors, the changing world of work, and social responsibility and ethics.

The New Economy

Today's economic arena that entrepreneurial organizations operate in is a lot different than it used to be. Current and potential entrepreneurs are facing new challenges and opportunities in an era where conventional wisdom regarding ways of doing things and what

(more than 2 million titles in print versus 300,000 music titles), and the publishing companies were not as ferociously competitive as the record companies. After pinpointing the product he would retail, Bezos piled his family's belongings into a moving van and ordered the drivers to head west. He told them he would contact them when he'd decided the destination. Bezos, his wife, and their Labrador retriever headed off in the same direction.

Eventually, they landed in Seattle. Why Seattle? Because it had a pool of talented computer professionals and it was near two major book wholesalers. From this convergence of elements, Amazon.com—Earth's Biggest Bookstore—was born. Now, seven years later, Bezos is transforming Amazon.com into one of the Internet's premier online shopping locations by expanding into videos, music, gifts, and numerous other products.

it takes to be successful no longer rules. Poised here in the early years of a new century, we need to examine some important characteristics of this economy: What forces are "driving" it? What are the implications? What will it take to be successful in this context? Figure 2-1 provides an overview. Let's take a closer look at these factors.

Drivers of the New Economy. What are the driving forces of the twenty-first-century economy? There are four that seem to be the most critical: (1) the information revolution, (2) technological advances and breakthroughs, (3) globalization, and (4) changing demographics. Let's discuss each of these more thoroughly.

1. If there's one driving force that has set the tone for this new economy, it's the information revolution. Not only is this revolution continuing to spread, it's also accelerating. Information is now readily available to practically anyone from anywhere on the globe at any hour of the day and in most any format. An investor in Los Angeles at 3 A.M. can check currency exchange rates for the yen, click on another software program, and e-mail instructions to a broker in London. A shopper in Shanghai with a fondness for maple syrup can indulge that passion by purchasing products from a small retail store in Vermont without ever physically stepping foot in the United States. How? By linking to its virtual storefront on the Internet. (Think of the chapter-opening case on Jeff Bezos and Amazon.com, a virtual bookstore.) The almost instant availability of almost any type of information has radically changed the nature of the economy. This in turn affects the context of entrepreneurship.

    Although information has always been a factor in producing goods and services, previously it had been applied only to the design and use of work tools, organizational processes, management systems, and products. A look

Figure 2-1

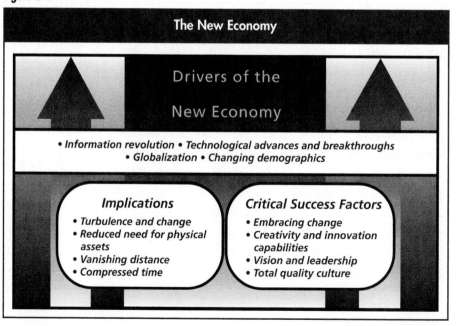

FYI

E-Commerce

Just how big is e-commerce? It's big and getting bigger! During 1998, nearly 9 million consumer households shopped online, generating some $7.8 billion in revenues. That revenue number is expected to be $108 billion by 2003. Sales revenue dollars are even larger for business-to-business e-commerce—$43 billion. That number is expected to balloon to $1.3 trillion by 2003. We're talking BIG here!

What exactly is **e-commerce**? The term is an abbreviation for electronic commerce, which refers to business sales transactions that take place online. E-commerce takes place within the realm of cyberspace and the only customer interactions are virtual, not face-to-face. If you've ordered a book from Amazon.com or shopped for a sweater at Lands End.com, you're an e-commerce participant.

What does an entrepreneur who wants to set up an e-commerce option need to do? The first step is getting an online account with an Internet Service Provider (ISP). Once you're on-line, surf around the Internet. Find out what others are doing. Make notes about what looks good and what doesn't; what seems to work and what doesn't. As soon as you've familiarized yourself with the Web, decide what you want it to do for you. Do you want just e-mail capability? Or do you want more information provided about your business? A Web site can consist of only one page or several pages. Once you've decided what you'd like your Web site to do, designing it is next. If your desired design is pretty simple, some ISPs will do this for you for free or a small fee. Or, if you want something more elaborate, you'll probably have to hire a Web page consultant or designer to help you. But, once your Web site is designed and online, your work isn't done. Service, service, service needs to be your mantra. Check your Web site constantly. Does it work? Can customers navigate through it easily with no or minimal problems? Are you servicing customer comments and orders promptly, efficiently, and accurately? Do you have technical support? These are just a few of the issues that an aspiring e-commerce entrepreneur needs to address. Although e-commerce may not be right for every entrepreneurial venture, its advantages present definite opportunities for others.

Sources: N. Pachetti, "Booting Up Your Business," *Time Select Business*, April 19, 1999; R. D. Hof, "What Every CEO Needs to Know About Electronic Business," *Business Week E.Biz*, March 22, 1999, pp. EB8–EB12; M. J. Mandel, "The Internet Economy," *Business Week*, February 22, 1999, pp. 30–32; T. McCollum, "E-Commerce Takes Off," *Nation's Business*, October 1998, pp. 34–37; and R. D. Hof, "The Net Is Open for Business—Big Time," *Business Week*, August 21, 1998, pp. 108–9.

back at history shows us that from the early days of the industrial revolution (the 1700s) up through what has often been called the "productivity" revolution (the early 1900s), information was primarily used to achieve organizational efficiency and effectiveness. However, what we're seeing today is information as *the* essential resource of production, not simply as a means to an end. In fact, today's economy has been described as the *Information Age*.

Since the development of the first transistors in the late 1940s, the information technology revolution has flourished. We now have **telecommuters** (individuals who are linked to a workplace by computers and modems); **virtual organizations** (organizations with little or no physical work space, no formal hierarchical structure, and individuals who contract to perform specific work as needed); and the Internet and World Wide Web where individuals and organizations communicate, research information, and conduct business transactions. It's a world made possible by information technology. However, the field of information is not the only one where we've seen incredible technological breakthroughs, which brings us to the second important driving force of the new economy: technological advancements and innovations.

2.   All organizations—regardless of size, type, or location—use some form of technology to do their work. What is **technology**? It's the use of equipment, materials, knowledge, and experience to perform tasks. Although some industries are by necessity more technology intensive (think, for instance, of electronics, telecommunications, software, pharmaceuticals, and so forth), even organizations such as the American Red Cross, your neighborhood grocery store, utility companies, and steel mills use technology. There's no doubt that technology is changing the way we work and the type of work we do.[3] Four major broad technological trends (see Table 2-1) that are affecting the context of entrepreneurship are the increasing rate of technological change and diffusion, the increasing commercialization of innovations, the increasing knowledge intensity, and the emergence of increasing returns.

The increasing rate of technological change and diffusion is a recognition that not only are technological advances happening more frequently, they're also being more rapidly adopted by organizations. This trend is important because it means that there are significant opportunities for creating and capturing value as new technologies are invented. However, it also means that entrepreneurs and their entrepreneurial ventures must keep up with technological change or get left behind.

The rapid rate of technological change also has had an impact on the competitive protection offered by patents, which brings us to our second major technological trend: the increasing commercialization of innovations. We're going to define **innovation** as the process of taking a creative idea and turning it into a product or process that can be used or sold. Some experts have cited growing evidence that the U.S. economy is in the early stages of a powerful new wave of innovation.[4] One possible measure of the increasing commercialization of innovations is the number of patents issued by the U.S. Patent and Trademark Office. Table 2-2 shows these figures. A **patent** is a legal property that allows its holder to prevent others from employing this property for their own use for a specified period of time. (We'll cover the different types of patents in Chapter 5.) Although the use of patents traditionally provided inventors and organizations with protection for technological discoveries that were the basis for proprietary products or services, this

TABLE 2-1   Major Technological Trends
■ Increasing rate of technological change and diffusion
■ Increasing commercialization of innovations
■ Increasing knowledge intensity
■ Emergence of increasing returns

TABLE 2-2	Number of Patents Issued, 1990–1998	
Year	**Number Issued**	**Percentage Increase**
1998	166,430	↑32.60%
1997	125,516	↑ 2.41
1996	122,561	↑ 7.11
1995	114,425	↑ .26
1994	114,126	↑ 3.70
1993	110,053	↑ 2.22
1992	107,663	↑ .77
1991	106,839	↑ 7.99
1990	98,937	

Source: U.S. Patent and Trademark Office (www.uspto.gov), "Issues and Patent Numbers." April 1999.

advantage is declining in significance because new technological advances can rapidly replace the technology that's currently protected by the patent.

Another significant trend in technology is the increasing dependence on knowledge intensity. Because technology—both the creation and the use of it—involves knowledge, the importance of it for entrepreneurial ventures has increased significantly. The implication is that as the use of technology increases, so does the need for knowledge. The reverse is true as well. As knowledge increases, so does the use of technology. For instance, even employees in traditionally labor-intensive jobs now must have more than manual dexterity skills and physical stamina. They need knowledge to operate the sophisticated equipment often found in today's manufacturing and service jobs. Successful entrepreneurial ventures in this "new" economy will capture and capitalize on knowledge.

The last important technological trend we want to look at is the emergence of *increasing* returns. Economists have long operated under the notion of *diminishing* returns—that is, the more you make or sell, the harder it is to keep doing so at continually increasing rates. On the other hand, increasing returns is the tendency for whatever product, process, or service is in the lead to get further ahead. For instance, if an organization uses a technology that gives it a small market lead, receives positive feedback, and locks customers into that technology, then that company has a significant market advantage. One of the best-known examples of the potential economic impact of increasing returns is Microsoft Corporation. Microsoft leveraged its 60 million DOS user customer base into Windows 95 and then into Windows 98 and Windows NT. Customers, for the most part, are "locked" into the Microsoft technology. Another interesting example of how increasing returns works is the QWERTY keyboard we all use for typing or word processing. Ergonomic experts say this arrangement of keys isn't the most efficient or effective for typing. However, because it has dominated data entry equipment for years, it's still the accepted standard. All kinds of organizations—

Rapid Review ◀◀|

✓ What are the four driving forces of the new economy?

✓ Describe the impact of the information revolution on the context facing entrepreneurs.

✓ Who are telecommuters? What are virtual organizations?

✓ What is e-commerce, and what role is it playing in the new economy?

✓ Define technology, and what technological trends are evident in the new economy?

✓ What is innovation, and how is it affecting the entrepreneurial context?

✓ What are patents, and why are they important in technology?

even service organizations—are attempting to capture the economic benefits of increasing returns by employing selective technology in providing their products and services.[5]

3. The third driving force of the new economy is **globalization**, the international linkage of economies and cultures that fosters a business and competitive situation in which organizations have no national boundaries. We've been hearing about the concept of globalization for so long now (you undoubtedly hear about it in every business class you take) that it almost seems a cliché. However, it is important and continues to be a dominant characteristic of the economic and business environment. More than ever, entrepreneurs are witnessing the globalization of the business landscape and are taking part in it. Here's one person's view of what this continuing global economic environment is all about: "As we move into the twenty-first century, business will become more internationalized. Your source of labor will be international; your source of financial support will be international; your market will be

Global Perspectives

During the 1990s, Japan and other East Asian countries were seen as technological powerhouses. Powerful corporations such as Sony, Samsung, and Matsushita pumped out product after product after product that "pushed" the technological edge. However, in the late 1990s, the Internet changed all that. Now, nimble entrepreneurs in the United States lead the pack while Asia's corporate giants are struggling to adapt. These corporate behemoths are also losing some of their brightest and savviest employees. These individuals are leaving their countries to become entrepreneurs,

intent on pursuing their dreams and using their knowledge and skills to create start-up ventures. For instance, Nobuhiro Michishita left Japan for the United States to pursue his cyberspace ideas. Now operating out of the International Business Incubator, a joint venture between San Jose State University and the city of San Jose, Mr. Michishita has started N&S Consulting, an Internet consulting company with offices also in Tokyo; Cyberspace Navigation, which markets Japanese-made toys over the Internet; and other entrepreneurial ventures. And he's not alone. A

number of other Asian entrepreneurs have migrated to where the opportunities are. But, don't make the mistake of thinking this geographical migration will continue permanently. The reality of a global economy is that Japan and other Asian countries can't afford to lose people like Mr. Michishita and thus are working to create a context that's more entrepreneur friendly. They're making changes to embrace the new marketplace dynamics.

Source: J. Kotkin, "New Home for a Lost Generation of Innovators," *New York Times,* March 28, 1999, p. 6BU.

international. Most companies now realize they cannot live by the domestic market alone."[6]

However, globalization is more than just producing, marketing, and distributing goods and services throughout the world. "It is a new way of thinking."[7] It's solving customers' needs no matter where the customer is. It's segmenting markets on a global basis and sourcing people, capital, technologies, and ideas from anywhere in the world. Globalization has transformed and continues to transform the new economy.

4. The fourth and final major driving force of the new economy is changing demographics. **Demographics**, very simply, are the physical characteristics of a population. It includes the kinds of information that the U.S. Census Bureau typically gathers in its census survey, such as gender, age, income levels, ethnic makeup, education, family composition, geographic locations, birthrates, employment status, and so forth. Gathering and analyzing demographic information isn't something that's done just in the United States. All industrialized, and most large semi-industrialized, countries collect census information. In addition, the United Nations collects a considerable amount of demographic information from around the world.

What kind of picture is this demographic information painting?[8] Five interesting trends are emerging! The first significant trend is that *the world's population is growing geometrically and at a very fast rate.* It took until about the year 1880 for the world's population to reach 1 billion people. It took only another 85 years to reach 3 billion. But, it took less than 30 years to reach 5 billion people in 1994. By the year 2020 (a short 26 years later), the world's population is expected to increase by another 3 billion people. Table 2-3 shows a forecast of the world's largest markets by the year 2015. Are you surprised by some of the countries indicated here? They may not be what you initially expected!

The second significant demographic trend is that *the world's population is getting older and younger at the same time.* In countries north of the equator, the average age of the population is increasing. However, in countries south of the equator, the average age of the population is decreasing as birthrates skyrocket. These southern locations are where you'll find the greatest concentration of young consumers, the fastest-growing incomes, and most of the world's unmet needs.

The third interesting demographic trend is that *the world's population continues on the move.* Migration within and between countries has always been a part of human history. However, even today, major migrations still occur, with approximately 60 million people worldwide moving annually. Ethnicity is no longer an important clue to a person's resident location. For instance, the growing proportion of Hispanics in the U.S. population reflects one of the most dramatic demographic shifts in American history. The number of Hispanics is increasing almost four times as fast as the rest of the population and is expected to surpass African Americans as the largest minority group by the year 2005. But the label *Hispanic* doesn't begin to capture the unique subcultures of this ethnic group. One estimate is that there are 17 different Hispanic subcultures including these examples: In Los Angeles, you'll find immigrant Mexicans, middle-class Mexicans, and barrio dwellers;

TABLE 2-3 The World's Largest Markets by the Year 2015

COUNTRY	POPULATION (in millions)
China	1,513
India	1,442
United States	300
Russia	300
Indonesia	286
Nigeria	281
Pakistan	267
Brazil	246
Bangladesh	235
Mexico	150
Japan	127
Ethiopia	127
Vietnam	117
Philippines	112
Zaire	99

Source: Reprinted from *The Shape of Things to Come* by R. W. Oliver. Copyright © 1999 McGraw-Hill. Reprinted by permission of the McGraw-Hill Companies.

in Texas, you'll find south Texans and Texas Guatemalans; in Miami, you have Miami Cubans and Miami Nicaraguans; and in Chicago, there are Chicago Puerto Ricans. These are just a few of the different subcultures in this one ethnic group.[9]

The fourth significant demographic trend is that *most of the world's economically active people live in cities and urban areas.* The vast majority of the world's population is urban. The world's five largest cities (Mexico City, Mexico—31 million; São Paulo, Brazil—26 million; Tokyo, Japan—26 million; New York, United States—22 million; and Calcutta, India—20 million) are more populous than many countries. This urban population is economically active, meaning most inhabitants are engaged in economic functions including producing, selling, and purchasing goods and services.

The final significant demographic trend we want to look at is *the division of the world's population into three broad groups.* Increasingly, the world's population can be defined by annual per capita income and lifestyle. Using these measures, we can identify three broad groups:

- The poor, which includes individuals with household incomes of less than $700 per year (about 1.1 billion people); these individuals account for a meager 2 percent of the world's income.
- The middle class, which includes individuals with family incomes of between $700 and $7,500 per year (about 3.5 billion people); these individuals earn about 33 percent of the world's income.

Littleton, Colorado. Springfield, Oregon. Pearl, Mississippi. Paducah, Kentucky. Names that are etched in our memories because of the unspeakable violence that happened in each of these locations. The national debate that has ensued from these tragedies has focused on the violence that children and teens are exposed to through film, music, video games, and the Internet. The video game industry, an industry ripe with entrepreneurs and entrepreneurial ventures, is trying to strengthen voluntary measures to shield children from inappropriate games. What social and ethical responsibilities do entrepreneurs have when there are tough societal questions being raised about the products being marketed? What would you do if you were a video game entrepreneur? How would you respond to the societal concerns being raised?

• The consumer class, which includes individuals with household incomes above $7,500 (about 1.1 billion people); these individuals claim about 64 percent of the world's income.

Each of these demographic trends is coloring the nature of the new economy. Like the other driving forces of the twenty-first-century economy, they are affecting the context within which entrepreneurs pursue their entrepreneurial ventures. What are the implications of these forces for entrepreneurs?

Implications of These Driving Forces. As you look back at Figure 2-1 (p. 34), you'll see that there are four major implications arising out of the driving forces of the new economy. These include continual turbulence and change, the reduced need for physical assets, vanishing distance, and compressed time. Let's examine each more closely.

1. *Continual turbulence and change.* Change, and for many organizations, turbulent change, is an undeniable reality in today's business environment. All organizations must deal with change, if not on a daily basis, then on an increasingly frequent basis. **Change** can be defined as any alteration in external environmental or internal organizational factors. Often changes in external factors stimulate the need for internal organizational changes. For instance, changes in technology (electronic mail and World Wide Web sites) have opened up new avenues for entrepreneurs who have created Web sites where electronic greeting cards can be purchased and sent electronically. The large corporate greeting card companies have been forced to rethink the way they do business. But meanwhile, several entrepreneurial greeting card ventures that recognized and acted on the changing technology have prospered. Or, take for instance, changing demographic trends. The baby boomlet (resulting from the large group of baby boomers who have had and are now having children), the increasing Hispanic population, and other demographic changes have forced entrepreneurs and other consumer goods marketers to alter the types of products they offer, the packaging of these products, and the promotional techniques used to sell these products. Organizations—entrepreneurial or not—are looking for rules to follow and yet are looking for ways to break the rules in order to prosper in this new economy where change is the norm, not the exception. Turbulence and change are the realities of the environmental context that entrepreneurs face.

2. *Reduced need for physical assets.* The economic context confronting business organizations even just a few years ago was one in which having a large number of physical assets (factories, equipment, inventory, and so forth) was crit-

Entrepreneurs in Action

Have you sent one of those cute and clever e-mail greeting cards to friends and family? If you have, you're one of millions of Internet users to do so. One of the most popular Web electronic greeting card sites—it was ranked the tenth most visited Internet site in February 1999—is Blue Mountain Arts (**www.bluemountain.com**). This Boulder, Colorado–based business started in 1996 when most businesses were still trying to figure out what the Internet was and how to take advantage of the technology. Stephen and Susan Polis Schutz and their son, Jared, are the three pillars of the company. Stephen and Susan, flower children of the 1960s who protested the Vietnam War and drove around California in an old car decorated with psychedelic hearts and flowers, provide the creativity and the passion behind the business. Jared provides the computer and business savvy. The challenge for Blue Mountain is to keep on top of the turbulent and dynamic changes that are characteristic of the cyberspace world.

Source: "Online Cards All in the Family," *Springfield News Leader,* April 12, 1999, p. 5A.

ical for financial success. The more assets you had, the more economically powerful you were. However, that's not the case in today's economy. Success in today's economy isn't reliant simply on physical assets. Instead, value can be found in intangible factors such as information, people, ideas, and knowledge. Think back to our chapter-opening case on Amazon.com, which generates sales in excess of $1.6 billion with fewer than 7,600 employees, minimal office and warehouse facilities, and little inventory. Instead, the company relies on the exchange of information and has found a way to capture value from that exchange.

3. *Vanishing distance.* The influence of physical distance on organizational decisions and actions has disappeared. Although geography traditionally played an important role in determining customers and competitors, that's no longer the reality! An entrepreneur's potential market can be found anywhere. The limitations once imposed because of physical distance have vanished. The world is your customer. But this also means that the world is your competitor. The opportunities—and challenges—for entrepreneurs have never been greater.

4. *Compressed time.* As the limitations of physical space have disappeared, so have the limitations of time. Whereas it used to take Pony Express riders weeks to deliver information via the mail, we now have the U.S. Postal Service delivering mail in two to three days, and even have overnight delivery services. But, as you already know, the time frame is even more compressed than that now. With electronic mail and interactive Web sites, we have

almost instantaneous delivery of information. This instant interactivity (between customer and business, between employees, between companies and suppliers, or between friends and family) has created a context within which there are no time-outs and no substitutions. If an organization doesn't stay on top of changes, its marketplace advantage will be only temporary, at best. Although it isn't easy to stay on top of changes, it's important! Take, for example, Dell Computer. It's been able to hold on to its marketplace advantage by understanding the benefits and challenges of compressed time. Michael Dell, founder and CEO of Dell Computer, has built a successful entrepreneurial venture on the basis of staying on top of changes through instantaneous interactivity. The company builds computers directly from buyers' requests. Then, using its lightning-fast inventory and purchasing cycles, Dell builds and ships out computers almost as soon as the customer's order is received. Also, Dell uses information from customers' orders to adapt to emerging trends way ahead of the curve. Dell is a good example of an organization that understands the external context and what it takes to be successful in this new economy. What does it take to be successful given the realities of the new economy?

Rapid Review ◀◀|

✓ What is globalization, and how is it affecting the entrepreneurial context?

✓ Why is it important for entrepreneurs to understand demographics?

✓ Describe five significant demographic trends that are impacting the nature of the new economy.

✓ What are the four major implications arising out of the driving forces of the new economy?

✓ What is change, and how is it impacting the entrepreneurial context?

✓ Why is there a reduced need for physical assets in the new economy?

✓ Describe how the concepts of vanishing distance and compressed time impact the entrepreneurial context.

Critical Success Factors. Four critical factors for succeeding in the new economy are shown in Figure 2-1 (p. 34): ability to embrace change, creativity and innovation capabilities, vision and leadership, and total quality culture. Let's look at why each of these success factors is critical.

If there's one word that captures the essence of this new economy, it's *change.* Do you like change? Few people enjoy, or even seek out, change. Most of us think change is scary. We like order, not chaos. We like the old and comfortable, not the new or the unknown. But change is a given in this new economy. Being successful in this kind of turbulent environment means not only being tolerant of change but also seeking it out and embracing it with open arms. As we know from Chapter 1, entrepreneurs are comfortable with change. They know that change not only brings opportunities to take advantage of but also brings challenges in dealing successfully with the changes. These uncertainties don't faze successful entrepreneurs, however, as they seek out change and enjoy it immensely.

The second critical success factor for this new economy is creativity and innovation capabilities. Here's an abbreviated statement of just how critical this success factor is: "Create and innovate or lose!" It's that simple. In this dynamic, chaotic world of technological change, information revolution, globalization, and changing demographics, entrepreneurs must be prepared to create new products and services and adopt state-of-the-art technology if their ventures are to compete successfully and survive. **Creativity**, the ability to combine ideas in a unique way or to make unusual associations between ideas, is an important capability.[10] A

FYI

Developing Your Creativity

If asked, many of us would say that we're not very creative. However, in a dynamic and turbulent environment, where changes are fast and furious, creativity is crucial! How can you become more creative? It's easier than you think!

Researchers who have looked at creativity say that being creative is a matter of deciding what you want to do, how you can do it, and how you can do it better. It involves the *process*, not just the outcome. So now that we've taken some of the pressure off—you don't *have* to be a Michelangelo or a Beethoven to be creative—what steps can you take to develop your creativity? Here are some specific suggestions to help develop your own creative abilities.

1. *Relax.* Some relaxation techniques include clearing your mind mentally, listening to classical music, meditating, telling a joke to someone, going off by yourself to someplace quiet, or stopping thinking about the problem and returning to it later.

2. *Exercise your mind.* This includes activities such as playing freely with ideas without any specific problem to solve, practicing concentrating on a single issue, trying to think of unique solutions to personal or work-related problems, and practicing becoming comfortable with not having complete control over problems or outcomes.

3. *Determine what you want to do.* This includes such things as taking time to understand an issue before even beginning to try resolving it, getting all the facts in mind, and trying to identify the most important facts.

4. *Look for ways to tackle issues.* This can be done by setting aside a block of time to focus on them; working out a plan for attacking them; establishing subgoals; imagining or actually acting out the issues; thinking of similar issues and how you solved them before; using analogies wherever possible (for example, could you approach your problem like a fish out of water and how it copes, or can you use what you do to find your way when it's foggy?) to help you resolve them; using different problem-solving approaches such as verbal, visual, mathematical, theatrical (for example, you might draw a diagram of the issue to help you visualize it better, or you might talk to yourself out loud describing the problem, or you might tell it as a story to someone else); trusting your intuition; and playing with different possible ideas and approaches (for instance, ask yourself what your grandmother might do if faced with this issue).

5. *Look for ways to do things better.* This may involve trying consciously to be more original, not worrying about looking foolish, eliminating or ignoring cultural taboos (such as gender stereotypes) that might influence your possible solutions, keeping an open mind, being alert to odd or puzzling facts, thinking of unconventional ways to use objects and the environment (for example, could newspaper or magazine headlines help you be more creative?), discarding usual or habitual ways of doing things, and striving for objectivity by being as critical of your own ideas as you are of others'.

Source: S. P. Robbins and M. Coulter, "Developing Your Creativity," *Management*, 5th ed. (Upper Saddle River, NJ: Prentice Hall, 1996), p. 209.

creative person or organization develops novel approaches to doing work or unique solutions to problems. But, it doesn't stop there. We know from our earlier chapter discussion that innovation is the process of taking a creative idea and then turning it into a useful product. An innovative person or organization is characterized by the ability to channel creativity into useful outcomes. Both capabilities, being creative and being innovative, are critical to entrepreneurial success in this new economy.

The third critical success factor involves vision and leadership. Think back to our chapter-opening case and Jeff Bezos's vision of Internet commerce. His interpretation of Internet usage and its potential for selling products compelled him to take dramatic action. Success in this new economy means visualizing what can be and pursuing this dream. A **vision** is a broad comprehensive picture of what an entrepreneur wants an organization to become. It's a statement of what the organization stands for, what it believes in, and why it exists. The vision provides a vibrant and compelling picture of the future. It presents a view beyond what the entrepreneurial venture "is" to what it "can be."[11] The vision is the embodiment of the entrepreneur's dream. You may think that the concept of a "vision" is pretty off the wall, hard to grasp, and weird—something that sounds good on paper, but isn't at all realistic or useful in improving an organization's performance. However, when an organizational leader—in this case, the entrepreneur—is able to articulate a distinct vision, all current and future decisions and actions are guided by this vision. It provides a marker in the vast array of potential directions an entrepreneur might pursue. By articulating a vision, the entrepreneur maps out an overall picture of where he or she would like the entrepreneurial venture to be in the future. Being successful in the tumultuous new economy requires this type of vision and the leadership to create, embrace, and convey it.

The final critical success factor for the new economy is having a **total quality culture**, in which all organizational resources and capabilities are engaged in a never-ending quest for greater quality in every single part of the organization.[12] Why is having a total quality culture so important? It's because quality is an absolute necessity in this new economy. Customers demand—and expect—it. There are too many other product or service options available to customers for organizations to ignore quality! Those who do, risk losing out. But, then, the question becomes, what is quality? How would *you* define it? Granted, the concept is not an especially easy one to describe. Each of us probably has his or her own perspective on what a "quality" product or service is—each correct in its own way. To help resolve this definitional dilemma, five different views of quality are illustrated in Figure 2-2. No matter which view you buy into, it's important that an entrepreneurial venture focuses all its resources and capabilities on the pursuit of quality in everything it does—in every decision and action. A total quality culture facilitates this pursuit.

There are many entrepreneurial opportunities and challenges associated with the realities of the new economy. However, not only do entrepreneurs need to be aware of these issues, they also need to know how legal factors are parts of the entrepreneurial context. That's what we're going to look at next.

Legal Environment

As we explore the context facing entrepreneurs, we can't ignore the impact of the legal environment. A society's laws and regulations provide the framework within

Figure 2-2

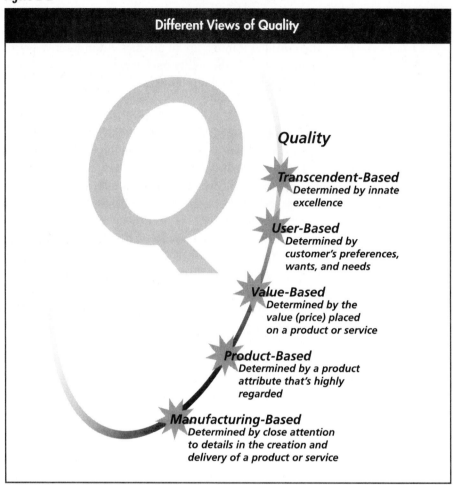

Different Views of Quality

Quality

Transcendent-Based
Determined by innate
excellence

User-Based
Determined by
customer's preferences,
wants, and needs

Value-Based
Determined by the
value (price) placed
on a product or service

Product-Based
Determined by a product
attribute that's highly
regarded

Manufacturing-Based
Determined by close attention
to details in the creation and
delivery of a product or service

Source: Based on D. Garvin, *Managing Quality* (New York: Free Press, 1988).

which its citizens can do or not do certain things. The legal environment both allows and prohibits certain decisions and actions. Obviously, entrepreneurs are affected by these legal issues and need to be aware of these factors before embarking on an entrepreneurial journey.

What first comes to your mind when you think of the legal environment? Is it laws and regulations and all the "red tape" that are a hassle to deal with whenever, for example, you have to renew your driver's license or car tags? Maybe it's forms and documents that must be completed, signed, and submitted by certain deadlines, such as the Internal Revenue Service's Form 1040. Perhaps it's Judge Judy and her strict courtroom rules, comments, and judgments. Well, believe it or not, the reality of the legal environment entrepreneurs must deal with isn't quite this cynical or negative! Yes, there are going to

Rapid Review ◀◀▌

✓ What are the four critical factors for succeeding in the new economy?

✓ Why is it important for entrepreneurs to be comfortable with change?

✓ What is creativity, and why is it important?

✓ How can you develop your creativity?

✓ What is vision? What role does it play in helping an entrepreneur succeed?

✓ Describe what a total quality culture is. Why is having one important?

Entrepreneurs in Action ▶

Skip Maggiora's vision was to provide a way for others to pursue their dreams. Dreams of being in a rock and roll band, that is. For a large number of baby boomers (that large demographic group of people born between the years 1946 and 1964), playing and singing in front of a live audience is a way, although fleetingly, to relive their reckless youth. Skip's company, Skip's Music located in Sacramento, California, provides a way for these rock star wannabes to take up music again. If they get hooked, Skip has the instruments for them to purchase. The program is called Weekend Warriors, and for $75 per person, the store puts people into a band and provides the instruments, a professional coach, and a sound-stage for four once-a-week rehearsals. Then, in the fifth week, Skip organizes a concert with four to six bands at a local hotel. He prints up tickets for the band members to give to family and friends. The bands' members become "stars" for a night. Skip has taken his Weekend Warriors plan national, which has helped boost his company's annual revenues to around $9 million.

Source: L. Armstrong, "Rocking Their Wallets," *Business Week Enterprise*, November 9, 1998, pp. ENT8–ENT10.

be certain things that you must do and certain things you absolutely cannot do. Pursuing your entrepreneurial dream means you'd better know and understand the legal constraints. Figure 2-3 illustrates several important legal issues affecting an entrepreneurial venture.

During the start-up stage, an entrepreneur faces certain legal issues. These can include determining the form of business organization, setting up appropriate records for tax purposes, negotiating leases and financing, drawing up contracts, and filing for patents, trademarks, and copyright protection. In each of these start-up activities, certain laws and regulations affect what an entrepreneur can and cannot do. An entrepreneur must be familiar with the relevant laws and regulations affecting the proposed venture. But the impact of the legal context on the entrepreneurial venture doesn't end there. When the entrepreneurial venture is up and running, there are legal issues associated with managing that ongoing business. For instance, human resource management laws and regulations may affect hiring, compensation, and performance appraisal decisions. Or, for example, safety laws and regulations may impact product design and packaging, workplace and equipment design and use, and environmental pollution control and species protection. Table 2-4 provides a brief description of some of the most recent laws and regulations (those enacted since 1970) that impact ongoing businesses. Although many laws may apply only when an organization reaches a certain size, the fact that entrepreneurial ventures are oriented toward growth means that entrepreneurs can face these legal issues fairly quickly. Entrepreneurs must also

Figure 2-3

Legal Issues at Different Stages

Entrepreneurial Venture

Legal Issues in Start-Up

- *Determine form of business organization*
- *Set up record keeping for tax purposes*
- *Conduct lease and financing negotiations*
- *Draw up contracts*
- *File for patents, trademarks, and copyright protection*

Legal Issues in Managing the Ongoing Business

- *Human resource management laws and regulations*
- *Safety laws and regulations (product, workplace, environmental)*
- *Financial and accounting laws and regulations*
- *Marketplace laws and regulations*

recognize with respect to the legal context that the federal government isn't the only source of laws and regulations. State and local governmental laws and regulations may also influence the ongoing operation of the entrepreneurial venture.

It should be clear to you by now that legal factors do play an important part in the entrepreneurial context. Before an entrepreneur proceeds with the entrepreneurial venture, it's important to know the pertinent laws and regulations. The next thing we need to examine in relation to the entrepreneurial context is how the world of "work" has changed and the implications for entrepreneurs.

Changing World of Work

Most people define *work* in terms of a job. You've probably worked at a job sometime during your life. Stop for a minute and think about what a "job" is. For most people, having a job implies regular work hours, written or orally communicated job descriptions that specify certain work responsibilities, regular and routine tasks that must be completed, and bosses who tell workers what needs to be done. Jobs can be described as the essence of predictability and security. There's only one problem with this view. It's no longer realistic given today's dynamic and turbulent environment! This image that we have of organizations with specific, rigid "jobs" that people work at just isn't appropriate or feasible anymore. This view might have been appropriate in an environment that was relatively stable and predictable. However,

TABLE 2-4 Selected Significant Legislation Regulating Business Since 1970	
Legislation	**Purpose**
Occupational Safety and Health Act of 1970	Requires employer to provide a working environment free from hazards to health
Consumer Product Safety Act of 1972	Sets standards on selected products; requires warning labels, and orders product recalls
Equal Employment Opportunity Act of 1972	Forbids discrimination in all areas of employer–employee relations
Americans with Disabilities Act of 1990	Prohibits employers from discriminating against individuals with physical or mental disabilities or the chronically ill; also requires organizations to reasonably accommodate these individuals
Civil Rights Act of 1991	Reaffirms and tightens prohibition of discrimination; permits individuals to sue for punitive damages in cases of intentional discrimination
Women's Business Development Act of 1991	Assists the development of small business concerns owned and controlled by women through a training program and a loan program that eases access to credit through the Small Business Administration (SBA) loan program
Family and Medical Leave Act of 1993	Grants 12 weeks of unpaid leave each year to employees for the birth or adoption of a child or the care of a spouse, child, or parent with a serious health condition; covers organizations with 50 or more employees
North American Free Trade Agreement of 1993	Created a free trade zone between the United States, Canada, and Mexico
U.S. Economic Espionage Act of 1996	Makes theft or misappropriation of trade secrets a federal crime
Electronics Signatures in Global and National Commerce Act of 2000	Gives online contracts (those signed by computer) the same legal force as equivalent paper contracts

today's world of work is changing and these changes are affecting the entrepreneurial context. We're going to look at two major areas of changes that have impacted the way people work. The first is the nature of the work they do and the second concerns the organizational setting within which work takes place.

The nature of work that people do in organizations has changed. The major change is that work is much more knowledge intensive. Knowledge has become an important component of task accomplishment, even in jobs that you might think traditionally don't require it—for instance, driving a truck or waiting tables. Today, employees are expected to use their mental abilities in addition to their physical ones. The application of knowledge to everything an organization's employees do has become necessary for prospering and even surviving in today's dynamic environment. In fact, an organization that has developed the continuous capacity to adapt and change by acquiring information and knowledge and incorporating these into decisions and actions is called a **learning organization**. A learning organization is one in which people look for new ways of thinking, are open to each other, understand how the organization really works, have a vision that everyone agrees on, and then work together to achieve that vision.[13] It's the type of organizational atmosphere that an entrepreneur needs to cultivate if he or she wants to be successful given today's environmental context. Although the knowledge-oriented nature of work today is a good example of how work has changed, it's also characteristic of the changed organizational setting within which work takes place. We also need to look at some other changes in the organizational setting.

As we know from our previous discussion of the driving forces behind the new economy, it's a fast-moving world out there! Traditional approaches to getting work done through rigid and inflexible job assignments just won't cut it anymore! Instead, the organizational setting necessary for succeeding in today's environmental context is one characterized by flexibility, temporariness, and independence. Instead of a "job," we have to think in terms of packets of skills and abilities applied to specific tasks. In fact, many of today's successful entrepreneurial organizations contend with the rapidly changing environment by doing their work using projects. A **project** is a one-time-only set of activities that has a definite beginning and ending point in time. As a need arises, people with the necessary skills and abilities are assigned work responsibilities to complete the project. As projects are completed, employees move to another one. It's an approach to work that recognizes the need to be flexible, temporary, and independent.

You may be asking yourself about now, so what? I just want to start my own business. How could these changes in our views about work possibly affect me? And that's a good question! Again, keep in mind that in this chapter we're looking at the context that's affecting entrepreneurial organizations. The demands imposed by the various components of the context will influence choices that you make about how work is going to get done in your entrepreneurial venture. The facts that the nature of work and the organizational setting within which work is done have changed will affect the way you do your work and if you have additional employees, the way they do their work. So, yes, the characteristics of the changing world of work are important to recognize and understand.

The final aspect of the environmental context that we need to look at involves the concepts of social responsibility and ethics. These are never easy issues to discuss, but they do play a significant role in influencing entrepreneurial decisions and actions.

Rapid Review ◀◀|

✓ Why is the legal environment an important part of the entrepreneurial context?
✓ What legal issues affect an entrepreneurial venture?
✓ Describe some of the important federal laws and regulations that impact businesses.
✓ How is the world of work changing?
✓ What impact are the changes in the work world having on entrepreneurial ventures?
✓ What is a learning organization, and why is this concept of interest to entrepreneurs?
✓ How might entrepreneurs use projects?

Social Responsibility and Ethics

How much and what type of social responsibility an organization should pursue has been a topic of heated debate for a number of years. **Social responsibility** is the obligation of organizational decision makers to make decisions and act in ways that recognize the interrelatedness of business and society.[14] Social responsibility assumes the existence of various **stakeholders**, individuals or groups who have a stake in or are significantly influenced by an organization's decisions and actions and who, in turn, can influence the organization. However, it's in the definition of "whom" organizations are responsible to that we find a diversity of opinions.

The traditional view of social responsibility was that organizations existed solely to serve the interests of one stakeholder group—the stockholders.[15] Milton Friedman has been the biggest advocate of this view. He argued that organizational social programs and actions must be paid for in some way, which adds to the costs of doing business. These costs have to be either passed on to customers in the form of higher prices or absorbed internally. In either case, profits might suffer because customers might buy less at higher prices or organizational costs would increase. Stockholders, the true "owners" of the organization, are interested in increasing profits and the return they're earning on their investments. You do need to understand, however, that Friedman didn't say that organizations shouldn't be socially responsible. In fact, he said they *should* be. Yet his argument was that the extent of the responsibility was to maximize stockholder returns.

However, the traditional—and purely economic—perspective of social responsibility has given way to a belief that organizations have a larger societal role to play and a broader constituency to serve than just stockholders alone. Possible organizational stakeholders are illustrated in Figure 2-4. Balancing the demands of these various stakeholders is, as you can well imagine, a complicated process because they often have a wide range of needs and conflicting expectations. Take just a minute and think about how an entrepreneurial organization could be socially responsible in each of these possible stakeholder relationships. There are numerous examples of organizations that believe in strong and socially responsible stakeholder relationships. For example, Ben and Jerry's Homemade, Inc., a successful entrepreneurial venture best known for its premium ice cream, has become a prototype of social responsibility with its efforts to promote world peace, preserve the environment, and support local businesses. Although social responsibility emphasizes the broad picture of an organization's societal interac-

Figure 2-4

> ### Entrepreneurs in Action
>
> Doing well by doing good. It's not just a nice thought at Blue Fish Clothing Inc. Jennifer Paige Barclay, who founded the business, has found a way to do just that. Her artistic clothes are made with natural dyes and pesticide-free cotton. She says her clothes are made from "products that are sourced responsibly." Her philosophy is to create artistic keepsake clothing *and* to emphasize social and environmental responsibility. Blue Fish clothing is fairly pricey ($58 and up for a T-shirt and $200 to $300 for a dress), but customers are loyal, loving the unique designs and the company's social philosophy.
>
> *Source:* J. Oleck, "Spinning Profits from Nice Threads," *Business Week Enterprise*, December 22, 1997, p. ENT6.

tions, it's also important that these interactions take place in a context of "doing the right thing." That's where the concept of ethics comes in.

By this time in your life, you've undoubtedly faced numerous ethical dilemmas, both in academics and, if you're employed, at your job. For instance, is it ethical to make a copy of inexpensive computer software for a friend who's short of money or to "donate" copies of completed homework assignments to your sorority or fraternity? Or say you're a telemarketing representative. Is it ethical for you to pressure customers to purchase a product just so you can win a prize? **Ethics** involves the rules and principles that define right and wrong decisions and behaviors. In other words, as we live our lives—attend school, work, engage in hobbies, and so forth—certain decisions and behaviors are ethically "right" and others are ethically "wrong." Considering the varied interpretations of right and wrong, you can see how ethics is a complex topic to address. However, ethical considerations do play a role in decisions and actions you will take with your entrepreneurial venture. You need to be aware of the ethical consequences of your decisions and actions. The example that you set, especially if you have other employees, can be profoundly significant in influencing behavior. For example, Charlie Wilson, founder of Houston-based SeaRail International Inc., made ethics a consideration in putting together guidelines for his sales representatives. He says, "Ethics is what's spearheading our growth. It creates an element of trust, familiarity, and predictability in the business. . . . You don't get a good reputation doing things that way [unethically]. And, if you do [act unethically], eventually customers won't want to do business with you."[16] The importance that entrepreneurs place on ethics can be seen in the results of a study of around 300 business owners and corporate managers. It showed that entrepreneurs generally have stricter ethical standards than do managers and are also better able to live by their beliefs, probably because they have more control over their decisions and actions. Only half of the entrepreneur respondents said that they would sacrifice personal ethics to achieve business goals as compared to 71 percent of the corporate managers.[17]

Being Ethical

As an entrepreneur, you'll undoubt-edly face ethical dilemmas. How will you deal with them? There are no easy answers to these types of dilemmas. However, the following guidelines might help you evaluate the ethical sit-uation more clearly.

1. Is the ethical dilemma what it appears to be? If you're not sure, you need to find out all you can about it.
2. Is the action you're considering legal? Is it ethical? If you're not sure, find out.
3. Do you understand the position of those who might be opposed to the action you're considering? Does their opposition sound reasonable?
4. Whom will your action(s) benefit? Harm? How much will it benefit or harm others? For how long?
5. Have you sought out the opinions of others who might have knowledge, training, or information about the situation and who could be objective?
6. Would you be embarrassed to have your action(s) made known to family, friends, neighbors, or others around you? How would you feel about having your action(s) reported in the local newspaper or on the evening news?

There are no correct answers to these ques-tions. But by using these guidelines, you should be better able to clarify whether your action(s) are ethically and socially responsible.

Sources: A. M. Pagano and J. A. Verdin, *The External Environment of Business* (New York: John Wiley, 1988), Chapter 5; and J. L. Badaracco Jr. and A. P. Webb, "Business Ethics: A View from the Trenches," *California Management Review*, winter 1995, pp. 8–28.

We've now looked at all the various contextual issues that might potentially affect entrepreneurs and their pursuit of entrepreneurship. Within this complex and dynamic environmental context, entrepreneurs need to be alert to certain trends and changes because of the potential opportunities they present. That's the next topic we're going to look at.

Rapid Review ◀◀|

✓ What is social responsibility?
✓ What are stakeholders, and what role do they play in entrepreneurial ventures?
✓ Describe the different types of stakeholders.
✓ Describe the traditional view of social responsibility, and describe the more contemporary view.
✓ What are ethics, and why are ethical considerations important to entrepreneurs?
✓ Describe the guidelines an entrepreneur can follow in order to be ethical.

IDENTIFYING ENVIRONMENTAL OPPORTUNITIES

The skyrocketing Internet usage that Jeff Bezos, our chapter-opening entrepreneur in action, observed is a prime example of identifying environmental opportunities. What exactly are **opportunities**? They're positive external environmental trends or changes that provide unique and distinct possibilities for innovating and creating value. Entrepreneurs need to be able to pinpoint these pockets of oppor-tunity that a changing context provides. Peter Drucker, a well-known management author, has identified seven potential sources of opportunity to look for in the external context.[18] These include the unexpected, the incongruous, the process need, industry and market structures, demographics, changes in perception, and new knowledge. Let's examine each of these more closely.

1. *The unexpected.* When situations and events are unanticipated, opportunities can be found. The event might be an unexpected success (positive news) or an unexpected failure (bad news). Either way, there can be opportunities for entrepreneurs to pursue. For instance, the publicized accidental skiing deaths of two well-known individuals (Sonny Bono and Michael Kennedy) proved to be a bonanza for ski helmet manufacturers as novice and seasoned skiers alike began to wear protective headgear. These events were unexpected and proved to be opportunities for entrepreneurs in that industry.

2. *The incongruous.* When something is incongruous, there are inconsistencies and incompatibilities in the way it appears. Things "ought to be" a certain way, but aren't. When conventional wisdom about the way things should be no longer holds true, for whatever reason, there are opportunities to capture. Entrepreneurs who are willing to "think outside the box"—that is, to think beyond the traditional and conventional approaches—may find pockets of potential profitability. Fred Smith, founder of FedEx, recognized the incongruity in the delivery of documents. His approach was: Why not? Who says that overnight delivery is impossible? Smith's answer to those incongruous questions was the creation of FedEx, now the world's largest express package delivery organization.

3. *The process need.* What happens when technology doesn't come up with the "big discovery" that's going to fundamentally change the very nature of some product or service? Well, what happens is that there can be pockets of entrepreneurial opportunity in the various stages of the process as researchers and technicians continue to work for the monumental breakthrough. Because they've not been able to make the full leap, opportunities abound in the tiny steps. A good example of this can be seen in the medical products industry. Although researchers have not yet discovered, for example, a cure for cancer, there have been many successful entrepreneurial ventures created and pursued as our knowledge about a possible cure continues to expand. The "big breakthrough" hasn't happened, but there have been numerous entrepreneurial opportunities throughout the process of discovery.

4. *Industry and market structures.* When changes in technology change the structure of an industry and market, existing firms can become obsolete if they're not attuned to the changes or are unwilling to change. Even changes in social values and consumer tastes can shift the structures of industries and markets. These markets and industries become open targets for nimble and smart entrepreneurs. The whole Internet realm provides several good examples of existing industries and markets being challenged by upstart entrepreneurial ventures. Think back to our chapter-opening case and how Jeff Bezos and Amazon.com have changed the book industry.

5. *Demographics.* We know from our earlier chapter discussion that the characteristics of the world's population—that is, demographics—are changing. These changes influence industries and markets by altering the types and quantities of products and services desired and customers' buying power. Although

> ### Entrepreneurs in Action
>
> One industry that's spawned a number of environmental opportunities for entrepreneurs (and threats for the established companies!) is the recorded music industry. Michael Robertson, chief executive of MP3.com, is one of the most controversial entrepreneurs. Robertson's revolutionary approach to music distribution seems incongruent with his conservative appearance and his evangelical Christian background. However, his company is making waves (sound waves, that is) by pursuing a new way of delivering music. MP3.com offers free music from over 7,000 artists over the Internet, and MP3's Web site gets around 250,000 visitors a day. That's a lot of eardrums! Robertson's approach to doing business is patterned after that of his idol, Steven P. Jobs, the legendary founder of Apple and Pixar. Robertson says, "I've got a lot of respect for him because he zigged when everybody else zagged, and that's what we're doing." By enthusiastically embracing the changing technology and being alert to opportunities, Robertson has blazed a trail in this rapidly changing industry.
>
> **Source:** A. Foege, "Capturing Ears on the Internet," *New York Times,* April 11, 1999, p. BU2.

many of these changes are fairly predictable if you stay alert to demographic trends, others are not as obvious. Either way, there can be significant entrepreneurial opportunities in anticipating and meeting the changing needs of the population. For instance, the burgeoning Hispanic population has spawned a number of new grocery products that cater to the tastes of this group.

6. *Changes in perception.* Perception is one's view of reality. When changes in perception take place, the facts do not vary, but their meaning does. Changes in perception get at the heart of people's psychographic profiles—what they value, what they believe in, and what they care about. Changes in these attitudes and values create potential market opportunities for alert entrepreneurs. For example, think about your perception of healthy foods. As our perception of whether or not certain food groups are good for us has changed, there have been product and service opportunities for entrepreneurs to recognize and capture.

7. *New knowledge.* As the "superstar" of entrepreneurship, new knowledge provides a significant source of entrepreneurial opportunity. However, not all knowledge-based innovations are significant. Some are downright trivial. Yet, as a source of opportunity, new knowledge ranks pretty high on the list! It does take more than just having new knowledge, though. It often takes the convergence of several pieces of new knowledge. You also have to be able to

Rapid Review ◀◀|

✓ What are opportunities?

✓ Why is the concept of opportunities important for entrepreneurs?

✓ List the seven potential sources of opportunity in the external environment.

✓ Describe how each of these seven sources can generate opportunities.

make products from the knowledge and to protect that important proprietary information from competitors.

The importance of understanding the entrepreneurial context and being alert to potential opportunities cannot be overemphasized! It's also important for entrepreneurs to understand the concept of competitive advantage. That's what we're going to discuss next.

UNDERSTANDING COMPETITIVE ADVANTAGE

Competitive advantage is important to successful entrepreneurial ventures. What is it? **Competitive advantage** is what sets an organization apart—in other words, its competitive edge. When an organization has a competitive advantage, it has something that other competitors don't, does something better than do other organizations, or does something that others can't.

Competitive advantage is a necessary ingredient for an entrepreneurial venture's long-term success and survival. Getting and keeping a competitive advantage is tough to do and getting tougher. The pursuit of competitive advantage leads to organizational success or failure. Although success is obviously the preferable choice, organizations don't choose to fail. Instead, poor performance can typically be traced to poor or nonexistent competitive advantage. What does it take to get, and keep, a competitive advantage? There are two different views on this.[19]

The first perspective—the industrial organization, or I/O, perspective—says that competitive advantage arises out of the ability to look at important external factors, analyze those factors for potential opportunities, and then base organizational decisions and actions on what was uncovered. The focus of analysis in the I/O view is external. According to this view, getting and keeping a competitive advantage is dependent on the ability to see external trends and changes and interpret and act on them.

The second view of competitive advantage is called the resource-based view (RBV) and emphasizes exploiting internal organizational resources and capabilities. The focus of analysis in this view is internal. According to the RBV, getting and keeping a competitive advantage is dependent on developing unique organizational resources and capabilities.

Resources are simply the assets an organization has for carrying out whatever work activities and processes it's in business to do. These resources (assets) can be financial, physical, human, intangible, and organizational. Financial resources include debt capacity, credit lines, available equity (stock), cash reserves, and other financial (monetary) assets. Physical assets are tangible assets such as buildings, equipment and fixtures, raw materials, office supplies, manufacturing facilities, and so forth. Human resources include the experiences, knowledge, skills, accumulated wisdom, and characteristics of the organization's employees. Intangible resources are such things as brand names, patents, trademarks, databases, copyrights, or registered designs. Finally, organizational resources include such things as organizational history, culture, work systems, policies, relationships, and the formal or informal structure being used. The resources are the "whats"—what the organization has or owns.

Capabilities, on the other hand, are the "hows"—the organizational routines and processes that determine how efficiently and effectively the organization transforms its inputs (resources) into outputs (products and services). A good example to illustrate how resources and capabilities differ is someone who's considered an excellent cook. This cook will own pots and pans, spices, equipment, and other cooking materials (that is, resources) to be used in preparing delicious meals. Likewise, an organization possesses resources that can be used to put together, hopefully, a sustainable competitive advantage. Although an organization's resources can be considered its "pantry of goodies," these assets are much more valuable as they're used by the entrepreneur or other organizational members in doing their work. By themselves, the resources aren't productive. Remember our gourmet cook—he has to combine the spices and food using the appropriate equipment to put together delicious meals. Likewise, the organization's resources have to be combined through its capabilities in order to do whatever it's in business to do. As organizational members work, combining resources and within the structure of these organizational routines and processes, they accumulate knowledge and experience about how best to get the most out of the resources.

However, creating organizational capabilities isn't simply a matter of assembling resources. Instead, capabilities involve complex patterns of coordination between people and between people and other organizational resources. In fact, some organizations never get the hang of it. They're never quite able to develop efficient and effective capabilities and struggle exhaustively to survive in an increasingly dynamic and competitive marketplace.

The thing for entrepreneurs to remember is that both the I/O and RBV perspectives are important to getting a sustainable competitive advantage. Because the external environment is continually changing (for instance, new competitors come and go, customers' tastes change, technology changes, and so forth), the source of sustainable competitive advantage—the "edge" an organization has over its competitors—is probably found in different places at different points in time. The internal organizational resources and capabilities needed to capitalize on these changes will vary also. Pursuing a sustainable competitive advantage by taking advantage of any positive changes (or buffering against negative changes) with the entrepreneurial venture's unique resources is what it all boils down to. That's the ever-changing, yet constant, challenge for the entrepreneur.

Rapid Review ◀◀|

✓ What is competitive advantage, and why is the concept important for entrepreneurs?
✓ Compare and contrast the two perspectives on getting and keeping competitive advantage.
✓ What are resources? What are capabilities?
✓ Describe the five types of resources an organization has.
✓ Describe the connection between resources and capabilities.
✓ Which of the two approaches to competitive advantage is more important to entrepreneurs? Explain.

CHAPTER SUMMARY

To be a successful entrepreneur in action, it's important to know about the context in which entrepreneurship takes place. It's also vital to understand the concepts of opportunities and competitive advantage.

Four main contextual issues have the potential to affect entrepreneurship in action: the new economy, legal factors, the changing world of work, and social responsibility and ethics. The driving forces behind the new economy include the information revolution, technological advances and breakthroughs, globalization, and changing demographics. These driving forces have given rise to four major implications: continual turbulence and change, the reduced need for physical assets, vanishing distance, and compressed time. As a result of these, success in the new economy requires the ability to embrace change, creativity and innovation capabilities, vision and leadership, and a total quality culture.

Entrepreneurs also must recognize the legal factors that are part of the environmental context. A society's laws and regulations provide the framework within which actions and decisions are both allowed and prohibited. Primarily, the entrepreneur must cope with legal issues during the start-up stage and, once the entrepreneurial venture is up and running, while managing the ongoing business.

The changing world of work also has had an impact on the context facing entrepreneurs. The major change in the nature of work that people do revolves around the fact that it's much more knowledge intensive than it used to be. Also, the organizational setting within which work takes place has changed. Today's workplace is characterized by flexibility, temporariness, and independence.

The final aspects of the environmental context that play an important role in influencing entrepreneurial decisions and actions are social responsibility and ethics. The traditional, and purely economic, view of social responsibility has given way to a belief that organizations have a larger societal role to play and a broader constituency to serve. Although social responsibility emphasizes the broad picture of an organization's societal interactions, it's also important that these interactions take place in a context of doing the right thing. That's where the concept of ethics comes in.

Within the complex and dynamic environmental context, entrepreneurs need to be alert to certain trends and changes because of the potential opportunities they present. There are seven potential sources of opportunities: the unexpected, the incongruous, the process need, industry and market structure, demographics, changes in perception, and new knowledge.

Finally, it's crucial for entrepreneurs to recognize the role that competitive advantage plays in successful entrepreneurial ventures. Getting and keeping a competitive advantage isn't easy. However, by recognizing the role that the external environment plays and the role that internal resources and capabilities play, an entrepreneur can pursue a sustainable competitive advantage.

KEY TERMS

⟫ *E-commerce:* An abbreviation for *electronic commerce*, which refers to business sales transactions that take place online.

⟫ *Telecommuters:* Individuals who are linked to a workplace by computers and modems.

⟫ *Virtual organizations:* Organizations with little or no physical work space, no formal hierarchical structure, and individuals who contract to perform specific work as needed.

- *Technology:* The use of equipment, materials, knowledge, and experience to perform tasks.
- *Innovation:* The process of taking a creative idea and turning it into a product or process that can be used or sold.
- *Patent:* A legal property that allows its holder to prevent others from employing this property for their own use for a specified period of time.
- *Globalization:* The international linkage of economies and cultures that fosters a business and competitive situation in which organizations have no national boundaries.
- *Demographics:* The physical characteristics of a population such as gender, age, income levels, ethnic makeup, education, family composition, geographic locations, birthrates, employment status, and so forth.
- *Change:* Any alteration in external environmental or internal organizational factors.
- *Creativity:* The ability to combine ideas in a unique way or to make unusual associations between ideas.
- *Vision:* A broad comprehensive picture of what an entrepreneur wants an organization to become.
- *Total quality culture:* An organizational culture in which all organizational resources and capabilities are engaged in a never-ending quest for greater quality in every single part of the organization.
- *Learning organization:* An organization that has developed the continuous capacity to adapt and change by acquiring information and knowledge and incorporating these into decisions and actions.
- *Project:* A one-time-only set of activities that has a definite beginning and ending point in time.
- *Social responsibility:* The obligation of organizational decision makers to make decisions and act in ways that recognize the interrelatedness of business and society.
- *Stakeholders:* Individuals or groups who have a stake in or are significantly influenced by an organization's decisions and actions and who, in turn, can influence the organization.
- *Ethics:* The rules and principles that define right and wrong decisions and behaviors.
- *Opportunities:* Positive external environmental trends or changes that provide unique and distinct possibilities for innovating and creating value.
- *Competitive advantage:* What sets an organization apart; its competitive edge.
- *Resources:* The assets an organization has for carrying out whatever work activities and processes it's in business to do.
- *Capabilities:* The organizational routines and processes that determine how efficiently and effectively an organization transforms its inputs (resources) into outputs (products and services).

SWEAT EQUITY

1. An article in *Business 2.0* ("Minds Over Matter," January 1999 issue) proposed that the new economy is based on brains, not brawn. In this new economy, intellectual (knowledge) capital is critical. According to author Don Tapscott, the only assets that count in this new economic arena are people assets—those with brains, knowledge, and the ability to think and innovate. People serve as the key to a sustainable competitive advantage. Your assignment is to research the topic of people as a competitive advantage. Using your research results, type up a bulleted list of important points you found (at least one page). Then, write up what you think the implications of this perspective might be for entrepreneurs. Be sure to cite your research sources!

2. Judo strategy just might be an appropriate description of what successfully competing in today's dynamic context requires. (See D. B. Yoffie and M. A. Cusumano, "Judo Strategy: The Competitive Dynamics of Internet Time," *Harvard Business Review*, January–February, 1999, pp. 71–81.) According to this description, a successful judo practitioner needs three things: rapid movement, flexibility, and leverage. Write a paper that addresses the following issues:
   - What do you think each of these characteristics refers to in relation to competing in today's dynamic context?
   - What role might these three characteristics play as entrepreneurs create and manage their businesses?
   - Find two examples of entrepreneurs in action who you feel fit the characteristics of a judo strategy. (Check out *Business 2.0, Fast Company, Inc.,* other news sources, or personal contacts.) Write a description of these entrepreneurial ventures: what they're doing and why you think they're good examples of a judo strategy.

3. In today's intensely competitive world, ethical business behavior isn't just something that's "good" to do—it's a valuable necessity. One thing an entrepreneur can do to behave ethically, and to encourage employees to behave ethically, is to have a written code of ethics. You're going to have the opportunity to create one! Research (using the library, Internet, or personal interviews with entrepreneurs) codes of ethics. Try to find out what should be in a code of ethics and perhaps even get some real examples. Then, create a code of ethics. Be prepared to provide your list of reference sources!

4. As an entrepreneur you need to recognize opportunities. Refamiliarize yourself with the seven potential sources of opportunity. Then, read through the five latest issues of any business or general news periodical (*Business Week, Inc., Fast Company, Time, Newsweek, Wall Street Journal,* and so forth). Use one or any combination of these magazines. Based upon your analysis, make a bulleted list of potential opportunities. Note which source of opportunity each of your items falls under. This assignment is going to require you to be really creative and open-minded. Look for the unusual connections and the unseen, yet potential, linkages. Have fun!

5. "We're from the government and we're here to help you." Does this phrase make you smirk knowingly? Well, an entrepreneur's best friend just may be the government. As we discussed in this chapter, legal factors both allow and prohibit certain behaviors and actions and, as such, affect the entrepreneurial context. But, the government can also be a source of immense help. Your

assignment is to do some research into the help for entrepreneurs offered by your local and state governments. Find out what types of entrepreneurial programs, assistance, and help are available in your community. Once you have collected this information, sort it according to start-up assistance and assistance for ongoing businesses. Write up a report describing what you have found.

ENTREPRENEURSHIP IN ACTION CASES

CASE #1: King of the Online Jungle

Entrepreneurship in Action case #1 can be found at the beginning of Chapter 2.

Discussion Questions

1. What source of opportunity seems to describe Jeff Bezos's idea for starting up Amazon.com? Explain your choice.

2. In the still-evolving world of the Internet, legal issues are often hard to pinpoint because it's such a new type of environ-

ment. What do you think would be the best way for an entrepreneur to deal with this type of legal uncertainty? Explain.

3. Go to Amazon.com's Web site (**www.amazon.com**) and find examples of how the company is being both socially responsible and ethical. Describe these and how they're examples of social responsibility or ethics.

CASE #2: Road Rules—Jobs on Tour

Whereas most college graduates are concerned (and justifiably so!) about getting that first job, two women stressing out over their own job searches decided to pursue a vision for helping students make their own job searches as stressless as possible. Rachel Bell and Sara Sutton decided to start JobDirect, a Stamford, Connecticut–based Internet job service for entry-level positions. (Check it out at **www.jobdirect.com**.) After doing some serious research into their idea and raising money from family and friends, they purchased a recreational vehicle, had it spray-painted to look like their Web site, and took off on their first promotional tour of college campuses. The RV was equipped with 15 laptops for students to type in their résumés. After cruising around 43 campuses, their database

soon contained the résumés of 5,000 young job seekers. (Their database now contains over 80,000 résumés.) JobDirect.com was on its way to ruling the road!

How does their business work? Job seekers put their résumés into JobDirect's database and are automatically notified by e-mail when a position is posted by an employer that meets specifications they have noted. Individuals can then get more information by clicking on links, and, if they like what they see, they can click on a response button to send their résumés to the employer. Students use JobDirect for free. More than 100 clients (including Price Waterhouse, Sun Microsystems, and Teach for America) pay fees to post jobs and search the database by student major, college, grade-point average, or other criteria. JobDirect's annual revenues are over $3 million.

Bell and Sutton have some clever marketing ideas to keep their company's name visible. The company dispatches its three RVs to college campuses twice a year and also sends them out on an extremely popular summer concert tour. The vehicles are equipped with beds and kitchens for the student employees who direct the activities when the RV arrives at a campus. JobDirect also gives away free mouse pads imprinted with the company name. There are more than 250 student representatives around the country talking up JobDirect's services to college students.

Although Bell and Sutton are enjoying their work immensely and have provided a desirable service for graduating college students, they have yet to graduate from college themselves! But, it's something both still intend to do!

Discussion Questions

1. How did the realities of the new economy contribute to the idea for this entrepreneurial venture? Given these realities, is JobDirect doing what it should to continue its success? (*Hint:* You might want to check out Figure 2-1.)

2. There are a number of online recruiting sources, so competitive advantage is obviously something that Bell and Sutton are concerned about. What would you tell them about getting and keeping a competitive advantage?

3. How might the changing world of work affect the service that JobDirect provides? Are these potential impacts positive or negative? Explain.

(*Source:* C. Adler, "Have Résumés, Will Travel," *Business Week Enterprise,* May 25, 1998, p. ENT18.)

CASE #3: Top-Secret Trash

Some of the largest companies in the United States (high- and low-technology types) depend heavily on Barry Grahek. What does he do? His company, Shred-All Document Processing, based in Jacksonville, Florida, is a high-security disposal company. The $10 million business shreds supersensitive documents and other products. It has ground up disk drives, prototype tires, computer disk drives, and of course, paper documents detailing product design and marketing.

High-security disposal is a supersensitive business. Grahek has to be sure to maintain the highest level of integrity because others are depending on him to protect their proprietary information. Shred-All offers not only shredding services but also recycling services for those companies who want to be fashionably correct. To provide this type of service,

Grahek has bonded workers, locked boxes for recycled documents, unmarked trucks, and high-security shredding facilities.

Shred-All's competitors are generally small local shops that serve only limited areas. Grahek has taken a different approach. He has signed up large corporations nationwide by offering to handle all their branches in states they serve. The big waste disposal companies (think of Browning-Ferris and Waste Management) haven't pursued this business because their strength tends to lie in volume, not in serving individual customized jobs. That individualized service is what Grahek's Shred-All does best. What makes the service even more attractive is that Shred-All can do it at about a third of what it would cost the customer to do in-house. It's a case of everyone coming out ahead!

Discussion Questions

1. Trash. It may not exactly be your idea of a product that would be affected by the dynamics of the changing entrepreneurial context. However, Barry Grahek and his company are both profiting from and impacted by the changes taking place in the entrepreneurial context. Explain.

2. What role would social responsibility and ethics play in a company such as Shred-All? How could Grahek ensure that his employees are acting responsibly and ethically?

3. How important is competitive advantage in this business because there seems to be little competition? Support your response.

(*Source:* J. Tanner, "Top Dog in Top-Secret Trash," *Business Week Enterprise,* May 13, 1996, pp. ENT12–ENT14.)

VIDEO CASE #1: Successfully Selling Bagels—in Japan

182,600 bagels a week. By anyone's count, that's a lot of bagels! But that's the number being sold in Japan by Jerry Shapiro's company, Petrofsky's Bagels. He predicted that number was about to double and perhaps to triple. Who would have thought there was a market in Japan for that distinct bagel taste? Yet, Japanese consumers obviously have developed a fondness for Petrofsky's bagels.

Jerry Shapiro has been described as a modern-day explorer. It's probably fitting that Jerry's business is based in St. Louis, Missouri, because that city has long been a jumping-off point for many famous historical explorers preparing to survey the western United States. Jerry's vision for exploring the world and expanding his business, though, was more international. He believed that there was a strong potential market for his bagels in Japan. Although having a vision is important, it takes more than having a vision to be successful. It takes putting the vision into action.

How did Jerry pursue his vision? How did he get the Japanese initially to try his bagels and then get them to continue buying them? He says that getting past that initial hurdle involved several things. First and foremost was a significant amount of taste testing. Although this step was time-consuming and tedious work, he knew he was on the right track when a couple of elderly Japanese professors who tasted Petrofsky's bagels said the bread dough reminded them of something sweet they had eaten when they were younger. Jerry also said that getting his product into Japan involved several trips to that country and finding the proper trading partner. Anticipating trends and needs of the Japanese market wouldn't be possible sitting in his office in St. Louis. Instead Jerry had to experience the unique characteristics of the Japanese market firsthand and had to develop a strong, long-term relationship with his company's trading partner. Although the amount of preparation and planning to get into the Japanese market may have seemed overwhelming at times, Jerry was committed to pursuing his business no matter how long it took.

After successfully implementing his vision, Jerry gives the following advice to others who wish to pursue such a plan for going into international markets: Put your plan in writing. Solicit customer participation. Finally, be prepared to do whatever it takes to build long-term relationships.

Discussion Questions

1. Do you think the globalization trend played a role in Jerry's decision to go into the Japanese market? Why or why not?

2. Jerry said that anticipating trends and needs of the Japanese market wouldn't be possible by sitting in his office in St. Louis. Do you agree? Is this an example of why it's important to understand the entrepreneurial context? Explain.

3. Jerry gave three pieces of advice for those who want to go into international markets. Evaluate each.

(*Source:* Based on *Small Business Today,* Show 104.)

VIDEO CASE #2: When You Care Enough to Send the Very Best

Although "caring enough to send the very best" may be the marketing slogan for the world's largest manufacturer of greeting cards, caring and compassion also are fitting descriptions of Judi Jacobsen's Madison Park Greeting Card Company of Seattle, Washington. The slogan, however, would have to change to "caring enough to *do* the very best." Judi's compassion is directed at the community where her business is located and at the people she employs.

At the age of 30, Judi decided to pursue a desire to paint. People who saw and bought her paintings told Judi that they would make good greeting cards. Taking that advice to heart, together with a partner, Judi started Madison Park Greeting Card Company. Today she sells her greeting cards in over 4,000 specialty shops around the United States. Madison Park employs 25 people and has reached the $3 million sales mark. The admirable part of this story is not just the fact that Judi was able to pursue her dream, but that she had a strong commitment to helping others. Her community involvement started with her decision to locate her business in a building in a rundown section of town in order to help revitalize the area. In addition, Judi has a strong and specific concern for her employees.

Judi's entrepreneurial philosophy is that one of the best things you can do for your people is to give them meaningful work. To put this into practice, she has hired Cambodian refugees who couldn't speak English but who could pack cards into boxes. She has hired hearing-impaired employees and displaced mothers for other jobs at Madison Park. Judi strongly believes that people count more than the bottom line. Although she understands that businesses must do well financially to be able to help others, having a balance between profits and people is important. She says, "If I had to choose people or profits, I'd put people first."

Discussion Questions

1. What types of values do you think Judi Jacobsen's Madison Park Greeting Card Company embraces?

2. What's your opinion of Judi's statement, "If I had to choose people or profits, I'd put people first"? What would this type of philosophy imply as far as business decisions and actions?

3. The greeting card industry is an intensely competitive one. What would you tell Judi about competitive advantage? Come up with a bulleted list of important points you'd want to make to her.

(*Source:* Based on *Small Business 2000,* Show 104.)

ENDNOTES

1. G. B. Knight, "How Wall Street Whiz Found a Niche Selling Books on the Internet," *Wall Street Journal*, May 15, 1996, p. A1; K. Rebello, "A Literary Hangout—Without the Latte," *Business Week*, September 23, 1996, p. 106; M. H. Martin, "The Next Big Thing: A Bookstore?" *Fortune*, December 9, 1996, pp. 168–70; M. Slovan, "Bound for the Internet," *Nation's Business*, March 1997, pp. 34–36; M. Krantz, "Amazonian Challenge," *Time*, April 14, 1997, p. 71; and J. Daly, "Running Scared," *Business 2.0*, April 1999, pp. 66–70.

2. D. R. Gnyawali and D. S. Fogel, "Environments for Entrepreneurship Development: Key Dimensions and Research Implications," *Entrepreneurship Theory and Practice*, summer 1994, pp. 43–62.

3. S. Kerr and D. Ulrich, "Creating the Boundaryless Organization: The Radical Reconstruction of Organizational Capabilities," *Planning Review*, September–October 1995, pp. 41–45.

4. M. J. Mandel, "You Ain't Seen Nothing Yet," *Business Week*, August 31, 1998, pp. 60–63.

5. W. B. Arthur, *Increasing Returns and Path Dependence in the Economy* (Ann Arbor, MI: University of Michigan Press, 1994); R. A. Bettis and M. A. Hitt, "The New Competitive Landscape," *Strategic Management Journal*, summer 1995, pp. 7–19; J. Alley, "The Theory That Made Microsoft," *Fortune*, April 29, 1996, pp. 65–66; and W. B. Arthur, "Increasing Returns and the New World of Business," *Harvard Business Review*, July–August 1996, pp. 100–109.

6. C. Mulhern, "Going the Distance," *Entrepreneur*, May 1998, p. 129.

7. R. W. Oliver, *The Shape of Things to Come: 7 Imperatives for Winning in the New World of Business* (New York: McGraw-Hill, 1999), p. 23.

8. Ibid., pp. 42–45.

9. L. Robinson, " 'Hispanics' Don't Exist," *U.S. News & World Report*, May 11, 1998, pp. 26–32.

10. This definition is based on T. M. Amabile, "A Model of Creativity and Innovation in Organizations," in B. M. Staw and L. L. Cummings (eds.), *Research in Organizational Behavior*, Vol. 10 (Greenwich, CT: JAI Press, 1988), p. 126.

11. D. I. Silvers, "Vision—Not Just for CEOs," *Management Quarterly*, winter 1994–1995, pp. 10–14.

12. J. Batten, "A Total Quality Culture," *Management Review*, May 1994, p. 61.

13. B. Dumaine, "Mr. Learning Organization," *Fortune*, October 17, 1994, p. 148.

14. D. J. Wood, "Corporate Social Performance Revisited," *Academy of Management Review*, October 1991, pp. 691–718.

15. M. Friedman, *Capitalism and Freedom* (Chicago: University of Chicago Press, 1962).

16. G. S. Stodder, "Goodwill Hunting," *Entrepreneur*, July 1998, p. 119.

17. E. Updike, "The Straightest Arrows," *Business Week Enterprise*, October 12, 1998, p. ENT2.

18. P. Drucker, *Innovation and Entrepreneurship* (New York: Harper & Row, 1985).

19. This discussion of the industrial organization perspective and resources-based views was developed from the following: R. Amit and P. J. H. Schoemaker, "Strategic Assets and Organizational Rent," *Strategic Management Journal*, January 1993, pp. 33–46; J. B. Barney, "Asset Stocks and Sustained Competitive Advantage: A Comment," *Management Science*, December 1989, pp. 1511–13; J. B. Barney, "Firm Resources and Sustained Competitive Advantage," *Journal of Management*, Vol. 17, No. 1, 1991, pp. 99–120; D. J. Collis and C. A. Montgomery, "Competing on Resources: Strategy in the 1990s," *Harvard Business Review*, July–August 1995, pp. 118–28; K. R. Conner, "A Historical Comparison of Resource-Based Theory and Five Schools of Thought Within Industrial Organization Economics: Do We Have a New Theory of the Firm?" *Journal of Management*, Vol. 17, No. 1, 1991, pp. 121–54; I. Dierickx and K. Cool, "Asset Stock Accumulation and Sustainability of Competitive Advantage," *Management Science*, December 1989, pp. 1504–11; M. A. Peteraf, "The Cornerstones of Competitive Advantage: A Resource-Based View," *Strategic Management Journal*, March 1993, pp. 179–91; M. Porter, *Competitive Strategy: Techniques for Analyzing Industries and Competitors* (New York: Free Press, 1980); M. Porter, *Competitive Advantage: Creating and Sustaining Superior Performance* (New York: Free Press, 1985); B. Wernerfelt, "A Resource-Based View of the Firm," *Strategic Management Journal*, Vol. 5, 1984, pp. 171–80; and B. Wernerfelt, "The Resource-Based View of the Firm: Ten Years After," *Strategic Management Journal*, March 1995, pp. 171–74.

3

RESEARCHING THE VENTURE'S FEASIBILITY

LEARNING OBJECTIVES

After reading this chapter, you should be able to:

1. Identify misconceptions about and realities of great ideas.
2. Describe different ways to generate ideas for entrepreneurial ventures.
3. Explain how to evaluate ideas.
4. Define competition and describe the different ways to view competition.
5. Discuss how to do a competitive analysis.
6. List and explain the various financing options entrepreneurs may choose from.
7. Explain how to evaluate the various financing options.
8. Discuss the guidelines for seeking financing.

ENTREPRENEURSHIP IN ACTION CASE #1

Shooting the Moon

Brenda Laurel had some great ideas for computer video games.[1] Because most video games were designed for and aimed at adolescent boys, she felt that a vast potential audience—preteen and young adolescent girls—was being missed. Laurel believed that girls could use video games to solve challenges and become immersed in complex situations where they had to use their knowledge and skills to resolve pressing issues. Her creation, the character Rockett Movado, became the star computer game character of Laurel's company, Purple Moon (**www.purple-moon.com**).

Rockett is a lot like her creator, a spunky heroine. Brenda Laurel was a game designer who worked for Atari in the early 1980s. Purple Moon evolved out of her belief that girls "played" differently than boys. She interviewed 1,000 girls to find out how to apply their principles of play to computer games. It soon became clear to her that girls were not turned off by the violence in boys' games as much as they found the dying and starting

The story of Purple Moon's rise and fall is an interesting illustration of the importance of researching an entrepreneurial venture's feasibility. It tells how an entrepreneur spotted an idea, evaluated its potential, and started a company. But sometimes, even with the best research, an entrepreneurial venture can't overcome the dynamics of the marketplace. However, we can't deny the fact that it is important for entrepreneurs to research the venture's feasibility. That's what we're going to cover in this chapter. We'll be looking at different ways to generate ideas for entrepreneurial ventures, how to evaluate those ideas, how to research and evaluate the competition, and finally, we'll explore the various financing options that entrepreneurs have.

GENERATING AND EVALUATING BUSINESS IDEAS

Even though research tells us that newer and smaller firms are less likely to engage in formal or structured environmental research, the fact is that generating and evaluating business ideas is an important step in the entrepreneurial process.[2] Some of you reading this book may already have fairly specific ideas about potential entrepreneurial ventures; others may know only in a broad sense what entrepreneurial direction you'd like to pursue; and the rest may not have any clue whatsoever! But, no matter your stage of entrepreneurial idea readiness, it's important for you to be able to generate and evaluate potential business ideas. Before we discuss how to do this, however, we need to address some misconceptions that you may have about ideas and what makes them great.

Misconceptions About and Realities of Great Ideas

Entrepreneurship books and magazines are filled with stories of entrepreneurs striking it rich because they had a good idea. These stories, however, tend to give the wrong impressions about great ideas—what they are and where they come from. These misconceptions about great ideas are summarized in Table 3-1.[3]

over again—a significant feature of most video action games—tedious and meaningless. The first Rockett game, "Rockett's New School," was introduced in 1997. Purple Moon used radically different game features such as emotional navigation and relationship hierarchies to position a product for girls in a market that had long been aimed at boys.

Unfortunately, even with the best ideas, research, and intentions behind it, Purple Moon's story does not have a happy ending. The company's attempt to "shoot the moon" turned out to be unsuccessful in the long run. Purple Moon was acquired by Mattel, the toy company, in the spring of 1999. Brenda Laurel blames Purple Moon's demise on tough competition, bad timing and, perhaps even unrealistic expectations about what the company could accomplish.

1. *Great ideas just appear out of nowhere.* Do you buy into the notion that a "light bulb" goes off as someone all of a sudden sees a unique, creative approach? That the whole process is almost an epiphany? The reality is that the best idea generators tend to do so in a structured, systematic way.

TABLE 3-1 Common Misconceptions About and the Realities of Great Ideas	
Misconception #1	**Reality #1**
■ Ideas just appear out of nowhere.	■ The most successful idea generators do so in a structured, systematic way.
Misconception #2	**Reality #2**
■ There are no stupid ideas.	■ The most powerful ideas often are resoundingly bad, at first glance.
Misconception #3	**Reality #3**
■ Customers will tell you what to do if you'll only listen.	■ Although customers can help identify unmet needs, there's much more involved with making an idea workable.
Misconception #4	**Reality #4**
■ We can generate all the ideas we'll ever need if we just sit down at a meeting.	■ Great ideas are best shaped through an ongoing dialogue.
Misconception #5	**Reality #5**
■ Getting ideas isn't the problem; implementing them is.	■ The problem is not carefully screening the ideas that are generated.

Source: Based on S. Greco, "Where Great Ideas Come From," *Inc.*, April 1998, pp. 76–86.

They don't wait for the bolt of lightning to hit them, but instead approach idea generation as a top-priority activity by devoting set periods of time to it.

2. *There are no stupid ideas.* In order to avoid hurt feelings or to prevent others from feeling that their contributions are not valued, the belief is that all ideas should be approached as worthy. The reality is that many ideas are bad. However, there's nothing wrong with that! Often, the most powerful ideas come from what, at first glance, seemed stupid or illogical.

3. *Customers will tell you what to do if you'll only listen.* Who better to have as a source of ideas than the people who will purchase your products? The only problem with this belief is that although customers can help identify unmet needs, there's much more involved with making a great idea workable.

4. *We can generate all the ideas we'll ever need if we just sit down at a meeting.* Getting people together at a meeting to discuss ideas and to feed off of each other's enthusiasm seems like a smart thing to do. However, generating great ideas shouldn't be restricted to a meeting. Great ideas are best shaped through an ongoing dialogue, not simply relegated to a specific place and time.

5. *Getting ideas isn't the problem; implementing them is.* There's a misconception that idea generation is the easy part of the process and that putting those ideas into action is the difficult part. However, the reality is that problems

arise from not screening carefully enough the ideas that are generated. If this were done, a lot of frustration could be minimized as ill-thought-out ideas could be screened out before even being implemented.

Now that we've cleared up some of the initial misconceptions you may have about ideas, it's time to look at the process involved with generating ideas.

Generating Ideas

Entrepreneurial ventures thrive on ideas. Generating ideas is an innovative, creative process. It's also one that will take some time, not only in the beginning stages of the entrepreneurial venture but also throughout the life of the business. As we look at the process of generating ideas, we're going to discuss where ideas come from, ways to generate ideas, and the roles of structured analysis and intuition.

Where Ideas Come From. Various entrepreneurship researchers have looked at the source of an entrepreneur's ideas. These studies of entrepreneurs have shown that the sources of their ideas are unique and varied. For instance, one survey cites "working in the same industry" as the major source—60 percent of respondents—of ideas for a company.[4] Our chapter-opening entrepreneur in action, Brenda Laurel of Purple Moon, would fit into this category because she had worked for a large video game designer before going out on her own. Another survey of 100 entrepreneurs who created some of the fastest-growing private companies in the United States had similar results.[5] The overwhelming majority (71 percent) of these respondents replicated or modified an idea gained through previous employment. The next largest percentage of survey respondents in this particular study (20 percent) said they got their ideas for an entrepreneurial venture from a serendipitous (coincidental) discovery. Included in this set of responses were comments such as "built temporary or casual job into a business," "happened to read about the industry," "wanted product or service as an individual consumer," and "thought up idea during honeymoon in Italy." Although a honeymoon in Italy may seem like a fun, but unusual, place to get an idea, actually it just confirms the fact that an entrepreneur needs to be open to ideas anyplace and at any time. But, as important as being alert and open to ideas is, it really doesn't tell you anything about where to look for ideas.

Entrepreneurs might use numerous idea sources. Figure 3-1 illustrates some of the more common sources and what to look for as you examine them. Let's look at the four main sources of ideas.

First on the list of sources is personal interests or hobbies. Many entrepreneurial ventures got their start because of an entrepreneur's love of doing something—restoring antique automobiles, scuba diving adventure tours, baking grandma's scrumptious praline brownies, or whatever. A successful entrepreneurial business might be built around your personal interests in a particular product or activity.

Another likely source of ideas, and a popular one as shown by the results of the entrepreneurial surveys described earlier, is an entrepreneur's work experiences, skills, and abilities. By tapping into the knowledge of a particular industry and market gained by working in it, an entrepreneur can pinpoint areas of potential opportunity. For example, if you've ever traveled, you've undoubtedly seen those ubiquitous suitcases with wheels. Now wasn't that a great idea! Well, Robert

Figure 3-1

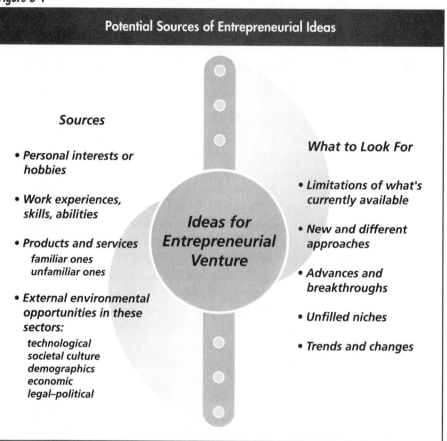

Potential Sources of Entrepreneurial Ideas

Sources

• *Personal interests or hobbies*

• *Work experiences, skills, abilities*

• *Products and services*
  familiar ones
  unfamiliar ones

• *External environmental opportunities in these sectors:*
  technological
  societal culture
  demographics
  economic
  legal–political

Ideas for Entrepreneurial Venture

What to Look For

• *Limitations of what's currently available*

• *New and different approaches*

• *Advances and breakthroughs*

• *Unfilled niches*

• *Trends and changes*

Plath created the first wheeled suitcase, the Travelpro Rollerboard, because in his job as an airline pilot he was constantly carrying his baggage from one place to another, and he was looking for a more convenient, comfortable way to do so. In the process of using his work-related experiences, he created not only a new product but also a whole new industry!

The third source of possible ideas is to look at products and services currently available, both familiar and unfamiliar ones. What products do you use every day? Do they do everything that you wished they would? What about products that you're not familiar with? Can you take what you are familiar with and apply it to those unfamiliar ones? This source of entrepreneurial ideas is quite similar to the investing philosophy of Peter Lynch, the legendary and successful Magellan mutual fund manager. He said that a contributing factor to his financial success was buying stock in companies whose products and services he or his family members used and thought were great.

The final source of potential entrepreneurial ideas is the external environment. As we discussed in Chapter 2, there are certain to be opportunities—positive trends or changes that provide unique and distinct possibilities for innovating and creating value—in the entrepreneurial context. You just have to look for them. These opportunities can be found in the technological, societal culture, demographics, economic, and legal–political sectors.

Entrepreneurs in Action

The distinctive crack of a wood bat as a ball goes sailing off of it is music to the ears of baseball fans everywhere. Wood baseball bats are also music to the ears of brothers Thomas and Kevin Lane. They are the owners of Carolina Clubs, a West Palm Beach–based company they founded in 1990 that manufactures custom wood baseball bats. At the time, they were still playing minor league baseball. Kevin, a pitcher, would hear teammates complain about the quality of their bats. He thought that his father, George, a skilled carpenter, might be able to help. Almost insulted at first, George made the bats and Kevin took them to his teammates. He didn't tell them at first where they came from. The first teammate to use one of the bats hit a double off the wall in center field. From then on, everyone wanted one. Approval of the bats for use by players in the major leagues came within a few months.

In order to compete with the major sporting goods companies, Carolina Clubs offers unparalleled customer service. The brothers have developed a profitable business that produces over 8,000 bats a year. Because the company's entire workforce consists mainly of family members, they sometimes have trouble keeping up with demand. But they love what they do, although both laughingly say they dream of stepping up to the plate in a major league uniform, Carolina Club in hand, and thrilling the crowd with that distinctive sound of bat hitting ball.

Source: P. Spiegel, "Batter Up!" *Forbes,* June 2, 1997, pp. 126–28.

Now that you know the potential sources of entrepreneurial ideas, what specific things should you look for? (Refer to Figure 3-1 again.) Basically, you look for the limitations of what is currently available, for new and different approaches, at scientific and technological advances and breakthroughs, for unfilled niches, and at trends and changes. Any of these characteristics could be a potential idea for an entrepreneurial venture. But, perhaps even this isn't enough. Even with the wide variety of idea sources, maybe you're finding it difficult to come up with an idea for your entrepreneurial venture. At this point, you may want to use some different, more structured methods to help generate ideas.

Ways to Generate Ideas. In this section, we're going to describe four different structured

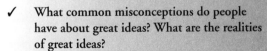

Rapid Review ◀◀|

✓ What common misconceptions do people have about great ideas? What are the realities of great ideas?

✓ What have various entrepreneurship researchers found with regard to the source of entrepreneur's ideas?

✓ Describe the four main sources of entrepreneurial ideas.

✓ What types of things should entrepreneurs look for in the main sources for ideas?

Trend Spotting

The skill of observing. Do you have it? Can you pick up on what people think is "hot" or popular? Faith Popcorn, an author and probably today's best-known trend spotter, actually says that you don't have to be a pro to be good at it. In fact, professionals may be constrained by rigid organizational structures and their past successes. So, how can you become more in tune with what's happening and hone your skills at trend spotting? Here are some suggestions:

1. Remember that valuable information is everywhere around you. Look for it everywhere and anywhere. Read magazines you don't normally read. Watch television shows or movies that you personally might not be interested in. Go to places. Do things. Talk to people. Information is the bread and butter of a good trend spotter.

2. File that information away. If your memory isn't as good as it should be, use note cards. What you write down doesn't have to be long and complex. It could be something as simple as "avocado seems to be a hot color" or "teens seem to be flocking to fitness programs" or whatever.

3. Determine whether the fads seem to be part of deeper, wider trends that can be good sources of entrepreneurial opportunity. You can do this by assessing whether the fad seems to have staying power, whether the fad is a reflection of a change in people's attitudes or behaviors, and whether you see the fad in more than a few places.

4. Test your ideas about trends on intelligent friends of various ages and incomes. Bounce your ideas off of them. What do they say? Make sure, however, that these people will be honest with you.

5. Don't expect trends to jump out at you. After all, if they were easy to spot, everyone would be doing it. You have to be alert, be open to new and unusual possibilities, and be willing to work at it. Don't worry if you miss a trend. After all, there will be more.

Source: R. Furchgott, "Trend-Spotting: Anyone Can Play," *Business Week Enterprise,* March 2, 1998, pp. ENT12–ENT16.

approaches you might use to help generate ideas: (1) environmental scanning, (2) creativity and creative problem solving, (3) brainstorming, and (4) focus groups. Keep in mind that although we're discussing these techniques in relation to generating entrepreneurial ideas, they're also useful for resolving any type of entrepreneurial challenge where an imaginative solution or new idea is needed.

Do you know the latest scoop on what's happening in the business world? Are you aware of the latest news headlines? Do you know what books or movies are popular right now? One technique that entrepreneurs can use to generate ideas is **environmental scanning**, the screening of large amounts of information to detect emerging trends. Here are some "ideas" to stimulate your own idea creation by scanning the world around you: Read your local and other major metropolitan newspapers such as the *New York Times,* the *Washington Post,* and others; read *USA Today;* read the *Wall Street Journal;* read popular consumer and news magazines; review the fiction and nonfiction best-seller lists; review government and consumer publications; subscribe to relevant trade publications; pay attention to commercials; watch and review the top prime-time television shows; browse through the magazine section of a bookstore; walk through a local shopping mall to see what's there; and so forth. The challenge of this method is not having too little information to scan; it's having too much. But, how are you going to know what's happening in the world, what people are thinking, what people are doing, if you're not staying alert to these things? Yes, this may seem like a lot of effort and work, but if you're serious about being a successful entrepreneur in action, it's energy well spent.

We introduced the concept of creativity in Chapter 2. We defined it as the ability to combine ideas in a unique way or to make unusual associations between ideas. Whereas traditional logical thinking is like a parallel railroad track—going on forever, but never meeting—creative thinking means linking new concepts in unusual ways. It means seeing new angles and unique approaches.[6] The whole field of creativity has extensive amounts of research and study behind it, way too much for us to look at here. Instead, what you need to understand about the role of creativity and creative problem solving as a structured technique for generating ideas is that a number of specific creativity approaches can be used. For instance, here are a few specific techniques: the checklist method in which the entrepreneur uses a list of questions or statements to develop new ideas; free association whereby the entrepreneur develops a new idea through a chain of word associations; attribute listing in which the entrepreneur develops a new idea by looking at the positive and negative attributes; and so on. Using any of these structured creative problem-solving approaches can help you unlock your creativity and generate potential entrepreneurial ideas. If you need more information about creativity, check out the topic at your local library or on the Internet.

One of the most familiar and widely used approaches to generating ideas is **brainstorming**, an idea-generating process that encourages alternatives while withholding criticism. Brainstorming is a relatively simple technique that is typically done with a group of people. In a brainstorming session, a group of people

News from the Internet

Having up-to-the minute reliable information delivered directly to your computer seems like the ideal answer to the entrepreneur's need for scanning the environment. Well, it's not a dream. It's a reality. Rather than having to initiate a search for specific information, these Internet news services bring specific information to you. You decide what type of information you need and use, and then design your personalized news service. Search and directory Web sites such as Yahoo!, Excite, and others have become gateways to news and information from leading sources. Many of these sources will also create personalized Web home pages for users, based on their personal interests with links to relevant information, content, and advertising. Other Internet news sources provide subscription services that are more personalized and help users monitor industries and competitors. Keeping on top of important news is becoming a critical necessity for entrepreneurs. These Internet-based information services can be a wonderful tool for entrepreneurs to scan the environment easily and effectively.

Source: T. McCollum, "All the News That's Fit to Net," *Nation's Business*, June 1998, pp. 59–61.

sits around a table. A group leader states the issue to be addressed in a way that all participants understand. Then members "freewheel" as many ideas as they can in a given time. Participants are encouraged to come up with as many ideas as possible and to build on each others' ideas. No criticism of ideas is allowed at the time of the brainstorming session. Instead, all ideas, no matter how illogical or crazy, are recorded for later discussion and analysis. It can be a frenzied, yet productive way to generate numerous ideas.

The final structured approach to generating ideas we want to look at is the use of **focus groups**. These groups of individuals provide information about proposed products or services in a structured setting. In a typical focus group, a moderator focuses the group discussion on whatever issues are being examined. For instance, a focus group might look at a proposed product and answer specific questions asked by the moderator. In other instances, the focus group might be given a more general issue to discuss and the moderator simply leads the discussion based on comments made by the group. Either way, a focus group can provide an excellent way to generate new ideas and to screen proposed ideas and concepts.

The Role of Intuition. We can't leave our discussion of generating ideas without looking at the role of intuition. **Intuition** is a cognitive process whereby we subconsciously make decisions based on our accumulated knowledge and experiences. It's been called that " 'aha' feeling you get when your internal search engine hits its mark."[7] You may know it better as "gut feeling." Researchers have shown that a person's intuition can be measured. Measure yours using the FYI box entitled "As Good As a Guess?" Although structured, methodical approaches to generating ideas are important, intuition can also play an important role. Intuition can be a powerful source of new ideas if you learn to use it. Maybe the best approach of all would be to combine the structured with the intuitive. After all, the two complement each other. Listen to that "inner voice" and then use more structured approaches to fine-tune your ideas.

Although generating ideas is an important process for entrepreneurs, it's only half the battle! You must look at your ideas carefully before taking action and proceeding any further with your entrepreneurial venture.

Evaluating Ideas

When you're in the market for a new stereo or maybe a new car, do you take the first one that you see? Most of us wouldn't. We shop around. We look at each possibility in order to determine which is going to best meet our needs and fit within our available budgeted funds. This process is just as important in evaluating entrepreneurial ideas. After all, we want to pursue the option that's going to allow us to best meet our goal(s) given the resources we have available. In this section we discuss why evaluation is important and then look at some different ways to evaluate ideas.

Why Is Evaluation Important? It may seem that evaluating ideas is a big waste of time, particularly when the environment is changing so rapidly. You may

Rapid Review ◀◀|

✓ What is environmental scanning? How can it be used to stimulate idea creation?
✓ Define creativity. Describe some specific techniques for enhancing creativity.
✓ What is brainstorming?
✓ How could focus groups be used to generate ideas?
✓ What is intuition, and what role does it play in generating ideas?

As Good As a Guess?

Rate your intuitive powers by taking the following quiz.

Complete the following quiz as honestly—and quickly—as you can. It will give you a gauge of how strong your gut instinct is.

1. When working on a project, do you prefer to:
   a) Be told what the problem is but left free to decide how to solve it?
   b) Get very clear instructions about how to go about solving the problem before you start?
2. When working on a project, do you prefer to work with colleagues who are:
   a) Realistic?
   b) Imaginative?
3. Do you most admire people who are:
   a) Creative?
   b) Careful?
4. Do the friends you choose tend to be:
   a) Serious and hardworking?
   b) Exciting and often emotional?
5. When you ask a colleague for advice on a problem, do you:
   a) Seldom or never get upset if he questions your basic assumptions?
   b) Often get upset if he questions your basic assumptions?
6. When you start the day, do you:
   a) Seldom make or follow a specific plan?
   b) Usually make a plan to follow first?
7. When working with numbers, do you find that you:
   a) Seldom or never make factual errors?
   b) Often make factual errors?
8. Do you find that you:
   a) Seldom daydream during the day and really don't enjoy it when you do?
   b) Frequently daydream during the day and enjoy doing so?
9. When working on a problem, do you:
   a) Prefer to follow the instructions or rules when they are given to you?
   b) Often enjoy circumventing the instructions or rules when they are given to you?
10. When you are trying to put something together, do you prefer to have:
    a) Step-by-step written instructions for assembly?
    b) A picture of how the item is supposed to look once it's assembled?
11. Do you find the person who irritates you the most is the one who appears to be:
    a) Disorganized?
    b) Organized?
12. When a crisis that you have to deal with comes up unexpectedly, do you:
    a) Feel anxious about the situation?
    b) Feel excited by the challenge?

HOW TO SCORE

First, total the number of "a" responses you circled for questions 1, 3, 5, 6, and 11. Second total the number of "b" responses you circled for questions 2, 4, 7, 8, 9, 10, and 12. Add the totals.

If you scored above an 8, your intuition is humming. If you scored above 10, you are an intuition superstar, in the top 10 percent of all Americans.

Source: By permission of Weston Agor, Ph.D. ENFP Enterprises, 5525 North Stanton Street, #18-D, El Paso, TX 79912.

think that if you take the time to evaluate your entrepreneurial idea you'll miss the quickly closing window of opportunity. However, evaluation gives you the chance to assess the soundness of your idea. We've come up with four reasons why idea evaluation is an important step in researching the venture's feasibility. (See Figure 3-2.)

The first reason why idea evaluation is important is that it forces the entrepreneur to decide what's important in this entrepreneurial venture. What are

Figure 3-2

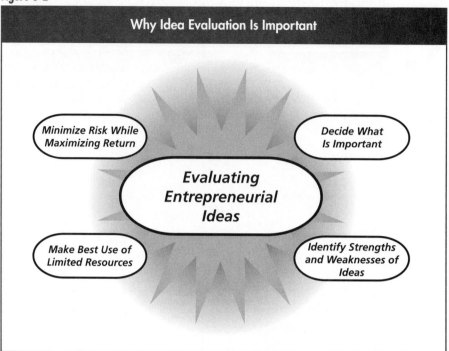

Why Idea Evaluation Is Important

Minimize Risk While Maximizing Return

Decide What Is Important

Evaluating Entrepreneurial Ideas

Make Best Use of Limited Resources

Identify Strengths and Weaknesses of Ideas

the goals of the entrepreneur in pursuing this venture? Think back to our chapter-opening case. Brenda Laurel's goal was to provide young adolescent girls with alternative video game experiences—ones that didn't have repetitive, mindless violence and that didn't feature typical "girl" activities. Any entrepreneurial ideas generated would be evaluated against this goal. Other entrepreneurs will have their own unique reasons behind wanting to pursue an entrepreneurial venture. Potential ideas should be evaluated against what's important to the entrepreneur.

The second reason why idea evaluation is important is that all ideas are not created equal! Some ideas that an entrepreneur comes up with will have better chances of success than others. By evaluating the strengths and weaknesses of each idea, the entrepreneur is forced to identify and assess the strong points and weak points. Think again of a time when you made a major consumer purchase. Did you look at the features of each alternative and assess the advantages and disadvantages? Why did you do this? By looking at the strengths and weaknesses of each alternative, you were getting information to help you make a better decision. When evaluating the strengths and weaknesses of entrepreneurial ideas, you're also getting and using information to help you make a better decision.

The next reason why idea evaluation is important has to do with the reality of limited resources. There are only limited amounts of money, people, time, or whatever other resources you may need in pursuing your entrepreneurial venture. By evaluating your entrepreneurial ideas, you can make sure that your choice(s) make the best use of those limited resources.

The final reason why idea evaluation is important has to do with the desire to minimize risk while maximizing return. What is **risk**? We're going to define it as the uncertainty surrounding decisions and actions about what will happen. **Return**, on the other hand, is the payback (financial or otherwise) that an entrepreneur hopes to gain from the entrepreneurial venture. Naturally, we'd like to have the least amount of uncertainty while getting the largest payback from our entrepreneurial decisions and actions. When an entrepreneur puts in the effort to evaluate potential entrepreneurial ideas, there's the opportunity to minimize the level of risk exposed to while maximizing the possible amount of payoff.

Here's some advice from a successful entrepreneur that summarizes the importance of idea evaluation. "In addition to having an idea for a better mousetrap, you have to understand it in a business context. You have to understand the industry, the market, the competition, and the necessary technology."[8] Now that we've looked at the reasons why idea evaluation is important, let's look at how it's done.

How to Evaluate Ideas. Evaluating entrepreneurial ideas revolves around personal and marketplace considerations. Each of these assessments will provide the entrepreneur with key information about the idea's potential.

In an entrepreneurial venture, the entrepreneur is the pivotal point around which all other decisions and actions are pursued. In evaluating potential ideas, it's important, therefore, to measure them against the personal considerations of the entrepreneur. Here are some questions to consider:[9]

- Do you have the capabilities for what you've selected?
- Are you ready to be an entrepreneur?

Entrepreneurs in Action

Jennifer Maxwell, cofounder and owner of PowerBar Inc., knows firsthand the importance of evaluating ideas. PowerBar, a $100 million company, got its start because of a bad case of stomach cramps. Brian Maxwell, a college athlete and top-ranked runner, was competing in the London Marathon. About halfway through the race—which, by the way, he was leading by about a minute—Maxwell began to experience cramps and finished in seventh place. Back in the United States, he met Jennifer Biddulph, also an accomplished runner and nutrition–food science student at the University of California at Berkeley. Trying to find a way to combat the cramp problem faced by athletes in all sports, Jennifer and Brian, who were now married, mixed hundreds of combinations of raw ingredients trying to find a snack bar that would digest easily and provide quick energy. They tried out the test bars on friends. After several "tests," the Maxwells finally hit on the right combination of fructose, oat bran, and milk protein. Today, PowerBar Inc. is a 250-person company that's intent on going the distance.

Source: "Entrepreneurial Excellence," *Working Woman*, May 1999, p. 48.

- Are you prepared emotionally to deal with the stresses and challenges of being an entrepreneur?
- Are you prepared to deal with rejection and failure?
- Are you ready to work hard?
- Do you have a realistic picture of the venture's potential?
- Have you educated yourself about financing issues?
- Are you willing and prepared to do continual financial and other types of analyses?

Although it's extremely important for an entrepreneur to evaluate ideas against personal considerations, it's equally important to assess them against marketplace considerations. Your decision about which entrepreneurial direction to go should not take place in a vacuum. Your idea will have to be viable in a competitive and dynamic marketplace. Consequently, the choice you make needs to be made with an eye to the market. The more market driven your venture, the greater the chances of success.[10] Here are some general questions to ask in relation to evaluating the marketplace potential:

- Who are the potential customers for your idea: who, where, how many?
- What similar or unique product features does your proposed idea have to what's currently on the market?
- How and where will potential customers purchase your product?
- Have you considered pricing?
- Have you considered how you will need to promote and advertise your proposed entrepreneurial venture?

These broad-based questions force an entrepreneur to at least think about the viability of the proposed entrepreneurial idea. Although the idea may appear great on paper, if there's no market for it, the chances of success are zero.

The final things we want to look at in this section on evaluating entrepreneurial ideas are two specific evaluation techniques an entrepreneur might use. One is called the four-questions approach and the other is a feasibility study.

The four-questions approach very simply suggests that evaluating entrepreneurial ideas revolves around four questions: (1) Do you love the business? (2) Are you skilled at the business? (3) Do you have experience at the business? (4) Is the business simply a fad or trend?[11] Each of these questions forces the potential entrepreneur to get beyond dreaming and to focus on specific issues. By answering these thought-provoking questions, the entrepreneur must examine whether or not he or she really has the personal characteristics (desires, skills, abilities) and marketplace considerations (fad, trend, or relatively long-term demand) in his or her favor. Another more structured evaluation technique is the feasibility study.

A **feasibility study** is a structured and systematic analysis of the various aspects of a proposed entrepreneurial venture designed to determine its feasibility. A well-prepared feasibility study can be an effective evaluation tool to determine whether or not an entrepreneurial idea is a potentially successful one. In addition, the feasibility study can serve as a basis for the all-important business plan. (We'll cover business plans in Chapter 4.)

What does a feasibility study include? It should give descriptions of the most important elements of the entrepreneurial venture and the entrepreneur's analysis of the viability of these elements. Figure 3-3 provides an outline of one possible approach to a feasibility study that covers eight different sections. These eight sections are an introductory section including historical background and brief summary of product, potential strengths and weaknesses, and other key information; accounting considerations; management considerations; marketing considerations; financial considerations; legal considerations; tax considerations; and an appendix with supporting charts, graphs, diagrams, layouts, résumés, and so forth.

Yes, the feasibility study covers a lot of territory. It takes a significant amount of time, effort, and energy to prepare it. However, isn't your potential future success worth an investment of time, effort, and energy? As stated previously, if done effectively, the feasibility study can make preparing and writing the business plan a whole lot easier.

Rapid Review ◀◀|

✓ Why is evaluating ideas important?

✓ What is risk? What is return? What role do they play in evaluating entrepreneurial ideas?

✓ What role do personal considerations play as an entrepreneur evaluates potential ideas? What role do marketplace considerations play?

✓ Describe the four-questions approach to evaluating entrepreneurial ideas.

✓ What is a feasibility study? Why is it a valuable tool in evaluating entrepreneurial ideas?

Now that you've thoroughly investigated your entrepreneurial idea(s) and have a fairly good assessment of the idea's strengths and weaknesses, it's time to look at others who might be doing the same or similar things that you're pursuing. That's the second part of researching the venture's feasibility—researching competitors and competitive advantage.

RESEARCHING COMPETITORS AND COMPETITIVE ADVANTAGE

Competition is everywhere. Very few industries or markets haven't experienced some form and degree of competitiveness. Researching your competition through competitor intelligence can be a powerful tool for entrepreneurs. **Competitor intelligence** is a process of gathering information on who competitors are, what they are doing, and how their actions will affect your organization. In this section, we're going to discuss these competitor intelligence issues: what competition is, how to determine who your competitors are, and competitive information—what information to get about your competitors and how to get it.

What Is Competition?

Competition is defined as organizations vying or battling for some desired object or outcome—typically, customers, market share, survey ranking, or needed resources. Although individuals also compete for desired objects or outcomes—getting the highest grade in a class, winning a race, or getting the desired job—we're looking at competition as it relates to organizations. What types of competition might an entrepreneurial venture face? This can be answered by looking at who our competitors are.

Who Are Our Competitors?

There are three ways to define possible competitors. The first approach, the industry perspective, identifies competitors as organizations making the same product or

Figure 3-3

Example of a Feasibility Study

FEASIBILITY STUDY

A. Introduction, historical background, description of product or service:
1. Brief description of proposed entrepreneurial venture
2. Brief history of the industry
3. Information about the economy and important trends
4. Current status of the product or service
5. How you intend to produce the product or service
6. Complete list of goods or services to be provided
7. Strengths and weaknesses of the business
8. Ease of entry into the industry, including competitor analysis

B. Accounting considerations:
1. Proforma balance sheet
2. Proforma profit and loss statement
3. Projected cash flow analysis

C. Management considerations:
1. Personal expertise—strengths and weaknesses
2. Proposed organizational design
3. Potential staffing requirements
4. Inventory management methods
5. Production and operations management issues
6. Equipment needs

D. Marketing considerations:
1. Detailed product description
2. Identify the target market (who, where, how many)
3. Describe place product will be distributed (location, traffic, size, channels, etc.)
4. Price determination (competition, price lists, etc.)
5. Promotion plans (role of personal selling, advertising, sales promotions, etc.)

E. Financial considerations:
1. Start-up costs
2. Working capital requirements
3. Equity requirements
4. Loans—amounts, type, conditions
5. Breakeven analysis
6. Collateral
7. Credit references
8. Equipment and building financing—costs and methods

F. Legal considerations:
1. Proposed business structure
   a. Type
   b. Conditions, terms, liability, responsibility
   c. Insurance needs: property, liability, personal, etc.
   d. Buyout, succession issues
2. Contracts, licenses, and other legal documents

G. Tax considerations:
1. Sales, property, employee
2. Federal, state, and local

H. Appendix—charts, graphs, diagrams, layouts, résumés, etc.

providing the same service. For instance, there's the oil industry, the supermarket industry, the package delivery industry, and the dental health care industry. The competitors in each of these industries are producing the same or very similar types of products or services. (To make sure you understand this approach, take a minute and try to name competitors in the personal computer industry, the video game industry, and the automobile industry.) Using this approach, an entrepreneur could assess the intensity of competition by looking at how many organizations there are in the industry and how much they differ from each other. Competition would be at its highest level when there are a number of competitors and they're not differentiated from each other. In other words, these competitors are all battling each other for the same desired outcome—for example, getting a customer to purchase their product or service, and not someone else's.

Another approach to defining who competitors are is the marketing perspective, which says that competitors are organizations that satisfy the same customer need. For example, if the customer need is entertainment, competitors might range all the way from video game designers to theme parks to movie theaters to the local community symphony orchestra. These are different industries but ones that are attempting to satisfy the same customer need. Under this perspective, the intensity of competition depends on how well the customer's needs are understood or defined and how well different organizations are able to meet that need.

The final approach to defining who competitors are is to use what is known as the strategic groups perspective. **Strategic groups** are groups of competitors following essentially the same strategy in a particular market or industry.[12] Within a single industry, you might find few or several strategic groups, depending on what strategic factors are important to different groups of customers. For instance, two strategic factors often used in grouping competitors are price (low to high) and quality (low to

Global Perspectives

Matthew Heyman, Adolfo Fastlicht, and Miguel Angel Davila, all Harvard Business School graduates, are reenergizing the Mexican movie theater industry. Starting from a class project requirement, the three founded a company, Cadena Mexicana de Exhibicion or Cinemex, which dominates the movie theaters in Mexico City. Of the 416 screens there, Cinemex has 147. Their entrepreneurial venture has succeeded because they understood what the marketplace wanted. As the Mexican government was lifting decades-old price controls on movie tickets, the trio saw their opportunity. The price-controlled market had discouraged theater owners from upgrading their facilities. Sound quality was terrible, as was the picture quality, and the food was cold, stale, and unappetizing. Middle-class Mexican moviegoers chose to stay at home in front of their VCRs. When the government lifted the price controls, Heyman and his partners bet that customers would pay for top-quality sound, image, and service. They were right! Even though competition is coming in, Cinemex is confident it can maintain its competitive lead by understanding the market and continuing to do what it does best.

Source: E. Malkin, "Movie Palace Coup," *Business Week Enterprise*, April 27, 1998, pp. ENT8–ENT10.

high). Competitors would then be "grouped" according to their price–quality strategies, with those following the same or similar approaches in the same strategic group. Take the automobile industry, for example. Saturn is not in the same strategic group as the Mercedes-Benz, but Lexus, BMW, and Jaguar are. The Kia Sportage sport utility vehicle would not be in the same strategic group as the Mercedes-Benz or the Lexus SUVs. Keep in mind that the important strategic factors, or strategic dimensions, used to determine an organization's competitors are different for every industry and can be different even for various industry segments. Table 3-2 lists some specific factors that might be used to distinguish strategic groups.

This approach says that the concept of strategic groups is important to understanding who competitors are because your most relevant competitors are those in your particular strategic group. Although competition might, and often does, come from organizations in other strategic groups, your main competitive concerns are those organizations in your own strategic group. The intensity of competition in this perspective then depends on how effectively each competitor has been able to develop a competitive advantage and on the competitive actions being used by each competitor to capture the desired outcome—be it customers, resources, or whatever.

No matter how we define our potential competitors, the fact remains that there are other organizations working hard to secure the same customers, resources, and other desired outcomes that you want. Now that we know who our competitors are, we need to look at what type of competitive information to get and where to get that information about what our competitors are doing.

Getting Competitor Information

Keep in mind that at this point you're still researching the viability of your entrepreneurial venture. By looking at what other competitors are doing, you can better understand how your proposed product or service would fit into the competitive arena and whether it's feasible. The first thing you need to decide is what type of competitive information you'd like. What would you like to know about your potential competitors?

What Type of Competitive Information Should You Look For? What you want to do is get a good feel for what your potential competitors are doing. Here are some possible questions you might research:

- What types of products or services are the competitors offering?
- What are the major characteristics of these products or services? What are their products' strengths and weaknesses?
- How do they handle marketing, pricing, and distributing?

TABLE 3-2   Possible Dimensions for Identifying Strategic Groups

▲ Price	▲ Market share
▲ Quality	▲ Product characteristics
▲ Geographic scope	▲ Profits
▲ Product line breadth–depth	▲ Any other relevant factor

- What do they attempt to do differently from other competitors? Do they appear to be successful at it? Why? Why not?
- What are they good at? That is, what competitive advantage(s) do they appear to have?
- What are they not so good at? What competitive disadvantage(s) do they appear to have?
- How large and profitable are these competitors?

These are just a few of the questions that you might ask about your potential competitors. Your goal is to get a good understanding of each one's competitive strengths and weaknesses. Then, you want to assess how your proposed entrepreneurial venture is going to "fit" into this competitive arena. Will you be able to compete successfully or is competitive intensity too extreme? Once you've decided what type of competitive information you'd like to have, you're ready to go out and find it. Where can you find this type of information?

Where to Get Competitive Information. It's not as difficult as you might think it would be to find information on competitors! You can use published financial sources; former employees; dealers, representatives, and distributors; suppliers; professional meetings; market surveys; trade fairs and exhibits; competitors' brochures; competitors' Web pages; technical analyses of competitors' products (called **reverse engineering**); comparison shopping; news stories found in newspapers or other publications; government studies; competitive intelligence firms; interviews with consultants; and so forth. One thing you should be concerned with as you gather competitive information, however, is whether or not your information gathering is ethical.

Questions and concerns that often arise about competitor intelligence pertain to the ways in which competitor information is gathered. Competitor intelligence becomes illegal spying when it involves the theft of any proprietary materials or trade secrets by any means. That's an easy one to understand. However, there's often a fine line between what's considered *legal and ethical* and what's considered *legal but unethical.* Some legal but ethically questionable methods are listed in Table 3-3.

Once you've gathered information on your competitors, you might want to organize it in some type of competitor analysis matrix. (See Figure 3-4 for an example.) List the competitors along the horizontal axis and the type of competitive information along the vertical axis. Fill in the actual information for each competitor in the appropriate cell. In this way, you would be able to compare your potential competitors easily. Also, this type of competitor analysis becomes an important part of your feasibility study and your business plan.

The **Grey** *Zone*   Here are some other techniques that have been suggested for gathering competitor information: (1) Pretend to be a journalist writing a story. Call up competitor's offices and interview knowledgeable personnel. (2) Dig through a competitor's trash. (3) Sit outside a competitor's place of business and count how many customers go in. (4) Get copies of your competitors' in-house newsletters and read them. (5) Call the Better Business Bureau and ask if competitors have had complaints filed against them and if so, what kind of complaints. (6) Have a friend call your competitors for a price list, a brochure, or other marketing information. Do you think these methods are ethical or unethical? Why? What ethical guidelines would you propose for entrepreneurs when doing competitor intelligence?

TABLE 3-3   Ethically Questionable Competitive Intelligence Methods

- Trying to get proprietary information by bribing individuals who once worked for competitors
- Questioning competitors' employees at technical meetings by disguising who you are and who you work for
- Going on false job interviews with a competitor
- Hiring a competitor's employee(s) away to obtain specific know-how or trade secrets
- Secret direct observation of a device or piece of equipment
- Conducting false job interviews with competitor's employees

The final part of researching the venture's feasibility is to look at the various financing options. This is not the final determination of how much funding you will need, where you will obtain these funds, or other specific financing information. However, it is important when researching the venture's feasibility to be aware of the various financing alternatives.

RESEARCHING FINANCING OPTIONS

Getting financing for your entrepreneurial venture is a lot like painting a room. A lot of the hard work is in the preparation. But if prepped right, the job goes fairly quickly and easily. What we're going to do in this section is "prep" the room by looking at the possible financing options. We're first going to describe the various options, then look at how to evaluate the options to determine what's best for your particular situation, and finally provide some general guidelines for preparing to seek funding.

Possible Financing Options

Chances are you're going to need funds to start your entrepreneurial venture. Have you thought about where those funds are coming from? A significant number of financing options are available to entrepreneurs—ranging all the way from personal resources to funds provided by others. Figure 3-5 shows the various options. Let's take a closer look at each.

Entrepreneur's Personal Resources. The entrepreneur's personal resources can be a good source of financing. What types of personal resources might an entrepreneur have access to? The following are the most common:

- Personal savings
- Home equity

Rapid Review ◀◀|

✓   What is competitor intelligence?

✓   What is competition?

✓   Describe the three different ways to define possible competitors. How is competitive intensity determined according to each of these three perspectives?

✓   What are strategic groups, and what types of strategic factors might be used to define a strategic group?

✓   What type of competitive information should an entrepreneur get, and what are some sources of competitive information?

✓   What is reverse engineering?

✓   What role should ethics play in competitor intelligence gathering?

✓   How might a competitor analysis matrix be helpful?

Figure 3-4

Example of a Competitor Analysis Matrix

Competitive Information	Business 1	Business 2	Business 3	Business 4
Products or Services Offered				
Product Strengths				
Product Weaknesses				
Competitive Advantage(s)				
Competitive Disadvantage(s)				
Other Competitive Information				

Figure 3-5

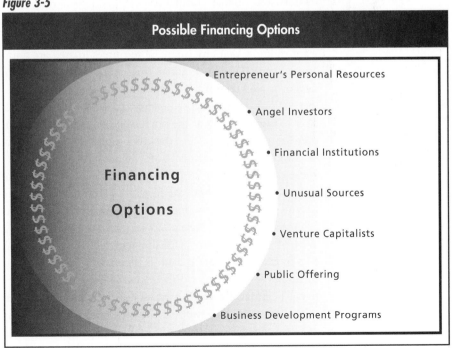

Possible Financing Options

Financing Options

- Entrepreneur's Personal Resources
- Angel Investors
- Financial Institutions
- Unusual Sources
- Venture Capitalists
- Public Offering
- Business Development Programs

- Proceeds from the sale of personal assets
- Life insurance policy loan
- Personal loans
- Credit cards
- Loans from family or friends

Of these possibilities, the credit card option has become a popular choice for entrepreneurs. A survey of entrepreneurs by the accounting and consulting firm Arthur Andersen in conjunction with the lobbying group National Small Business United found that 47 percent of entrepreneurs have used credit cards as a financing option.[13] Although credit cards are not a cheap way to finance a business (with interest rates running anywhere from 18 percent to 22 percent a year), they are easy and quick to use and widely available.

Each of these personal sources of funds allows the entrepreneur to maintain more control over the entrepreneurial venture but also exposes the entrepreneur to more personal risk. You need to decide if you can live with this risk. You're risking your personal financial assets, your credit record, and your personal relationships with family and friends. Is this acceptable? Keep in mind, however, that some entrepreneurs have no other options. They cannot get a loan, provide sufficient equity ownership, or qualify for other types of assistance. Under those circumstances, the entrepreneur's personal resources are the only choice.

Financial Institutions. Another possible alternative for financing the entrepreneurial venture is to look to financial institutions. Financial institutions provide **loans**, financial resources made available by a financial institution that are paid back, including the principal amount plus interest, by the borrower over a certain period of time. The borrower is charged a certain interest rate as the cost for borrowing the funds. Financial institutions that provide loans include banks, savings and loan institutions, credit unions, life insurance firms, other commercial lenders, and finance companies.

Getting a loan can be tricky, particularly for new start-ups! A new entrepreneurial venture represents uncertainty. Financial institutions like certainty. They want to know that any financial resources loaned are going to be paid back in full and on time. Usually, the loan will have to be secured by (backed by) either business or personal assets. If the loan is not repaid, these assets become the financial institution's property to sell to pay off the loan. Loan decisions are made only after a careful review of the borrower and the financial track record of the entrepreneurial venture. Often, these decisions are based on both quantifiable information and subjective information. The entrepreneur has to make a good impression and provide adequate supporting documentation that justifies why the loan is a good idea. This is where the feasibility study and the business plan will come in handy. These written reports will document that you have thought through your proposed venture and are aware of the opportunities and challenges awaiting you. What if you just do not have the necessary track record, assets, or other ingredients to get a loan from a bank or financial institution? This is where a U.S. Small Business Administration (SBA) guaranteed loan might be an appropriate alternative. The **Small Business Administration (SBA)** is a government agency devoted to the enhancement, support, and education of entrepreneurs and small business owners–managers. (Check out its Web page at **www.sba.gov**. It's full of great information!)

An SBA-guaranteed loan assures that 80 percent of the amount loaned to the entrepreneur's business will be repaid by the SBA if the entrepreneur cannot pay it. This guarantee permits the bank to make a more risky loan than it might otherwise make. The procedure to obtain a SBA loan is similar to that of a regular bank loan in that the entrepreneur has to complete loan application forms. But, in addition, government forms and documentation are required. Often, there are banks in a city that specialize in these types of loans and are equipped to assist the entrepreneur in filling out the needed loan forms correctly, minimizing the amount of time for the government's processing, and approving (or denying) the loan. An entrepreneur would need to inquire to find out whether there is a financial institution that specializes in SBA loans.

Although banks are the most common source for obtaining loans, entrepreneurs can't overlook the other financial institution possibilities. These include savings and loan institutions, credit unions, life insurance firms, other commercial lenders, and finance companies. Although the decision criteria may be stricter at

FYI

New Sources for Funding

Although most of the traditional funding sources for entrepreneurial ventures are the most likely ones to pursue, there are some sources that provide new solutions to the perennial financing challenge faced by entrepreneurs. Here are just a few of these:

1. *SBA Express.* This is another initiative of the U.S. Small Business Administration. It's a streamlined process for bank-qualified business owners. They can borrow up to $150,000 through an SBA-backed loan without going through the typical application process. An answer is guaranteed within 36 hours. One difference, though, is that these loans are guaranteed at only 50 percent of their value, so many lending institutions have yet to offer this service.

2. *Community banks.* As competitors in the banking industry continue to merge with each other, entrepreneurial ventures looking for financing from these megabanks often get shortchanged. Many times, the best chance for these businesses is to look to local, community banks where a long-term banking relationship can be established.

3. *Microloans.* These loans typically range from hundreds of dollars to the low six figures. Because many financial institutions consider microloans too small to be worth the effort, these may be difficult to find. But, if you need only a small amount of financing, ask about one.

4. *Third-party loan guarantees.* Sometimes a loan approval can be gained if a third party (family or close friend) cosigns for the loan. If this is something you're reluctant to ask someone close to you to do, there are financial sources that will consider cosigning your loan for a fixed fee or a percentage of the face value of the loan.

5. *Strategic partnership.* Perhaps a financing alternative might be to look to a corporate partner. The corporate partner benefits by having access to new technology or a niche market that's too small for it to pursue profitably on its own. Of course, the entrepreneur benefits by getting the needed financing.

Source: J. A. Fraser, "How to Finance Anything," *Inc.*, March 1999, pp. 32–48.

these financial institutions, the process for getting a loan from any of these will be similar to getting one from a bank.

Venture Capitalists. The next alternative source for financing is **venture capital**, which is external equity funding provided by professionally managed pools of investor money. Whereas banks and other financial institutions provide debt (loan) financing that is paid back, the venture capitalist provides equity (ownership) financing. In other words, the entrepreneur is giving up some amount of ownership in the entrepreneurial venture in return for financing from the venture capitalist. Venture capitalists get their funds and additional financial returns back if and when their equity stake rises in value.[14] Many venture capitalists also provide more than access to funding; they provide consulting services to entrepreneurs. Although each venture capital fund has its own investment criteria, most will provide capital only to entrepreneurial ventures that are "well beyond a scribble on a napkin."[15] As with other attempts to obtain external financing of any type, debt or equity, the entrepreneur needs to be well prepared with a thorough feasibility study and business plan.

Angel Investors. An **angel investor** is a private investor, a wealthy individual, who offers financial backing usually in high risk–high reward opportunities. The angel is looking to invest in entrepreneurial ventures that have the potential to provide high rates of return but also have the risk of failing dramatically without any chance of earning back the investment. But the angel is willing to take that risk because of the potentially high reward.

As with venture capital financing, an angel investor is an equity investor. The angel provides funds in return for some ownership stake in the entrepreneurial venture. If the venture is profitable and its market value rises, the angel's investment increases in value. Because they're dealing personally with the entrepreneur, many angels do have a personal interest in the venture as well. They want to see the entrepreneurial venture succeed and are willing to provide advice and assistance as needed. Although angels may indeed seem like the answer to an entrepreneur seeking funds, there are some cautions about angel investors.[16] Some angels may be looking for a quick turnaround of their money and will, in effect, destroy the business to get it back out. Some supposed angels are less-than-desirable individuals with suspicious backgrounds and intentions. In other instances, angel

Global Perspectives

Kanwal Rekhi has become the dominant investor in, and adviser to, several start-up businesses in Silicon Valley's Indian community. Rekhi made his millions selling his own start-up company, Excelan, in the late 1980s. Since that time, he has funded 12 small start-ups, all but one started by Indian immi-

grants. His $5 million initial investment has returned him $20 million from selling parts of the companies he has backed. Individuals in Silicon Valley call Rekhi a "very important player" and a wonderful adviser to the intelligent, ambitious, and hard-working Indian entrepreneurs, many of them

immigrants. His funding and his advice have helped a number of fledgling companies get up and running.

Source: J. Pitta, "The Venture Capitalist from Kanpur," *Forbes,* July 6, 1998, pp. 162–63.

Rapid Review ◀◀|

✓ What types of personal resources might an entrepreneur have access to for financing? Which seems to be a popular choice and why?

✓ What types of financial institutions provide funds to entrepreneurs? How do they provide these funds?

✓ Describe an SBA-guaranteed loan.

✓ What is venture capital? Why would venture capitalists be interested in financing entrepreneurial ventures?

✓ What is an angel investor? What cautions are appropriate when dealing with an angel investor?

investors may feel that their equity investment permits them to tell the entrepreneur how to run the business. So, just be cautious. Although an angel investor can, indeed, seem to be the answer to financing problems, be aware up front what the angel's motivations, stipulations, and intentions are.

Public Offering. Rather than offering equity stakes to private venture capitalists or angel investors, an entrepreneur may choose to do a public offering of ownership stakes in the entrepreneurial venture. This is done through an **initial public offering (IPO)**, an investment vehicle that is the first public registration and sale of a company's stock. The IPO allows an entrepreneur to raise a much larger pool of funds than is possible through the other approaches. In fact, stories of Internet companies going public and raising hundreds of millions of dollars in funds has many potential entrepreneurs with big dollar signs in their eyes salivating at the prospect! However, keep in mind that what is being offered for sale is ownership—ownership of the entrepreneurial venture. With the acquired funds come certain requirements and expectations. A brand-new start-up faces overwhelming hurdles in going the IPO route. Without a proven track record, the new entrepreneurial venture has nothing to entice potential investors. Underwriters (an investment banking firm that actually manages the whole stock-offering process) and attorneys want to see a strong management team, a competent board of directors, standardized procedures, outstanding employees, and a host of other characteristics. Often, an IPO—the process and event of "going public"—is the culmination of years of hard work and long-delayed financial rewards for an entrepreneur. However, this doesn't mean that a brand-new entrepreneurial venture can't pull it off, but the probability of obtaining financing through an IPO is highly unlikely.

Business Development Programs. The next type of financing can be found in various business development programs. These programs are designed to help entrepreneurs get their feet on the ground; to provide funding and other types of assistance in those crucial early stages of the entrepreneurial venture. We're going to look at four different programs and what they offer: Small Business Investment Companies (SBICs), Small Company Offering Registration (SCOR), business incubators, and Angel Capital Electronic Network (ACE-Net).

1. *Small Business Investment Companies (SBICs).* The U.S. Congress authorized the creation of SBICs in 1958.[17] Since then, SBICs have invested over $13 billion in entrepreneurial businesses. Some of those businesses—such as FedEx, America Online, Apple Computer—have gone on to become huge market successes. The Small Business Administration licenses private investment firms as SBICs. These SBICs get their money from their owners and from individual investors. To become an SBIC, a firm must have at least $5 million of its own capital and obtain a special license from the government.[18] The SBIC can then sell certain government-guaranteed bonds and borrow money at attractive rates

from the SBA to put into entrepreneurial ventures. An SBIC will generally take more risk than a bank will. The funds are repaid through a regular stream of payments, but the SBIC may also reserve the right to purchase stock in the new venture if it succeeds. However, SBICs are barred by federal law from buying a controlling interest in the entrepreneurial venture. A specialized type of SBIC called an SSBIC (Specialized Small Business Investment Company) offers financing to businesses owned by socially or economically disadvantaged individuals. These programs offer help to entrepreneurial ventures that might have no other financial options to pursue.

2. *Small Company Offering Registration (SCOR).* A SCOR is a do-it-yourself public offering.[19] The concept was created by the North American Securities Administrators Association and the American Bar Association to encourage entrepreneurs and other small business owners to take advantage of the U.S. Securities and Exchange Commission's Rule 504. Rule 504 permits the sale of securities worth up to $1 million in a 12-month period without being subject to SEC reporting requirements. The registration form is called a U-7 and was designed to be completed by business owners rather than by securities lawyers and investment banking firms. (The U-7 registration form and an accompanying manual are available free on the North American Securities Administrators Association Inc. Web site at **www.nasaa.org**. Click on the Help for Small Business button.) Sounds like an entrepreneur's financing dream, right? Despite its many professed advantages, nothing about a SCOR is simple. Although the form is the same in all the states that allow SCOR financing, the SCORs are administered by state securities commissions, and laws vary from state to state. In addition, there are expenses associated with the document's preparation. Most states require that financial statements be reviewed or audited by a certified public accountant. Then, there's the time spent on becoming familiar with the program and completing the preparation, filing, and marketing processes. Because of the lack of publicity about it and the lack of standardization among states, the SCOR program hasn't been as popular as first envisioned. However, it does provide another financing option for an entrepreneur.

3. *Business incubators.* Are you familiar with an incubator? It protects newly born animals (and humans) in a controlled environment and ensures that they're off to a healthy start. **Business incubators** serve much the same purpose—they nurture new entrepreneurial ventures in a controlled environment and ensure that they get off to a strong start. Many incubators are found in conjunction with universities, although not always. Most incubators provide their start-up companies with common office space, equipment, professional services (such as attorneys and accountants), managerial advice, and encouragement. We're including this as a financing option because it is a way for an entrepreneur to minimize his or her initial financial investment.

4. *Angel Capital Electronic Network (ACE-Net).* The ACE-Net is sponsored by the Small Business Administration's Office of Advocacy. It's simply a listing service that provides information to private investors on promising entrepreneurial ventures seeking to raise $250,000 to $5 million.[20] For anyone seeking less than $250,000, the SBA warns that the costs involved may offset a significant amount of the funding received. Investors must have a net worth

Entrepreneurs in Action

In Fort Collins, Colorado, a not-for-profit group, the Fort Collins Virtual Business Incubator, is nurturing a number of new entrepreneurial companies in the hopes that new jobs will be created in this community of 110,000. There's just one unique thing about this incubator—it's a virtual one. What it provides is the services of professionals (lawyer, accounting, marketing firm), free management advice, and encouragement from volunteer experts and businesspeople. What it does not provide is physical space for companies to set up business. This approach is unlike most incubators, which provide office or work space for the entrepreneurial venture. However, the fledgling entrepreneurs seem to think this approach works just fine. For example, Maury Willman, cofounder of Ergonomic Health Systems, which makes software to help companies improve workplace ergonomics and safety, says she got into the incubator to "surround herself with knowledge and excitement." Willman maintains that even though she may not be receiving the typical services of an incubator, she is receiving valuable advice and assistance. Another incubator client, Kristin Romberg, sales director for Infusion Technologies, which makes custom software for telephone call centers, says that the incubator's services were a "tremendous value" for her company. This approach, "an incubator without walls," is becoming another option for entrepreneurial ventures.

Source: W. R. Long, "Warmth, but No Walls, in This Incubator," *New York Times*, January 17, 1999, p. BU7.

of at least $1 million or an annual income of more than $200,000. Entrepreneurs pay $450 annually to be listed and must meet certain qualifications. You can access the site at **www.ace-net.org**. Entrepreneurs and investors wishing to have access to this service must first enroll in the system. An application may be downloaded from the ACE-Net Web site. Once the form is completed, it must be mailed, along with the enrollment fee, to the nearest network operator. The local network operator will then issue a password providing access to the secure ACE-Net Web site. A majority of states have adopted new initiatives allowing companies raising less than $1 million on ACE-Net to use a short-form listing that significantly reduces the amount of effort required to get listed. This allows a company to file a simplified single listing along with its business plan. ACE-Net is fast becoming the primary information source linking entrepreneurs to angel investors.[21]

Unusual Sources. Although we've covered traditional and even some new Internet-based financing sources, there are even more unusual sources. For instance, one is a television show called *MoneyHunt* where entrepreneurs get 10

Rapid Review ◀◀|

✓ Describe an IPO. Is it a viable financing option for a new entrepreneurial venture? Explain.

✓ What is an SBIC? How is this program different from other venture capitalists?

✓ What is SCOR? What are the advantages and drawbacks of this form of financing?

✓ How is a business incubator a financing option for entrepreneurs?

✓ Describe the ACE-Net.

✓ What other unusual financing sources might an entrepreneur explore?

minutes to tell their story and persuade a panel of experts why they deserve financing. *MoneyHunt* is a half-hour show that airs on public television on about 130 stations nationwide.[22] Other unusual financing sources can be found in judged competitions at places such as MIT's Sloan School of Management's $50,000 Entrepreneurship Competition or the Wharton School's Venture Fair.[23] These competitions provide opportunities for would-be entrepreneurs to get exposure to potential investors and to get financing.

Now that we've covered all the possible financing sources, how do you evaluate the financing options? That's what we're going to discuss next.

Evaluating Financing Options

Remember at this point, the entrepreneur is still looking at and assessing the venture's feasibility. It doesn't help just to know what financing options there are. Which option(s) are the best? The evaluation of financing options boils down to three words: control, risk, and reward.

One issue in evaluating the financing options is the amount of control the entrepreneur wants. To keep the highest level of personal control means financing the entrepreneurial venture through personal resources. When the entrepreneur has to look elsewhere for financing, some level of control is sacrificed because he or she either is in debt to someone or someone has been offered ownership (equity) percentages in the business. However, the flip side to the control issue is that of risk. Using personal resources for financing the entrepreneurial venture exposes the entrepreneur to personal risk. But, this doesn't mean that there are no risks involved with the other sources of financing either. Debt (loan) financing and equity (ownership) financing also carry degrees of risk. What the entrepreneur has to do is weigh the risk he or she is willing to live with. Another important consideration in weighing the risk is the potential reward. If the entrepreneur hopes to maximize personal reward(s) from the entrepreneurial venture, personal resources would be the best choice. Under this option, the rewards (profits or business value) are not "shared" with anyone else. The other financing options are going to require some percentage of the rewards in return for putting up the money for the business.

The various combinations of control, risk, and reward are different for each of the financing sources that we've covered. Table 3-4 summarizes these combinations.

Guidelines for Seeking Financing

You can take certain steps to ease the difficulties of seeking out potential financing. As we said earlier in the chapter, *preparation* is the key.

1. *Write a feasibility study and then a business plan.* These two documents show potential financing sources that you have thought through your idea, you've researched the competition and marketplace, and you've identified the key elements of getting this proposed entrepreneurial venture up and running.

TABLE 3-4   Evaluating the Financing Options

	Personal Control	Personal Risk	Potential Reward
Personal resources	High	High	High
Financial institutions (debt financing)	Low to medium	Low	Low to medium
Venture capitalists (equity–debt financing)	Low to medium	Low	Low to medium
Angel investors (equity financing)	Low to medium	Low	Low to medium
Public offerings (equity financing)	Low	Low	Low to high
Business development programs	Low to medium	Low	Low to medium
Unusual sources	Low to high	Low	Low to high

2. *Get professional advice and help.* Although the last thing you may want to do is spend resources, this is important. Getting the advice of an accountant, attorney, or other professional consultant can pay for itself by saving you time and making sure you have covered every base and have what you need. Usually a financing source (bank, venture capitalist, or other source) will want to see financial statements and other documents with verified information.

3. *Get references.* Even entrepreneurs need references—someone who is willing to attest to their character, skills, experiences, or whatever. Be ready to provide these names and contact information.

4. *Go do it.* You've researched the venture's feasibility. You've prepared whatever supporting documents and information you can. Now, as the popular advertising slogan says, "Just Do It!"

Rapid Review ◀◀|

✓ Why is it important for entrepreneurs to evaluate the various financing options?

✓ What role do control, risk, and reward play in an entrepreneur's evaluation of the financing options?

✓ Describe the various combinations of control, risk, and reward for each of the financing sources.

✓ What role does preparation play in seeking financing? Explain.

✓ List and explain the guidelines for seeking financing.

CHAPTER SUMMARY

It's important to research an entrepreneurial venture's feasibility. Doing this entails generating and evaluating business ideas, researching and evaluating competitors, and exploring and evaluating the various financing options.

Generating and evaluating business ideas is an important step in the entrepreneurial process. Entrepreneurial ventures thrive on ideas. Generating ideas is an innovative, creative process. There are four main sources of ideas. First is personal interests or hobbies. Many entrepreneurial ventures got their start because of an entrepreneur's love of doing something. Another popular source is an entrepreneur's work experiences, skills, and abilities. The third source is to look at products and services currently available, both familiar and unfamiliar ones. Finally, opportunities in the external environment can be a source of potential entrepreneurial ideas.

How do entrepreneurs evaluate these ideas? They should look at the limitations of what is currently available, for new and different approaches, at scientific and technological advances and breakthroughs, for unfilled niches, and at trends and changes. If these suggestions don't work, the entrepreneur might try any of four different structured approaches to generate ideas. These include environmental scanning, creativity and creative problem solving, brainstorming, and focus groups.

Although generating ideas is an important process, it's only half the work. Evaluating ideas is important, also. Evaluating ideas revolves around personal and marketplace considerations. Two specific evaluation techniques include the four-questions approach and a feasibility study.

Once the entrepreneur has investigated an entrepreneurial idea and has a fairly good assessment of its strengths and weaknesses, it's time to look at the competition. Researching the competition through competitor intelligence activities can be a powerful tool for entrepreneurs. In assessing the competition, it's important to know who the competitors are, what information to get on competitors, and how to get that information.

The final aspect of researching the venture's feasibility is to look at the various financing options. There are seven possible sources: the entrepreneur's personal resources, financial institutions, venture capitalists, angel investors, public offering, business development programs, and unusual sources. Each of these sources will vary in terms of the control, risk, and reward it offers.

KEY TERMS

⟿ *Environmental scanning:* A technique for generating ideas that involves the screening of large amounts of information to detect emerging trends.

⟿ *Brainstorming:* A technique for generating ideas that encourages participants to dream up alternatives while withholding criticism.

⟿ *Focus groups:* An approach to generating ideas that uses groups of individuals who provide information about proposed products or services in a structured setting.

⟿ *Intuition:* A cognitive process whereby we subconsciously make decisions based on our accumulated knowledge and experiences; sometimes called "gut feeling."

⟿ *Risk:* The uncertainty surrounding decisions and actions about what will happen.

⟿ *Return:* The payback (financial or otherwise) that an entrepreneur hopes to gain from the entrepreneurial venture.

⟿ *Feasibility study:* A structured and systematic analysis of the various aspects of a proposed entrepreneurial venture designed to determine its feasibility.

- *Competitor intelligence:* A process of gathering information on who competitors are, what they are doing, and how their actions will affect your organization.
- *Competition:* Organizations vying or battling for some desired object or outcome—typically, customers, market share, survey ranking, or needed resources.
- *Strategic groups:* Groups of competitors following essentially the same strategy in a particular market or industry.
- *Reverse engineering:* Technical analyses of competitors' products.
- *Loans:* Financial resources made available by a financial institution that are paid back, including the borrowed amount and interest charges, by the borrower over a certain period of time.
- *Small Business Administration (SBA):* A government agency devoted to the enhancement, support, and education of entrepreneurs and small business owners–managers.
- *Venture capital:* External equity financing provided by professionally managed pools of investor money.
- *Angel investor:* A private investor, a wealthy individual, who offers financial backing usually in high risk–high reward opportunities.
- *Initial public offering (IPO):* An investment vehicle that is the first public registration and sale of a company's stock.
- *Business incubators:* A business development program that nurtures new entrepreneurial ventures in a controlled environment to ensure they get off to a strong start.

SWEAT EQUITY

1. "It is important to choose a business or profession that fulfills your unique purpose or passion in life. It is much easier to succeed at something you enjoy." Do you agree with this statement? Why or why not? Write a paper explaining your position. Be sure to examine your personal philosophy about this and how this might affect your pursuit of an entrepreneurial venture.
2. In the June 1999 issue of *Business 2.0* (p. 14), four entrepreneurs gave their thoughts on the role that striking it rich plays in entrepreneurship. Take each one and discuss it. Do you agree? Disagree? Why? What are the implications? Now, which fits your own personal beliefs? Why?
   - "Striking it rich is simply the pinnacle of success for ambitious people who express themselves through creativity in business. It's not the money, it's what the money represents. Were I a seal, it would be fish, lots of fresh fish" (Derick M. Bulkley, founder and CEO, The SeriousCollector.com).
   - "Striking it rich for an entrepreneur means they have more money, but less passion. They now get to hang out with lawyers, accountants, investment advisors, an occasional IRS auditor, and other exciting types they have spent most of their life trying to avoid" (Len Batterson, CEO, Batterson Venture Partners).
   - "Entrepreneurship is not about the money. What drives entrepreneurs—what drives me—is the desire to build a company from scratch, to create

something unique from anything else on the market that delivers long-lasting value. You can't assign a monetary value to that kind of quest" (Sonia Khademi, CEO, CableSoft).

- "Striking it rich is not the keystone of the entrepreneurial arch. However, it does build family, investor, and personal fulfillment that helps to support the portal's structure on many levels (Jeff Kleck, Ph.D., CEO, Neoforma.com).

3. Generation X. This term is often used to describe the cohort of 60 million–plus Americans born between 1964 and 1978. Generation Xers are the group of people born after the all-too-familiar baby-boom generation. In the early 1990s, this group was stereotyped as the "slackers"—no ambition, no drive, no desire to succeed. However, this isn't descriptive of this group at all. In fact, Xers are earning and spending more and more every year. That's good news for entrepreneurs because Xers tend to be independent and individualistic. They don't gravitate to the well-known brand-name products, but instead search out the entrepreneurial upstarts. What do you know about Generation X? Research this group. Look at its demographics, attitudes, characteristics—whatever you can find. Using a bulleted-list format, put this information into a report.

4. We know that economic, demographic, and social trends provide significant opportunities for entrepreneurship. However, trends in business do, too. Here's a list of business trends. Think of how each of these trends impacts entrepreneurship and some potential entrepreneurial ideas that could arise from it.

   Business Trends:
   The computer revolution
   The Internet–World Wide Web
   Downsizing
   Outsourcing
   Abundant financing
   Globalization
   Quality improvement programs

5. Trends can be a powerful source for entrepreneurial ideas. However, how do you know when something is really a trend and not simply a fad? For instance, think of the "clear" colas. Why did these turn out to be a fad? Do some research on trends and fads. Write a report that includes suggestions for entrepreneurs as it relates to understanding trends and fads.

ENTREPRENEURSHIP IN ACTION CASES

CASE #1: Shooting the Moon

Entrepreneurship in Action case #1 can be found at the beginning of Chapter 3.

Discussion Questions

1. Where did the idea for Purple Moon come from? Is this a good source for entrepreneurial ideas? Why or why not?

2. Purple Moon did exhaustive market research (over 25 studies), but still failed as an independent business. What's your explanation? What are some possible reasons why this happened? Does this mean that competitor intelligence is useless? Explain.

3. Design a competitor intelligence report that Brenda Laurel could use. You don't have to find the information. Just describe what types of information you would include. For each type of information, be sure to explain why you would want to have it.

CASE #2: Tooth Wars

The battlefield is your mouth. Or more precisely, your teeth and gums. Helping people keep those teeth and gums clean and healthy is a huge market! David Giuliani, founder and CEO of Optiva Corporation, was about to stake his career and savings on the home-dental-care appliance of the future.

An engineer by training, Giuliani had spent 12 years at Hewlett-Packard, working his way up to section manager. But he wanted more. He wanted to "try his hand at the tiller." He left H-P for an executive post with a medical-imaging company and when an opportunity came to head up one of its subsidiaries, a digital radiography business, he jumped at it. However, because he still wanted something more entrepreneurial, he quit. Now on his own, Giuliani developed a handheld ultrasound device that could measure bladder volume. He eventually built that product into a 70-employee division of a company that was eventually acquired by Abbott Laboratories. Although he stayed on as an executive, Giuliani was searching for his next entrepreneurial challenge.

Meanwhile, two University of Washington professors, David Engel and Roy Martin, were looking for someone with entrepreneurial experience to help them market a prototype sonic toothbrush they'd developed. A sonic toothbrush is based on the premise that a sound-wave-based device could effectively clean the plaque and tartar that are the major causes of dental disease. Engel and Martin had hoped that a large personal health care company would pick up their technology and bring it to market. However, industry giants such as Procter & Gamble, Johnson & Johnson, Sunbeam, Squibb, and 25 other companies declined, pointing to the fact that the U.S. Patent Office was filled with the sad stories of other home sonic toothbrushes that had been tried and failed. What Engel and Martin felt they had, though, was a technology that did work—that did blast teeth and gums with sound waves to keep them clean and healthy. But they needed someone to help them get their prototype up and running. When they spread the news around that they were looking for a sharp businessperson with a knowledge of high-tech medical equipment who could help them build a company, Giuliani's name kept coming up. The three met, and Giuliani's introduction to the prototype in the lab sold him on the deal. The University of Washington, to which Engel and Martin had assigned the patent rights under a standard employee agreement, granted the new company lifetime rights to the patent in exchange for partial ownership.

At the beginning, Giuliani kept his day job with Abbott, but his free time was spent tinkering with the prototype. The results were discouraging. The strip of metal and ceramic that held the toothbrush bristles kept breaking, and it required too much power to produce the needed vibrations. Giuliani was about to give up. But one day, while walking along the beach, he watched as the waves washed over the sand, slowly eroding the beach. That process of nature was the key product design breakthrough Giuliani had been looking for! Maybe what the product needed was sound waves traveling through fluid, which would then erode away plaque. Giuliani went back to his cofounders and told them the idea of a sonic toothbrush was a great one, but they had to abandon the prototype and try a new approach.

After consulting with various engineers, Giuliani came up with a new design: sort of like a tuning fork driven by a vibrating electromagnetic field that would provide power to the brush head. Engel and Martin spent hours in the lab observing how the vibrating brush head churned up a mixture of toothpaste and saliva on artificial teeth. When the vibrations were tuned to 520 strokes per second (middle

C on the musical scale), the churned-up fluid would start to erode plaque, even when the brush itself wasn't making contact with the teeth. In theory, this meant that the plaque-cleaning action could take place between teeth and under the gum line, the places where other toothbrushes failed to go. The trio began to believe that their product could really be hot!

The next step was finding financing, always a big challenge. But Giuliani was able to get nearly half a million dollars from about 25 different investors. He didn't want to bring in venture capital or angels because he didn't want to risk losing control of the company down the road.

It was more than a year after getting financing that the toothbrush design was perfected into one that was manufacturable. The product became Sonicare, and the company, now called Optiva Corporation, set up its first assembly line in August 1992. For a high-tech product, production was pretty low-tech. A high-school student on summer vacation was hired to cut the brush-head bristles with a pair of tiny scissors and to assemble the rest of the product. Eventually, they began producing about 20 units a day. Since that time, Optiva has grabbed 33 percent of the $184 million electric toothbrush market in the United States. It has passed one major competitor, Interplak, and trails behind only Braun, another large competitor, which holds 37 percent of the market.

Discussion Questions

1. Describe the process of idea development behind Sonicare, Optiva Corporation's sonic toothbrush.

2. Would research-oriented universities be a good source of potential entrepreneurial ideas? Do some research on this topic

and write up a short report outlining the advantages and drawbacks of this idea source.

3. One of the misconceptions about great ideas is that they come out of nowhere. How do you explain the fact, then, that Giuliani "saw" the connection between a process of nature (waves hitting the beach and eroding the sand) and his redesign of the company's prototype?

4. What is your opinion of Giuliani's approach to the company's financing needs? What suggestions might you have given him?

(*Sources:* D. H. Freedman, "Sonic Boom," *Inc. 500 1997*, 1997, pp. 36–41; and C. Caggiano, "A Simple Plan in a Complex World," *Inc.*, February 1999, p. 45.)

CASE #3: Fun with Foam

Tad Wiginton of Round Rock, Texas, has a kid's dream job. He gets to play with styrofoam all the time and shape it into fanciful, fun objects. His company, Capitol Foam, Inc., carves and assembles plastic-foam designs for billboards nationwide. Its sculptures have included a 23-foot-high Timberland hiking boot (it weighed nearly half a ton), an 18-foot-high gumball machine that contained gumballs the size of beach balls, and a giant diaper pin. The three-dimensional designs are one-of-a-kind and some have won awards. The diaper pin, for instance, won a prestigious ADDY award from the American Advertising Federation.

The foam sculptures sell for $2,000 to $10,000. The desired shape is carved from huge blocks with wood-carving tools and electric hot knives. If something doesn't look right, it's cut off, carved on another piece of foam, and glued on. Each sculpture then receives an application of paint and a protective coating before being shipped to the customer. In addition to the sculptures, Capitol Foam makes its own special formula protective coating. This coating is distributed by an East Coast company to theatrical and film scenery designers from Broadway to Hollywood. The company also sells foam shapes to builders for use in moldings, arches, and columns.

Wiginton didn't plan on cutting and shaping polystyrene when he graduated from college with a computer science degree. However, he had received a grant from the U.S. Department of Education to create a computer system to make raised letters. He developed a computer-controlled machine with a hot wire that cut through foam like a hot knife cutting through butter. When his device wasn't accepted, he decided to use it for carving letters, logos, and signs out of foam for department and craft stores. One day, out of the blue, an ad agency called and wanted to know if he could make a 15-foot-long Starship Enterprise for a billboard advertising a TV station in Chattanooga, Tennessee. Wiginton agreed, although he had no idea how he was going to do it. The foam spaceship won an award for the TV station. Wiginton and Capitol Foam were on their way to foam fun!

Discussion Questions

1. Is the way the idea for this entrepreneurial company arose typical? Explain.

2. Which approach to defining who competitors are would be most appropriate for Capitol Foam? Support your choice.

3. No feasibility study was done for Capitol Foam, but still it has succeeded. So, why would an entrepreneur need to do a feasibility study?

(*Source:* A. Ebbers, "Foam Follows Function," *Nation's Business,* April 1999, pp. 62–63.)

VIDEO CASE #1: Shopping the World

From his home in Tampa, Florida, Jimmy Fand shops the world . . . literally. As the owner of The Tile Connection, North America's largest ceramic tile importer, Fand scours the world for different and unique tile. He got into this business because he found such poor selections and high prices when he was shopping for ceramic tile for a home he was building for his family in Tampa. Growing up in Colombia, where tile is a common fixture in homes and offices, he knew there had to be better choices than he was finding. He decided to go into business himself and search out and import tile from foreign tile manufacturers. His global searches have led him to high-quality tile manufacturers in Spain, Portugal, Colombia, Brazil, Argentina, Japan, Turkey, and other places all around the world.

Fand's background is quite interesting, as well. He came to New York City at the age of 19 and found the city to be a truly exciting place that fulfilled his every expectation of a large cosmopolitan city. Despite the fact that he was a high-school dropout, Fand went on to complete three university degrees. It's likely that his success and confidence in being a global businessperson come from his willingness to absorb new experiences.

Before starting The Tile Connection, Fand gained considerable experience and wisdom through his involvement in other business ventures. He has developed a set of principles that he has successfully applied at The Tile Connection. He knows that market research can give him an edge on competitors, and he strives hard to understand what types of tile are likely to be popular with his customers. Fand has also learned that proper money management and strict financial controls are crucial. He takes pride in the excellent credit rating he has built up with his vendors over the years.

Fand is proud of his business success, and he knows he has earned it himself through hard work and effort. "I'm self-made," he says. "A lot of people are used to getting things for free, but only those who work hard for those things are able to appreciate them." But he also values "the ability to be a human being." He says it's important, "to think in terms of the needs of others. To create, to raise your family with very high standards, and to raise them with a high degree of education."

Discussion Questions

1. How did Jimmy Fand get the idea for his business, The Tile Connection?

2. Would the fact that Fand operates globally affect his analysis of competitors? Discuss.

3. Evaluate the business principles that Jimmy Fand has successfully used to guide his business. How do they relate to what we discussed in this chapter?

4. Pretend that Jimmy Fand has asked you to consult with him about the viability of

his proposed business. Describe the types of things you would want to discuss with him.

(*Source:* Based on *Small Business 2000, Show 405.*)

SMALL BUSINESS 2000 — VIDEO CASE #2: Scrubs with a Smile

If you've ever been in a hospital, they're a familiar sight: the green or blue baggy outfits worn by doctors, nurses, orderlies, and technicians. These scrub suits, or as they're more commonly known, "scrubs," typically are two-piece outfits with v-necks, pullover tops with a patch pocket, and drawstring pants. For years, scrubs were purchased in mass quantities by hospitals and issued to employees who arrived at work in street clothes and changed in locker rooms. These uniforms were made from a cotton-polyester-blend fabric designed to withstand the extremely hot laundering temperatures that were believed to be necessary for thorough sanitation. A few years ago, however, studies showed that germs were not transmitted through health care workers' clothing. Rather, it was found that thorough hand washing was the key to stopping the spread of infection. At the same time, hospital administrators were facing increased pressure to cut costs. One solution was to transfer the responsibility for buying and maintaining scrubs to nurses and other staff employees. Employees began wearing their own scrubs to work.

These trends created an opportunity for Sue Calloway, a nurse in a San Diego hospital. Sue had enjoyed sewing for most of her life and continued to sew even after fulfilling her lifelong ambition of becoming a nurse. Rather than buying scrubs that looked like all the other drab ones, Sue sewed her own. She added subtle styling touches and chose 100 percent cotton fabrics with bright colors and designs. When Sue began wearing her home-made scrubs to work in 1988, all her co-workers wanted to know where she had gotten them. She explained that she had made them herself. Sue recalls, "All my friends wanted them. I never said 'no,' and I just kept sewing and taking orders."

For several years, Sue continued her nursing job and sewed at home in her spare time. In 1992, her husband Rocky encouraged her to quit sewing part time and turn her hobby into a full-time business. She did, and what a good decision that was!

Today, Sue devotes all her time to the design and marketing of scrubs, surgical dresses, and other apparel items for health care workers. Most of the actual sewing is now outsourced to another company. She has registered the brand name S.C.R.U.B.S., which stands for Simply Comfortable Really Unique Basic Scrubs. Her years of experience enable her to add whimsical touches to her products, such as S.C.R.U.B.S. featuring flying pigs. Sue says, "Sometimes when you work in a high stress environment, it's like, 'When pigs fly, I'll get to it.'" Her customers get the subtle humor.

Early on, Sue found a partner who could help steer S.C.R.U.B.S. in the right direction. Steve Epstein, a long-time family acquaintance, had extensive experience and expertise in the apparel industry. Steve convinced her that the large number of health care professionals represented a significant opportunity. His conservative projections of how the business could grow exceeded Sue's expectations. To support the new venture, Sue, Rocky, Steve, and Steve's wife Ida borrowed money from their friends, used their credit cards, and sold their cars. Although it was touch-and-go early on, Steve's projections, optimism, and confidence in Sue turned out to be justified. Not only was there a market to be tapped, but Sue had the right product for that market. As Steve explains, "The product is unique, it's different, and it addresses a genuine need in the community."

S.C.R.U.B.S. has since grown to a $6-million-a-year business. It relies mainly on mail order to reach its customers. However, it has opened up nine retail stores in shopping malls across the country. Now Callaway's apparel is catching on beyond the health care market. Retirees, teachers, and vacationers who want attractive, easygoing clothes for everyday activities are snapping up the products. S.C.R.U.B.S. is continuing to bring smiles to the faces of its growing base of customers!

Discussion Questions

1. Describe how the idea for S.C.R.U.B.S. evolved. Be sure to look at each of the idea sources that played a part in the idea for the business.

2. How did Sue and her cofounders address the financing challenge? What are the benefits and drawbacks of the approach they took?

3. This market obviously is ripe for competition. One competitor can be found at **www.scrubs.com**. Go to this site and gather competitive information. Make a bulleted list of your important points.

4. The S.C.R.U.B.S. product has been described as "unique, different, and addressing a genuine need." How important are these characteristics in researching the feasibility of an entrepreneurial idea? Explain.

(*Sources:* Based on C. Goodman, "Medical Garb with a Smile," *Nation's Business*, May 1999, pp. 65–67; and *Small Business 2000, Show 404.*)

ENDNOTES

1. L. Bannon, "Mattel's Barbie Gains New Friend, Rockett, Who's Really Serious," *Wall Street Journal*, March 19, 1999, p. A3; and A. Harmon, "With the Best Research and Intentions, a Game Maker Fails," *New York Times*, March 22, 1999, p. C1.

2. S. I. Mohan-Neill, "The Influence of Firm's Age and Size on Its Environmental Scanning Activities," *Journal of Small Business Management*, October 1995, pp. 10–21.

3. S. Greco, "Where Great Ideas Come From," *Inc.*, April 1998, pp. 76–86.

4. S. Greco, "The Start-Up Years," *Inc. 500*, October 21, 1997, p. 57.

5. A. Bhide, "How Entrepreneurs Craft Strategies That Work," *Harvard Business Review*, March–April 1994, pp. 150–61.

6. A. H. Anderson and P. Woodcock, *Effective Entrepreneurship* (Cambridge, MA: Blackwell Publishers, 1996).

7. R. Wild, "Naked Hunch," *Success*, June 1998, p. 54.

8. D. Phillips and C. E. Griffin, "Good Advice," *Entrepreneur*, December 1997, p. 58.

9. A. W. Hiam and K. W. Olander, *The Entrepreneur's Complete Sourcebook* (Paramus, NJ: Prentice Hall, 1996), pp. 23–37.

10. T. Burns, *Break the Curve: The Entrepreneur's Blueprint for Small Business Success* (London: International Thomson Business Press, 1999), p. 21.

11. T. Severance, *Business Start-Up Guide* (Oceanside, CA: Tycoon Publishing, 1998), p. 31.

12. See M. E. Porter, *Competitive Strategy* (New York: Free Press, 1980), Chapter 7.

13. R. Ho, "Small Businesses Take Charge of Credit by Using Cards as a Financing Option," *Wall Street Journal*, November 19, 1998, p. A2; and "Charge!" *Success*, March 1999, p. 13.

14. B. Zider, "How Venture Capital Works," *Harvard Business Review*, November–December 1998, pp. 131–39.

15. B. Solomon, "Something Ventured, Something Gained," *Working Woman*, May 1999, p. 64.

16. S. Gruner, "The Trouble with Angels," *Inc.*, February 1998, pp. 47–53.

17. J. Pryde, "A Lending Niche Helps Small Firms," *Nation's Business*, February 1998, pp. 52–53.

18. D. R. Evanson, "Lending Over Backwards," *Success*, July 1998, pp. 54–58.

19. R. Reynes, "Financing for Do-It-Yourselfers," *Nation's Business*, May 1998, pp. 38–40.

20. S. Nelton, "Using the Internet to Find Funds," *Nation's Business*, August 1998, pp. 35–36.

21. "SBA's ACE-Net Pairs Small Companies with Investors," *Springfield Business Journal*, March 1–7, 1999, p. 13.

22. T. Post, "You Bet Your Life," *Forbes*, June 1, 1998, p. 142; and J. Schembari, "In a Gong Show for Start-Ups, the Best Business Plan Wins," *New York Times*, March 21, 1999, pp. 1.

23. D. Foote, "Show Us the Money!" *Newsweek*, April 19, 1999, pp. 43–45.

4

PLANNING THE VENTURE

LEARNING OBJECTIVES

After reading this chapter, you should be able to:

1. Describe what organizational vision and mission are.
2. Explain the importance of having an organizational vision and mission.
3. Discuss how to develop an organizational vision and mission.
4. Define organizational culture.
5. Describe the various aspects of organizational culture.
6. Explain why it's important for an entrepreneur to understand organizational culture.
7. Explain the various components of a business plan.
8. Prepare a business plan.

ENTREPRENEURSHIP IN ACTION CASE #1

Cleaning Up at SOL

As one of northern Europe's most admired companies, SOL Cleaning Service, located in Helsinki, Finland, isn't what you might expect.[1] The company's headquarters, located in a renovated film studio, positively "explodes" with color, creativity, and chaos. Walls are painted bright red, white, and yellow, and employees wander the halls talking on bright yellow high-tech portable phones. These bright and energetic surroundings might seem tailor-made for creative, artistic businesses (such as software designers, or advertising executives), but SOL competes in a basic, grungy, and unglamorous business—industrial cleaning. It's a high-energy, fast-paced, knowledge-driven organization whose business is scrubbing hospital floors, making hotel beds, and sweeping grocery store aisles.

The philosophy of Liisa Joronen, SOL's owner, is "In a service business, if you're not happy with yourself, how can you make the customer happy?" Answering that question has made Joronen's company wildly successful, and the company's unique culture has played an important role.

SOL's culture is characterized by five values. The first value is that hard work has to be fun. Joronen believes that because few

104

Although it may seem far-fetched to view a company with 3,500 employees and $60 million in revenues derived from industrial cleaning as entrepreneurial, SOL Cleaning Service is about as entrepreneurial as they come. The company is pursuing opportunities, is characterized by innovative practices, and has profitability and growth as its main goals—all hallmarks, we know, of entrepreneurial ventures. As an entrepreneurially oriented company, SOL has enjoyed a great deal of success. An important part of SOL's continued success is its recognition of the importance of organizational cultural values in guiding what it does and how it conducts its business. In this chapter we're going to look at organizational culture issues as well as at the importance of developing a vision and mission and developing and writing the business plan. These activities are important steps in the planning of the entrepreneurial venture that need to be addressed before the venture is formally organized and launched.

DEVELOPING ORGANIZATIONAL VISION AND MISSION

The importance of an organization's vision and mission is perhaps best stated by one of the century's most noted and prolific management authors, Peter Drucker, who said, "A business is not defined by its name, statutes, or articles of incorporation. It is defined by the business mission. Only a clear definition of the mission and purpose of the organization makes possible clear and realistic business objectives."[2] Even the Bible references the importance of vision in Proverbs 29:18, which states, "Where there is no vision, the people perish." Before a new entrepreneurial venture is organized and launched, the entrepreneur must give serious thought to the organizational vision and mission. In this section, we're going to look at what the organizational vision and mission are, why they're important, and how you develop them.

What Are the Organizational Vision and Mission?

Although many people view organizational vision and mission as one and the same, we don't. There are some distinct differences between the two concepts, and we're going to address them separately.

We introduced the concept of organizational vision in Chapter 2 as we looked at it as one of the critical factors for succeeding in the new economy. Just to review, a **vision** is

people dream of becoming a cleaner, the keys to keeping her employees satisfied on the job are fun and individual freedom. The second cultural value that characterizes SOL is that there are no low-skill jobs. The company invests significant amounts of time and money in training employees. Another unique value of SOL is that people who set their own targets shoot for the stars. SOL employees have significant amounts of responsibility. Joronen's philosophy is that people will set targets higher for themselves than what anyone would set for them. The fourth value that SOL stresses is that loose organizations need tight measures. Although Joronen believes in employee autonomy, she is a fanatic about performance measurement and accountability. Finally, SOL believes that great customer service demands cutting-edge technology. SOL may be in a "low-end" business, but that doesn't mean it has to be low-tech.

a broad comprehensive picture of what an entrepreneur wants an organization to become. The vision provides a vibrant and compelling picture of the future, and presents a view beyond what the entrepreneurial venture "is" to what it "can be." The vision becomes the embodiment and statement of the entrepreneur's dream. When an organizational leader—in this case, the entrepreneur—articulates a distinct vision, all current and future decisions and actions are guided by this vision. By articulating this vision, the entrepreneur maps out an overall picture of where he or she would like the entrepreneurial venture to be in the future. For instance, at Microsoft, Inc., another highly successful entrepreneurial organization, the vision of "a computer on every desk" has guided organizational decisions and actions throughout the company's history of rapid and turbulent growth.

Whereas organizational *vision* provides an overall picture of where the entire organization would like to be in the future, a **mission** is a statement of what the various organizational units do and what they hope to accomplish in alignment with the organizational vision. These organizational units typically include common work activities, departments, projects, work groups, and so forth—for instance, a marketing department, a customer service team, an employee relations work group, or a purchasing project. An organization will have only one vision, but potentially several missions that contribute to the pursuit of the vision. A work unit's mission statement provides a focus for that particular area. Although the mission is not as comprehensive and broad as the statement of vision, it still provides an overview of the unit's purpose, what it does, and its goals. Each of the specific mission statements should also align with the organizational vision. Table 4-1 provides some examples of companies' vision and mission statements.

Why Are Organizational Vision and Mission Important?

The importance of developing an organizational vision and mission cannot be overemphasized for several reasons. Ideally, with the development of organizational vision and mission, an entrepreneur will have a broad framework that allows him or her and any additional organizational members to know what they're doing and why they're doing it. What results is a comprehensive and unified view of these important elements—that is, what the entrepreneurial venture is doing and what it hopes to become. The vision and affiliated statements of mission, then, provide direction and guidance for making decisions and taking actions. By expressing and clarifying the desired values, these statements can also serve to establish a general tone or climate for the organization. These desired values also become an important basis for the organizational culture as we'll discuss in an upcoming section. In addition, these statements serve as a focal point for the entrepreneur and any other organizational members to identify and clarify the organization's purpose and direction. There are no misunderstandings about what this organization is going to do (or is doing) and what it hopes to become. A final point about the importance of organizational vision and mission statements is that researchers who have studied organizational vision and mission statements have found that high-performing organizations have more comprehensive and thorough statements than do low-performing organizations.[3] This is further support for the importance of developing viable and appropriate organizational vision and mission statements.

TABLE 4-1   Sample Vision and Mission Statements

PRIME INC.

OUR MISSION

Is to prosper while providing excellent service to our customers

PRIME VALUES

CUSTOMERS: Finding, serving, and keeping customers guarantees our existence.

SERVICE: We will provide quality service that meets or exceeds our customers' requirements.

VALUE: We will price our service at rates that are a true value to our customers.

PROFIT: To remain free and provide security for our company and associates, we must earn a profit.

Courtesy of Prime Inc.

THE BAMA COMPANIES, INC.

OUR MISSION

People helping people be successful.

OUR VISION

To delight our customers with the **Bama experience** . . . again and again by setting the **standard**, and being the **best** in our **products**, our **service,** and our **people**.

Courtesy of The Bama Companies, Inc.

AIRE-MASTER

MISSION

To provide invaluable services that enhance the customer's image of quality.

VALUES

Positive mental attitude • Teamwork and communication • Concern for others • Going the extra mile • Innovative thinking • Training and education • Honesty • Reliability • Excellence • Constant improvement

Courtesy of Aire-Master

BASS PRO SHOPS

MISSION STATEMENT

To be the leading merchant of outdoor recreational products, inspiring people to love, enjoy, and conserve the great outdoors.

Courtesy of Bass Pro Shops

Entrepreneurs in Action

Bruce Brown's vision involved bugs. Not the creepy, crawly types with feelers and feet, but the types that invade computers. Computer bugs are Brown's passion. As these bugs have proliferated and as good technical help has become scarce, his *BugNet* newsletter fills an important need of corporate and personal computer users. (Check the newsletter out at **www.bugnet.com**.) *BugNet* makes its money from subscriptions, syndication, and licensing deals, and has been profitable from almost the very beginning. Each week, *BugNet*'s editors wade through numerous user complaints. The approximately 10 percent of problems that are judged to be the most serious or widespread are researched and reported to subscribers. From a vision to a viable venture—now there's nothing "buggy" about that at all!

Source: E. Updike, "Killer Applications," *Business Week Frontier*, April 26, 1999, pp. F28–F29.

Rapid Review

✓ What is organizational vision?
✓ What is organizational mission?
✓ How are organizational vision and mission similar? Different?
✓ Why is it important to develop organizational vision and mission statements?

Now that we recognize how important the organizational vision and mission are to the entrepreneurial venture, how are they developed? That's what we're going to discuss next.

How Do You Develop Vision and Mission Statements?

In order to answer this question, we first need to look at the process an entrepreneur can follow in developing the organizational vision and mission statements. Then, we address what should be included in these statements. The assumption that we're making is that these statements do need to be written. If the proposed dreams, desires, values, and ideas remain only in the entrepreneur's head and are never written down in some formal document, the potential for having a unified direction and framework for making decisions and taking actions is lost.

The Process of Developing Organizational Vision and Mission. It can be difficult to express in writing the things that are important parts of the organizational vision and mission. The entrepreneur may have a good idea of what the entrepreneurial venture is going to do but describing that "vision" in words can prove frustrating. The best way to start is to first of all believe in and commit to the importance of having these formal stated documents. Unless an entrepreneur personally is "sold" on the wisdom of having articulated an organizational vision and mission, there's not going to be the commitment of time or energy to developing them. There's no doubt that it will take some effort to create statements that capture the essence of the entrepreneurial venture and that do so in a way that's clear, concise, and motivational. But the effort is worth it! Once an entrepreneur has accepted that statements of vision and mission are important, what next?

The next step in developing the vision and mission(s) for the entrepreneurial venture is finding examples of ones already being used by other organizations, large and small. These statements usually can be found in company brochures, posted on walls at the organization's place of business, printed in annual reports, on a Web site, and in a variety of other places. If there are organizations that you particularly admire, ask the owners for a copy of their vision and mission statements. Look at what these organizations have included in their statements. Use these as a guide to the key points or important values that you would like to see included in your own statements.

Finally, once you've had an opportunity to examine and study sample statements, write your own. This means writing them down on paper! Don't just keep them in your head. Actually put them in writing. Then, look carefully at what you've written. Have other people close to you and whose judgment you trust—family, friends, professional advisers—look at what you've developed. Evaluate if the proposed statements capture the spirit of what you want your entrepreneurial venture to be and to become. Do the statements describe what is unique about your organization? If there are other key decision makers in the entrepreneurial venture, they should play an active role in developing and writing the vision and mission statements as well.

Important Components of Organizational Vision and Mission Statements. As you examine organizational vision and mission statements, one thing may strike you immediately, and that's the fact that they vary in length, content, format, and specificity. However, there are some common elements. Let's look at what both the organizational vision and the organizational mission statements should include.

What should an organizational vision include? Four components have been identified as important to organizational vision.[4] These are illustrated in Figure 4-1. First is that the vision be built on a foundation of the organization's core values and beliefs. These values and beliefs address what's fundamentally important to the organizational founders, such as conducting business ethically and responsibly, satisfying the customer, emphasizing quality in all aspects, or being a leader in technology. The vision should emphasize whatever those core values might be. Although a statement of values won't guarantee success for an entrepreneurial venture, it can provide the entrepreneur and any other future or current employees with a sense of expectations. For example, if employees know that outstanding customer service is valued by the organization, they can then make decisions and act in ways that champion customer service. Look back at our chapter-opening case and reexamine SOL's core values and the ways in which work decisions and actions are affected.

Second, the vision should elaborate a purpose for the organization. Any organization—large or small, profit or not-for-profit—must have a unique purpose for even existing. Specifying the purpose entails asking questions such as: Why is this organization in business? What is its intent? What is its *reason for being* in existence as an organization? This may seem an easy thing to do, but it's

Figure 4-1

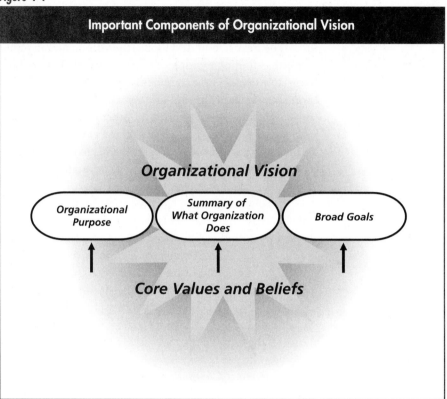

Important Components of Organizational Vision

Organizational Vision

Organizational Purpose | Summary of What Organization Does | Broad Goals

Core Values and Beliefs

not! An entrepreneur must think long and hard about the purpose of the entrepreneurial venture.

The third component of organizational vision is a brief summary of what the organization does. Although the vision shouldn't provide explicit details about what the organization does (this is best done through the mission statements, which we'll discuss shortly), it should explain what it's doing to fulfill its purpose. This is a good time to say that although the concepts are related, there is a difference between an organization's purpose and what it does. For example, there may be several organizations that have the purpose of ecological preservation, but the way they go about carrying out that purpose (that is, what they do) may be entirely different.

The last component of organizational vision is that it should specify broad goals. **Goals** are outcomes or end results that are desired by individuals, groups, or entire organizations. Goals provide targets that all organizational members work toward meeting. Goals serve to direct the entrepreneur and any other organizational members toward a common and unified end. The organization's vision can and should be a guiding force in every decision as goals are developed and pursued.

We've covered all the important elements of an organizational vision statement. Now, what about the mission statement(s)? What should be included in them?

Nine specific components are recommended to be included in every statement of mission.[5] These are illustrated in Figure 4-2. Here's a brief explanation of each of them.

Values-Based Management

Having a core set of values can influence the way an organization does its business. **Values-based management** is an approach to managing an entrepreneurial venture that entails establishing, promoting, and practicing shared values. An organization's values reflect what it stands for and what it believes in. For example, at Tom's of Maine, an entrepreneurial manufacturer of natural personal care products, the company's shared values have become part of the overall way the business is operated. Every decision at Tom's is evaluated in light of the values found in its Statement of Beliefs and Mission Statement.

Shared organizational values serve at least four main purposes: These shared values (1) guide decisions and actions, (2) shape employee behavior, (3) influence marketing efforts, and (4) help build team spirit in organizations. As you can see, shared organizational values can prove highly beneficial to an organization. Now, how can these shared values be developed?

As any venture that uses values-based management will tell you, it's not easy to establish the shared organizational values. At Tom's of Maine, the process involved everyone in the company. All the employees, working in groups of four to six, took a long, hard look at defining "who we are" and "what we are about." But the commitment by Tom's employees to developing shared values didn't stop there. They realized that they were actually to use the values they had helped define. They found that those shared values really mattered. Entrepreneurs who believe in the importance of shared values might follow these suggestions in developing them: (1) Involve everyone in the company. (2) Allow individual departments or units to customize the values. (3) Expect and accept employee resistance or uncertainty. (4) Keep the statement of values short. (5) Avoid trivial statements of values. (6) Leave out religious references. (7) Challenge the stated values. (8) Live the stated values.

Sources: G. P. Alexander, "Establishing Shared Values Through Management Training Programs," *Training and Development Journal*, February 1987, pp. 45–47; A. Farnham, "State Your Values, Hold the Hot Air," *Fortune*, April 19, 1993, pp. 117–24; and R. Kamen, "Values: For Show or for Real," *Working Woman*, August 1993, p. 10.

The first component is customers. Describe who the specific organizational or work unit's customers are. The next one is products or services. Define the major products and services of the organizational or work unit. The third component is markets. Explain where the organizational unit competes geographically. Next is technology. Describe if and how the organizational unit is technologically current. The fifth one is concern for survival, profitability, and growth. Explain how the organizational unit is committed to growth and financial viability. The next component is philosophy. This may be one of the harder ones to address because it should describe the basic beliefs, values, aspirations, and ethical priorities of the organizational unit. This philosophy should, and does, arise out of the vision statement. The values that are expressed in the mission statement should align with those in the vision statement. The next one is self-concept. Describe the organizational unit's competitive advantage. Explain what it has that competitors do not or that it does better than competitors. Next is concern for public image. Tell how the organizational unit is responsive to soci-

Figure 4-2

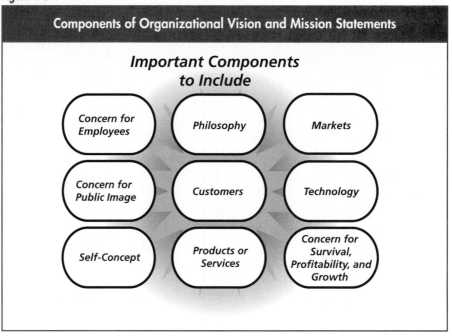

Components of Organizational Vision and Mission Statements

Important Components to Include

- Concern for Employees
- Philosophy
- Markets
- Concern for Public Image
- Customers
- Technology
- Self-Concept
- Products or Services
- Concern for Survival, Profitability, and Growth

etal, community, and environmental issues. If the organizational unit has employees, the final component should be concern for employees. Describe how and why employees are valuable assets of this organizational unit. These nine components are simply recommendations for what should be included in the mission(s). Some may apply; others may not. It is important, however, for an entrepreneur to at least examine each of these areas even though they may turn out to be inappropriate for describing what is happening in a specific organizational or work unit.

Much of what is expressed in the written statements of vision and mission make up the essence of organizational culture. It's important for entrepreneurs to understand what organizational culture is and how it influences the entrepreneurial venture. We're going to look at organizational culture issues next in our exploration of planning the entrepreneurial venture.

Global Perspectives

Entrepreneurship in Europe is not as easy as it could be. However, opportunities are beckoning, and European political entities are beginning to see entrepreneurs as part of a solution to unemploy- ment. One dedicated entrepre- neur, Roman Koidl, has started five companies with combined annual revenues of around $5.9 million and has more planned. In spite of the external obstacles he faces, Koidl remains focused on the organizational vision and mis- sions for his businesses.

Source: J. Kahn, "Suddenly, Startups Are Chic," *Fortune,* February 15, 1999, p. 110.

Rapid Review ◀◀|

✓ Describe the process of developing organizational vision and mission.

✓ What four components should an organizational vision include?

✓ What is values-based management, and what role might it play in organizational vision?

✓ What are goals?

✓ List the nine specific components that are recommended to be included in organizational mission statements.

ORGANIZATIONAL CULTURE ISSUES

When you go into a particular business, do you get a certain impression about what is important and about the way work is done by organizational members? Do you get the feeling that employees are excited and motivated by what they do, or that employees are there just because it's a paycheck coming in? Does it seem that customers are important and valued, or that customers are seen as intrusions on getting work done? Do you get the feeling that this organization is warm, relaxed, and open, or that this organization is structured, inflexible, and very rigid? Do you get the feeling that this organization is more formal or more informal? Just as individuals have personalities, an organization also has a personality. This personality is called *culture.* Just as every person has his or her own unique personality, every organization has a unique personality. In this section, we're going to explain what organizational culture is, describe the different dimensions of organizational culture, look at the source of culture, examine how organizational culture is learned by organizational members, and discuss why it's important for entrepreneurs to understand organizational culture.

What Is Organizational Culture?

Exactly what is **organizational culture**? It's the beliefs, values, and behavioral norms shared and practiced by organizational members. Even in an entrepreneurial organization that includes only the entrepreneur, certain beliefs, values, and behavioral norms will influence how decisions are made and work is completed. These shared beliefs, values, and behavioral norms that make up an organization's culture determine, to a large degree, what organizational members think is important and the way they do their work. When confronted with a problem, the organizational culture influences what organizational members do about it because of the "way we do things around here."

This definition of culture implies a couple of things. First, culture *is* a perception. Individuals perceive the culture of the organization on the basis of what they see, hear, or experience within the organization. Even though organizational members may have different backgrounds or work in different areas in the organization, they tend to describe the organization's culture in similar terms. That's what we mean by the *shared* aspect of culture. Organizational members share these values, beliefs, and behavioral norms. Second, organizational culture is a *descriptive* term. This means that culture is concerned with how organizational members perceive an organization, not with whether they like it. Culture describes rather than evaluates. What exactly, though, is the culture describing? Let's take a look at the dimensions of organizational culture.

Dimensions of Organizational Culture

Research into organizational culture suggests that seven dimensions capture the essence of an organization's culture.[6] These dimensions, as illustrated in Figure 4-3, have been described as follows:

Figure 4-3

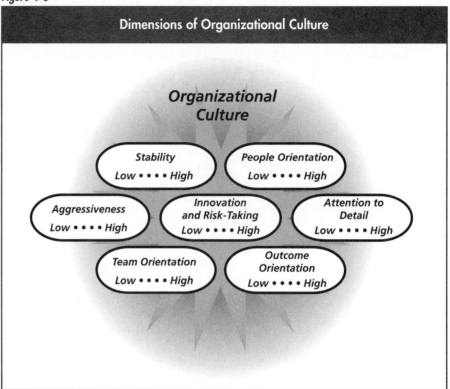

Dimensions of Organizational Culture

Organizational Culture

Stability
Low • • • • High

People Orientation
Low • • • • High

Aggressiveness
Low • • • • High

Innovation and Risk-Taking
Low • • • • High

Attention to Detail
Low • • • • High

Team Orientation
Low • • • • High

Outcome Orientation
Low • • • • High

1. *Innovation and risk-taking.* The degree to which employees are encouraged to be innovative and take risks.
2. *Attention to detail.* The degree to which employees are expected to exhibit precision, thorough analysis, and attention to detail.
3. *Outcome orientation.* The degree to which results or outcomes are considered more important than the techniques and processes used to achieve those outcomes.
4. *People orientation.* The degree to which organizational decisions take into consideration the effect on organizational members.
5. *Team orientation.* The degree to which organizational work is done in teams rather than by individuals.
6. *Aggressiveness.* The degree to which organizational members are aggressive and competitive instead of easygoing and cooperative.
7. *Stability.* The degree to which organizational decisions and actions emphasize maintaining the status quo as opposed to growing.

As shown, each of these cultural dimensions exists on a continuum from low to high. Describing an organization on these seven dimensions provides a composite picture of its culture. In many organizations, one cultural dimension often takes precedence over the others and essentially shapes the organization and the way organizational members do their work. The personalities of these organizations reflect the cultural dimension that is valued and prized. For instance, an organization may have a strong attention-to-detail personality. Or, it may have a strong people-orientation personality. Look back at our chapter-opening case. Based on the story, what type of personality would you say SOL has? In other words, which cultural dimensions are valued and highly regarded?

The Source of Culture

An organization's values, customs, traditions, and ways of doing things are largely due to what's been done before and the degree of success it has had with these. The original source of an organization's culture usually reflects the beliefs, values, and vision of the founder(s). Because the founder has the original idea, he or she also may have certain biases about how best to accomplish the idea. The founder is not constrained by previous customs or approaches. This person establishes the early culture of the organization by projecting an image of what the organization should be. The small size of the new organization also helps the founder(s) instill the vision in organizational members as they come on board. These people either "buy into" the culture or they don't join the organization.

Let's look at an example of an individual who had an immense influence on shaping his organization's culture. Yvon Chouinard is the founder of the outdoor gear company Patagonia, Inc. Chouinard is an avid extreme adventurer and approached the business in a laid-back, casual manner. For instance, he hired employees not on the basis of any specific business skills they might have had, but because he had climbed, fished, or surfed with them. Employees were friends, and work was treated as something fun to do. In a speech Chouinard gave a few years ago, he uttered his legendary line, "Let my people go surfing!" Although Patagonia is now a $125-million-a-year company with more than 500 employees, its culture still reflects Chouinard's values and philosophy. How did Patagonia's 500 employees "learn" the organizational culture? As an entrepreneurial organization grows and organizational members are hired, they soon learn the "way things are done around here." How? That's what we're going to discuss next.

Rapid Review ◀◀|

- ✓ What is organizational culture?
- ✓ Describe the two implications of the definition of culture.
- ✓ List and explain the seven dimensions of organizational culture.
- ✓ How do these dimensions describe an organization's culture?
- ✓ Where does an organization's culture come from?

How Organizational Culture Is Learned

The culture of the organization is transmitted to organizational members in a number of ways, most importantly through stories, rituals, material symbols, and language. These stories, rituals, material symbols, and language give the culture life. They are the ways through which we see, experience, and learn about an organization's culture. In this section, we'll also take a look at the role that physical surroundings play in reinforcing and supporting the organizational culture.

Stories. Organizational "stories" typically contain a narrative of significant events or people including such things as the founders and how they started the business, organizational members breaking the rules and succeeding through taking risks, rags-to-riches successes, reactions to past mistakes and what happened to individuals who made mistakes, and other key organizational events. These stories help tie together the present with the past, provide explanations and legitimacy for current practices, and exemplify what's important to an organization.

The stories can play an important role in passing on key values and expectations to organizational members.

Rituals. Rituals are repetitive sequences of activities that express and reinforce the key shared values of the organization, and what goals are most important. For example, one of the best-known organizational culture rituals takes place at the annual meeting of another well-known entrepreneurially oriented company, Mary Kay Cosmetics. Looking like a cross between a circus and a Miss America pageant, the meeting takes place over a couple of days in a large auditorium, on a stage in front of a large, cheering audience, with all the participants dressed in glamorous evening clothes. Salespeople are rewarded for their success in achieving sales goals with an array of flashy gifts including gold and diamond pins, furs, and pink Cadillacs. This ritual serves as a motivator to organizational members by publicly acknowledging outstanding sales performance. It also reinforces the determination and optimism of the founder, Mary Kay Ash, who overcame personal hardships, founded her own company, and achieved material success. It conveys to the salespeople that they too can achieve success through hard work and reaching their sales goals. But a ritual doesn't have to be elaborate to instill and reinforce the key corporate values. It may be something as simple as a Friday afternoon celebration at the end of a successful week. The important thing is that the rituals express and reinforce the desired values.

Material Symbols. Material symbols can include, for example, office location, office furnishings, office size, employee lounges and workout facilities, tech-

Entrepreneurs in Action

In many entrepreneurial organizations, work practices that began as simple management moves have evolved into cultural rituals. For instance, at AGI, Inc., a Melrose Park, Illinois, design and print firm, CEO Richard Block has consistently promoted open debate and the "combustive rub of ideas." He has tried to create an environment ripe for experimentation and one that urges employees to take responsibility for a problem rather than working to conceal it. In the spirit of such an environment, Block opens himself up to lively interrogation at a monthly company-wide meeting. The toughest questioner gets a prize! At Visual In-Seitz of Rochester, New York, it's a Thursday afternoon production meeting held at a bar. At these meetings, employees share problems and tips, track performance, and voice complaints. Because the company's employees deal with very short deadlines and demanding customers (they create business presentations for corporations), stress was very high. The off-site production meetings were a way to defuse the stress and still focus on making sure customers received superior products and service.

Source: J. Case, "Corporate Culture," *Inc.,* November 1996, pp. 42–53.

nological equipment, or reserved parking spaces. Who gets these material symbols conveys to organizational members who is important and the kinds of behavior (for example, risk-taking, conservative, individualistic, team player) that are expected. If the organization takes the approach that all organizational members share in the material symbols, it's conveying that egalitarianism is important. For example, a story on the national evening news told about the owner of a long-distance phone company based in New Jersey who provided all his employees who had been there a certain number of years with a year's lease on a brand-new BMW automobile.[7] The entrepreneur explained his actions by saying that he wanted to reward employees who stayed with him because he was spending around $1 million a year training new employees. It was actually cheaper for him to lease, insure, and license these automobiles to keep his current employees than it would have been for him to retrain new ones continually. What expectations, values, and acceptable behavior would these BMWs convey to new employees and to employees who hadn't yet been there the specified number of years?

Language. Many organizations and even units within organizations use a special language as a way to identify members of a culture. By learning this "language," members attest to their acceptance of the culture, and in so doing, help preserve it. Over time, organizations often develop unique terminology to describe equipment, key personnel, suppliers, customers, or products that are related to this business. This unique terminology can act as a common denominator that unites members of the organization. In turn, this special language makes people feel like they're part of something unique and that they need to preserve that uniqueness by "using" the language.

Role of Physical Surroundings. As we're looking at planning the entrepreneurial venture, we can't forget that the organization's physical work space plays a role in organizational culture. The way an organization arranges and decorates its physical surroundings should reinforce its culture. For instance, if collaboration among organizational members is an important and valued behavior, then the way the work space is arranged should support open and continual discussion. Or, if innovativeness is an important company value, the work space should encourage and allow people to experiment and to be innovative. Think back to our chapter-opening case and how SOL's physical surroundings—bright, colorful, open, high-tech—reinforced its core values. There's no doubt that the physical work space can play an important role in reinforcing and supporting the shared values, beliefs, and behavioral norms.

The Importance of Understanding Culture

Many people don't like to think about organizational culture because it's not an easy thing to see or describe or explain. Yet, when you walk into a business, you *do* get a feeling for its culture. You can just tell *something* about what the people there think is important. That's one reason why an entrepreneur needs to understand organizational culture—because culture defines what the business considers important and what it considers unimportant. Every organization has some kind of culture, basically because it includes human beings and humans have values, beliefs, and expectations. These values, beliefs, and expectations become the organizational culture, which, in turn, influences what people do and say, and how they do it because they know it's important or unimportant.

Building a Healthy Culture

A healthy organizational culture—one that nurtures, supports, encourages, and motivates organizational members—can be an important advantage for companies. If organizational members don't feel as strongly about the organization as the founders or the key decision makers do, then it's time to take action to get them to feel that way. In other words, it's time to give your organizational culture a checkup and to prescribe some healing medicine! How can you build a healthy culture? Even though every organizational situation is different, you can follow some general guidelines to achieve a healthy culture. These guidelines include the following:

1. *Change has to start at the top.* If the present organizational culture is sick—that is, it's not working—and cultural change is needed, the person at the top is the one who will have to champion this change.

2. *Think about your culture when hiring.* Job applicants need to be aware of the organization's values, beliefs, and expectations so they know what they're getting into. Cultural "fit" between employee and organization is critical.

3. *Two-way communication is important.* Sharing information is a way to discover problems and to resolve them. It's a way of acknowledging that "we're all in this together."

4. *If you don't believe in it, don't fake it.* If certain values and beliefs are important, make sure that your actions support your words. For instance, don't profess to believe in individual participation in decision making and then not ever give employees the opportunity to make decisions. Nothing can sicken an organizational culture faster than not backing up your words with actions.

Although nurturing your organizational culture may seem a waste of time and effort, keep in mind that a healthy culture can support a long and productive organizational life—just as a healthy body supports a long and productive personal life!

Sources: J. Case, "Corporate Culture," *Inc.*, November 1996, pp. 42–53; and M. Barrier, "Building a Healthy Company Culture," *Nation's Business*, September 1997, pp. 57–59.

Another reason why understanding culture is important is that culture can be a source of competitive advantage. Maybe an entrepreneurial venture can't compete on the basis of having the most complete product line with every style, color, and variation under the sun or by having numerous locations, but maybe it can have a culture that rewards employees for innovativeness or teamwork or whatever else the organization thinks is important. For example, Amy's Ice Creams, a chain of premium ice cream shops in Austin and Houston, has a unique culture that sets the stores apart and contributes significantly to their success.[8] Employees at Amy's Ice Creams are encouraged to entertain customers. They juggle with their serving spades, toss scoops of ice cream to one another behind the counter, and dance on the countertops. They often offer free ice cream to any customer who will sing, dance, recite a poem, or mimic a barnyard animal. They might be wearing pajamas (because it's sleepover night) or there might be colorful pulsating strobe lights throughout the store (because it's disco night). They wear costumes. They express their individuality. They create fun. It's a culture that employees embrace as enthusiastically as do the customers. Amy Miller, the entrepreneur behind Amy's Ice Creams, had to find a way to keep her ice cream shops from becoming just another commodity product amid a vast array of competitors. She believed that the way to do that was to sell an experience that the customer wouldn't forget. In order to do that, she had to create and nurture a culture that made employees *want* to provide those unforgettable customer experiences. As Amy Miller discovered, having the right culture can help an organization resolve critical competitive advantage issues.

The final reason it's important for entrepreneurs to understand organizational culture is that the culture serves as a powerful guide for decisions and actions. As we said earlier, the shared values and beliefs that are the organizational culture should be stated in the organizational vision and mission statements. Organizational members know from those statements what the organization believes and what it values. They know what's expected of them and what guidelines they should use as they make decisions and take actions. In this sense, the organizational culture shapes behavior and serves as a guide to what's acceptable and what's not.

Whereas planning for the vision and mission statements and the organizational culture may entail looking at factors (that is, values, beliefs, and so forth) that are hard to describe and understand, the final aspect of planning the entrepreneurial venture isn't quite as abstract, although it, too, may involve some uncertainties! It's the process of developing and writing the business plan.

Rapid Review ◀◀|

- ✓ List and describe each of the ways that organizational culture is learned by organizational members.
- ✓ What role do physical surroundings play in organizational culture?
- ✓ Why is it important for entrepreneurs to understand organizational culture?
- ✓ What does it take to build a healthy organizational culture?

DEVELOPING AND WRITING THE BUSINESS PLAN

For many would-be entrepreneurs, developing and writing a business plan is a daunting task. However, a good business plan is magical. It pulls together all the elements of the entrepreneur's vision into a single coherent statement. The business plan requires careful planning and creative thinking, but, if done well, can be a convincing document that serves many functions. In this section we're going to look at what's involved with developing and writing an effective—a magical—business plan.

Why Is a Business Plan Important?

Satchel Paige, the famous baseball pitcher, once said, "If you don't know where you're going, any road will take you there." As an entrepreneur, you *want* to know where you're going. You want to *choose* that road, not just take any one. The process of developing and writing a business plan will help identify and clarify many of the issues that need to be addressed as an entrepreneurial venture is organized, launched, and managed. Preparing the business plan is an important outcome of the planning process. Let's look at this important planning process.

The process of planning involves deciding where you want to go, how to get there, and what to do to reduce (as much as possible) any uncertainties. It's a way of thinking about the future where planning serves as a bridge between the present and the future—that is, between where we are currently and where we would like to be. To make this concept clearer, think of the college degree you would like to obtain someday. You've had to plan your courses semester by semester so that you complete the required ones in the correct sequence for getting that desired degree. Perhaps you've followed a degree program—a type of planning document—that outlines where you are currently and where you would like to be. That "plan" serves as the bridge between the present and the future until one day that goal of graduating with a college degree is attained. For an entrepreneurial venture, one document that results from the planning process is a **business plan**, which is a written document that summarizes a business opportunity and defines and articulates how the identified opportunity is to be seized and exploited. The process of developing and writing a business plan involves critically analyzing where your venture currently is and where it's headed. That business plan, then, becomes a blueprint and road map for operating the business. It serves as a "living" document that guides organizational decisions and actions throughout the life of the business and isn't used just once as a start-up tool.

As you might be able to conclude so far, the business plan is an important document for entrepreneurs. It serves the five main purposes shown in Table 4-2. We're going to discuss each of these purposes separately.

The first purpose of a business plan is that it's a development tool for the organizational founders. As the organizational founders identify and assess opportunities, the structured outline of a business plan forces them to address important issues. Rather than just blindly and wildly pursuing ideas, the business plan provides a check and balance for the founders. This type of structured start-up planning by entrepreneurs has been widely studied by researchers, who, for the most part, agree that this type of planning can be beneficial.[9]

The business plan's second purpose is that it is useful for helping clarify the venture's vision and mission. As we discussed earlier in this chapter, organizational vision and mission statements are an important element in planning the entrepreneurial venture. As portions of the business plan, these statements describe and explain to others what this entrepreneurial venture is about. Again, the founders are "forced" into carefully considering their organizational purpose, values, and expectations.

The third purpose that the business plan serves is that it defines planning and evaluation guidelines for managing the ongoing entrepreneurial venture. As we stated earlier, the business plan is a living document that should be used beyond the start-up phase. It should guide decision makers on planning and evaluating issues throughout the life of the business. It also should help clarify what the goals and plans are (planning) and should help define how goal attainment is going to

---

TABLE 4-2 **Purposes of a Business Plan**	
■ Development tool for organizational founders	■ Tool for securing financial resources
■ Vision and mission clarification	■ Tool for guiding growth
■ Planning and evaluation guidelines	

be measured (evaluating). However, we need to be aware of the fact that although a business plan attempts to define a desirable future path for the venture, unexpected factors can—and often do—significantly alter that path. But even given the fact that uncertainties exist, *not* having some type of plan would make coping with and managing the uncertainties even more challenging for an entrepreneur.

Helping an entrepreneur to secure needed financial resources is the next purpose that business plans serve. Potential lenders and investors absolutely will require some type of financial analysis and projections before making a decision on whether or not to provide a loan or to invest capital in the entrepreneurial venture. These people are not going to provide money without some analysis of current and future financial data. Again, the structured nature of a business plan forces an entrepreneur to perform these important calculations and projections. This is often the hardest part for an entrepreneur in preparing a business plan, but it is a critical component to include because any potential outside financing will depend on it.

The final purpose of the business plan is that it's an effective tool for guiding growth. We know already that what characterizes an entrepreneurial venture is its focus on growth. Although some entrepreneurs may get lucky and growth just sort of "happens" to their organizations, you don't want to bank your future on luck. A well-written business plan can lay the foundation for growth to happen. As we've said before, the business plan provides the road map for pursuing the opportunities that await. A successful entrepreneur doesn't want to "take just any road," but needs to plan for the future and the future growth of the venture through developing a strong business plan.

Entrepreneurs in Action

Mark Gentile had a good idea for a business. He had money to start the business. He also had good partners. But, he swears that one other thing was essential to his successful start-up: a written business plan. Mark's company, Odyssey Software, sells "middleware"—software that links mainframe computers and computer peripherals of different brands. Working as a programmer of custom software, Mark saw an opportunity for a product that could work with many different types of equipment. Odyssey Software was born. But, he knew that in order to compete in the turbulent software market, a solid business plan was needed. So Mark invested the time and effort to complete one. His business plan not only helped him clarify his goals but also helped him find financing. As Mark understood, a good idea was only the beginning! The business plan helped shape that good idea and continues to be an effective road map for the business.

Source: "Company Finds Plan Central to Success," *Springfield News-Leader*, December 7, 1997, p. 12B.

Now that we've looked at the important purposes that business plans serve, what's included in a business plan? That's what we need to look at next.

What Should the Business Plan Include?

A thorough, complete, and *effective* business plan is usually of considerable length. Yes, it takes time and effort to complete, but as we've just seen, the business plan serves many important purposes for the entrepreneur. It's a critical tool in successfully launching and managing the entrepreneurial venture. Practically all those who have written about entrepreneurs and entrepreneurial issues have their own ideas about what should be included in a business plan.[10] We think a good business plan needs to include six major areas. These are executive summary, analysis of the opportunity, analysis of the context, description of the business, financial data and projections, and supporting documentation. Each of these sections will be explained next. (A suggested outline for a business plan is provided in the Killer Apps Appendix at the end of the book.)

Executive Summary. Some experts recommend that the executive summary go at the beginning of the business plan so that readers will know what key points are being made in the document whereas others recommend that it go at the end of the business plan in order to summarize what's been presented. Both of these arguments make sense, so you need to decide which you feel more comfortable doing. The key thing is that the report includes an executive summary. What information should be included in the executive summary? It should summarize the key points that the entrepreneur wants to make about the entrepreneurial venture. These might include brief statements of vision and mission; primary goals and objectives; history of entrepreneurial venture including, perhaps, a time line; key people involved in the venture; nature of the business; concise product or service descriptions; explanation of market niche, competitors, and competitive advantage; proposed strategies; and financial information. Some have suggested that obvious concerns and challenges be presented in the executive summary as well. The important thing to remember about the executive summary is that it should be concise and comprehensive. The reader should be able to obtain all the significant information highlights about the entrepreneurial venture from this section. The rest of the business plan, then, fleshes out this information.

Analysis of Opportunity. Remember our discussion in Chapter 3 of how important the identification and analysis of opportunities are to entrepreneurial ventures. In this section of the business plan, you want to present the details of your analysis of the perceived opportunity. Essentially, this means (1) sizing up the market by describing the demographics of the target market—who the customers are, how many of them there are, what values and expectations they have, how the product or service will meet their needs, and so forth; (2) describing and evaluating industry trends—what the current status of the industry is, what the trends in the industry are, evaluation of the industry growth rate (is it a growing, stable, or declining industry), what it takes to be successful in this industry, and so forth; and (3) identifying and evaluating competitors—who they are, what competitive strengths and weaknesses they have, what they are doing currently, and so forth. If, in the process of researching the venture's feasibility, a feasibility study were completed—as in Chapter 3, we recommended be done—the information included in it can be the basis for the material in this section of the business plan. You must show that you have thoroughly researched this market and that you know as much as possible about the advantages and drawbacks of this proposed opportunity.

Analysis of the Context. Whereas the opportunity analysis focuses on the opportunity in a specific industry and market, the context analysis takes a much broader perspective. Entrepreneurial opportunities exist in a context, and in this section of the business plan, you need to address this context. What should be included here? You should describe broad external changes and trends. These external factors would include an analysis of the macroeconomic environment such as the state of the economy, current and forecasted inflation, current and forecasted interest rates, and any other important economic trends that might significantly impact the entrepreneurial venture; an evaluation of any current or proposed governmental rules and regulations that might potentially impact the entrepreneurial venture; an analysis of any broad technological trends not related to the specific market or industry that might affect the entrepreneurial venture; and, if appropriate, a description of global changes and trends that potentially might have an impact on the entrepreneurial venture.

Description of the Business. In the previous sections of the business plan, you've described the "what's"—what you see as the potential opportunity you hope to capture and exploit. You've described and evaluated the significant trends and changes that might affect the entrepreneurial venture. Now, you're ready to explain the "how's"—the specifics of how you will capture and exploit this opportunity. Specifically, what this section describes is how you're going to organize, launch, and manage the entrepreneurial venture. This section provides a thorough explanation of the following: vision and mission statements and a description of the desired organizational culture; marketing plans including overall marketing strategy, pricing, sales tactics, service–warranty policies, and advertising and promotion tactics; product development plans such as an explanation of development status (prototype availability) and tasks, difficulties and risks, and anticipated costs; manufacturing and operations plans such as a description of proposed geographic location, facilities and improvements, equipment, and work flow; human resource plans including a description of key management persons, composition of board of directors including their background experience and skills, current and future staffing needs, compensation and benefits, and training needs; and an overall schedule and timetable of events.

Financial Data and Projections. Every effective business plan contains financial data and projections. Although these financial calculations and interpretations may be difficult to do, they are absolutely critical. No business plan is complete without financial information. What, then, should be included in this section? Financial plans should cover at least three years and contain projected income (profit and loss) statements, pro forma cash flow analysis (monthly for the first year and quarterly for the next two), pro forma balance sheets, breakeven analysis, and cost controls. If you anticipate equipment purchases or other major capital expenditures, list the items, costs, and what collateral you have available. In your financial projections and analyses, provide notes of explanation whenever the data seem contradictory or questionable. Try to make your financial projections as realistic as possible. Research materials costs, product prices being charged by competitors, and any other quantitative information that will add to the validity and reliability of your data. Although much of the financial analysis is based on assumptions, if you back up your assumptions with logical reasoning and appropriate analysis, you can minimize the inherent problems of making assumptions.

Supporting Documentation. You may have had professors say to you, "Support what you say . . . support, support, support." I know I've said this to my students numerous times. Supporting documentation *is* an important component of an effective business plan. Back up your descriptions with charts, graphs, tables, photographs, or other visual tools. In addition, you'll want to provide information (personal and work related) about the key participants in the entre-

Calculating Breakeven Point

One of the most important calculations that you'll need to do for your business plan is breakeven point. **Breakeven point** identifies the level of sales at which total revenue is just sufficient to cover total costs and represents that point above which the business begins to make a profit. This is one of the most basic and simple business concepts, yet is one that many would-be entrepreneurs fail to examine. How do you calculate it?

To compute breakeven point (*BE*), you need to know the unit price of the product being sold (*P*), the variable cost per unit (*VC*), and total fixed costs (*TFC*). Variable costs change in proportion to output and typically include raw materials, labor costs, and energy costs. Fixed costs are expenses that do not change as output volume changes. It doesn't matter whether you produce 0 or 100 units, these costs must be covered. Examples are such costs as insurance premiums, rent, and property taxes. Once you know these figures, breakeven point can be calculated as follows:

$$BE = \frac{TFC}{P - VC}$$

This formula tells us that (1) total revenue will equal total cost when we sell enough units at a price that covers all variable unit costs and (2) the difference between price and variable costs, when multiplied by the number of units sold, equals the fixed costs.

Let's work through an example. Assume that Charlie's Photocopying Service charges $0.10 per photocopy. If fixed costs are $27,000 per year and variable costs are $0.04 per copy, Charlie can compute his breakeven point as follows: $27,000/($0.10 − $0.04) = 450,000 copies, or when annual revenues are $45,000 (450,000 × $0.10).

Breakeven analysis can help an entrepreneur determine that level of sales needed to reach the desired profit. It can also help tell how much volume has to increase to break even if the business is currently operating at a loss and how much volume can be lost and still break even if the business is currently operating profitably. As you can see, breakeven point can be an important piece of information to know.

preneurial venture. Through these supporting documents, you can provide additional details about the information being presented in the actual business plan.

Writing the Business Plan

Explaining your business on paper can be an intimidating challenge! Moving from the unabashed exuberance and excitement over the potential of "this great idea" to the harsh reality of describing it in concrete, specific, and explicit terms can prove to be exhausting physically and mentally. However, certain software templates, books, and Web sites (check out **www.moneyhunter.com** as one example) can help entrepreneurs write business plans. Keep in mind, however, that when you're using these tools, you're following a standardized format that might not adequately describe your unique situation. Be sure that you tailor and amend the business plan template appropriately to fit what you're doing.

Just as the idea for an entrepreneurial venture takes time to germinate, so does the writing of a good business plan. It's important to put serious thought and consideration into the plan and to develop one that has all the necessary elements. Because this process can take several days, be prepared to spend whatever time and effort is needed. You don't need to be a professional writer to come up with a solid business plan, but you do need to be able to write clearly and concisely. The resulting document should be something that will serve as a road map for current decisions and, if revised and updated, for future decisions as well.

Rapid Review ◀◀|

- ✓ What is a business plan?
- ✓ Why is a business plan important?
- ✓ What five purposes does the business plan serve?
- ✓ List and describe the six major areas that should be included in a business plan.
- ✓ What is breakeven point? How is it calculated?
- ✓ What are some important things to remember about the actual writing of the business plan?

FYI

Writing a Successful Business Plan

We now know that a business plan is a critically important document. How can you create a business plan that's going to win a Pulitzer prize? Okay, so they don't give Pulitzers for business plans. How can you write a business plan that's going to "wow" whoever reads it and that's going to serve as an effective road map for the long-term success of your entrepreneurial venture? What makes for a successful business plan? (See outline in Killer Apps Appendix at end of book.) Here are 10 characteristics:

- Clear, realistic financial projections
- Detailed market research
- Detailed competitor research
- Descriptions of key decision makers
- Thorough summary
- Proof of vision
- Good formatting and clear writing
- Brief and concise
- Writing that demonstrates an understanding of the importance of the bottom line
- A plan that captures "you"

Source: L. Elkins, "Tips for Preparing a Business Plan," *Nation's Business*, June 1996, pp. 60R–61R.

CHAPTER SUMMARY

There are three important issues to address when planning the entrepreneurial venture. These include developing vision and mission statements, thinking about the type of desired organizational culture, and developing and writing the business plan.

An organizational vision is a broad comprehensive picture of what an entrepreneur wants an organization to become. It provides an overall picture of where the entire organization would like to be in the future. A mission is a statement of what the various organizational units do and what they hope to accomplish in alignment with the organizational vision. An organization will have only one vision, but potentially several missions that contribute to the pursuit of the vision. These statements are important for the following reasons: (1) They provide a broad framework that allows entrepreneurs to know what they're doing and why. (2) They offer direction and guidance for making decisions and taking actions. (3) The desired values become a basis for the organizational culture. (4) They serve as a focal point for the entrepreneur and any other organizational members to identify and clarify the organization's purpose and direction. (5) These statements may contribute to higher performance levels. The organizational vision should include four components: core values and beliefs, organizational purpose, brief summary of what the organization does, and broad goals. The mission statement(s) should describe nine components: customers; products or services; markets; technology; concern for survival, profitability, and growth; philosophy; self-concept; concern for public image; and concern for employees.

Organizational culture is the beliefs, values, and behavioral norms shared and practiced by organizational members. These shared values and beliefs determine, to a large degree, what organizational members think is important and the way they do their work. An organization's culture can be described using seven different dimensions: innovation and risk-taking, attention to detail, outcome orientation, people orientation, team orientation, aggressiveness, and stability. An organization's culture usually reflects the beliefs, values, and vision of the founder(s). This person (or persons) actually establishes the early culture of the organization by projecting an image of what the organization should be. The culture of an organization is transmitted to organizational members in a number of ways. The most important ways include stories, rituals, material symbols, and language. The organization's physical surroundings also reinforce and support the organizational culture.

Developing and writing a business plan is a daunting task. However, a good business plan is essential. A business plan is a written document that summarizes a business opportunity and defines and articulates how the identified opportunity is to be seized and exploited. The business plan serves five purposes: (1) It's a development tool for the organizational founders. (2) It is useful for helping clarify the venture's vision and mission. (3) It defines planning and evaluation guidelines for managing the ongoing entrepreneurial venture. (4) It can help an entrepreneur secure financial resources. (5) It's an effective tool for guiding growth. The business plan should include six major areas: executive summary, analysis of the opportunity, analysis of the context, description of the business, financial data and projections, and supporting documentation.

KEY TERMS

▸ *Vision:* A broad comprehensive picture of what an entrepreneur wants an organization to become.

▸ *Mission:* A statement of what the various organizational units do and what they hope to accomplish in alignment with the organizational vision.

▸ *Goals:* Outcomes or end results that are desired by individuals, groups, or entire organizations.

▸ *Values-based management:* An approach to managing an entrepreneurial venture that entails establishing, promoting, and practicing shared values.

▸ *Organizational culture:* The beliefs, values, and behavioral norms shared and practiced by organizational members.

▸ *Business plan:* A written document that summarizes a business opportunity and defines and articulates how the identified opportunity is to be seized and exploited.

▸ *Breakeven point:* The level of sales at which total revenue is just sufficient to cover costs and represents that point above which the business begins to make a profit.

SWEAT EQUITY

1. Do you agree or disagree with the following statements? Discuss.

   • "A good business plan won't make you succeed."
   • "A business plan has the ability to prevent you from wasting your time on something that can't succeed."
   • "You should write a business plan even if you don't need outside financing."

2. Do an Internet–World Wide Web search of five different company sites (large or small). Look for the following information and then write a report describing what you found. Be sure to provide the Web site addresses for each of the companies you research.

   • What can you tell about this company's culture from its Web site? What clues did you observe?
   • Were there any descriptions of stories, rituals, material symbols, language, or physical surroundings included on the Web site? If so, describe. If not, create and describe an appropriate ritual and material symbols that this company might use.
   • Was a vision or mission statement included on the Web site? If so, what is it? If not, what do you think this company's vision or mission statement might say?

3. Get into small teams (three or four per team). Select one of the two start-up companies described below. Then complete the required tasks at the end of the descriptions.

   Company A
   Yes, pet owners tend to be a pretty sentimental bunch, and yes, they tend to buy lots of stuff for their beloved pets. (Every year people spend $9 billion worldwide to feed their pets compared with $6 billion for baby food.) However, there's little competition for gourmet pet snacks—custom-blended snacks made

of all-natural ingredients. Three Dog Bakery of Kansas City, Missouri, is out to change the face of pet snacks by offering gourmet doggy biscuits made up of a delicious blend of garlic, spinach, and carrots (**www.threedog.com**).

Company B
The leafy flowering perennials called hostas are a blooming success for Eagle Bay Hosta Gardens in Sheridan, New York. The three-acre sanctuary of bridges, ponds, arbors, and a faded red barn contains 800 hosta varieties and 15,000 plants. Customers can see how the plants they're buying will eventually look. In addition, hosta research is done at Eagle Bay. New hosta varieties are monitored for flower color, form, height, uniqueness of the leaf pattern, and resistance to slugs (**www.vinetime.com/eaglebaygardens/**).

To Do
Write an organizational vision statement and a mission statement for your chosen start-up. Write an executive summary for the company you chose. Write an abbreviated business plan outline. Your team must be prepared to present its information to the rest of the class. Make sure you cover all the necessary areas because others will be trying to find "holes" in your business plan material.

4. Do an Internet–World Wide Web search using any search engine for the phrase *business plan*. Link to 10 entries from your search and write an analysis of what each site has to offer. Be thorough, descriptive, and critical. Be sure to identify the Web site address in your analysis.

    Now, do the same thing for the phrase *organizational culture*. Write an analysis of 10 entries from this search.

5. Organizations have their own unique personalities—that is, their cultures. Visit seven different organizations (you might even want to try one or two not-for-profit ones) and observe the physical surroundings. Make note of work arrangements, what's on the walls, how you're greeted or treated, interactions between employees, and any other cultural clues that you might observe about this organization. Write up a description of what you observed at each business. Now, compare this information to the seven dimensions of organizational culture we discussed in the chapter. What type of organizational culture would you say each organization exhibits?

ENTREPRENEURSHIP IN ACTION CASES

CASE #1: Cleaning Up at SOL

Entrepreneurship in Action case #1 can be found at the beginning of Chapter 4.

Discussion Questions

1. Using Figure 4-3, describe SOL's organizational culture.

2. Would the five values that characterize SOL's culture be as effective in other types of organizations? Why or why not?

3. Describe how you think new employees at SOL might learn the culture.

CASE #2: Serious Business

At Empower Trainers and Consultants, associates (there are no "employees") take organizational culture very seriously. Michael and Caroline May have built a successful company where people dress up as "sparkle" fairies, candy is tossed around at meetings, Foosball competitions are held in hallways, and mistakes are publicized, not ridiculed or criticized. Culture is an important component of Empower's way of doing business.

Empower provides computer training, applications development, and Internet instruction to clients around Overland Park, a suburb of Kansas City, where it is based. When May started his company, he brought with him thoughts and ideas from previous jobs and from reading about and interacting with other successful entrepreneurs. He knew what he wanted his company to be like. The company's 21-word mission statement—To become number one or number three in all markets we serve and to make this company fun, fast, and fulfilling—can be recited by everyone at Empower. Now, you may be asking yourself, why number one or number three? May explains that you should never settle for second best and being number three gives you something to shoot for (ideas he borrowed from Jack Welch, CEO of global powerhouse General Electric).

There are numerous other unusual cultural characteristics of Empower. For example, there's Sparkle. Sparkle captures in one word the sort of personality an Empower associate is always expected to project. Sparkle the Fairy (a character dreamed up by Susan Burden, the first employee hired by Michael and Caroline) will appear and shower associates with glitter and recite a poem: "This Sparkle Power I give you today/Will empower you in a special way/We hope you will always keep this in mind/To make Empower one of a kind." Every other Tuesday at the company's regular company-wide team meeting, everyone recites the poem and new associates get sparkled by a team of Sparkle Fairies. Or, take, for instance, what happens if someone uses the word *employee, boss,* or *manager.* The offender must pay $5 a word into a big yellow crayon bank. The money collected (averaging about $75 a year) goes to charity. Issues that affect everyone are put to a majority-rule vote. Written policies are few and far between. One important written policy, however, is the Cookie and Bagel–Doughnut Policy (68 words long—more than three times as long as the mission statement), which prohibits raids on the refreshments served to client students who are at the company's offices taking computer training. Then, there's the shared belief that to be successful, first and foremost, business should be fun. Finally, there's the attitude toward making mistakes. May says, "If you're not making seven mistakes a day, you're just not trying hard enough." Associates at Empower are encouraged to post "Today's List of Mistakes" on a piece of paper that has, of course, seven lines. The feeling is that mistakes that are hidden can become real land mines ready to explode at any time.

Although Empower's culture may sound curiously strange (to be polite), it works for the company! The company's distinctive and effective culture has enabled it to build the kind of workplace that attracts and keeps scarce and top-of-the-line technical talent.

Discussion Questions

1. Evaluate Empower's mission statement. How would you interpret it? Does it include what it should? According to our definitions, would this be a mission or a vision statement? Explain.

2. Describe and evaluate the examples of organizational rituals, language, and shared values. Would these work in other types and sizes of organizations? Explain.

3. Some busy entrepreneurs know that culture is important but feel that they don't have the time to create a distinctive culture. They outsource (hire outside consultants) to come in and do it. What would be the benefits and drawbacks of this approach?

(*Source:* N. K. Austin, "The Cultural Evolution," *Inc. 500,* 1997, pp. 72–80.)

CASE #3: Breaking Even

Calculating breakeven point is an important task for entrepreneurs. For each of the examples given, calculate breakeven point in dollars *and* in units. Show your calculations.

Company A
Smith and Smith Inc. manufactures scented potpourri. Annual fixed costs are $10,000. Direct labor is $1.50 per unit and direct material is $.75 per unit. The selling price is $4.00 per bag.

Company B
Deborah Biggs makes wooden canoe paddles. Her annual fixed costs are $8,000. Direct costs are $8.00. The selling price of the paddles is $12.50 per paddle.

Company C
Symetrix manufactures customized wooden puzzles. The puzzles are priced at $15 per unit. Total fixed costs are $1,000. Variable costs are $10 per puzzle.

VIDEO CASE #1: Casting a Long Shadow

SMALL BUSINESS 2000

"All companies are shadows of their leader." This statement was made by Tom Velez of CTA, who has proven to have a huge shadow indeed. He has provided the strong leadership that guided his company as it grew from nothing to $150 million in sales revenues. What can Velez teach us?

The Velez family emigrated from Ecuador to the United States, and both of Tom's parents were uneducated. However, his father deeply believed in the power of education and also felt strongly about music. With these

family values, it's not surprising that Velez attended the Juilliard School of Music. However, he soon realized that, although he was a good violinist, he would never be great. He began to look at other possibilities. At the time, there weren't many opportunities for Hispanics, but Velez knew that mathematics was easy for him. This self-knowledge guided his job search. He eventually ended up in a job at the National Aeronautics and Space Administration (NASA) and went on to get his Ph.D. in mathematics at Georgetown

University. Mathematics was a core skill that NASA needed in writing computer programs and understanding the physical phenomena coming from the data being gathered from space exploration. Velez's skills seemed tailor made. In addition to his study of mathematics, Velez had studied philosophy. One of the philosophical ideas he took to heart was the idea of creative genius—that is, a person who makes things happen. Because of NASA's mission and reputation, he expected to find many creative geniuses there. Instead, he found that it was only a few people who made the biggest difference. From NASA, Velez went on to work at Martin Marietta, a large defense contractor.

Velez soon left Martin Marietta to form CTA with a partner. What does CTA do? It provides information systems and resource management capabilities to the U.S. government. How has Velez encouraged in his organization the type of creative genius he considers so important to success? His approach has been based on the belief that people aren't always attracted to paychecks. Instead, they're attracted to challenge, to opportunities, and to organizational culture. He advises

finding a way to build a team incrementally and to be a leader. As a leader, admit you're not the best. Admit you need the team's help and then reward those creative geniuses. How? Give them ownership in the business; give them freedom. And, he says, remember that creating the culture you want your business to have is a day-by-day, month-by-month, year-by-year process.

Discussion Questions

1. What role do you think Velez's pursuit of creative genius plays in the type of organization he has created? Explain.
2. Do you agree with Velez's philosophy that people aren't always attracted to paychecks? Discuss. What implications might this have for other entrepreneurs?
3. What factors do you think shaped Velez's approach to leading CTA? Explain.
4. Evaluate the statement, "All companies are shadows of their leader." What do you think it means? What are the implications for entrepreneurs?

(*Source:* Based on *Small Business 2000, Show 107.*)

VIDEO CASE #2: Not Just Toying Around

The toy industry, like all others, has its good points and its bad points. One person who's trying to take advantage of the good points—what he sees as the many growth opportunities in the toy industry—is an individual by the name of Charlie Woo, of Los Angeles.

Woo and his family came to the United States from Hong Kong in the late 1970s. To support the family, his mother and father initially opened a restaurant but found that venture to be too time consuming. They looked to

start another business and decided that the toy business looked like a good one. By using their contacts in Hong Kong and by bringing their four sons into the business, the Woo family opened ABC Toys. The company's initial goal was to manufacture and distribute toys to small wholesalers who couldn't get products from the large toy makers because they didn't buy enough volume. ABC Toys had identified a specific niche and hadn't intended to compete with Mattel, Hasbro, or other major toy manufacturers. Charlie, who was just about to complete his Ph.D. in Physics, found himself making a major career switch—from physics to toys.

ABC Toys purchased several dilapidated warehouses on a blighted corner of downtown Los Angeles. Charlie's vision was to encourage other small toy manufacturers and distributors to rent these buildings and by all working together, to create a "Toy Town." In the beginning, ABC Toys was located there by itself. But Charlie reasoned that this wholesale district would enable customers to come to one location, shop comparatively, and he hoped, end up buying more products than they would if they had to travel to separate stores. As more and more small toy companies joined ABC Toys in Toy Town, word soon spread and customers began coming from all over. Now, there are more than 400 wholesale toy dealers within a few blocks of each other in Toy Town. These companies together employ around 4,000 people and sell more than $1 billion of toys, half of that outside the United States. There are two large operations (each employing almost 500 people), but most of the businesses in Toy Town are one-warehouse operations run by ethnic Chinese, Mexicans, and Koreans.

In 1989, Charlie and one of his brothers spun off a separate business called Megatoys. This company now employs around 30 people and has hit $15 million in sales. And

Charlie isn't finished yet! Part of his plan for Toy Town and Megatoys involves expanding the number of customers they serve. Why? He believes that there is still good potential for growth in his business since the changing global trade environment is opening up many potentially profitable areas. After all, in this business, you can't just toy around!

Discussion Questions

1. What role does a founder play in the vision for an entrepreneurial venture? Assess Charlie Woo's role in ABC Toys and Toy Town.

2. Charlie wants to continue Megatoys' growth. Would a business plan be necessary? Explain. What would a business plan for his business need to include?

3. We know that growth is a distinguishing characteristic of entrepreneurial ventures. What challenges does an entrepreneur face in maintaining an organization's culture as it grows? How can an entrepreneur meet these challenges?

4. Charlie has asked you to make a presentation to his employees about the importance of organizational vision and mission. Draw up a list of the main ideas you'd want to tell them.

5. Write a vision statement for Toy Town and for Megatoys.

(*Sources:* Based on *Small Business 2000, Show 107* and J. Micklethwait and A. Wooldridge, "Toy Story," *Fortune*, June 26, 2000, pp. 258–72.

ENDNOTES

1. G. Imperato, "Dirty Business, Bright Ideas," *Fast Company Web Page*, **www.fastcompany.com**, April 16, 1997.
2. F. David, *Strategic Management* (Upper Saddle River, NJ: Prentice Hall, 1999), p. 79.
3. J. Pearce II and F. David, "Corporate Mission Statements: The Bottom Line," *Academy of Management Executive*, May 1987, p. 110.
4. D. I. Silvers, "Vision—Not Just for CEOs," *Management Quarterly*, winter 1994–1995, pp. 10–14.

5. This section is based on information in David, *Strategic Management*, pp. 89–90.

6. C. A. O'Reilly III, J. Chatman, and D. F. Caldwell, "People and Organizational Culture: A Profile Comparison Approach to Assessing Person–Organizational Fit," *Academy of Management Journal*, September 1991, pp. 487–516; and J. A. Chatman and K. A. Jehn, "Assessing the Relationship Between Industry Characteristics and Organizational Culture: How Different Can You Be?" *Academy of Management Journal*, June 1994, pp. 522–53.

7. T. Brokaw, *NBC Evening News*, June 18, 1999.

8. J. Case, "Corporate Culture," *Inc.*, November 1996, pp. 42–53.

9. G. J. Castrogiovanni, "Pre-Startup Planning and the Survival of New Small Businesses: Theoretical Linkages," *Journal of Management*, Vol. 22, No. 6, 1996, pp. 801–22.

10. Here's a short list of resources on writing business plans: C. M. Brown, "The Do's and Don'ts of Writing a Winning Business Plan," *Black Enterprise*, April 1996, pp. 114–22; L. Elkins, "Tips for Preparing a Business Plan," *Nation's Business*, June 1996, pp. 60R–61R; S. Hodges, "How to Write a Business Plan," *Nation's Business*, August 1997, p. 36; and W. A. Sahlman, "How to Write a Great Business Plan," *Harvard Business Review*, July–August 1997, pp. 98–108.

5

ORGANIZING THE VENTURE

LEARNING OBJECTIVES

After reading this chapter, you should be able to:

1. List the three major ways to organize a business legally.
2. Explain the benefits and drawbacks of each of the six forms of business organization.
3. Describe the other legal issues that entrepreneurs face.
4. Explain the importance of choosing an appropriate organizational structure.
5. Describe the different decisions in organizational design.
6. Discuss the advantages and disadvantages of each of the types of organization structure.

ENTREPRENEURSHIP IN ACTION CASE #1

The Idea Factory

Bill Gross has always been motivated by the challenge of something new.[1] He has been starting companies since 1975, when he was just 16 years old. To help pay his way through Cal Tech, Gross built and sold plans for a solar heating device, started a successful stereo equipment company, and then sold a major software upgrade to Lotus. In 1991, he started Knowledge Adventure, a company that designed and created educational software. He sold the company in early 1997 to CUC International for a cool $100 million. Gross's newest business venture is a factory unlike any you've ever seen. It's an *idea* factory!

The mission of Gross's idealab! (**www.idealab.com**) is to develop individual ideas into highly focused and successful Internet businesses. Gross and his key decision makers believe that to succeed in the dynamic Internet market, companies must have the ability to execute their ideas rapidly. idealab! provides this by allowing these start-ups to tap into the services, support, and knowledge of individuals and organizations that have extensive experience in starting

Bill Gross's idealab! is a successful experiment in providing a nurturing climate for entrepreneurial start-ups. It's also an example of the different types of unique organizational designs that an entrepreneurial venture can take. Once the organizational vision and mission statements have been written, the organizational culture issues addressed, and the business plan written, it's time to put the plan into action. One of the first steps in executing the plan is deciding the best way to organize the venture. Organizing the venture involves determining the legal form of business organization, addressing other legal issues, and then choosing the most appropriate organizational design. We're going to discuss these topics in this chapter.

LEGAL FORMS OF BUSINESS ORGANIZATION

The first organizing decision that an entrepreneur must make is a critical one. It's the form of legal ownership for the venture. The two primary factors that affect this decision are taxes and legal liability. As an entrepreneur, you want to minimize the impact of both of these factors on your entrepreneurial venture. So, it's important to know, examine, and evaluate the advantages and drawbacks of each of the legal forms of business organization. You want to make an educated decision—a decision in which you choose a form of legal organization that's going to help you fulfill your goals for the entrepreneurial venture. The right choice can protect you from legal liability as well as save tax dollars, in both the short run and the long run.

What alternatives are available? There are three basic ways to organize your entrepreneurial venture: sole proprietorship, partnership, and corporation. However, when you include the variations of these basic organizational alternatives, you end up with six possible choices, each with its own tax consequences, liability issues, and pros and cons. These six choices are sole proprietorship, general partnership, limited liability partnership, C corporation, S corporation, and limited liability company. Let's look carefully at each one. Table 5-1 summarizes the basic information about each organizational alternative.

Sole Proprietorship

A **sole proprietorship** is a form of organization in which the owner maintains sole and complete control over the business and is personally liable for business debts. There are no legal requirements for establishing a sole proprietorship other than obtaining necessary local

Internet companies. idealab! combines the best elements of a small, nimble company with the financial strength and wisdom of a much larger organization and shares these benefits with its portfolio companies. How does idealab! work?

Many of idealab!'s talented employees are entrepreneurial computer whizzes and other creative types from nearby Cal Tech, the Art Center College of Design, and Hollywood. Gross has a pool of about 25 programmers and Web site graphic designers who are on call for assisting the start-up companies. The members of this talent pool can be quickly assembled into what Gross calls "Internet start-ups in a box." This arrangement enables Gross to move very quickly from idea to execution—a capability that's critical in the fast-changing world of the Internet and Web. It's an unusual organizational arrangement, but one that seems to work well!

TABLE 5-1   Legal Forms of Business Organization

Structure	Ownership Requirements	Tax Treatment	Liability	Advantages	Drawbacks
Sole proprietorship	One owner	Income and losses "pass through" to owner and are taxed at personal rate	Unlimited personal liability	■ Low start-up costs ■ Freedom from most regulations ■ Owner has direct control ■ All profits go to owner ■ Easy to go out of business if necessary	■ Unlimited personal liability ■ Personal finances at risk ■ Miss out on all kinds of business tax deductions ■ Total responsibility ■ May be more difficult to raise financing
General partnership	Two or more owners	Income and losses "pass through" to partners and are taxed at personal rate; flexibility in profit–loss allocations to partners	Unlimited personal liability Personal assets of partners are at risk	■ Ease of formation ■ Pooled talent ■ Pooled resources ■ Somewhat easier access to financing ■ Some tax benefits	■ Unlimited personal liability ■ Divided authority and decisions ■ Potential for conflict ■ Continuity of transfer of ownership
Limited liability partnership (LLP)	Two or more owners	Income and losses "pass through" to partners and are taxed at personal rate; flexibility in profit–loss allocations to partners	Limited, although one partner must retain unlimited liability	■ Good way to acquire capital from limited partners	■ Cost and complexity of forming can be high ■ Limited partners cannot participate in management of business without losing liability protection
C corporation	Unlimited number of shareholders; no limits on types of stock or voting arrangements	Dividend income is taxed at corporate and personal shareholder levels; losses and deductions are corporate	Limited	■ Limited liability ■ Transferable ownership ■ Continuous existence ■ Easier access to resources	■ Expensive to set up ■ Closely regulated ■ Double taxation ■ Extensive record keeping ■ Charter restrictions
S corporation	Up to 75 shareholders; no limits on types of stock or voting arrangements	Income and losses "pass through" to partners and are taxed at personal rate; flexibility in profit–loss allocations to partners	Limited	■ Easy to set up ■ Enjoy limited liability protection and tax benefits of partnership ■ Can have a tax-exempt entity as a shareholder	■ Must meet certain requirements ■ May limit future financing options

TABLE 5-1	Legal Forms of Business Organization (Cont.)				
Structure	**Ownership Requirements**	**Tax Treatment**	**Liability**	**Advantages**	**Drawbacks**
Limited liability company (LLC)	Unlimited number of "members"; flexible membership arrangements for voting rights and income	Income and losses "pass through" to partners and are taxed at personal rate; flexibility in profit–loss allocations to partners	Limited	■ Greater flexibility ■ Not constrained by regulations on C and S corporations ■ Taxed as partnership, not as corporation	■ Cost of switching from one form to this can be high ■ Need legal and financial advice in forming operating agreement

business licenses and permits. In a sole proprietorship, income and losses "pass through" to the owner and are taxed at the owner's personal income tax rate. However, the liability issue is the major concern of sole proprietorships. The sole proprietor has unlimited personal liability for any and all debts of the business.

The advantages of the sole proprietorship revolve around the ease of formation and the freedom to run your business as you please. There are low start-up costs associated with a sole proprietorship. As the owner–proprietor, you have direct control of what you do, when you do it, and how you do it (within legal and regulatory guidelines, of course). Another advantage of the sole proprietorship is the fact that all profits and losses go directly to the owner. A final advantage of this form of business organization is that it is easy to shut down if that becomes necessary. There are no buyout agreements of other owners or shareholders to worry about. If you choose to go out of business, you just do it.

The biggest disadvantage of the sole proprietorship is **unlimited liability**—the obligation to personally repay all debts incurred by the business, which means the potential to lose more than just what the owner has invested in a business. Personal assets, such as a house or a car, may have to be sold to cover the business debts. Although this is the primary disadvantage of the sole proprietorship—and it's a major one—there are also other disadvantages. One is the fact that as a sole proprietor, you forfeit different kinds of business deductions on income taxes that are available only to corporations. Because these deductions lower the amount of income taxes paid, the effective tax rate increases. Another disadvantage is that although you have the freedom and control to run your business the way you want, you also have total responsibility. You are limited by your personal skills and capabilities, which can prove overwhelming at times. Finally, another disadvantage of the sole proprietorship is the fact that it may be more difficult to raise financing. Many financial institutions are reluctant to lend money to sole proprietors because the ability to repay the loan is dependent solely on that individual.

General Partnership

A **general partnership** is a form of business organization in which two or more business owners share the management and risk of the business. Legally, you can have a partnership without a written agreement. However, problems are inevitable in any partnership, no matter whether the partners are family members or good friends. A written partnership agreement drafted by legal counsel is highly recommended. Without a written partnership agreement, a partnership operates according to the rules of the Uniform Partnership Act (UPA) in the state in which the partnership is operating. The intent of the UPA is to resolve issues and problems among partners. Rather than relying on some standardized solution, it's a good idea to invest the necessary resources and money to draft a solid partnership agreement up front. Each partner has much to gain from making sure that the partnership starts off with a written partnership agreement.

How does a general partnership compare in terms of the two major organizational issues—taxes and liability? In a general partnership, income and losses "pass through" to the partners and are taxed at each partner's individual personal tax rate. As with the sole proprietorship, the partners are exposed to unlimited personal liability. Each partner's personal assets are at risk under this arrangement as well.

One advantage of this form of organization is that, even with a written partnership agreement, it is relatively easy to form. As with the sole proprietorship, the partnership simply needs the appropriate business licenses and permits. Another advantage of the general partnership that the sole proprietorship does

FYI

The ABCs of Perfect Partnerships

Setting up a partnership involves some interesting and challenging issues. One of these issues is the use of a written partnership agreement. The formal contract between the partners forming a partnership is called the **articles of partnership,** wherein the obligations and responsibilities of each business owner are outlined. It's also a good idea to cover the following issues in the partnership agreement: name, location, and purpose of the partnership; the personal contribution of each partner in cash, services, or other assets; the decision-making authority of each partner and situations when consensual decision making is required; work responsibilities of each partner; duration of the partnership; distribution of profits or losses; compensation of each partner; dispute resolution procedure; procedure for adding any new partner(s); procedure for dissolution of partnership; and process of dealing with death or disability of a partner.

Another issue that partners need to be aware of, particularly if they do *not* have a written partnership agreement, is the provisions of the Uniform Partnership Act (UPA). The UPA covers most legal issues concerning partnerships and provides a minimal amount of protection and regulation, especially in the following areas: agreement between partners regarding assignment of partnership property; voting rights because each partner is to have one vote, regardless of ownership percentage; keeping accurate records with each partner having the right to examine them; the responsibility of each partner to be loyal to the partnership and not do anything to harm the partnership intentionally; the right of partners to draw on their share of their profits; and agreement about salaries and dealing with losses. The intent of this law was to settle potential problems that came up between partners who had no written partnership agreement.

Source: T. Hatten, *Small Business* (Upper Saddle River, NJ: Prentice Hall, 1997), pp. 50–53.

not have is the pooling of talent and resources. Working together, the partners may be able to do more than each partner is able to do on his or her own. Along these lines, the pooling of resources may make it easier to access outside financing. Financial institutions may be more willing to provide funds because more than one person is involved. Finally, there are some tax benefits to the general partnership. Each partner reports partnership income on an individual income tax return, and the business does not pay any taxes as its own entity.

What about disadvantages of the general partnership? As with the sole proprietorship, the biggest disadvantage is the unlimited personal liability. Each partner is liable for all business debts, which means personal assets are at risk. In a partnership, you can be held liable for the negligence of your partner(s). Because each partner has the ability to enter into contracts to incur debt, sell assets, or take other actions, you should know what you're getting into with a partner. (Another reason why a partnership agreement is a good idea!) In addition, a big drawback of the partnership arrangement is the divided authority and decision making. In a sole proprietorship, you're the decision maker. In a partnership, there are other viewpoints and perspectives to consider. The divided authority and decision making can lead to conflicts. This can be particularly serious if the partners disagree on important core business issues such as future business direction or philosophy. Finally, other disadvantages of this form of organization are the facts that the continuity of the partnership and the transfer of ownership are more complicated. What happens when one partner wants to sell out and the other one doesn't? What happens when one partner wants to shut down the business and the other one doesn't? Or what happens if one partner dies or becomes incapacitated in some way? These dissolution scenarios should be dealt with up front at the creation of the partnership. Although it may seem strange to talk about dis-

Entrepreneurs in Action

You've probably heard the old admonishment about never going into business with family or friends. But, can best friends in life be best friends at work also? Gail Tessler and Norma Menkin are living proof that it can happen! As partners and co-presidents of Gainor Staffing, a temporary and permanent staffing firm located in New York City, Gail and Norma have survived pregnancies, recessions, chicken pox, and undesirable silent partners whom they eventually bought out. Each woman brings a particular strength to the business. Norma is best at courting clients, making speeches, and envisioning the big-picture strategies. Gail is happiest when she's digging into spreadsheets and data analysis. Even though they have had their disagreements, both women know that they have a rarity in partnerships. They're thankful that this particular partnership arrangement has worked successfully for them.

Source: R. D. Schatz, "A Perfect Blendship," *Business Week Enterprise*, March 1, 1999, p. ENT 20.

solving a partnership right when it's being formed, that is the best time to address these issues.

Limited Liability Partnership (LLP)

The **limited liability partnership (LLP)** is a form of legal business organization in which there are general partner(s) and limited liability partner(s). The general partners actually operate and manage the business. They are the ones who have unlimited liability. There must be at least one general partner in an LLP. However, there can be any number of limited partners. These partners are usually passive investors, although they can make management suggestions to the general partners. They also have the right to inspect the business and make copies of business records. The limited partners are entitled to a share of the business's profits as agreed to in the partnership agreement, and their only risk is the amount of their investment in the LLP.

An LLP faces a similar tax situation as does a general partnership. Income and losses "pass through" to the partners and are taxed at personal rates. The partnership agreement outlines the percentage each partner is to receive. The liability issue is a distinguishing feature of the LLP. Although at least one general partner must have unlimited liability, the limited partners are liable only up to the amount of their investment in the LLP.

The main advantage of the LLP is that it is a good way for an entrepreneur to raise capital. Because the limited partners are risking only a "limited" amount of liability, they view the investment in the LLP as a good source for potential financial returns, and the general partners have the opportunity to obtain funds without having to go through a financial institution.

The biggest disadvantage of this form of organization is the cost and complexity of forming the LLP. A written agreement among all partners is required by most states under the Revised Uniform Limited Partnership Act. Drafting this agreement can be almost as complex as the process involved with incorporating a business. Another disadvantage is the stipulation that limited partners cannot participate in the management of the partnership without losing their liability protection.

Rapid Review ◀◀

✓ What are the two primary factors that affect the decision about type of legal ownership, and what are the three basic ways to organize an entrepreneurial venture?

✓ What is a sole proprietorship, and what are its advantages and disadvantages?

✓ What is a general partnership, and what are its advantages and disadvantages?

✓ What are articles of partnership? What does the Uniform Partnership Act do?

✓ What is a limited liability partnership, and what are its advantages and disadvantages?

C Corporation

Of the three basic types of ownership (sole proprietorship, partnership, and corporation), the corporation (also known as a "C corporation") is the most complex to form and operate. A **corporation** is a legal business entity that is separate from its owners and managers. Many entrepreneurial ventures are organized as a **closely held corporation**, which, very simply, is a corporation owned by a limited group of people who do not trade the stock publicly. Whereas the sole proprietorship and partnership forms of organization do not exist separately from the person(s) who own and manage them, the corporation does. The corporation functions as a distinct legal entity and, as such, can make contracts, engage in business activities, own property, sue and be sued, and of course, pay taxes. A corporation must operate in accordance with its charter and the laws of the state in which it operates. These laws do vary by state. What does it take to incorporate?

The process of incorporation can be quite complex. Although many states do allow entrepreneurs to incorporate without legal assistance, this may not be the best choice. Getting an attorney to help with this process can save a lot of frustration. Even though you may not want to spend the money to get legal assistance, making a mistake in incorporating could end up costing you more in the long run than the legal fees charged for the job. The process of incorporation involves some specific activities. You must prepare **articles of incorporation**, a document that describes the business and is filed with the state in which the business is formed. Articles of incorporation typically include the following information:

1. *The name of your company.* This name must be registered with the state in which it will operate. By registering your company name, you're preventing others from using your name and ensuring that you're not using another company's name. Your chosen corporate name must reflect the type of business and should not be deceptive.

2. *The purpose of your business.* You must state the intended nature of your business. This should not be a problem to include if you have written organizational vision and mission statements. Some states do allow very general information in this section, which lets the entrepreneur change the nature of the business without going through the process of reincorporating.

3. *The names and addresses of the incorporators.* This is pretty self-explanatory. Be aware that some states require at least one of the incorporators to reside in the state.

4. *The names and addresses of the corporation's initial officers and directors.* The individuals elected as corporate officers and directors must be identified.

5. *The address of the corporation's home office.* You must establish corporate headquarters or offices in the state from which you receive your charter or register as an out-of-state corporation in your own state.

6. *The capital required at the time of incorporation.* Some states require that a newly formed corporation deposit in a financial institution the specific percentage of the stock's par value prior to incorporating.

7. *Capital stock to be authorized.* The types of stock and the number of shares the corporation wants to be authorized to issue must be specified. This doesn't mean that this number of shares must be issued, but the corporation is authorized to issue up to this amount. In addition, the rights, preferences, or limits of each class of stock must be specified in this section.

8. *Corporate bylaws.* **Bylaws** are the rules and regulations that govern the management and operation of the corporation. The bylaws must stipulate the rights and powers of shareholders, directors, and officers; the time and place for the annual shareholder meeting; the number needed for a quorum (the number of people who must be present at corporate meetings in order to conduct business); the process for election and compensation of board of directors; the dates of the corporation's fiscal year; and the individuals within the corporation who have authorization to sign contracts.

9. *Corporation's time horizon.* Most corporations are set up with the intention of operating indefinitely. However, you may specify a duration for the corporation's existence.

10. *Miscellaneous information.* Some other information that may be included in the articles of incorporation is restrictions on transferring shares (many closely held corporations want to maintain control over their ownership) and provisions for preemptive rights (if shareholders are granted any).

The main tasks involved in writing the articles of incorporation are naming a **board of directors** (individuals elected by the shareholders to represent their interests), adopting bylaws, electing corporate officers, and issuing stock. You must also decide whether to incorporate as a C corporation, an S corporation (described in the next section), or a limited liability company (also described in a later section).

The tax treatment of a corporation is one of the considerations an entrepreneur must look at in deciding whether or not to incorporate. If business profits are distributed as dividend income, this income is taxed at both the corporate and the personal shareholder levels. This is often referred to as the problem of double taxation. However, the trade-off is that the entrepreneur has limited personal liability because as a legal entity, the corporation assumes any liabilities of the business.

The corporation has other advantages in addition to the major one—that is, limited liability. One of these other advantages includes transferable ownership. Because the corporation's shares can be bought and sold, ownership can be transferred. This also means that the corporation enjoys continuous existence. If something happens to one of the owners, the business does not have to cease operations as is the case with sole proprietorships and partnerships. In addition, corporations typically have easier access to financial and other types of resources. Because the corporate entity has its own assets, which could be sold if necessary, financial institutions are often more willing to lend money.

However, there are some significant disadvantages to the corporate form of organization. We've already discussed one of the major ones—the double taxation problem. Other disadvantages are that corporations are expensive to set up, they're more closely regulated, extensive records must be kept, and the corporate charter restricts what can and cannot be done.

S Corporation

The **S corporation** (also often called a subchapter S corporation) is a specialized type of corporation that has the regular characteristics of a C corporation but is unique in that the owners are taxed as a partnership as long as certain criteria are met. The S corporation has been the classic mechanism for getting the limited liability of a corporate structure without incurring corporate tax. New legal interpretations by federal agencies have relaxed some of the strict criteria for being an S corporation. What are the current criteria regarding S corporations?[2]

1. S corporations can now have as many as 75 shareholders (150 including spouses) instead of the former 35 (70 including spouses). This means that several families plus employees can now share ownership of a business.

2. An S corporation can now have a tax-exempt entity (such as an employee stock ownership plan or pension plan) as a shareholder.
3. Any trust that owns shares in an S corporation can now have multiple beneficiaries rather than just one. This new type of trust is called an "electing small business trust" and it can "sprinkle" income—that is, it can allocate its income unevenly to the owners.

Some legal criteria for being an S corporation have remained the same. These include the following:

1. The S corporation must be a domestic corporation.
2. The S corporation cannot have a nonresident alien as a shareholder.
3. The S corporation can issue only one class of common stock, which means that all shares carry the same rights, except in the case of voting rights, which may differ. Very simply, what this means is that an S corporation can issue both voting and nonvoting common stock.

Violating any of these criteria (new or old) automatically terminates a company's S status. If the criteria are satisfied, the business owner(s) must annually elect S status within 75 days of the beginning of the tax year—which is usually around March 15. This is done by filing Internal Revenue Service Form 2553. All the corporation's shareholders must consent to being an S corporation. Getting legal and accounting advice on this decision is highly advised because there are some legal loopholes that can be used during the annual S status election.

The tax treatment for an S corporation is the same as for a partnership. Income and losses are not incurred at the corporate level, but instead "pass through" to the owners who are taxed at their personal rate. However, the S cor-

---

Entrepreneurs in Action

Black Cat Computer Wholesale of Amherst, New York, had tried pretty much every form of legal organization in its five years of operation. It started as a sole proprietorship, became an S corporation, and then switched to a C corporation. Owner Deborah Williams said that selecting the right legal form for her company was a struggle because the company was growing so fast that it was tough to figure out which structure made sense at the time. Williams admitted that her accountant during the company's fast-growth phase wasn't qualified to advise her. Growth was happening so quickly and Williams became concerned about limiting her personal liability. Fortunately, the switches from one organizational form to another were relatively simple. However, as this example illustrates, this decision is an important one.

Source: J. A. Fraser, "Perfect Form," *Inc,* December 1997, pp. 155–58.

poration does enjoy the limited liability of a regular corporation. In fact, this limited liability is a significant advantage of the S corporation form of organization. Another advantage is that it's relatively easy to set up an S corporation as long as the legal criteria are met. In addition, the new stipulation that tax-exempt entities can be shareholders in the S corporation is a significant advantage. This means that a business's employees can be owners through an employee stock ownership plan or a pension plan.

The disadvantages of the S corporation are few. One is, of course, the fact that to be an S corporation, your business has to meet certain criteria. If these criteria are not met, the S election is jeopardized. The other disadvantage is that an S corporation may limit future financing options because of its treatment of income and losses. Because income flows through to the owners, financial institutions may be reluctant to lend money.

Limited Liability Company (LLC)

The **limited liability company (LLC)** is a relatively new form of business organization that's another hybrid between a partnership and a corporation. The LLC offers the liability protection of a corporation, the tax benefits of a partnership, and no restrictions such as on an S corporation. For instance, an LLC is not limited to 75 shareholders, it can have foreigners as shareholders, and it can have more than one class of stock. An LLC should be seriously considered if the owner(s) need flexibility in the legal structure of the business, desire limited liability, and prefer to be taxed as a partnership rather than as a corporation.

An LLC must have at least two owners (called "members"). These members are offered limited liability, just like in a corporation. In addition, the LLC does not pay income taxes. Income and losses "flow through" to the owners, who are taxed on their share of the LLC's income.

The biggest advantage of the LLC is the flexibility that it gives owners. In addition, the fact that the LLC is not constrained by the regulations on C and S corporations is an advantage. Finally, the absence of double taxation is an advantage of this organizing approach.

The main drawback of this approach to organizing is that it's quite complex and expensive to set up. Legal and financial advice is an absolute necessity in forming the LLC's operating agreement. The **operating agreement** is the document that outlines the provisions governing the way the LLC will conduct business. It's similar to a corporation's bylaws.

Summary of Legal Forms of Organization

The decision on the legal form of organization is a big one and one that should not be approached lightly. This decision can have significant tax and liability consequences down the road. Although the legal form of organization can be changed, it's not an easy thing to do. An entrepreneur needs to think

Rapid Review ◀◀|

✓ What is a corporation? A C corporation? A closely held corporation?

✓ What are articles of incorporation, and what do they typically include?

✓ What are bylaws? What is a board of directors?

✓ What is an S corporation? What criteria must be met in order to be an S corporation?

✓ What is a limited liability company? What criteria does an LLC have? What is an operating agreement?

✓ List the advantages and disadvantages of the corporate form of organization, the S corporation, and the LLC.

carefully about what's important, especially in the areas of flexibility, taxes, and amount of personal liability. As we've mentioned, it's a good idea to get legal and accounting advice on this decision. There are also other legal issues that an entrepreneur must deal with where professional advice may be necessary or highly recommended. Let's take a look at some of these legal issues.

OTHER LEGAL ISSUES

It's often said with a humorous laugh that entrepreneurs have three choices when it comes to legal issues: Learn nothing but hire good lawyers; learn nothing and avoid lawyers; or learn enough to know when legal advice is needed. The best approach is the last—know enough about legal issues to know when professional legal advice is needed. You don't want to bury your head in the sand when it comes to legal issues. There are too many risks associated with doing something illegal, even if it were unintentional. Ignorance of the law is not a valid excuse. We're going to discuss four legal issues that impact organizing the entrepreneurial venture: choosing a business name, patents, contracts, and employment law. In addition, we're going to look briefly at some miscellaneous legal topics.

Choosing a Business Name, Slogan, or Design

You may be asking yourself why choosing a business name, slogan, or design is a legal issue that entrepreneurs must deal with. Although it may seem that your business is entitled to pick any name it wants, that's not the case. In fact, it's an important legal issue. Legal problems can arise if you choose a name that another company has trademarked or has registered as a corporate name with the appropriate state agency. A **trademark** is a form of legal protection for a distinctive word, name, phrase, logo, symbol, design, slogan, or any combination of these elements. It's a good idea to do a trademark search before choosing a name, logo, or slogan. Doing a trademark search has gotten a lot easier with the advent of the Internet. Two of the biggest trademark search companies on the Internet are Thomson & Thomson (**www.thomson-thomson.com**) and Corsearch (**www.corsearch.com**). These Web sites charge a fee, although what you'll get for that fee is a check of federal and state registrations, Internet domain names, and common-law listings found in phone books and trade publications.[3] You can also conduct a trademark search yourself using *The Trademark Register of the United States*, which is available in many libraries or by using other similar directories. A search of registered corporate names would have to be done through the state agency where corporations are registered. By investigating name and trademark information, you will have a good basis for arguing that you did act with due diligence if you should ever get in trouble for using another business's name. But, hopefully, if you've conducted a thorough search, you won't ever have to worry about that anyway.

Once you've found a name that you like and that's clear, what then? You can choose that name for your business and do nothing, but it's probably worthwhile to register the name with the federal government. The cost (as of mid-1999) is $245 to apply to the United States Patent and Trademark Office for a trademark name that will cover you anywhere in the United States as well as on the Internet. The forms needed for filing are available on the agency's Web site (**www.uspto.gov**) and are so user friendly that you probably won't even need legal advice to fill them out.

Patents

In Chapter 2, we briefly covered patents. Remember that a **patent** is a legal property that allows its holder to prevent others from employing this property for their own use for a specified period of time. A patent protects an invention. It's valid for up to 20 years from the date you file for the patent. There are three different types of patents. A **utility patent**, the most common type of patent, covers inventions that work uniquely to perform a function or use. For instance, if you invented a new device to administer medications, you would apply for a utility patent. However, if you came up with a unique or new form, shape, or design of an existing

---

FYI

The ABCs of Trademarks and Patents

Here are some frequently asked questions and answers about trademarks and patents:

● *Is a service mark the same as a trademark?*

A service mark is the same except that it identifies and distinguishes the source of a service rather than of a product.

● *How are trademarks, patents, and copyrights different?*

A trademark protects a distinctive word, name, phrase, logo, symbol, design, slogan, or any combination of these elements. A patent protects an invention. A copyright protects an original artistic or literary work.

● *When can I use the "TM," "SM," and "®" symbols?*

Anyone who claims rights in a mark may use the TM (trademark) or SM (service mark) designation with the mark to alert the public to the claim. It isn't necessary to have a registration or even a pending application to use these designations. This claim may or may not be valid. The registration symbol (®) may be used only when the mark is registered in the Patent and Trade Office.

● *How long does a trademark registration last?*

For a trademark registration to remain valid, an Affidavit of Use ("Section 8 Affidavit") must be

filed between the fifth and sixth year following registration. Assuming that this affidavit of use is filed correctly, registrations granted before November 16, 1989, have a 20-year term and registrations granted on or after November 16, 1989, have a 10-year term. These timing periods are also true for the trademark renewals.

● *What do the terms* patent pending *and* patent applied for *mean?*

These terms are used by a manufacturer or seller of an article to inform the public that an application for a patent on that article is on file in the Patent and Trademark Office. The law imposes a fine on anyone who uses these terms falsely to deceive the public.

● *If two or more persons work together to make an invention, who is granted the patent?*

If each person had a share in the ideas forming the invention, they are joint inventors and a patent will be issued to them jointly on the basis of a proper patent application. If one person has provided all of the ideas of the invention and the other has only followed instructions in making it, the person who contributed the ideas is the sole inventor and the patent application and patent will be in his or her name alone.

Source: Information found on the Web pages of the United States Patent and Trade Office (**www.uspto.gov**).

object, you would want to get a **design patent**. For instance, if you came up with a stapler that performed the standard function of stapling but looked like a frog, you would want to apply for a design patent. The final type of patent is a **plant patent**, which covers new strains of living plants such as flowers, trees, or vegetables.

You need to know that you can't patent everything. You can't patent, for example, an abstract idea, a purely mental process, or a process that you can simply perform using pencil and paper. Also, naturally occurring things cannot be patented. To be patentable, an invention must be a process, a machine, a manufacture, a composition, or an improvement in these. In addition to meeting the requirement of being in this "statutory" class (that is, being a process, a machine, a manufacture, a composition, or an improvement in these), an invention must satisfy three additional requirements to be patentable. These include (1) *novelty*—the invention must be a new idea and physically different in at least some small way from what already exists; (2) *nonobviousness*—the invention must be a new or unexpected development, which means that it would not be obvious to someone skilled in the technology of a particular field; (3) *usefulness*—the invention must have some obvious use, or in the case of design, must be ornamental. Once you feel that your invention has met these tests, what then?

The first thing to do before filing a patent application is to conduct a patent search. This search will tell you whether other patents have already been issued that reveal or suggest your invention. You can either do the search yourself or hire a patent agent or patent attorney. If you choose to do the search yourself, you can go to a library that has been designated as a Patent and Trademark Depository Library, or if you have Internet access you can search online (see **www.uspto.gov** or **www.patents.ibm**). If you want to hire someone to do this search, professional patent researchers will do the search for you. Whichever approach you take, this search should be thorough in order to prevent later problems.

If you complete your search and find nothing that indicates your invention has already been patented, you're ready to submit a patent application. A patent application is a complex legal document and the federal agency (the United States Patent and Trade Office—USPTO) responsible for reviewing these applications highly recommends they be completed by someone trained to prepare such documents. There are specific requirements set forth by the USPTO for both content and format of the patent applications. (You can read through the requirements at the USPTO Web site at **www.uspto.gov**.) If you've invented a new way to do something or a new design, doesn't it make sense to protect it? Although this professional advice may be expensive, not having it may be even more so. Protecting your invention(s) that you hope to turn into a viable—and potentially profitable—entrepreneurial venture is absolutely critical. One thing you can do is adhere to the rigorous patent application process requirements.

Contracts

A **contract** is an agreement that creates legal obligations and is enforceable in a court of law. Organizing and then managing an ongoing entrepreneurial venture may entail executing different types of contracts. The commonness and potential variety of contracts that an entrepreneur may deal with means knowing something about contract law. Although it's highly recommended again that you enlist professional legal advice regarding the writing and execution of contracts, there's some basic knowledge about contracts with which you should be familiar.[4]

There are four essentials of a contract. One is *mutual assent*, which means that both parties must agree to the contract. Another is *consideration*, that is, both parties must do or pay something as stated in the contract. The third is *legality of object*, which means that the contract cannot force the parties to do something illegal. The final contract essential is *capacity of the parties*, that is, all parties to the contract must be legally able to perform their part of the contract. For instance, minors, people of unsound mind, intoxicated persons, or drugged persons can legally get out of contracts. In addition, contract law has specific understandings about which contracts must be in writing to be legally binding, what a breach of contract is, and interpretation of contracts. There's much more to contract law than what we've discussed here, and that's why it's a good idea to get legal advice on preparing any contracts that your business may need.

Employment Laws

Employment laws cover hiring and firing, employee policies, employee compensation and benefits, discrimination, workers' compensation, workplace health and safety, family and medical leave, and other employer–employee relationships. New rulings and interpretations in any of these areas further complicate what you can and cannot do regarding any aspect of employment. If you're a sole proprietor, you obviously do not have to worry about employment laws. However, if your organization is going to have other employees, you need to be familiar with employment law. Again, it's highly recommended that you seek professional legal advice in employment law matters. It can be an expensive proposition if an employee sues and you're found to be at fault. A survey of small company executives indicated that most were attempting to forestall legal complaints by establishing clear guidelines and procedures. (See Figure 5-1.)

Other Miscellaneous Legal Issues

You may have to deal with other miscellaneous legal issues when organizing your entrepreneurial venture or while managing the ongoing venture. These may

Global Perspectives

Although Khe Sanh in central Vietnam is probably best remembered as the site of a bloody siege at the U.S. military base stationed there during the Vietnam War, a different type of "war" is being fought there now. It's a business war. Barefoot peasants have been transformed into prosperous coffee capitalists. From being an unknown in the coffee industry, Vietnam now is the world's number three exporter of coffee. However, the region's thriving entrepreneurs have had to endure a legal tangle of governmental permits and bribes. One official stated that anyone who wants to invest in this region has to get 47 separate permits, each requiring a bribe. Despite the legal challenges, Vietnamese entrepreneurs are charging ahead and spurring the region's economic development.

Source: B. Fulford, "Capitalism Creeps into Vietnam," *Forbes*, May 17, 1999, pp. 174–76.

Figure 5-1

A Survey of Ways Small Business Owners Are Preventing Employee Lawsuits

Action	Approximate percentage of respondents who have done this
• Wrote employee manual or handbook	80%+
• Trained supervisors	60%+
• Wrote grievance policies	58%
• Hired consultants	53%

Source: "Staying on the Right Side of the Law," *Business Week Frontier,* April 26, 1999, p. F7.

Rapid Review ◀◀|

✓ What legal issues might arise in choosing a business name, slogan, or design?

✓ What is a trademark, and how can entrepreneurs do a trademark search?

✓ What is a patent? Describe the three different types of patents.

✓ What are the requirements for being able to patent an invention, and what are the steps involved in getting a patent?

✓ What is a contract? Describe the four essentials of a contract.

✓ How might employment laws affect an entrepreneurial venture?

✓ What other miscellaneous legal issues might an entrepreneur have to deal with?

include sales laws, trade secrets laws, securities laws, credit laws, consumer protection laws, pension and fringe benefit laws, and antitrust laws. In any of these areas, professional legal advice can be valuable, particularly if it relates to a major business concern. The key is to be aware of when you need legal advice—that is, learn enough to know when legal advice is needed.

ORGANIZATIONAL DESIGN ISSUES

The choice of an appropriate organizational structure is an important activity when organizing the entrepreneurial venture. No other topic in creating and designing organizations has undergone as much change in the past few years as that of organizational structure. Think back to our chapter-opening case on idealab! and its unique structural design. What does that type of structural design do for this organization and why does it seem to work? Those are some of the topics we want to look at in this section. We first need to understand something about the process of organizing.

What Is Organizing?

In the field of management, organizing is one of the four basic functions of managers (planning, leading, and controlling are the other three) and is defined as the process of creating an organization's structure. Just what is an organization's structure? An **organizational structure** is the formal framework within which work is divided, grouped, and coordinated. Organizational structure is similar to the human skeleton. The bones in your skeleton are the mechanism for supporting and holding together your various body parts so you can do things such as stand, sit, run, walk, write, dance, and so forth. The "bones" that are the organizational structure are the mechanisms for supporting and holding together the various parts of the organization so work can be done. However, one difference is that whereas the bones in the human skeleton can be seen and felt, an organization's structure cannot. We can see a visual representation of the organization structure with an **organizational chart**. However, the organizational chart simply portrays the division and grouping of various work activities (horizontal levels) throughout the organization and who's in charge (vertical levels) in the organization. The process of developing or changing the organizational structure is called **organizational design**. Knowing something about organizational design is important for entrepreneurs because the work that the people in the entrepreneurial venture will perform must be divided, grouped, and coordinated in some way. As the entrepreneurial venture is organized, decisions must be made about the most appropriate organizational design.

Organizational Design Decisions

The whole purpose behind organizational design is making sure that the organization's work gets done efficiently and effectively. In a sole proprietorship, there's not much to organizational structure because the sole proprietor is the one who makes sure the work gets done. There's no need to divide, group, or coordinate the work. However, if an entrepreneurial venture has more than one person involved, decisions about who does what need to be made. As the venture grows, these design decisions arise as more employees join the organization. Organizational design involves decisions about six key elements: (1) How much work specialization is needed? (2) Is departmentalization needed and what type? (3) Who's going to be in charge and who reports to whom? Or, in other words, what is the chain of command? (4) How many employees will supervisors manage—that is, what is the span of control? (5) Are organizational decisions going to be centralized or decentralized? (6) How much formalization—rules and procedures—is necessary?[5] Let's take a closer look at each of these important organizing elements.

Work Specialization. **Work specialization** describes the degree to which work tasks are divided into separate jobs. It's also known as division of labor. The essence of work specialization is that an entire job is not done by one individual but instead is broken down into various steps, and each step is completed by a different person. Individual employees perform one part of an activity rather than the entire activity. Work specialization has been around for a number of years and has both advantages and drawbacks. (See Table 5-2.) The advantages are mainly economic and revolve around increasing work efficiency and productivity. The drawbacks are mainly human and stem from the fact that individuals don't want to do the same thing over and over. Today, work specialization is viewed as an important organizing mechanism, but not as a source of endlessly increasing productivity. There will come a point in the entrepreneurial venture when work responsibilities must be divided. However, keep in mind the potential drawbacks of making jobs too narrowly specialized.

TABLE 5-2   Advantages and Drawbacks of Work Specialization

Advantages—Economic	Drawbacks—Human
■ Efficient use of employee skills	■ Boredom
■ Employee skills can improve because of repetition	■ Stress
■ Easier and less costly to train employees	■ Fatigue
■ Minimizes resource waste	■ Poor work quality
■ Encourages development of specialized equipment and machinery	■ Lower productivity
	■ May lead to absenteeism and turnover

Departmentalization. When an organization grows to the point where more than one person is working on a particular function, it may be time to departmentalize. **Departmentalization** very simply describes the basis on which specialized work tasks (jobs) are grouped. Once jobs have been divided up through work specialization, they are grouped back together so that common tasks can be coordinated. Although every organization will have its own unique way of classifying and grouping common work activities, there are some general approaches to departmentalization. One of these approaches is by *job function*. For instance, a hotel might be departmentalized around housekeeping, front desk, maintenance, restaurant operations, reservations and sales, human resources, and accounting. Departmentalization by function can be used in all types of organizations and will reflect each organization's unique work functions. Another approach to departmentalization is by *product* in which jobs are grouped by product line. For example, an accounting firm might have departments oriented toward its "products"— tax preparation, management consulting, auditing, and so forth. An organization might also choose to departmentalize on the basis of *geography* or location. For instance, it might have a southwest region, a midwest region, and a southeast region. Another approach to departmentalization is on the basis of *process*, or grouping jobs on the basis of how products or customers "flow" through the business. For example, a cabinet manufacturer may have departments for the various work processes involved in designing and manufacturing wood cabinets: sawing, planing, milling, assembling, lacquering, sanding, finishing, inspecting, and shipping. Finally, the *customer* approach might be used if there are common groups of customers that the organization seeks to serve. For instance, an office supply firm might be departmentalized on the basis of retail customers, wholesale customers, and governmental customers. One trend that's evident in the ways that organizations are departmentalizing is the use of **cross-functional teams**. These teams are hybrid groupings of individuals who come from various specialties or functions and who work together on tasks. Those tasks might include designing a new product, preparing a long-term marketing plan, or creating a new layout for the office. Entrepreneurial ventures are particularly fertile grounds for cross-functional teams because of the need for flexibility in assigning and coordinating work.

Chain of Command. In designing an appropriate organizational structure, it's important to know who has ultimate decision-making authority, who has the authority to perform what tasks, and who reports to whom. These are all issues in determining the chain of command. Strict adherence to a formal chain of command where individuals have to get permission from their supervisor before doing something may not be the best approach for a nimble and flexible entrepreneurial organization. Instead, the solution to the command-and-control issue for many entrepreneurial organizations is to empower employees. **Empowerment** is increasing the decision-making discretion of individuals. In an empowered organization, individuals are free to resolve problems as they arise, are encouraged to approach doing their work the way they feel is best because they do have more detailed knowledge about it, and are encouraged to think for themselves rather than being told what to do. Being empowered, however, doesn't mean making decisions and doing work just any way you want. All decisions and actions should be aligned with the organizational purpose and goals. However, that's where the vision and mission statements and the behavioral expectations inherent in the organizational culture help shape what employees do and how they do it. Although employee empowerment can be an attractive alternative in resolving organizational chain-of-command issues, keep in mind that effective empowerment doesn't just happen. It's not a coincidence that empowerment efforts are almost always coupled with extensive training. Enhancing employees' skills, abilities, and confidence through training increases the likelihood that any empowerment efforts will succeed.

Span of Control. As the number of organizational employees increases, an organizational structure decision may have to be made regarding the number of employees a manager can effectively and efficiently supervise. This organizational design concept is called the **span of control**. The span of control concept is important in organizational design because, to a large degree, it determines how many vertical levels and managers an organization will have. Wider spans (supervising a greater number of people) are more efficient in terms of cost because you need fewer managers. But at some point, wider spans become inefficient because the manager loses track of what's going on and employees may make costly mistakes. Organizational design theorists now recognize that many factors influence the appropriate number of employees a manager can efficiently and effectively supervise. These factors revolve around the skills and abilities of the manager, the skills and abilities of the employees, and the work that must be done. The more skilled and able the manager and the employees, the wider the span can be. The trend in organizations, large and small, has been toward larger spans of control. These wider spans of control allow organizations to control costs, cut overhead, speed up decision making, increase flexibility, and empower employees.

Centralization–Decentralization. In an organization, decisions are being made constantly and continuously. These decisions determine what gets done, when, how, and so forth. The organizational design concept of centralization–decentralization addresses where these decisions are being made. **Centralization** describes the degree to which decision making is concentrated in the hands of a few people. **Decentralization** describes the degree to which decision making is delegated to other organizational members. Our earlier discussion of employee empowerment is an example of how decision making is being decentralized in organizations. The nature of the entrepreneurial environment favors a more decentralized approach as entrepreneurial ventures need the ability to respond quickly to rapidly changing circumstances. The entrepreneurial venture needs to be nimble and flexible and decentralization supports this. In addition, the small size of an entrepreneurial organization may limit any attempts to centralize decision making. When there are not many organizational members, it's kind of hard to keep decision making concentrated to just a few. In addition, in a small organization, the overlapping job duties and high need for coordination would not be conducive to centralization.

Formalization. The last organizational design issue we need to look at is **formalization**, the degree to which jobs are standardized and the extent to which employee behavior is dictated by rules and procedures. If an organization is highly formalized, employees will have little discretion over what is to be done, when it's to be done, and how they should do it. In organizations with high formalization, there would be explicit job descriptions, lots of organizational rules, and clearly defined procedures for doing work. On the other hand, when formalization is low, the way employees do their jobs is fairly nonstructured, and employees have a great deal of freedom in how they do their work. There are few rules and procedures. Even in organizations with low formalization, however, this doesn't mean that the workplace is a free-for-all. Some degree of formalization is necessary for planning and controlling purposes. Employees have to know what they're supposed to be doing and how their work performance is being measured. Within these parameters, though, employees would be free to do their work in the way they felt was best.

Summary. As we stated at the beginning of this section, organizational design decisions revolve around amount and type of work specialization, amount and type of departmentalization, approach to chain of command, width of span of control, amount of centralization or decentralization, and degree of formalization. We've discussed the various design options. Now, how do these design options translate into actual organizational structures? What types of organizational structures might an entrepreneur use? That's what we want to look at next.

Types of Organization Structures

An entrepreneur might choose from two generic types of organizational structures.[6] (See Figure 5-2 for a comparison.) One is the **mechanistic organization**, which is a rigid and tightly controlled structure characterized by high specialization, rigid departmentalization, clear chain of command, narrow span of control, high formalization, limited information networking throughout the organization, and little participation in decision making by employees. A mechanistic-type structure tends to be focused on efficiency and cost minimiza-

Structuring the Entrepreneurial Firm

At some point, successful entrepreneurs find that they cannot do everything alone. More people are needed. The entrepreneur must then decide on the most appropriate structural arrangement for effectively carrying out the organization's activities.

Without some type of suitable organizational structure, the entrepreneurial venture may soon find itself in a chaotic situation.

In many small firms, the organizational structure tends to evolve with very little conscious and deliberate planning by the entrepreneur. For the most part, the structure may be very simple—one person who does whatever is needed. As the entrepreneurial venture grows and the entrepreneur finds it increasingly difficult to go it alone, employees are brought on board to perform certain functions or duties that the entrepreneur cannot handle. These individuals tend to keep doing those same functions as the company grows. Then, as the entrepreneurial venture continues to grow, each of these func-

tional areas may require managers and employees.

With the evolution to a more deliberate structure comes a whole new set of challenges for the entrepreneur. All of a sudden, he or she must share decision making and operating responsibility. This is typically one of the most difficult things for an entrepreneur to do—letting go and allowing someone else to make the decisions. After all, he or she reasons, how can anyone know this business as well as I do? Also, what might have been a fairly informal, loose, and flexible atmosphere that worked well when the organization was small may no longer be effective. Many entrepreneurs are greatly concerned about keeping that "small company" atmosphere alive even as the organization grows and evolves into a more structured arrangement. But having a structured organization doesn't necessarily mean giving up flexibility, adaptability, and freedom. In fact, the structural design may be as fluid as the entrepreneur feels comfortable with and yet still have the rigidity it needs to operate efficiently.

Figure 5-2

Mechanistic and Organic Organization Structures

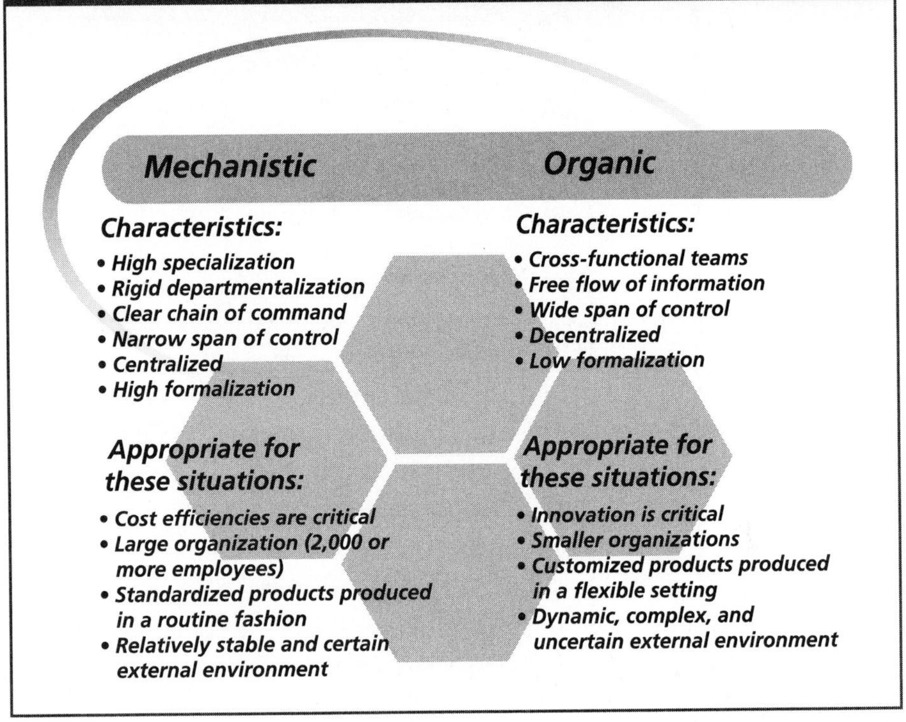

Mechanistic

Organic

Characteristics:
- High specialization
- Rigid departmentalization
- Clear chain of command
- Narrow span of control
- Centralized
- High formalization

Characteristics:
- Cross-functional teams
- Free flow of information
- Wide span of control
- Decentralized
- Low formalization

Appropriate for these situations:
- Cost efficiencies are critical
- Large organization (2,000 or more employees)
- Standardized products produced in a routine fashion
- Relatively stable and certain external environment

Appropriate for these situations:
- Innovation is critical
- Smaller organizations
- Customized products produced in a flexible setting
- Dynamic, complex, and uncertain external environment

tion. The impact of differing personalities, human judgments, and ambiguity are minimized because these are seen as inefficient and inconsistent. In direct contrast is the **organic organization**, which is a structure that's highly adaptive and flexible with little work specialization, minimal formalization, and little direct supervision of employees. Rather than having standardized jobs and regulations, the organic organization is flexible, which allows it to change rapidly as needs require. Although organic organizations do have division of labor, the jobs people do are not standardized. Organizational employees are highly trained and empowered to handle diverse job-related problems. Employees in this type of organization require minimal formal rules and little direct supervision. Their high levels of skills and training and the support provided by other highly skilled and trained team members make formalization and rigid organizational controls unnecessary. When is a mechanistic design preferable and when is an organic one more appropriate?

A mechanistic structure would be preferable when cost efficiencies are critical to the organization's competitive advantage; for large organizations where more specialization, departmentalization, centralization, and rules and regulations are needed for control; if the organization produces standardized products in a routine fashion; and where the external environment is relatively stable and certain. An organic structure would be more appropriate when innovation is critical to the organization's competitive advantage; for smaller organizations where rigid approaches to dividing and coordinating work aren't necessary; if the organization produces customized products in a flexible setting; and where the external environment is dynamic, complex, and uncertain.

> ### Entrepreneurs in Action
>
> In the business of developing special effects used in movies, Cinnabar Inc. was a good example of an organic-type organization. Because it operated in a dynamic and complex industry, speed and flexibility were critical. Employees of the company, located in Burbank, California, and Orlando, Florida, were accustomed to all the bells and whistles of virtual communication to help them do their jobs. Cyberspace became the point of contact with each other and with customers. However, when founder Jonathan Katz saw his company's revenues dropping off, he came to the conclusion that the lack of face-to-face contact with clients was having a negative impact on sales. He had his employees quit relying solely on their electronic tools to communicate and return to personally visiting directors, producers, and art directors at the movie production companies. The lesson: Although technology provides flexibility, speed, and agility, it still can't replace good old-fashioned human contact. Even an organic-type organization needs a balance.
>
> *Source:* M. Ballon, "The Technocrats," *Inc,*, February 1999, p. 55.

Given the realities of the new economy and the changing world of work (as we discussed in Chapter 2), it's not surprising that many entrepreneurial organizations are looking for more flexible and adaptable organizational designs. For instance, Bill Gross's company, idealab!, described in the chapter-opening case, is a perfect example of a company that's uniquely organized to take advantage of the dynamic realities of the Internet market. It moves rapidly to capture market opportunities that it sees. Although its structural arrangement is rather unusual, that arrangement fosters and supports the effective and efficient accomplishment of the organization's often chaotic work. Entrepreneurial organizations are using some new structural designs that don't fit the traditional mold. One of these new models is a **virtual organization**, which is a network of independent companies linked by common goals and information technology. In a virtual organization, each company contributes its core competencies and skills as markets are pursued. The benefit of the virtual organization is that it's extremely fluid and flexible. As opportunities arise, the virtual organization ramps up to take advantage of them. The virtual organization is possible only because of the information technology that links the various companies. Sharing information both within and across companies is important to the ultimate success of a virtual organization. Another of these "new" organizational designs is called a **boundaryless organization**. This type of organization is one whose design is not defined by, or limited to, horizontal, vertical, or external boundaries imposed by a predefined structure.[7] Although they're similar in terms of being flexible and fluid, the main difference between a boundaryless and a virtual organization is that a boundaryless organization involves a single organization whose design minimizes the structural boundaries within and outside the organization. The virtual organization, on the other hand, refers to several organizations linked together by technology in a virtual arrangement. The term *boundaryless organization* was coined by an entrepreneurially oriented manager of a large and successful corporation: Jack Welch, chairman of the global corporate giant, General Electric. Despite GE's enormous size, Welch wanted to eliminate vertical and horizontal boundaries *within* GE and break down barriers *between* the company and its external stakeholders. He passionately believed that by getting rid of these boundaries, his company could be more responsive and flexible and, ultimately, more successful. Although the idea may sound odd, many of today's most successful organizations are finding that they can effectively operate best in today's environment by remaining flexible and *un*structured. The ideal structure for them is *not* having a rigid, predefined structure. Instead, the boundaryless organization seeks to eliminate the chain of command, have limitless spans of control, and replace rigid department lines with empowered teams.[8] The boundaryless organization functions efficiently and effectively by breaking down the artificial boundaries created by a fixed structural design.

Throughout this chapter, we've looked at the issues involved with organizing the entrepreneurial venture. From deciding the legal form of business organization to dealing with other important legal issues to choosing an appropriate organizational design, an entrepreneur has important organizing issues to address. Rather than haphazardly or mindlessly jumping right into an entrepreneurial venture, it's important for an entrepreneur to think carefully about the best approach—that is, the approach that will allow work to be performed efficiently and effectively.

Rapid Review ◀◀|

✓ What is an organizational structure, organizational chart, and organizational design?

✓ What are the six key decisions in organizational design? Describe the main issues to be addressed in each of these areas.

✓ Compare and contrast mechanistic and organic organizations.

✓ What is a virtual organization? A boundaryless organization?

CHAPTER SUMMARY

One of the first steps in executing the business plan is deciding the best way to organize the entrepreneurial venture. Organizing involves determining the legal form of business organization, addressing other legal issues, and then choosing the most appropriate organizational design.

The two primary factors that affect the decision about the form of legal ownership are taxes and legal liability. The right choice can protect you from legal liability as well as save tax dollars. The three basic ways to organize your entrepreneurial venture are sole proprietorship, partnership, and corporation. When you add in the variations of these organizational alternatives, you end up with six possible choices, each with its own tax consequences, liability issues, and pros and cons. These six choices are sole proprietorship, general partnership, limited liability partnership (LLP), C corporation, S corporation, and limited liability company (LLC). The decision on the legal form of organization is a big one that should not be approached lightly. An entrepreneur needs to think carefully about what's important, especially in the areas of flexibility, taxes, and the amount of personal liability.

Some other legal issues that entrepreneurs must deal with include choosing a business name, patents, contracts, and employment law. Choosing a business name can bring about legal problems if you pick a name that another company has trademarked or has registered as a corporate name with the appropriate state agency. A trademark is a form of legal protection for a distinctive word, name, phrase, logo, symbol, design, slogan, or any combination of these elements. A patent protects an invention. There are three different types of patents: utility patent, design patent, and plant patent. Filing a patent application involves a number of steps. Another legal issue that entrepreneurs may deal with includes contracts. A contract is an agreement that creates legal obligations and is enforceable in a court of law. Finally, entrepreneurs may have to deal with employment laws that cover hiring and firing, employee policies, employee compensation and benefits, discrimination, workers' compensation, workplace health and safety, family and medical leave, and other employer–employee relationships.

The choice of an appropriate organizational structure is another important activity when organizing the entrepreneurial venture. As the entrepreneurial venture is organized, decisions must be made about six key organizational design issues: How much work specialization is needed? Is departmentalization needed and what type? Who's going to be in charge and who reports to whom? How many employees will supervisors manage? Are organizational decisions going to be centralized or decentralized? How much formalization is necessary? An entrepreneur might choose from two generic types of organizational structures. A mechanistic organization is one whose structure is rigid and tightly controlled and is characterized by high specialization, rigid departmentalization, clear chain of command, narrow span of control, high formalization, limited information networking, and little participation in decision making. An organic organization, on the other hand, is a structure that's highly adaptive and flexible with little work specialization, minimal formalization, and little direct supervision of employees.

KEY TERMS

➠ *Sole proprietorship:* A form of organization in which the owner maintains sole and complete control over the business and is personally liable for business debts.

➠ *Unlimited liability:* The obligation to personally repay all debts incurred by the business.

➠ *General partnership:* A form of business organization in which two or more business owners share the management and risk of the business.

➠ *Articles of partnership:* The formal contract between partners forming a partnership.

➠ *Limited liability partnership (LLP):* A form of legal business organization in which there are general partner(s) and limited liability partner(s).

➠ *Corporation (C corporation):* A legal business entity that is separate from its owners and managers.

➠ *Closely held corporation:* A corporation owned by a limited group of people who do not trade the stock publicly.

➠ *Articles of incorporation:* A document that describes a business and is filed with the state in which the business is being formed.

➠ *Bylaws:* The rules and regulations that govern the management and operation of the corporation.

➠ *Board of directors:* Individuals elected by shareholders to represent their interests.

➠ *S corporation:* A specialized type of corporation that has the regular characteristics of the C corporation but is unique in that the owners are taxed as a partnership as long as certain criteria are met.

➠ *Limited liability company (LLC):* A relatively new form of business organization that's another hybrid between a partnership and a corporation.

➠ *Operating agreement:* The document that outlines the provisions governing the way the LLC will conduct business.

➠ *Trademark:* A form of legal protection for a distinctive word, name, phrase, logo, symbol, design, slogan, or any combination of these elements.

➠ *Patent:* A legal property that protects an invention.

➠ *Utility patent:* The most common type of patent, which covers inventions that work uniquely to perform a function or use.

➠ *Design patent:* A patent that covers a unique form, shape, or design of an existing object.

➠ *Plant patent:* A patent that covers new strains of living plants.

➠ *Contract:* An agreement that creates legal obligations and is enforceable in a court of law.

➠ *Organizational structure:* The formal framework within which work is divided, grouped, and coordinated.

➠ *Organizational chart:* A visual representation of the organizational structure.

➠ *Organizational design:* The process of developing or changing the organizational structure.

➠ *Work specialization:* The degree to which work tasks are divided into separate jobs. Also known as division of labor.

➠ *Departmentalization:* The basis on which specialized work tasks (jobs) are grouped.

➠ *Cross-functional teams:* Hybrid groupings of individuals who come from various specialties or functions and who work together on tasks.

➠ *Empowerment:* Increasing the decision-making discretion of individuals in organizations.

➠ *Span of control:* The number of employees a manager can effectively and efficiently supervise.

➠ *Centralization:* The degree to which decision making is concentrated in the hands of a few people.

➠ *Decentralization:* The degree to which decision making is delegated to other organizational members.

➠ *Formalization:* The degree to which jobs are standardized and the extent to which employee behavior is dictated by rules and procedures.

▐▶ *Mechanistic organization:* A rigid and tightly controlled structure characterized by high specialization, rigid departmentalization, clear chain of command, narrow span of control, high formalization, limited information networking, and little participation in decision making by employees.

▐▶ *Organic organization:* A structure that's highly adaptive and flexible with little work specialization, minimal formalization, and little direct supervision of employees.

▐▶ *Virtual organization:* A network of independent companies linked by common goals and information technology.

▐▶ *Boundaryless organization:* An organization whose design is not defined by, or limited to, horizontal, vertical, or external boundaries imposed by a predefined structure.

SWEAT EQUITY

1. A custom-made candle business owned and operated by high-school students in Ozark, Missouri, has broken a national Junior Achievement sales record. The JA company surpassed $16,000 in sales in its one year of operation. The student president of the company said, "Organization was the toughest part. You learn real quick what works and what doesn't."

    - What is your interpretation of this remark? Do you agree or disagree? Why?
    - What are the implications for entrepreneurs who are looking at organizing their entrepreneurial ventures?
    - Contact your local Junior Achievement office to set up interviews with one or two student-run businesses. Discuss with them their experiences in organizing the business. What problems did they run into? How did they resolve these problems?

2. Go to the U.S. Patent and Trademark Office Web site (**www.uspto.gov**). Pick any of the topics there and compile a bulleted list of 10 items of important information. Be prepared to share your information with the class.

3. Visit with a business law professor or an attorney and ask about the importance for entrepreneurs of understanding contracts. What types of contracts might an entrepreneur face? What types of problems might arise? How can these problems be minimized or averted? Write a short report detailing the information you learned. Be prepared to share your information with the class.

4. Interview five different entrepreneurs as to their form of legal organization. Ask them why they chose that particular form of legal organization. A survey will be conducted in class to see what the most common forms of organization are.

5. Discuss the following statement in a short paper. What's your interpretation? What are the implications for entrepreneurs?

    > Over the course of time, many entrepreneurs can build their business to a particular size. But then they're unable to get it to the next level.

ENTREPRENEURSHIP IN ACTION CASES

Entrepreneurship in Action case #1 can be found at the beginning of Chapter 5.

Discussion Questions

1. How does idealab! deal with the six key elements of organizational design?

2. Is idealab!'s organizational design more of a mechanistic- or an organic-type structure? Explain.

3. Why do you think idealab!'s unique structural design works?

CASE #2: Virtually Yours

Selling ergonomic computer desks in chains such as OfficeMax and Wal-Mart doesn't exactly sound like a chaotic business in which adaptability and flexibility in organizational structure would be critical to marketing success. However, Mahmoud (Max) Ladjevardi and Bibi Kasrai (a husband-and-wife team), co-owners of Soho Inc., have found that being a virtual organization has been a wise decision.

Ladjevardi founded Soho in 1994. Although he didn't enter the business with the intent of being a virtual company, Max thought to himself, "Can I add that much value building all aspects of the company myself?" His answer was a clear and resounding "no!" So, Max and Bibi chose to handle sales and marketing out of their home office in La Jolla, California. Two employees in Milford, Massachusetts, handle orders and back office operations. Everything else is out-sourced. The company has contracts with 14 suppliers around the country: a wood fabricator in North Carolina, a metal manufacturer in Georgia, a bracket supplier in Ohio. These suppliers ship finished parts to a warehouse in Chicago where the components are boxed and shipped to customers. The company

spends no money on advertising but instead offers promotional discounts to retailers to garner premium shelf space or full pages in catalogs. With the approach Max and Bibi have chosen, they can fill orders for 10 desks or 10,000. Says Max, "If I can earn a profit with four people, why would I want to do it with ten?" Their biggest expense is the variable cost of materials. However, they have no money tied up in a factory, machinery, or warehousing space.

Max and Bibi know that their most valuable asset is the patent on their wood-and-metal desk units with adjustable shelves. A Soho desk allows users to set their own keyboard and monitor heights even if they choose to sit on the floor or stand up. In the huge market for computer desks, ergonomic designs appeal to individuals concerned about the physical ailments arising from sitting in front of a computer for an extended period of time. Well aware of the fact that the ergonomic desk patent expires in 2013, the duo are dreaming up new devices for Soho.

Discussion Questions

1. Using information from the chapter, describe Soho's organizational design.

2. Why do you think this type of organizational structure has worked for Soho? Would it work for other types of organizations? Why or why not?

3. This case is a good example of the importance of patent protection. What will Max and Bibi have to do to protect that asset now and in the long run?

4. Do some research (library or Internet) on outsourcing. What are its advantages? Its drawbacks?

(*Sources:* D. Morse, "Where's the Company?" *Wall Street Journal*, May 21, 1998, p. R19; and L. Gallagher, "The Virtual Startup," *Forbes*, August 9, 1999, p. 78.)

CASE #3: Who Needs an Attorney?

Thoughts of drowning while surfing in Baja, California, prompted James Evans to purchase a surfboard leash quick-release device. After finding nothing suitable on the market, Evans decided to invent one himself using fabric and rubber. When his fellow surfer pals enthusiastically endorsed his invention, Evans decided to patent it. Many people have this type of inspiration but when faced with the sum (anywhere from $3,000 to $10,000) they would spend on a patent attorney—more than they would possibly ever earn from royalties on the patent—they don't pursue their idea.

As a journalist for a California legal publication and author of *Law on the Net*, a book about legal resources on the Internet, Evans knew how to avoid the expense. He first checked into the Patent Office home page (**www.uspto.gov**). He searched the site using the keywords *surfboard, leash*, and *quick release* and found only four patents for inventions similar to his. With a few more clicks, he had the names of the patent holders, the dates of issuance and patent numbers, and summaries of how the inventions worked. Then he went to the IBM patent site (**www.patents.ibm**), which had sketches. After his Web search, Evans decided that the four other surfboard leash snaps weren't similar enough to pose a threat to his patent. (One used a buckle, another a pin, a third a

snap, and the fourth a foot-activated pressure release. Evans's invention used Velcro.)

The next step Evans took was to file a patent application using a book and software sold by Nolo Press. With this, he wrote a detailed description of his invention. This information, two pages of graphics, four Patent Office forms, and the filing fee were submitted to the Patent Office. Once this required material is submitted, it takes at least a year for the government agency to decide whether to issue a patent.

Discussion Questions

1. Do you think it's a good idea for individuals to do their own patent search and application? Why or why not? (Look at the advantages and disadvantages of doing so.)

2. Pretend you're an official at the USPTO looking over this application. Using the information in the chapter, does this invention meet the requirements to be patentable? Explain.

3. Go to the Nolo Press Web site (**www.nolopress.com**). Search for information on patents. Did you find this information helpful? Why or why not?

(*Source:* S. Adams, "Be Your Own Patent Lawyer," *Forbes*, October 20, 1997, pp. 188–90.)

VIDEO CASE #1: Caring Entrepreneur

Although caring may not be a word most people would normally associate with entrepreneurs, Cheryl Womack of Kansas City, Missouri, has built a $45 million company by caring about her customers and her employees. She started her business—VCW Inc., which she laughingly says stands for Very Cute Women—in 1981 in the basement of her home with one telephone and call waiting. What does VCW Inc. do? It's in the business of overseeing the National Association of Independent Truckers. VCW offers cost-effective insurance coverage, retirement benefit plans, low-interest credit cards, and other benefits to approximately 8,000 (out of 300,000 total) independent truck drivers who belong to this association. In addition, many large motor carriers who hire independent drivers also are her customers.

Womack's customers are a unique breed, indeed! Independent truck drivers "move the world" as they haul cross-country in their 18-wheelers most of the products we use every day. Independent truck drivers also are businesspeople who must run their businesses effectively and efficiently or they won't survive in this intensely competitive industry. How does VCW show that it cares about its customers? It provides an answer to a problem that many of them face: where to find cost-effective insurance coverage and other types of financial protection that other insurance companies refuse to carry. Womack believes that if you can help solve a customer's problem, you'll be successful. She and her employees have been successful at solving their customers' problems and caring about them by providing outstanding customer service. But Womack's caring approach doesn't stop with her customers. It extends to her employees as well.

Her most telling statement about her organizational philosophy is that "everything I do here is designed to cultivate and grow employees." From the beautifully designed offices to the formal dinners and travel experiences she provides, Womack sees her role as a mentor for employees, not as a boss. She wants her employees not only to do their jobs but also to recreate, redesign, and expand them. Employees can earn $1,000 for proposing suggestions that help them do their job better. VCW Inc. also has a profit-sharing plan that gives employees a stake in the company's ability to make a profit. Womack also recognizes that employees need more than financial caring. To that end, she provides on-site day care for employees' children, and employees enjoy delicious home-cooked meals at the office prepared by an employee who started at VCW in customer service but who had always dreamed of having a cooking job. Cheryl strongly believes in the power of such benefits to show employees that she cares about them and wants them to be committed and productive at their jobs.

Discussion Questions

1. In this industry, would a mechanistic- or an organic-type organization design be more appropriate? Explain your answer.
2. In the company's dealings with customers, what types of legal issues might arise? How about in dealing with employees?
3. How do you interpret Cheryl Womack's statement, "everything I do here is designed to cultivate and grow employees"? What are the organizational design implications?

(*Source:* Based on *Small Business 2000*, Show 110.)

VIDEO CASE #2: The Bean Queen

There's the Bean Queen. There are Bean Counters. And, there are Human Beans. All found at Buckeye Beans and Herbs in Spokane, Washington. Jill Smith is the Bean Queen. She's a self-proclaimed hippie artist turned entrepreneur who started her company in 1983 with an investment of $1,000. From that small, inauspicious beginning, Buckeye Beans now has sales revenues approaching $8 million and employs 50 people (human beans). Buckeye Beans has been quite innovative in expanding its product line. The product line, which started out with one product, Buckeye Bean Soup, now includes a line of all-natural soups, chili, bread mixes, and pasta. It pioneered the special-occasion-shaped pasta; that is, pasta shaped like Christmas trees, hearts, bunnies, dolphins, leafs, grapes, baseballs, and even golf balls. But what strikes you most about Buckeye Beans isn't its unique products—it's the unusual organizational approach that melds this company together.

That unusual organizational approach is reflected in the company's simple mission statement: *Make people smile.* Jill's belief is that cooking should be fun and that the experience of cooking can be a fun escape, not a drudgery. That's why the first ingredient listed on all Buckeye's product packages is a cup of good wine for the cook. Buckeye's strategy that its products go beyond just a simple bag of beans and instead serve as entertainment is also seen in the company's HEHE principle: humor, education, health, and environment.

That's what Jill, husband Doug, and other Buckeye employees believe in and value.

Many of Buckeye's employees are family members and long-time friends. They share like values. Although Jill admits that her organizational approach wouldn't work for every organization, she does think it's important for entrepreneurs to identify their basic values and what they're trying to accomplish. She suggests asking what kinds of values are important and what kind of organization is desired. For Buckeye Beans, the approach has been to create a "different" type of company—a new model—in which the business is run and employee and customer relationships operate on the basis of trust, confidence, loyalty, and working hard together to get something done.

Discussion Questions

1. What would be the advantages and drawbacks of having an organization filled with family members and friends? Will this approach continue to be effective and efficient as the organization grows? Explain.

2. Trust, confidence, loyalty, and working hard together are important values. However, can an organization be designed to provide the type of environment that promotes these values? How?

3. Take the six key elements of organizational design and describe the approach that Buckeye Beans is taking with each.

(Source: Based on Small Business 2000, Show 203.)

ENDNOTES

1. E. Matson, "He Turns Ideas into Companies—At Net Speed," *Fast Company*, December–January 1997, pp. 34–36; J. Useem, "The Start-Up Factory," *Inc.*, February 1997, pp. 40–52; A. Marsh, "Promiscuous Breeding," *Forbes*, April 7, 1997, pp. 74–77; L. Armstrong and R. Grover, "Bill Gross, Online Idea Factory," *Business Week*, June 29, 1998, pp. 100–2; D. Clark, "Entrepreneur Launches New Firm to Help Web Shoppers Provide Billing Information," *Wall Street Journal*, November 25, 1998, p. B7; and idealab! Web page (**www.idealab.com**).

2. L. Saunders, "Freedom Day for Small Business," *Forbes*, February 22, 1999, pp. 128–30.

3. "Ask Success," *Success*, August 1998, p. 29.

4. W. D. Keller, *The Essentials of Business Law, I* (Piscataway, NJ: Research and Education Association, 1998), pp. 64–74.

5. See, for example, R. L. Daft, *Organization Theory and Design*, 6th ed. (St. Paul, NJ: West Publishing, 1998).

6. T. Burns and G. M. Stalker, *The Management of Innovation* (London: Tavistock, 1961); and D. A. Morand, "The Role of Behavioral Formality and Informality in the Enactment of Bureaucratic versus Organic Organizations," *Academy of Management Review*, October 1995, pp. 831–72.

7. For additional readings on boundaryless oganizations, see "The Boundaryless Organization: Break the Chains of Organizational Structures," *HR Focus*, April 1996, p. 21; R. M. Hodgetts, "A Conversation with Steve Kerr," *Organizational Dynamics*, spring 1996, pp. 68–79; and J. Gebhardt, "The Boundaryless Organization," *Sloan Management Review*, winter 1996, pp. 117–19. For another perspective on boundaryless organizations, see B. Victor, "The Dark Side of the New Organizational Forms: An Editorial Essay," *Organization Science*, November 1994, pp. 479–82.

8. R. W. Keidel, "Rethinking Organizational Design," *Academy of Management Executive*, November 1994, pp. 12–27; R. Ashkenas, D. Ulrich, T. Jick, and S. Kerr, *The Boundaryless Organization: Breaking the Chains of Organization Structure* (San Francisco: Jossey-Bass, 1995); P. LaBarre, "The Seamless Enterprise," *IW*, June 19, 1995, pp. 22–34; D. Ulrich and S. Kerr, "Creating the Boundaryless Organization: The Radical Reconstruction of Organization Capabilities," *Planning Review*, September–October 1995, pp. 41–45; and A. Majchrazk and Q. Wang, "Breaking the Functional Mindset in Process Organizations," *Harvard Business Review*, September–October 1996, pp. 93–99.

6

LAUNCHING THE VENTURE

LEARNING OBJECTIVES

After reading this chapter, you should be able to:

1. Explain the purposes of goals.
2. Describe the characteristics of good goals.
3. Describe the kinds of goals that entrepreneurial ventures might pursue.
4. Explain how to set goals.
5. Discuss the importance of strategies to entrepreneurial ventures.
6. Describe the coordinative relationship between goals and strategies.
7. Explain specific technology and operations, marketing, information systems, and financial and accounting strategies.

ENTREPRENEURSHIP IN ACTION CASE #1

The King of Underwear

Nicholas Graham is the king of underwear and the self-proclaimed "Chief Underpants Officer."[1] His Joe Boxer brand of underwear has grown into a global brand on the strength of its exceptionally wacky and fun boxers and briefs. Underwear, sleepwear, and loungewear for men, women, and kids represent the company's core business.

The San Francisco–based Joe Boxer Company (**www. joeboxer.com**) was founded in 1985 on the premise that the most basic and utilitarian element of men's clothing should be remade to reflect humor, fashion, and the shifting trends in American culture. Over the years, Graham has guided his company with a bold plan and specific goals. He understood that the clothing industry (even the "under" clothing industry) was intensely competitive and being successful in such an environment would require bold strategic choices.

The company firmly believes in innovation and creativity and

You might be saying to yourself about now, "What a strange company!" However strange and wacky it may appear, Nicholas Graham's Joe Boxer Company has carved a successful niche for itself. From his original idea to change the way the world looked at men's underwear to the unique Joe Boxer Cab program, Graham has fashioned an assortment of strategies to launch and operate his entrepreneurial venture. In this chapter, we're going to look at the process of launching an entrepreneurial venture. Once the venture has been planned and organized, it's time to get it actually going. Doing that involves establishing goals and strategies for the organization's key work activities. These key work activities typically revolve around technology and operations methods, marketing, information systems, and financial and accounting systems. As we look at each of these key areas, we'll be examining the specific types of strategies that entrepreneurs might choose. Before we get into the specifics in these areas, however, we need to explore what's involved with establishing goals and strategies.

ESTABLISHING GOALS AND STRATEGIES

Without goals and strategies, there would be no coherent organizational decisions or direction. Once the vision and mission are outlined, the business plan crafted, and the organizational legal and structural decisions made, it's time for the entrepreneur to think about more specific issues of what the entrepreneurial venture hopes to accomplish and how it will do so. Rather than rushing headfirst into the unknown with no thought given to the future (even in the dynamic, often chaotic environments of entrepreneurial ventures), it's important to take the time to establish goals and strategies. In this section, we're going to discuss what goals and strategies are and the process entrepreneurs use in developing them.

Goals

Remember that we defined **goals** earlier in Chapter 4 as outcomes or end results that are desired by individuals, groups, or entire organizations. Although some individuals make a distinction between goals and objectives—they maintain that goals are more general and objectives are more specific—we're going to use the terms *goals* and *objectives* interchangeably. But no matter what we call them, why is it important to have goals? Goals serve three main purposes. (See Figure 6-1.)

Purposes of Goals. First, goals direct the entrepreneur

emphasizes these core values in product design, merchandising, marketing, customer service, and all business functions. However, in this business, marketing and publicity strategies are the bread and butter of Joe Boxer's operation. For instance, in 1994, Graham launched the world's largest e-mail message center on a billboard in Times Square. This type of marketing approach is critical to Joe Boxer's identity as a fun, wacky, and exciting entrepreneurial business. Many of the company's marketing strategies are tied in to socially responsible activities. One of its newest marketing innovations is the Joe Boxer Cab that cruises the streets of New York and San Francisco. The best part is that 100 percent of the cab fares collected go to breast cancer research through General Motors' charity venture Concept:Cure. Graham states that "I guess the more people talk about you, the better. Joe Boxer is very eccentric."

Figure 6-1

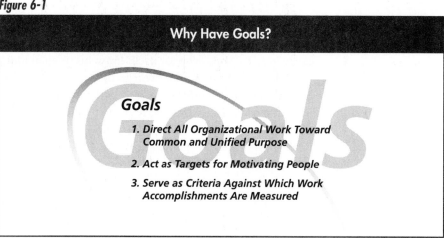

Why Have Goals?

Goals

1. *Direct All Organizational Work Toward Common and Unified Purpose*

2. *Act as Targets for Motivating People*

3. *Serve as Criteria Against Which Work Accomplishments Are Measured*

and any other organizational members toward a common and unified organizational purpose (remember, this common and unified purpose is known as the organizational vision). Goals can help organizational members understand where the organization is going and why it's vital to get there. This is particularly important for entrepreneurial ventures in which, in the chaotic and uncertain environment, it may be easy to lose sight of what we're doing. Another reason goals are important is that they provide targets organizational members may be motivated to work toward accomplishing.[2] Motivation, very simply, is the willingness to put forth effort in the accomplishment of some activity. Don't you work a little harder, aren't you a little more motivated, when you have a goal you're trying to reach? Maybe it's getting an A grade in a course you're taking or getting that term paper done one week before it's actually due. Whatever the goal might be, it serves as a target that you put forth effort and work hard to meet. The same is true for organizational goals, except in this case, the goals may revolve around completing an advertising campaign for a new product or finding ways to lower shipping expenses. Finally, goals serve as criteria against which work accomplishments and performance are measured. How do you know how efficiently or effectively you're doing something if there's nothing to measure against? Goals provide that measurement standard. They give us some guide as to what we should be working to accomplish. How would an entrepreneur know whether he has been successful in his efforts without some way of measuring and comparing what was done? Goals serve as a way to measure success. Actual work outcomes and results are measured against whatever goals were established. For example, did revenues increase by x amount? Was the product development schedule met? Was cash flow positive? Without something to measure against, we'd never know whether what we're doing is the best thing for us to be doing or whether we're doing it the best possible way.

As you can see, goals do play an important role in an entrepreneurial venture for several reasons. But it's also important to understand that there are different types of goals an entrepreneur needs to establish. Let's take a look at these.

Types of Goals. At first glance, it might seem that a business organization would have only one objective—to make a profit. However, it's not quite that simple. All organizations have different types of goals. Because there are a variety of work activities to be pursued in an entrepreneurial venture and because no one single measure can evaluate whether an organization is successful, entrepreneurs need to establish several goals. (See Figure 6-2.)

As you can see, there are four ways to describe the goals of an entrepreneurial venture: breadth, time frame, specificity, and area. The breadth category covers how broad-based or narrow the organizational goals are. **Organization-wide goals** are ones that establish broad purposes, apply to the entire entrepreneurial venture, and seek to successfully position the venture in terms of its environment. These goals are broad in nature and tend to encompass the entire spectrum of what the entrepreneurial venture hopes to accomplish. These organization-wide goals stem from the organizational vision and provide broad targets for organizational members to accomplish. On the other hand, **operational goals** are ones that specify details associated with accomplishing the organization-wide goals. The operational goals are much narrower in their focus and serve to subdivide the organization-wide goals into more specific targets.

Time frame is another way to describe an entrepreneurial venture's goals. By definition, a goal is something to be accomplished in the future. What this category of goals describes is how far away that "future" is. The difference in years between short term and long term has shortened considerably. It used to be that long term meant anything over seven or even ten years. Try to imagine what you

Figure 6-2

would like to be doing in seven years, and you can begin to appreciate the difficulty of establishing goals that far in the future. Therefore, we're going to define **long-term goals** as ones with a time frame beyond three years.[3] **Short-term goals** are ones that cover one year or less. Goals in between these two categories can be referred to as intermediate-term goals, but they aren't normally specified. Although these time classifications (that is, three years and one year) are fairly common, any desired time frame can be designated by the entrepreneur. Whatever time frame is used, entrepreneurs do need to have both long-term and short-term goals. Long-term goals provide a coherent and unified target for the entrepreneurial venture whereas short-term goals provide the stepping-stones to the future. It's like building a house where you have the long-term goal of having a solid, functional, and enjoyable living space. But to get to that point, you have to accomplish certain short-term goals along the way, such as getting the foundation poured, the plumbing installed, and the floors carpeted. The accomplishment of these short-term goals contributes to the accomplishment of the long-term goal. It's the same thing with an entrepreneurial venture in which it's important to accomplish the short-term goals in order to reach the long-term goals.

The next category describes how specific the organizational goals are. **Specific goals** are ones that are clearly defined and leave no room for interpretation. There's no ambiguity and no problem with misunderstanding about what is intended to be accomplished. Although it may seem preferable to have goals as specific as possible, there are drawbacks to having specific goals. They require clarity and a sense of predictability that typically do not exist in an entrepreneurial environment. When uncertainty is high and decision makers must be flexible

---

Entrepreneurs in Action ▶

Wiley Mullins is a good example of how entrepreneurs must set goals on the road to success. He knew his Healthy Southern Classics line of food seasonings was a winner if he could just get supermarkets to sample them. But first he had to overcome their reluctance to try fat-free and cholesterol-free versions of seasonings for traditional southern cooking. With no proven demand track record for his products, Mullins had an uphill battle. However, he first set a short-term goal to get into one major food chain and to work from there. He also had a long-term goal of seeing his face on his packages smiling down at customers from gleaming grocery shelves all across the country. Today, Mullins has 15 employees and annual revenues of around $9 million. You can see Wiley's face smiling on his packages found in a number of top grocery chains including Safeway, Stop & Shop, and Wal-Mart.

Source: B. Deterline, "A Man for All Seasonings," *Smart Money*, April 1999, pp. 155–58.

in order to respond to unexpected changes, it is preferable to use **directional goals**, which are flexible enough to provide focus and general guidelines but do not lock decision makers into specific courses of action. The flexibility of directional goals must be weighed against the loss of clarity provided by specific ones.

One thing that you may have noticed after reading the descriptions of these first three categories of goals (organization-wide versus operational, long term versus short term, and specific versus directional) is the strong similarities among them. Well, you're very perceptive! In fact, organization-wide goals tend to be long term and directional whereas operational goals tend to be short term and specific. The important thing to recognize is that entrepreneurs need to establish both broad, directional, long-term goals *and* narrow, specific, short-term goals. All these different types of goals are needed in the last category of goals we need to examine—areas of organizational work.

The final category of types of goals covers the various areas of organizational work. The most common organizational work areas include technology and operations methods, marketing, and financial. (Please note that the human resource area is an important work area, also. However, we don't cover it here because we think it's so important that a whole chapter is devoted to it—Chapter 8.) Therefore, an entrepreneur would want to set technology and operations goals, marketing goals, and financial goals. But, be aware that not all organizations do the same type of work. Entrepreneurs should establish area goals for the particular types of work activity that characterize their entrepreneurial ventures. So whether the venture is a restaurant, a software design firm, or a medical equipment laboratory, the area goals should reflect the specialized work that is done.

Now that we've discussed all the types of goals that are important for an entrepreneur to establish, we need to look at how these goals are developed. What's involved in the process of setting goals? However, before we explain the steps in the goal-setting process, we need to look at the characteristics of "good" goals.

Characteristics of Good Goals. Goals are not all created equal! Some goals are better than others. How do you tell the difference? What makes a goal a "good" goal? Table 6-1 outlines the characteristics of good goals.

A good goal should be written in terms of outcomes rather than actions. The desired end result is the most important element of any goal and, therefore, the goal should be written to reflect this. Next, a goal should be measurable and quantifiable. It's much easier to determine if a goal has been met if it's measurable. For instance, suppose one of your goals is to "produce a high-quality product." What exactly do you mean by high quality? Because there are numerous ways to define quality, you

TABLE 6-1 Characteristics of Good Goals	
▲ Written in terms of outcomes rather than actions	▲ Challenging yet attainable
▲ Measurable and quantifiable	▲ Written down
▲ Clear as to a time frame	▲ Communicated to all organizational members

should be stating specifically how you will measure whether or not the product is high quality. This means that even in areas where it may be difficult to quantify your intent, you should try to find some specific way or ways to measure whether that goal is accomplished. Otherwise, why have the goal if you can't measure whether it's met? In line with specifying a quantifiable measure of accomplishment, a good goal should also be clear as to a time frame. Although open-ended goals may seem preferable because of their supposed flexibility, in fact, goals without a time frame make an organization less flexible because you're never sure when the goal has been met or when you should call it quits because the goal will never be met regardless of how long you work at it. A good goal will specify a time frame for accomplishment. Next, a good goal should be challenging yet attainable. Goals that are too easy to accomplish are not motivating and neither are goals that are not attainable even with exceptional effort. To provide high levels of individual motivation, goals should be challenging yet attainable. Next, good goals are written down. Although actually writing down goals may seem to be a ridiculous waste of time, the process of writing the goals forces the entrepreneur to think them through. In addition, the written goals become visible and tangible evidence of the importance of working toward something—something specific that is important to the entrepreneur to accomplish. After all, if it isn't important enough to identify and accomplish, why have the goal in the first place? Finally, good goals are communicated to all organizational members. This may not be necessary in an entrepreneurial venture with one person (the entrepreneur), but becomes extremely important as additional people join the organization. It's crucial that these individuals know what end results are being pursued. Particularly, in a growing entrepreneurial venture, goals need to be communicated so everyone is aware of them. This, in turn, helps ensure that all organizational members are "on the same page" and working in ways to ensure the accomplishment of the organizational goals.

The question now becomes How do I set good goals? What process do I follow in establishing organizational goals? Figure 6-3 illustrates the seven steps in the goal-setting process.

The Goal-Setting Process. Sitting down and writing out goals is not something that most entrepreneurs look forward to doing. However, as we've discussed, it is important to have written goals. The process of writing goals can be made easier by following these seven steps.

Step 1. Review the organizational vision and mission(s). These broad statements of what the entrepreneurial venture's purpose is and what it hopes to accomplish provide an overall guide to what the entrepreneur and other organizational members think is important. As we stated in Chapter 4, the vision and mission are future oriented (just like goals

The **Grey** *Zone* One potential ethical dilemma that entrepreneurs need to be aware of as they work on setting good goals is the focus on outcomes rather than actions. Although it's important in writing good goals to identify the desired end result, you don't want to give the impression that achieving this goal is important even if you have to act unethically or irresponsibly to do so. When organizational (or individual) performance results are evaluated only on outcomes, there are increased pressures to do "whatever is necessary" to look good by achieving the desired outcomes. How can entrepreneurs get the best of both worlds—the desired focus on end results and being ethical and responsible while achieving these ends? What would you recommend that entrepreneurs do to deal with this ethical dilemma?

Figure 6-3

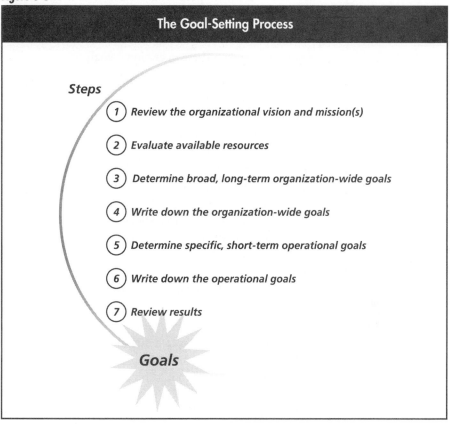

The Goal-Setting Process

Steps

1. *Review the organizational vision and mission(s)*

2. *Evaluate available resources*

3. *Determine broad, long-term organization-wide goals*

4. *Write down the organization-wide goals*

5. *Determine specific, short-term operational goals*

6. *Write down the operational goals*

7. *Review results*

Goals

are). Therefore, it's important to review these statements before writing goals because organizational goals should be established in light of what the vision and mission statements profess.

Step 2. Evaluate available resources. You wouldn't want to set goals that are impossible to achieve given your available resources. Even though goals should be challenging, they should be realistic. After all, if the resources you have to work with won't allow you to achieve a goal no matter how hard you try or how much effort is put forth, that goal shouldn't be set. That would be like the person with a $50,000 annual income and no other financial resources setting a goal of building a $1 million house in two years. No matter how hard he or she works at it, it's not going to happen!

Step 3. Determine individually or with input from other organizational members broad, long-term organization-wide goals. In order for these organization-wide goals to provide an entrepreneur with a sense of what the overall entrepreneurial venture hopes to achieve, they should be measurable and indicate a time frame; for instance, achieving a 2 percent market share penetration within three years or bringing out a new product every year for the next four years.

Step 4. Write down these organization-wide goals. You already know why written goals are important!

Step 5. Determine individually or with input from other organizational members specific, short-term operational goals. These goals reflect the desired outcomes in the various areas of operational work activities and are congruent with the organization-wide goals. They should be measurable, specific, and include a time frame.

Step 6. Write down these operational goals.

Step 7. Review results and whether goals are being met. Make changes as needed. Given the fast-paced dynamic nature of entrepreneurial organizations, this can be a real challenge. However, to keep from focusing resources and efforts on nonimportant activities and to keep from wasting resources, it's important to know whether the established goals are being achieved. Because the established goals serve to direct efforts, energies, and resources in appropriate ways, if we know that the goals aren't being met, we can redirect our activities and resources.

Now that we have a well-defined set of goals, what next? At this point, the entrepreneur should develop specific strategies to accomplish the goals.

Strategies

In this section, we want to discuss why strategies are important to entrepreneurial ventures and introduce the different types of strategies entrepreneurial ventures might pursue. However, before we can do this, we first need to know exactly what a **strategy** is. We're going to define it as a plan of action for accomplishing organizational goals. Specific strategies need to be developed so the venture's long-term organization-wide goals and short-term operational goals can be achieved. They do, indeed, play an important role in how well the entrepreneurial venture ultimately performs.[4]

Why are strategies important to entrepreneurial ventures? They are important to develop because they provide the "how's" of goal achievement. Whereas the goals themselves indicate "what" it is the entrepreneur hopes to accomplish, the strategies outline "how" the goals are going to be met. The goals and strategies must coordinate with each other in order for the venture to run smoothly. This relationship is illustrated in Figure 6-4.

As we've stated many times, the organizational vision and mission statements provide a broad overview of what the entrepreneurial venture is going to do and how it's going to do it. Using the vision and mission statements as guides, the organization-wide goals are developed. From these broad goals, then, the operational goals are developed. The operational goals are pursued through the development and implementation of various operational strategies. If the strategies are effective, the operational goals are achieved. The achievement of these goals, then, becomes the mechanism for the accomplishment of the organization-wide goals. This is what is known in management theory as the **means–end chain**, the integrated collection of organizational goals in which higher-level goals (*ends*) are inextricably linked to lower-level goals and strategies because these lower-level goals and strategies serve as the *means* for accomplishing those organization-wide ends. Using our previous example of an organization-wide goal of achieving a 2 percent market share penetration within three years, we would need to specify operational goals and strategies probably in the areas of marketing, product development, and technology and operations methods (or in whatever other operational areas we feel are critical) in order to be able to achieve that organization-wide goal. If the short-term operational goals aren't

Figure 6-4

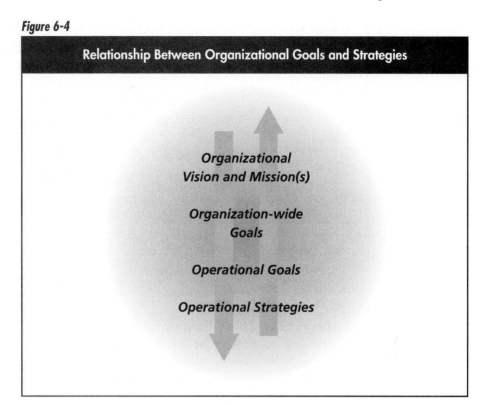

Relationship Between Organizational Goals and Strategies

*Organizational
Vision and Mission(s)*

*Organization-wide
Goals*

Operational Goals

Operational Strategies

achieved through the implementation of various operational strategies, there's no way that the long-term organization-wide goals are going to be met. The strategies are the ways organizational goals are pursued and ultimately achieved.

What we need to look at next are the various operational areas that entrepreneurs must address. As we study these, we'll be discussing the different strategic choices that entrepreneurs must consider. We're going to look first at the area of technology and operations methods.

Rapid Review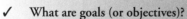

✓ What are goals (or objectives)?

✓ What purposes do goals serve?

✓ Describe the four categories of organizational goals and the types of goals within each category.

✓ What characteristics do good goals have?

✓ Outline the steps in the goal-setting process.

✓ What is a strategy?

✓ Why are strategies important to entrepreneurial ventures?

✓ Describe the connection between goals and strategies.

TECHNOLOGY AND OPERATIONS METHODS

By this point in your life, you've obviously purchased and used an incredible number and variety of products and services. Where do these products come from? How do they get made? You may have produced some yourself—for example, if you've ever grown produce in a garden, built a bookshelf out of wood and bricks, fashioned a wreath out of twigs and grapevines, or baked a loaf of bread—but most of the products we consume and use are produced (made) by someone else. The process of creating products (goods and services) in which organizational inputs (resources) are transformed into outputs is called **production**. The production process

Figure 6-5

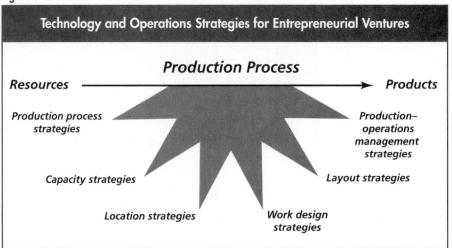

used to create physical (tangible) products is fairly obvious. However, even the creation of services requires some types of transformation activities. What are these *transformation activities* used to create products and services? Very simply, they are the various technology and operations strategies. So whether our entrepreneurial venture is producing goods or services, we need to decide what technology and operations strategies we'll use to produce our product or service. What we'll look at in this section are some of the common strategic choices in this area. Figure 6-5 illustrates the possible technology and operations strategies.

Production Process Strategies

How are you going to transform your available resources into the products or services that your entrepreneurial venture will market? In other words, what's the "best way" to produce the desired products? Different organizations use different approaches to do this, but all involve a certain production process strategy. The production process strategy decision focuses on the approach that the entrepreneurial venture will use to transform resources into goods and services. The goal of your production process strategy is to find a way to produce your products or services so they meet (or exceed) customer expectations in light of cost and other organizational constraints. Your decision(s) in this area involve choosing the most appropriate production process strategy given the nature of your product. The type of process strategy you choose will have a long-run effect on how efficient your production activities are as well as the flexibility, cost, and quality of the products you're producing. There are three possible choices:

1. The *process-focused* strategy is one in which the organization's technology and operations methods are organized around the processes necessary to produce a customized product or service. This strategy would be appropriate for situations where the entrepreneur is producing high-variety, low-volume products such as gourmet meals, specialized print jobs, or custom-designed Web pages. In this strategy, the most important production decisions are focused on the actual processes used in producing the custom-made, specialized

products. That is, the entrepreneur must carefully consider the way the product or service is produced and make sure that production process design decisions are focused on the actual process itself.

2. A *product-focused* strategy is one in which the organization's technology and operations methods are organized around the products or service. This strategy would be appropriate for producing high-volume, low-variety products—for example, computer chips, potato chips, or wood chips. With this strategy, the most important production decisions are focused on the actual products, not on the process used to make them. The production process would not have to be complex because the products being produced are not complex. Instead, this approach means making sure that the production process supports the efficient production of these products.

3. The *repetitive-focused* strategy is one that falls somewhere between process focused and product focused. In this production approach, standardized component parts, typically called modules, are used to assemble standardized products. There's more customizing of the product than in the product-focused strategy, but not as much as in the process-focused approach. An example would be an assembly line where motorcycles are produced to customer specifications using standardized component parts. Or, another example might be a fast-food restaurant where the product is assembled to a customer's order using standardized components (same-size buns, same-size hamburger patty, measured amounts of condiments).

Which production process strategy is most appropriate for the entrepreneurial venture depends on the volume and variety of products being produced. The entrepreneur must also consider factors such as how important it is to keep costs low, to provide high levels of quality, or to meet specialized customer needs better. Looking at all these technology and operations factors is important in choosing the most appropriate production process strategy.

Entrepreneurs in Action

Sometimes the most appropriate production process strategy may be *not* to do it yourself. For Cherie Serota and Jody Gardner, co-owners of New York–based maternity clothing manufacturer Belly Basics, outsourcing certain work proved to be the best approach for them. **Outsourcing** involves subcontracting services and operations to other organizations that can do the job better or less expensively. However, even though Serota and Gardner were able to outsource certain production functions, they found through trial and error that they would not outsource anything that had to do with creative and design tasks.

Source: S. Greco, "Go Right to the Outsource," *Inc.*, February 1999, p. 39.

Capacity Strategies

Another important technology and operations strategy involves production capacity. Capacity is the maximum possible output of an organization in a given time period. It's a constraint on how much product can be produced by the entrepreneur or the entrepreneurial venture. Capacity influences how much physical space and equipment are needed to produce the desired number of products. After all, you don't want to have too much or too little capacity. That could prove to be a significant financial drain on your entrepreneurial venture—either you're losing money because you don't have enough product because you lack the space to produce more or you're paying for too much space you don't need. Some strategic decisions associated with determining appropriate production capacity include demand management and capacity management. Let's look first at demand management.

How do entrepreneurial organizations "manage" demand? They'll use strategies such as staffing changes (adding or laying off employees), adjusting equipment (purchase, lease, or sell), improving work methods to be more efficient, or redesigning the product so more (or fewer) can be produced. Another factor that may need to be considered in managing demand is whether there's a seasonal demand for your venture's products. If there is, capacity will likely need to expand during the time of high demand (unless you happen to have excess capacity) and shrink during non-seasonal times. It's important for the entrepreneur when considering demand management strategies to also consider strategies for managing capacity. These strategic choices work hand-in-hand and should complement each other.

Capacity management involves decisions about how to use the current facilities and equipment effectively and efficiently. Part of this strategy involves knowing breakeven point, which we discussed in Chapter 4. You want to make sure you have enough capacity to support the production level necessary to reach breakeven point. On the other hand, though, you don't want to have too *much*

Global Perspectives

Although market sales success is something that most entrepreneurs work hard to achieve, this success can bring about production challenges, especially in terms of capacity to produce the desired demand. Carla Haeussler Baudillo of Puerto Rico had this problem, albeit a good one! Baudillo's company, Carla's Sweets Corporation, produces bite-size miniatures of merengue, a favorite Caribbean dessert. When she first whipped them up, the desserts sold like hotcakes at her parents' gourmet café. With this initial positive reaction from customers, Baudillo went from store to store and soon landed accounts with the island's top grocery stores and movie theater chains. However, all this sales success meant larger and larger production facilities. During the first five years of her business's operations, the company moved four times because it outgrew its current facilities. Both demand management and capacity management strategies were important to the company's continued success.

Source: J. P. Marino, "Success Is Sweets," *Business Week Enterprise*, March 1, 1999, p. ENT22.

capacity, either. Paying for excess capacity and equipment would not be a wise use of an entrepreneurial venture's often limited resources. Finally, part of the capacity management strategy may involve forecasting future capacity requirements in order to assure that facilities and equipment are available when needed. It's important to do some planning ahead in order to have the necessary space and equipment.

Location Strategies

One of the most important technology and operations decisions for entrepreneurs is where to locate. The decision basically boils down to this: Will you operate your entrepreneurial venture out of your home or from another location? Because the choice of location significantly influences costs and revenues, the objective of your location strategy should be to maximize the benefits and minimize the costs of locating in a particular area. What factors may affect the location strategy of an entrepreneurial venture? It's important to consider labor costs and availability (if your organization needs or may someday need additional employees), proximity to needed raw materials and suppliers, proximity to markets (customers), state and local government policies and regulations, environmental regulations, availability and cost of utilities, site costs (lease or buy), transportation availability, and quality of life issues. Each of these factors can influence what is the most appropriate choice for locating the entrepreneurial venture. Keep in mind that one or some of these factors may be more critical than others to your organization and thus be more important to your decision about where you choose to produce your product.

Work Design Strategies

What are work design strategies and why are they important to the technology and operations decisions of the entrepreneurial venture? First of all, these strategies are important to the technology and operations methods of the entrepreneurial venture because they determine who can do what work, when they can do it, and under what conditions. They, very simply, address the way your entrepreneurial venture's work is going to be done. Some of the more common work design strategies that entrepreneurs may choose involve job specialization (tasks are divided up into specialized components with organizational employees performing one or a couple of these specialized components), job enlargement (organizational employees are given a number of tasks to do rather than specializing in just one), job enrichment (organizational employees are given the responsibility for doing the task *and* responsibilities for planning and controlling), ergonomics (designing physically efficient and safe work approaches), work methods (determining the processes and procedures for performing tasks), and motivation and incentive systems (deciding how individuals will be rewarded for their efforts in completing assigned tasks). Work design often also involves establishing standards for different jobs and different levels of output for those jobs. Organizational employees need to know what work output (quantity and quality) is desired and expected.

Layout Strategies

How a facility is arranged has a significant impact on operational efficiency. The objective of an entrepreneurial venture's layout strategy is to design a layout that's economical and meets the requirements of product design and volume, process equipment and capacity, quality of work life for organizational employees, and building and site constraints. There are six potential layout strategies:

1. The *fixed-position layout* is one in which the product remains stationary and requires workers and equipment to come to the work area. Some examples include building a bridge, erecting an apartment building, building sailboats, or dousing a burning oil well fire.

2. The *process-oriented layout* is appropriate for low-volume, high-variety products in which the focus is on the processes being used to create the product or service. Some examples might include a medical clinic, a cafeteria kitchen, or a job shop that produces thermostats.

3. The *office layout* positions workers, equipment, and office spaces to provide for movement of information. Some examples include an insurance company, an advertising agency, or a computer software design firm.

4. The *retail–service layout* arranges people and equipment according to customers' needs and behaviors. Obviously, the objective behind any retail layout is to maximize profitability per square foot of shelf space or floor space—that is, putting the products where customers are going to try and buy. Examples might include a grocery store, a clothing store, or an office-products store.

5. The *warehouse layout* is designed to find the optimum trade-off between product handling cost and warehouse space. Examples include any type of warehouse, storage, or distribution facility.

6. The *product-oriented layout* is organized around a product or group of similar high-volume, low-variety products. In this type of repetitive, continuous production, it's important to have layout arrangements that maximize people and machine utilization. Examples might include a meatpacking facility or a furniture manufacturer.

Rapid Review

✓ Describe transformation activities and how they relate to production.

✓ What are the three possible production process strategies and how are they different?

✓ What is outsourcing?

✓ What are the strategic decisions associated with capacity?

✓ What factors affect the location strategy of an entrepreneurial venture?

✓ What are the different work design strategies, and why are they important to entrepreneurial ventures?

✓ Describe the six potential layout strategies.

✓ What types of strategies might be needed in the area of managing operations?

By looking at the various options, the entrepreneur can determine which layout strategy will best fit the demands and requirements of the production process being used in the entrepreneurial venture. An appropriately designed layout strategy can make the production process as efficient as possible.

Production and Operations Management Strategies

An entrepreneur might use other types of technology and operations strategies that are associated with the production process. For instance, the entrepreneur may need to make some strategic decisions about using a just-in-time production system, purchasing management procedures, inventory management systems, project management procedures, or maintenance management. Each of these strategies is aimed at making the venture's production process as efficient and effective as possible.

Once strategies for the technology and operations area have been determined, the entrepreneur is ready to look at developing some appropriate marketing strategies. We know how the product is going to be produced, now how do we market it? That's the area we want to look at next.

MARKETING STRATEGIES

An entrepreneurial venture's marketing strategies are critical. **Marketing** is defined as a process of assessing and meeting an individual's or group's wants and needs by creating, offering, and exchanging products of value. The two biggest factors in marketing are the two Cs—customers and competitors. All the entrepreneurial organization's marketing strategies are directed at effectively and efficiently managing these two groups. The main marketing strategies we're going to discuss involve segmentation or target market selection, differentiation, and marketing mix (the 4 Ps: product, pricing, promotion, and place). Let's look at some of the most common strategic options for each of these areas. (See Table 6-2.)

Segmentation or Target Market Selection Strategies

Every market consists of potential or actual customers. These customers may differ in one or more ways. These differences can be used to segment a market. Market segments are large, identifiable groups within a market. At the most basic

---

TABLE 6-2   Marketing Strategies for Entrepreneurial Ventures

Segmentation Strategies

- Geographic
- Demographic
- Psychographic
- Behavioral

Target Market Selection Strategies

- Single segment concentration
- Selective specialization
- Product specialization
- Market specialization
- Full market coverage

Differentiation Strategies

- Product itself
- Services
- Personnel
- Image

Marketing Mix Strategies

- Product
  - New product development
  - Product line
  - Brand
  - Packaging and labeling
  - Product life cycle decisions
- Pricing
  - Markup pricing
  - Target return pricing
  - Perceived-value pricing
  - Value pricing
  - Going-rate pricing
  - Sealed-bid pricing
  - Geographical pricing
  - Price discounts and allowances
  - Promotional pricing
  - Discriminatory pricing
  - Product mix pricing

- Promotion
  - Advertising
  - Billboards
  - Point-of-purchase displays
  - Symbols and logos
  - Packaging inserts
  - Sales promotion
  - Public relations
  - Personal selling
  - Direct marketing
- Place
  - Channel choice
  - Market logistics
  - Inventory
  - Transportation modes/carriers

level, an entrepreneurial venture may choose a marketing strategy either to segment (divide) the market into different groups or to treat it as one homogeneous market. If entrepreneurs choose to segment their markets, they can select from several different segmentation variables. The major strategic choices for segmenting consumer markets are *geographic* (region, city or metropolitan area, population density, and climate); *demographic* (age, gender, family size, family life cycle, income, occupation, education, religion, race, and nationality); *psychographic* (social class, lifestyle, attitudes toward various societal situations, and personality); and *behavioral* (occasion of product use, benefits, user status, usage rate, loyalty status, readiness to purchase, and attitude toward product). If the entrepreneurial venture sells products or services to the business market, the major strategic approaches to segmenting these markets include demographic (industry type, company size, and location); operating variables (technology, user–nonuser status, and customer capabilities); purchasing approaches (purchasing department, power structure, nature of existing relationships, general purchasing policies, and purchasing criteria); situational factors (urgency, specific applications, and size or order); and personal characteristics (buyer–seller similarity, attitudes toward risk, and loyalty). Once possible customer segments have been identified, the next step is to determine which ones are the most attractive targets for selling our product.

Target market selection can take one of five possible strategic approaches: (1) *Single segment concentration* is when the entrepreneur selects a single segment (out of all possible segments) to target. (2) *Selective specialization* means the entrepreneur chooses to serve a number of equally attractive and appropriate segments that have little or no common characteristics. (3) The *product specialization* strategy is one in which the entrepreneurial venture concentrates on making a certain product that's sold to several segments. (4) In the *market specialization* strategy, the organization serves many needs of a particular segment or customer group.

(5) The *full market coverage* strategy means that the entrepreneurial venture is attempting to serve all customer groups (segments) with all the products they might need or desire.

After deciding the segmentation and target market selection strategies for the entrepreneurial venture, an entrepreneur has a good idea of the customer group (or groups) that he or she hopes to target. However, the design of appropriate marketing strategies doesn't stop here. Now, the entrepreneur must decide how to get that customer group to notice his or her product over others' products. That's where the differentiation strategies come in.

Differentiation Strategies

Because the vast majority of marketing takes place in competitive markets, entrepreneurs must look for ways to differentiate their products from those of competitors. How? Four basic differentiation strategies have been identified: (1) *Differentiating the product itself* by emphasizing features, performance, conformance, durability, reliability, repairability, style, and design. (2) *Differentiating on the basis of services offered* such as delivery, installation, customer training, consulting service, repair, and other miscellaneous factors. (3) *Differentiating by personnel* because of their competency, courtesy, credibility, reliability, responsiveness, and communication ability. (4) *Differentiating by image* through focusing on symbols such as a logo, color identifier, or famous person; through written and audiovisual media; through atmosphere features such as building design, interior design, layout, colors, or furnishings; or through sponsored events or causes.

Although the choice of differentiation strategy is obviously an important one, there's more for the entrepreneur to decide. That "more" is the marketing mix strategies.

Marketing Mix Strategies

The marketing mix strategies get into the specific details of what product is going to be offered to customers, how it will be priced, how it will be promoted, and where it will be placed so customers can get it. These are the 4 Ps often referred to in marketing—that is, product, price, promotion, and place. We'll look at each of these separately.

An entrepreneurial venture's *product* strategy involves several aspects. One important one is how the organization approaches new-product development. New products can include original products, improved products, modified products, or new brands. Once new-product ideas have been developed, the organization may have different strategies for developing and testing the actual product. If the proposed product passes these stages, then the entrepreneur must decide how much and what type of market testing to use, requiring the use of different strategies. Strategic product decisions at this point also involve the width (how many different product lines to offer), depth (how many variations of a product to offer), length (how many different products to offer within the product line), and consistency (how closely related the product lines and products are). There also may be product strategy choices that involve brand decisions such as whether to use a brand name, a brand sponsor, and what type of brand strategy to pursue. Other product strategies involve packaging and labeling decisions. Once the product is out in the market, then product strategies concern managing the vari-

Figure 6-6

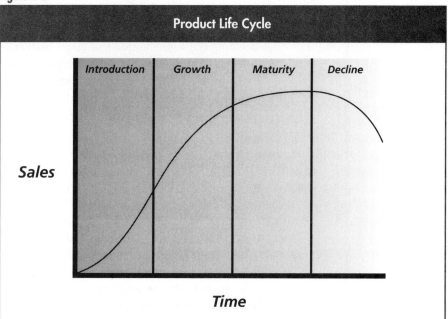

ous stages in the product life cycle (PLC). The PLC concept is a recognition that a product's sales rise and decline, bringing about the need for different strategies for coping with these ups and down. (See Figure 6-6 for an example of what a typical PLC curve looks like. The various stages of the PLC might require changes not only in the product strategy but also in the other P strategies as well.

Entrepreneurs in Action

In an expanding market saturated with products, how does a new company with no profits and little to spend on marketing get customers' attention? Packaging was the answer for Fountainhead Water Company. Company president Kevin McClanahan wanted a product packaging breakthrough—a design with dual appeal—one that was an unusual two-liter size (the recommended daily amount to drink) and elegant enough for the dinner table. The first package prototype turned off consumers who said it looked too much like a bottle of bleach. The company's second choice was a tall, elegant-looking fluted bottle. This design has won awards from industry groups and kudos from consumers. As one of Fountainhead's distributors said, "You can have the best water, from a 3,000-year-old well, but that doesn't sell it. The bottle does." Although its package strategy has been important to Fountainhead's success, the other marketing mix strategies have played an important role, also.

Source: E. Updike, "Selling the Sizzle of . . . Water?" *Business Week Enterprise*, April 27, 1998, p. ENT12.

The choice of *pricing* strategies is an important one! It depends on the entrepreneur's pricing objectives (survival, maximum current profit, maximum current revenue, maximum sales growth, maximum market skimming, product–quality leadership, or other). It also is influenced by the customers' demand for the product, costs of producing and marketing the product, and competitors' prices. Based on these factors, the entrepreneur may choose one of the following pricing strategies: *markup pricing* (pricing by adding a standard markup), *target return pricing* (to achieve a targeted or desired return), *perceived-value pricing* (based on the customers' perception of value), *value pricing* (based on charging low prices for high-quality products), *going-rate pricing* (based largely on what competitors are charging), or *sealed-bid pricing* (based on expectations of how competitors will bid). Other pricing strategy decisions to be made by the entrepreneur include geographical pricing, price discounts and allowances, promotional pricing, discriminatory pricing, or product mix pricing. Also, even though an entrepreneur may establish what he or she believes is an effective pricing strategy, competitive and marketplace dynamics may require increasing or lowering prices, thus creating a need to change the current pricing strategy from time to time.

A good overall marketing strategy requires strategies for *promotion* of the product. Common strategies for promotion involve the use of the various marketing communication and promotion tools. These include advertising (print and broadcast media ads, brochures and booklets, posters and leaflets, billboards, point-of-purchase displays, symbols and logos, packaging inserts, and many others); sales promotion (contests, games, sweepstakes and lotteries, premiums and

Entrepreneurs in Action

Diamond wholesaler Glenn Rothman faced a significant marketing challenge. As one of several thousand diamond wholesalers, he had to find a way to create a consumer brand. That way was a new Japanese method of cutting diamonds. With this process, the cut stones viewed under low magnification refracted light in a way that appeared to give off a pattern of eight heart-shaped sparkles at the bottom of the diamond and eight arrow-shaped fire bursts through the top. Diamonds cut this way are referred to as "hearts-and-arrows" diamonds. Rothman knew he had found his marketing strategy. He changed the name of his company from Di-Star to Hearts on Fire. Then, to get consumers to shell out more money for his branded Hearts on Fire diamonds, Rothman started distributing a handheld cylindrically shaped magnifying glass so they could see the pattern of hearts and arrows. He also started giving training sessions for the stores that carried his line of diamonds. These marketing strategies helped Rothman increase his overall sales and his gross profit margins.

Source: B. Nelson, "Stones on Fire," *Forbes,* August 9, 1999, pp. 74–78.

gifts, sampling, fairs and trade shows, exhibits, demonstrations, coupons, rebates, trading stamps, product tie-ins, and others); public relations (press kits, speeches, annual reports, charitable contributions, sponsorships, community relations, lobbying, community events, company magazine, and others); personal selling (sales presentations, sales meetings, incentive programs, samples, and others); and direct marketing (catalogs, mailings, telemarketing, electronic shopping, or TV shopping). What are the most appropriate promotional strategies? It depends on the target audience and the marketing communication objectives. What am I wanting to communicate to whom? Once this is determined, then the appropriate message, communication channels, promotion budget, and promotion mix strategies can be designed.

The final aspect of the marketing mix strategies involves specific *place* or distribution strategies. What's involved with the place strategy? One important aspect for the entrepreneur to determine is the choice of channels for distributing the venture's product or service. Strategic alternatives include the *type* of intermediary to use (such as wholesaler, dealer, direct sales, value-added reseller, mail-order marketer, etc.) and the *number* of intermediaries to use (exclusive distribution, selective distribution, or intensive distribution). Another important aspect of the place strategy involves the actual physical distribution of the product—also referred to as market logistics. Normally, there are four logistics strategies to decide. The first is determining how customer orders will be processed. Next, we must decide what warehousing arrangements (if any) are most appropriate. Then, decisions about inventory (when to order and how much to order) must be addressed. Obviously, decisions about the inventory strategy must be coordinated with the technology and operations strategy so that finished products are available when needed, in the style and design needed, and at an appropriate cost. Finally, place strategy involves decisions about transportation modes and carriers that will get the product to where it's needed.

The choices of appropriate marketing strategies in all these areas are obviously important decisions for the entrepreneur. Effectively managing customers and competitors through well-designed marketing strategies should help an entrepreneurial venture achieve its goals. The next major types of strategies we want to look at are the information system strategies.

Rapid Review ◀◀|

✓ Define marketing.

✓ What are the two Cs of marketing?

✓ Describe the segmentation strategies for consumer markets. For business markets.

✓ What are the five possible strategic approaches to target market selection?

✓ How could entrepreneurs differentiate their products from those of competitors?

✓ Describe the specific strategies associated with each of the 4 Ps of the marketing mix.

INFORMATION SYSTEM STRATEGIES

You would probably agree that information affects how effectively and efficiently you get your schoolwork done. Well, it also affects how organizational members do their work and how effectively and efficiently they get it done. Without information, the payroll clerk wouldn't know what deductions to make from paychecks; the sales representative wouldn't know what prices to quote a potential customer; or the production manager wouldn't know how this month's quality levels compared to last month's. It's essential to have information to make

TABLE 6-3	**Information Systems Strategies for Entrepreneurial Ventures**

System Technology	Type of Information System
■ Manual	■ Transaction processing system
■ Computer based	■ Office automation system
	■ Knowledge work system
	■ Management information system
	■ Decision support system
	■ Executive support system

decisions and to carry out work duties. How does an entrepreneur get information? If there are other organizational members, how will they get information? That's what an information system does. An **information system** is defined as a set of interrelated components used to collect, process, store, and disseminate information to support decision making, analysis, and control in organizations. Two strategic decisions associated with the entrepreneur's choices of an information system are the choice of system technology and the choice of what type (or types) of information system to have. Table 6-3 summarizes possible information system strategies.

System Technology

The choice of system technology is actually pretty simple—the information system can be either manual or computer based. A manual system uses simple pencil-and-paper technology to collect, store, process, and disseminate information. A computer-based system relies on computer hardware and software to do

Entrepreneurs in Action

Sometimes computers *don't* make your life easier! Roger Bergen of The Nature Company, a national retailer based in Berkeley, California, believed that technology could solve any problem. The company spent a fortune on computer systems that became obsolete before it "grew" into using them. Bergen said, "We never had a system that everyone could rely on. I saw employees create manual systems to support the computer system." The company's response was to buy more technology. Although information systems can be a useful and important tool for entrepreneurial ventures, entrepreneurs need to think about their information system strategies before jumping in feet first and investing significant money.

Source: S. Greco, "A Question of Human Nature," *Inc.*, February 1999, p. 55.

the same. Which approach an entrepreneur chooses to use depends on how important the collection and manipulation of information is to effectively and efficiently running the business. For instance, is it critical that the entrepreneur have rapid access to information from all operational areas? Is it crucial that other organizational members have rapid access to information to help them do their jobs effectively and efficiently? Is it critical that various organizational units share information? All these factors will influence the extent to which an entrepreneurial venture uses a computer-based or a manual system. As prices of computer-based systems continue to fall and computing power continues to rise, many entrepreneurial ventures have chosen a computer-based information system because of the easy access to information and the more sophisticated analyses that can be done with the information.

Types of Information Systems

An entrepreneurial venture's information system isn't just one single system because no one system can provide all the information needed. Instead, an organization will have many different types of information systems satisfying different information needs. Six different types of information systems are possible strategic choices. The first type is called a *transaction processing system (TPS)*. This type of information system tracks day-to-day work (transactions) being completed in various work areas such as payroll, sales tracking, or production scheduling. The next type of information system is an *office automation system (OAS)*. This system includes any of the organization's paperwork such as letters, invoices, press releases, newsletters, schedules, and so forth. More and more, this type of information gathering and exchange is done through word processing, electronic mail, and desktop publishing software. The remaining types of information systems are increasingly sophisticated in what they do. Although they may not be entirely appropriate for an entrepreneurial venture, we need to introduce them. A *knowledge work system (KWS)* is used primarily by an organization's knowledge workers (engineers, analysts, designers, research scientists, and so forth). A KWS provides ways to promote and use new knowledge and innovations in the organization through such elements as product design graphics, legal database searches, or financial data analysis. The *management information system (MIS)* is used by an organization's managers for planning, controlling, and decision making. The MIS typically summarizes and reports the organization's work activities but differs from the TPS because it summarizes a series of time periods, not simply the day-to-day transactions. A *decision support system (DSS)* allows for powerful data analysis and allows decision makers to change assumptions and information to see what impact these changes have on the outcomes. Finally, the last type of information system is an *executive support system (ESS)*, which would be used by an organization's upper-level managers to aid in making unstructured, comprehensive, broad, and complex decisions.

It's important for an entrepreneur to choose appropriate strategies for the efficient and effective collection and use of information. Without information, it's going to be hard to run the business successfully. One area that provides pretty important information for the entrepreneurial venture is the financial and accounting area, which we discuss next.

FINANCIAL AND ACCOUNTING STRATEGIES

This last group of strategies concerns choices about how financial and accounting data are collected and used. The four broad areas we'll be looking at are evaluating financial performance; financial forecasting, planning, and budgeting; financing mix; and other financial management decisions. Possible financial and accounting strategies are summarized in Table 6-4.

Evaluating Financial Performance

How is an organization's financial performance usually evaluated? By looking at the financial statements and evaluating the information that's on them. These financial statements include specific pieces of information about the organization's operations. The typical financial statements include the income statement, the balance sheet, and a cash flow statement. By themselves, the financial statements show only results. To evaluate financial performance, we have to look closer at what the statements are telling us. Financial ratios are the principal tool for financial analysis. The financial ratios standardize financial information so that comparisons can be made from time period to time period or of the organization to its industry. The strategic choices in terms of evaluating financial performance revolve around what types of analysis to do, how often to analyze, and how much analysis to do. Quite often, this is dictated by securities laws and regulations and not entirely open to individual choice, particularly for entrepreneurial ventures whose stock may be held publicly. Even if financial analysis isn't mandated, though, the fact remains that an organization needs to have in place some

---

TABLE 6-4   Financial and Accounting Strategies for Entrepreneurial Ventures

Evaluating Financial Performance

- What type of analysis?
- How often to analyze?
- How much analysis?

Financial Forecasting, Planning, and Budgeting

- What type of forecast?
- How often to forecast?

Financing Mix

- Short-term versus long-term funding sources
- Permanent or temporary sources

Other Financial Management Decisions

- Capital budgeting
- Stock dividend policy
- Cash flow management
- Cash and marketable securities management
- Accounts receivable and inventory management
- Term loans or leases

mechanism and procedure for evaluating financial performance. Without this information, an entrepreneur would have little knowledge of how the organization is performing, at least from a quantitative and financial standpoint. We'll cover some of the basic financial analysis techniques in the next chapter as we discuss ways to measure performance.

Financial Forecasting, Planning, and Budgeting

Financial forecasting is used to estimate an entrepreneurial venture's future financial needs. Once forecasts are developed, an entrepreneur can plan and budget according to the forecasts. The most popular type of financial forecast—because it's fairly easy to do—is the percent of sales method. With this approach, you would first convert each expense, asset, or liability to a percentage of current sales. Then, you would forecast the future level of sales. Using this forecasted level of sales, you would estimate the potential levels of an expense, asset, or liability using that same calculated percentage of sales. The resulting numbers provide the basis for operational planning and budgeting. This approach can help an entrepreneur identify the changes that result from an increasing (or perhaps even a decreasing) level of sales. With this information, plans and budgets can be developed to support the expected level of sales.

Other types of financial forecasting models tend to be more sophisticated and may not be entirely appropriate for the unique situations facing entrepreneurial ventures. The strategic choices in terms of financial forecasting, planning, and budgeting—just as with the strategic choices in evaluating financial performance—revolve around the choice of financial models and how often they're used.

Financing Mix

The financial mix strategies concern decisions about the entrepreneurial venture's financial and capital structure. In making decisions about the optimum financial structure, entrepreneurs must look at (1) how they want to divide the total fund sources between short- and long-term components and (2) what proportion of total financing they want to be from permanent sources. Answers to these two questions will determine what financing mix strategies the entrepreneur uses. Other factors that may influence this strategic choice include how much debt capacity the venture has, whether or not it has reached its optimum amount of debt, the stage in the business cycle, and the amount of risk the venture faces. All of these factors will affect the types and maturities of the various financing options an entrepreneur has to select from.

Other Financial Management Decisions

Other possible financial management strategic decisions involve choices about investing in long-term assets (capital budgeting decisions—when and how), stock dividend policy (how much, how often), cash flow management (how much, how often), cash and marketable securities management (what do we do with our excess cash—put it in the bank or invest it in marketable securities), accounts receivable and inventory management (how do we efficiently and effectively collect accounts receivable and manage our inventory), and lease–purchase decisions (do we buy or lease needed equipment and facilities). In each of these financial

Rapid Review ◀◀|

✓ What is an information system?

✓ What are the two possible strategic choices in system technology?

✓ Describe the six different types of information systems.

✓ What strategic choices are there in terms of evaluating financial performance?

✓ What strategic choices are there in terms of financial forecasting, planning, and budgeting?

✓ Describe what financial mix strategies cover.

✓ What other financial management strategies might entrepreneurs need?

areas, there are strategic choices to make. The entrepreneur must decide what to use and how to implement it.

Each of the operational areas that we've looked at is important for entrepreneurs to develop appropriate strategies. Without appropriate strategies in these areas, the short-term operational goals will not be met nor will the organizational goals be achieved. Joe Boxer Company could not have achieved the levels of success that it has without goals and strategies. Although we've discussed goals and strategies from the perspective of launching the entrepreneurial venture, keep in mind that setting goals and pursuing them through appropriately chosen strategies is an ongoing challenge for entrepreneurs.

CHAPTER SUMMARY

Once the entrepreneurial venture has been planned and organized, it's time to actually get it going. Doing that involves establishing goals and strategies for the organization's key work activities.

Without goals and strategies, there would be no coherent organizational decisions or direction. Goals are the outcomes or end results that are desired by individuals, groups, or organizations. Goals serve several purposes for organizations, and organizations will have different types of goals. Four ways to describe the goals of an entrepreneurial venture are: breadth (organization-wide or operational), time frame (long term or short term), specificity (specific or directional), and work area (most common ones are technology and operations methods, marketing, and financial). Goals are not all created equal: Some are better than others. There are several characteristics of good goals. Sitting down and writing goals is not something that most entrepreneurs look forward to doing; however, it is important to do so. The process can also be made easier by following the steps in the goal-setting process. Once the goals have been identified, it's time to look at how these goals will be accomplished.

A strategy is a plan of action for accomplishing organizational goals. Specific strategies need to be developed so the entrepreneurial venture's long-term organization-wide goals and short-term operational goals can be achieved. Strategies and goals are linked because the operational goals are pursued through the development and implementation of various operational strategies. The achievement of the operational goals, then, becomes the mechanism for the accomplishment of the organization-wide goals.

Strategies are needed in various operational areas of the entrepreneurial venture. The production area is one of these operational areas. The technology and operations strategies include production process strategies, capacity strategies, location strategies, work design strategies, layout strategies, and production and operations management strategies. Another operational area is marketing. Marketing strategies include segmentation and target market selection strategies, differentiation strategies, and marketing mix strategies. The information system strategies must also be addressed. These include system technology strategies and types of information systems. Finally, financial and accounting strategies must be decided. These include strategies for evaluating financial performance, financial forecasting strategies, financing mix strategies, and strategies involved with other financial management decisions.

KEY TERMS

▭▶ *Goals:* Outcomes or end results that are desired by individuals, groups, or entire organizations.

▭▶ *Organization-wide goals:* Goals that establish broad purposes, apply to the entire entrepreneurial venture, and seek to successfully position the venture in terms of its environment.

▭▶ *Operational goals:* Goals that specify details associated with accomplishing the organization-wide goals.

▭▶ *Long-term goals:* Goals with a time frame beyond three years.

▭▶ *Short-term goals:* Goals that cover one year or less.

▭▶ *Specific goals:* Goals that are clearly defined and leave no room for interpretation.

▭▶ *Directional goals:* Goals that are flexible enough to provide focus and general guidelines but do not lock decision makers into specific courses of action.

▭▶ *Strategy:* A plan of action for accomplishing organizational goals.

▭▶ *Means–end chain:* The integrated collection of organizational goals in which higher-level goals (*ends*) are inextricably linked to lower-level goals and strategies because these lower-level goals and strategies serve as the *means* for accomplishing those organization-wide ends.

▭▶ *Production:* The process of creating products (goods and services) in which organizational inputs (resources) are transformed into outputs.

▭▶ *Outsourcing:* Subcontracting services and operations to other organizations that can do the job better or less expensively.

▭▶ *Marketing:* A process of assessing and meeting an individual's or group's wants and needs by creating, offering, and exchanging products of value.

▭▶ *Information system:* A set of interrelated components used to collect, process, store, and disseminate information to support decision making, analysis, and control in organizations.

SWEAT EQUITY

1. A survey of 7.4 million small businesses about their technology usage showed that small firms are big technology spenders. During 1998, small business organizations spent around $57.3 billion on computers and related goods. However, not all types of small businesses are investing in technology. Banking and financial-type firms led the pack in spending, followed by legal services, insurance, manufacturing, business services, and retail trade. Even though retailers, as a percentage, were at the bottom, their overall total

spending exceeded that of financial firms because retailers far outnumber other types of businesses.

- What do you think the information from this survey is saying? What are the implications for (a) entrepreneurs and (b) companies selling computers and related products to entrepreneurs?
- How might each of these categories of small businesses be using technology?
- How can small businesses get the most out of their dollars spent on technology?
- What role should the business's goals and strategies play in spending on technology?

(***Source:*** *Cnnfn* Web page [**www.cnnfn.com**], February 5, 1999.)

2. Electronic commerce is a hot topic these days. Many entrepreneurial ventures are taking the plunge. Says one expert, "Start-ups see selling products or services online as a way to generate revenue quickly." The market appears to be there. The Forester Group, a research firm, forecasts that electronic commerce sales could reach $108 billion by 2003, which would account for about 6 percent of the total retail market.

   Research the topic of electronic commerce and how it relates to entrepreneurial ventures. Write a two- to three-page bulleted list that identifies key points about e-commerce, its potential, its drawbacks, and any other relevant information. Be sure to cite your information sources.

3. Pricing is something that many entrepreneurs don't put a lot of thought into. However, determining how much to charge for a product or service can spell the difference between financial success or failure. Interview three to five entrepreneurs (preferably from different types of businesses and industries) and ask how they established their pricing strategy. Your survey results will be combined with what other students in your class found. Then, graph the totals and write a short report on pricing strategy for entrepreneurial ventures.

4. Here are some ideas suggested as ways to fire up an organization's marketing strategies:
   - Start a product-of-the month program.
   - Offer short educational classes to actual and potential customers on how to use your product or service.
   - Insert lottery tickets into mailings to customers and make follow-up calls with the winning number.
   - Keep the reception desk area stocked with candy, toys, and yo-yos so customers and employees perceive that everyone is relaxed and having fun.
   - Conduct on-line focus groups to find out what customers think.
   What do you think of these suggestions? Now, break into small groups, identify a type of entrepreneurial venture, and come up with your own list of creative marketing strategies. (Be sure to think in terms of the 4 Ps and the other marketing strategies.) Be prepared to share these with the class.

5. Staying in touch with customers. This would seem to be a pretty important strategy for entrepreneurs. MXG Media, Inc., a company founded in 1997, sells clothes and accessories via the Internet (at **www.mxgonline.com**) and

through a hybrid publication called a "magalog"—that is, it's part magazine, part catalog. This magalog is sent to 500,000 teen girls every quarter. In such an intensely competitive market, MXG has found a way to keep in touch with its fickle customers. It hires teen girls to work after school answering letters, doing interviews, and creating advertising copy that sounds authentically teen. Then, at the start of every fashion season, it brings 30 teen girls into its offices and has them spend a hypothetical $150 each. These "pretend" purchases determine which items will appear in the next issue of the magalog.

a. Find some data on the number of teenage girls and their disposable income. Is it increasing or decreasing? What are the implications for MXG Media and its strategies?

b. Go to the company's Web site. What's your assessment of the site? Is it a good marketing tool? Why or why not?

(**Source:** C. Waxler, "Guys with Moxie," *Forbes*, May 31, 1999, pp. 130–31.)

ENTREPRENEURSHIP IN ACTION CASES

CASE #1: The King of Underwear

Entrepreneurship in Action case #1 can be found at the beginning of Chapter 6.

Discussion Questions

1. Put yourself in Nicholas Graham's place. What types of long-term goals might you have for the company?

2. Which of Joe Boxer's strategies appear to be the strongest and most effective? Support your answer.

3. What other strategies would be important to a company such as Joe Boxer?

CASE #2: Sportsman's Paradise

The most popular tourist site in Missouri isn't what you might expect. It's not the Arch in St. Louis nor is it Harry Truman's home in Independence. Instead, you would have to travel to the southwest corner of Missouri to Springfield to Bass Pros Shops Outdoor World. More than 4 million people visited the 300,000-square-foot store in 1998, including Zimbabwe's 12-member national fishing team. Although most of the visitors to the retail store are dedicated to hunting and fishing, many come just to see the incredible sights. There's a four-story waterfall, rifle and archery ranges, four aquariums, an indoor driving range, a putting green, and a 17,000-square-foot wildlife museum with a world-class collection of stuffed animals. The visitors can get their hair cut at the four-chair barbershop and then arrange to have a fishing lure made out of the hair clippings. They can eat at McDonald's or at the Hemingway's Blue Water Café, whose showpiece is a 30,000-

gallon saltwater aquarium. However, despite all these fascinating attractions, the heart (and soul) of the store is row after row of guns, decoys, tents, rods, reels, lures, campers, clothing, and other sportsman and outdoors equipment. One floor of the massive store showcases boats—speedboats, houseboats, pontoon boats, fiberglass boats, and aluminum boats. There's something for everyone to gaze at and enjoy.

Johnny Morris, the founder of Bass Pro Shops, was born and raised in Springfield. He opened the original store in a small corner of his father's liquor store. From that humble beginning, the company has grown to be a significant player in the sportsman and outdoors market. Morris did it through a strategy of never allowing the customer to have a dull moment. His retailing approach has been one of excitement and entertainment. The flagship store's design (and ultimately the design of the other stores) was developed from trips to different stores to pinpoint their appeal. One visit to L.L. Bean in Freeport, Maine, was particularly memorable. Morris felt that if that store could draw well over 3.5 million visitors a year to the middle of nowhere, then he could do that, and better, in Springfield.

The privately owned Bass Pro Shops Inc. is now pursuing a strategy of trying to duplicate the flagship store's success. Stores have opened in Atlanta, Chicago, Fort Lauderdale, the Florida Keys, Grapevine (Texas), Detroit, Charlotte, Katy (Texas), Nashville, and Orlando. Another store in Cincinnati was to open in 2000. Each of these new sites was chosen with a discerning eye for location. Although none of the new stores is as huge as the original, all are still enormous, complete with waterfalls and aquariums. There's also something new happening at the original store in Springfield. Right next to the store, the $40 million American National Fish and Wildlife Living Museum and Aquarium is scheduled to open in 2001. This museum is expected to attract a large number of visitors. Morris also continues to look for new opportunities. He says, "I'd be happy to add two or three stores a year, if we can resist the temptation to grow faster than our ability to maintain our quality."

Discussion Questions

1. What role do you think goals and strategies have played in the success of Bass Pro Shops Inc.? Give some examples.

2. To be a successful entrepreneurial venture in this industry, which strategies would have to be particularly effective? Now, using information in the case and from the company's Web site (**www.basspro.com**), how do Bass Pro Shops' strategies seem to measure up? Explain your answer.

3. Evaluate Johnny Morris's statement at the end of the case. What do you think it means? What are the implications for setting goals and strategies?

(*Sources:* E. McDowell, "Adventures in Retailing," *New York Times*, March 20, 1999, p. B1; and author's personal experiences at Bass Pro Shops.)

CASE #3: Impossible Dream?

Linda Froelich's dream has turned out to have nightmarish overtones. She had created a product and, convinced that it was a winner, set about getting her patented invention onto store shelves only to find the shelves soon crowded with knockoffs of her invention. Her product is a simple paper clip design that she called the SuperClip. The SuperClip is little more than a very large paper clip. However, it neatly holds up to 100 sheets of paper, is easier to use, and is less bulky than the old standard bulldog or butterfly clips.

Even with a very simple product, Froelich believed that she had done everything right. She was awarded a patent in July 1994 (No. 5329672) for her unique design, which was a quantum leap over the prior design. With an early sale to Office Depot (a national office-supply chain with over 582 stores), she was convinced that she was about to crack the mainstream office-supply market. However, she soon discovered that the office-supply industry is dominated by a handful of very large companies. These companies have found it easy to design around her patent and have not hesitated to do so. Froelich was stunned. She says, "I felt everyone would love this product as I have. I was naïve. I believed this product was so good I wouldn't have a problem."

The SuperClip is produced by Froelich and her husband through their family business, Ace Wire Spring & Form Company, based in McKees Rocks, Pennsylvania. (Check out their Web site at **www.acewire.com**.) For over 60 years, Ace has custom-manufactured wire forms such as bucket handles, paper racks, and springs that go into varied products from screen doors to M-1 tanks. The company has annual sales of more than $5 million. Although these markets were nowhere similar to the office-supply business, Linda felt that her paper clip design was so unique and superior that it was worth pursuing. The realities have been a harsh lesson.

With imitation supersize clips found everywhere, pallet upon pallet of the SuperClips languish in the back storeroom of Ace. The large office-supply industry competitors have priced their imitations so much lower that Linda's product can't compete. But she's not giving up just yet. Although Linda and her husband pride themselves on being American manufacturers, they have made the decision to go to offshore production of the SuperClip. That way they'll be able to meet competitors' prices and hopefully be able to provide better quality. In addition, they've decided to extend the product line by introducing the SuperClip in various colors to appeal to school and office markets. They also hope to offer a midsize paper clip that can function as a money clip. Ace has landed contracts with the federal government for the SuperClip, and the Arthritis Foundation has endorsed it because of its ease of use for people with arthritis. In addition, Linda has been trying to get a large national fast-food chain to give away SuperClips as a back-to-school promotion. She's not at all ready to give up—not any time soon at least, no matter how bad the dream seems.

Discussion Questions

1. What do you think went wrong with the Froelichs' entrepreneurial venture?

2. Could goals and strategies have prevented the problems? Explain.

3. What advice might you give the Froelichs? What advice could you learn from the Froelichs' experiences?

(*Source:* E. O. Welles, "Clipped!" *Inc.*, December 1997, pp. 96–109.)

VIDEO CASE #1: Drawing the Perfect Inventory System

George Granoff, owner of The Art Store, a retail art supply store with five locations in California, has put together an inventory control system that allows him to efficiently and effectively keep his stores stocked with 17,000 art supply items. Granoff, who had no background or experience in art or in art supplies, used his extensive retailing experience and knowledge of product scanning, bar coding, just-in-time inventory, and other retail inventory control techniques to bring The Art Store online.

The Art Store operates and maintains its enormous level of in-store inventory with no "back room." (In retailing language, this means there's no product being stored in a back room; all inventory owned is out on the floor.) As Granoff readily admits, it's an enormous challenge to stay in stock day in and day out with that number of items and no back room and no warehouse. He says he's been able to do it because of organization and technology.

The area that was most important to Granoff was installing point-of-sale scanning at the front end (checkout counters) of the store and bar coding all 17,000 items. When a customer takes merchandise to a cash register to check out, the cashier scans the bar-coded products and the encoded information is recorded and compiled. In addition, when an employee out in the store runs across empty product space—that is, an empty shelf, bin, or rack—he or she scans the bar code information and a written order for that item is automatically initiated. The order information is immediately transmitted over the phone lines to the manufacturer. In most cases, the ordered item is at the store within two days.

Granoff admits that his computer system is the company's workhorse. It handles the merchandising function as well as all of the company's other important business functions, such as payroll, budgeting, and so forth. Without the technology, it would have been impossible for The Art Store to grow or even to keep in stock and on hand the products its customers want. After all, being a successful retailer means having the products that customers want when they want them. If you can't do that, you won't be around very long!

Discussion Questions

1. What are some advantages of the type of computerized inventory control system that The Art Store uses? What are some disadvantages?

2. Would it be important for an entrepreneurial venture's strategies to be coordinated with each other? Explain. Are The Art Store's various strategies (production, marketing, information systems, and financial–accounting) tied together? How?

3. What do you think Granoff meant when he said that it is organization and technology that have enabled him to monitor 17,000 inventory items?

(*Source:* Based on *Small Business 2000, Show 303.*)

VIDEO CASE #2: Virtual Flowers

Here at the beginning of a brand-new century, merchandise transactions in cyberspace account for a fraction of total retail sales revenues. However, the dollar amount of these transactions continues to increase every year. Although the Internet and World Wide Web are household words now, that wasn't the case just a few years ago. The early days of interactive advertising, selling, and marketing distribution are just a fragment of what they are today. Entrepreneur Bill Tobin saw opportunities in the burgeoning online world. His entrepreneurial venture, started in 1989, was targeted at selling fresh flowers to the online user.

Tobin had to fight to convince others that the time was ripe for what he called a "new transactional paradigm." "Everybody said it couldn't be done," Tobin recalls. "Everybody said it won't work." Even though Tobin had an impressive track record of business success, he still had a hard time selling his idea. But that was then, and the online retailing world is different today.

Today, PC Flowers (**www.pcflowers. com**) prospers and, thanks to the Internet, can serve customers worldwide. It has become, in Tobin's words, "the most comprehensive floral and gift service in the interactive world." One reason for Tobin's success is that he understands how dramatically different online retailing is from traditional retailing. He explains, "You must earn the right of the consumer to tell them about your message. You can't be as intrusive as traditional channels and means of advertising. This is a highly educated user. This is a consumer who is use to a laser-beam approach to what they want, a consumer who won't put up with a waste of his or her time. Online consumers

are far more demanding than traditional consumers."

Shoppers are also savvy enough to know that many online retailers have lower overhead costs than do retailers who have made substantial investments in "bricks and mortar." Therefore, Tobin points out, online shoppers expect lower prices. Another crucial difference is that online consumers have much more control than do traditional consumers. Tobin described this as the "sword of Damocles"—if an online customer is unhappy with something, that dissatisfaction can be shared with millions of other online users with just a few keystrokes. To ensure the highest level of customer satisfaction, Tobin has designed PC Flowers with the best graphics and the best navigational tools in the industry. Online shoppers also demand security when they use credit cards to pay for their orders. Tobin is aware that the general public doesn't have a high degree of confidence in Internet security. However, most Internet retailers do use highly effective forms of electronic encryption when uploading customers' credit card information. Tobin insists that Internet transactions are actually more secure than are traditional methods of using credit cards such as giving out credit card information over the phone.

Tobin's online enterprise boasts other state-of-the-art features such as cutting-edge "push–pull" technology that changes screen images automatically without prompting from the online shopper. In 1994, Tobin expanded the scope of his business to include greeting cards, balloons, stuffed bears, gift baskets, and gourmet food items. The company is now known as PC Flowers and Gifts. Tobin's market research told him that, in the United

States, men don't send flowers to other men, women don't send men flowers, and kids under age 13 don't get flowers. His response: Offer customers the opportunity to build balloon arrangements online that are delivered by the FTD network. He is also looking at other ways to add value to marketing flowers.

Despite his success, Tobin still has ambitious plans for the future. He says, "An entrepreneur is like a dog with a bone. He doesn't drop it until there's not a scrap of meat on it. He stays with it. He's focused. He's driven and cannot sleep, cannot eat until he accomplishes that goal." Summing up his business philosophy, Tobin says, "An entrepreneur is one of the biggest gamblers in the world. But he gambles in an area where he figures he controls the odds, as opposed to the house controlling the odds." He continues, "I understand the Internet, and I understand where I want to go with it. The Internet gives me the opportunity to take my business forward into one hundred new areas. It's a wide-open, free-for-all highway—it's the autobahn of opportunity."

Discussion Questions

1. What production strategies does Tobin's company use? Give examples.
2. What marketing strategies does Tobin's company use? Give examples
3. What are some of the key differences between online retailing and traditional retailing? How might these differences affect choices of (a) production strategies, (b) marketing strategies, and (c) information system strategies?
4. Evaluate all of Tobin's quotes in the last paragraph of the case. What are the implications for entrepreneurs in setting goals and strategies?

(*Source: Small Business 2000, Show 102.*)

ENDNOTES

1. "Photo Opportunities," *Inc.*, May 1999, pp. 104–5; and materials from Joe Boxer Company Web site (**www.joeboxer.com**), August 4, 1999.
2. J. C. Naylor and D. R. Ilgen, "Goal Setting: A Theoretical Analysis of a Motivational Technique," in B. M. Staw and L. L. Cummings (eds.), *Research in Organizational Behavior*, Vol. 6 (Greenwich, CT: JAI Press, 1984), pp. 95–140; E. A. Locke, "Facts and Fallacies About Goal Theory: Reply to Deci," *Psychological Science*, January 1993, pp. 63–64; and M. E. Tubbs, D. M. Boehne, and J. S. Dahl, "Expectancy, Valence, and Motivational Force Functions in Goal-Setting Research: An Empirical Test," *Journal of Applied Psychology*, June 1993, pp. 361–73.
3. J. D. Hunger and T. L. Wheelen, *Strategic Management*, 5th ed. (Reading, MA: Addison-Wesley, 1996), p. 143.
4. N. Capon, J. U. Farley, and J. M. Hulbert, "Strategic Planning and Financial Performance: More Evidence," *Journal of Management Studies*, January 1994, pp. 105–10; S. Hart and C. Banbury, "How Strategy-Making Processes Can Make a Difference," *Strategic Management Journal*, May 1994, pp. 251–69; and D. J. Ketchen Jr., J. B. Thomas, and R. R. McDaniel, "Strategic Planning and Firm Performance: A Synthesis of More Than Two Decades of Research," *Academy of Management Journal*, December 1994, pp. 1649–65.

7

MANAGING PROCESSES

LEARNING OBJECTIVES

After reading this chapter, you should be able to:

1. Describe the steps in the decision-making process.
2. Explain the different styles of decision making.
3. Describe different ways to measure and evaluate performance.
4. Describe the commonly used financial statements and financial ratios.
5. Explain cash flow analysis.
6. Detail what is involved in a SWOT analysis.
7. Tell why stimulating change is important to entrepreneurial ventures.
8. Describe the different roles entrepreneurs play as change agents.
9. Explain how creativity and innovation can be managed.
10. Define quality and describe how it can be managed.
11. Detail what a world-class organization is.

ENTREPRENEURSHIP IN ACTION CASE #1

Swatting the Bugs

As any motorcyclist knows, bugs can be a real annoyance when out enjoying the open road. Well, for John Healy—owner of *Vintage Bike* magazine and Coventry Spares, Ltd., a motorcycle parts business located in Holliston, Massachusetts—the annoying bug wasn't the kind that splatters on the helmet or the windshield, but the Y2K kind that created havoc for computer systems because of the date change from 1999 to 2000.[1] Healy, a successful entrepreneur, never

thought the Y2K bug could infect his small computer systems, but he was mistaken.

After hearing about his sister's experience with trying to rent a car with her driver's license that had a 2000 expiration date and the computer crashing because it couldn't handle the "00" date, Healy knew he had better check his company's computer systems. He checked out the computer that held the subscriber database for his *Vintage Bike* magazine and got the frightening

Although the momentous change in years from 1999 to 2000 is now just a memory, for entrepreneurs such as John Healy, the date change was a situation that needed attention. Once an entrepreneurial venture is launched, continual situations arise that need the attention of the entrepreneur. The successful entrepreneur needs to be able to manage the various processes of an ongoing venture. Managing processes is what we're going to look at in this chapter. We'll first examine the all-important decision-making process and look at some characteristics of different decision-making styles. Next, we'll look at different ways of measuring and evaluating performance. Based upon performance results, the entrepreneur may need to stimulate and manage change, which is also a topic we'll look at. Finally, we're going to discuss some contemporary issues facing entrepreneurs as they manage the processes of an ongoing business. These include managing creativity and innovation, managing quality, and becoming a world-class organization. Because everything that an entrepreneur does in managing processes involves making decisions, we're going to look first at the all-important decision-making process.

MAKING DECISIONS

One thing that all entrepreneurs do, regardless of size, type, location, or age of their entrepreneurial ventures, is make decisions. A **decision** is a choice made between two or more alternatives. When you choose where to eat for lunch, you're making a decision. When you choose which classes or which professors to take, you're making decisions. Entrepreneurs are faced with making decisions day in and day out, although their decisions aren't usually as simple as deciding between tacos or cheeseburgers. How are decisions made? What's involved with making decisions? Let's look at the decision-making process to try and help us understand these issues.

The Decision-Making Process

From the initial context analysis to determine and evaluate entrepreneurial opportunities to the point of designing and implementing strategies, the entrepreneur has been making decisions. The decision making doesn't stop there. Decisions are continually made in the day-to-day ongoing operation of the entrepreneurial venture. Although many of these decisions may be relatively simple and straightforward, they still

"Not valid date" message. It was time for Healy to take some serious action to prepare his business to smoothly navigate the December 31, 1999, passage to January 1, 2000.

Although Healy had invested in technology for his growing business, he, like many other business owners, had thought the Y2K scare would not impact him. When his little experiment with his computer software showed otherwise, Healy tackled the problem with the same inventive-ness that characterized his business. The 2000 date bug spurred him to action. Doing some programming work himself and using the services of a consultant, Healy got his computer systems in shape. Now, as that magic date passed, Healy breathed a sigh of relief with the knowledge that through effectively managing the problem, he had swatted an annoying, and potentially disruptive and expensive, bug.

Figure 7-1

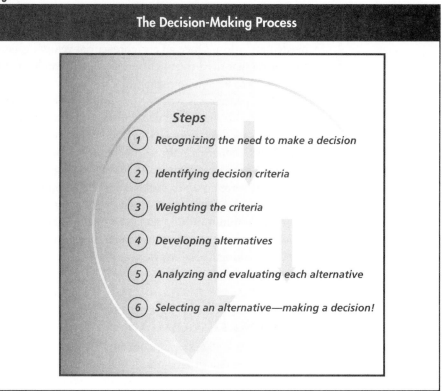

The Decision-Making Process

Steps

1. *Recognizing the need to make a decision*

2. *Identifying decision criteria*

3. *Weighting the criteria*

4. *Developing alternatives*

5. *Analyzing and evaluating each alternative*

6. *Selecting an alternative—making a decision!*

involve making a choice. How are decisions made? The process of making decisions involves a series of six steps. (See Figure 7-1.)

Step 1 is *recognizing the need to make a decision*. The need to make a decision comes about because of a problem or an opportunity. A **problem** is a situation where there's an inconsistency between actual and desired results. An **opportunity** is an optimistic possibility or positive trend. In either situation, the entrepreneur must recognize that a decision needs to be made—that is, must be aware that performance is not up to par or that performance can be improved if opportunities are exploited. (In later sections of this chapter, we're going to discuss ways to analyze and evaluate performance results and trends.) Once the entrepreneur has identified a problem or opportunity that needs attention, step 2 is *identifying decision criteria* that will be important in addressing the situation. That is, the entrepreneur must determine what's relevant or important in making a decision. Whether they are explicitly stated or not, every decision maker has criteria that guide his or her decisions. These criteria reflect the entrepreneur's interests, values, and personal preferences. Keep in mind that not all the criteria identified will be equal in importance. So step 3 in the decision-making process is *weighting the criteria* so they have the appropriate priority in making choices. Step 4 is *developing alternatives*, which often demands creative and innovative thinking. In step 5, the entrepreneur needs to critically *analyze and evaluate each alternative*. He or she would do this by appraising the alternative against the important and relevant criteria identified earlier. The strengths and weaknesses of each alternative become apparent as they are compared to the weighted criteria. Step 6 in the decision-making process is *selecting an alternative*. Once an alternative has been selected, it would be implemented and, after an appropriate period of time, evaluated to see whether the problem or opportunity had been addressed.

Now, how realistic is this decision-making process? Is that actually what an entrepreneur should—or would—do every time there's a decision to be made? The answer probably would be "yes" if every decision-making situation were one where the decision maker could be this rational and precise because this approach is going to lead to a wide variety of choices from which the best alternative is chosen. However, in reality, several factors limit just how rational a decision maker can be. Not that we want to imply that the decision-making process just presented is useless. It isn't, and most entrepreneurs probably do try to be as rational as possible as they make decisions. In addition, many types of entrepreneurial decisions do lend themselves to the preciseness and thoroughness of the rational decision-making process. But, we also need to recognize that certain factors influence just how rational decision makers are (and can be) as they make decisions.

Factors That Influence the Rationality of Decision Making

We're going to look at four factors that influence how rational an entrepreneur can be in making decisions. These include individual differences in information processing ability and capacity, individual decision-making style, the role of intuition, and the type of decision-making condition.

Individual Differences in Information Processing Ability.

The first factor we want to discuss that determines rationality in making decisions is individual differences in the ability to process information. Think about how you respond when you're presented with large amounts of information. Then, think of someone close to you. Does this person respond in the same way? Some people would stress out under these circumstances; others would break the information into smaller parts and deal with it this way; still others might be able to process the information without any problem whatsoever. People differ in their ability to absorb, analyze, and process information. Some people reach what is known as "information overload" more quickly than do others. In an entrepreneurial venture, the entrepreneur is juggling a number of problems and taking in so much information that always following a rational systematic decision-making process may be impossible to do. Instead, entrepreneurs cope with the complex information demands of decision making by behaving in a way that allows them to be rational within certain limits. This approach to decision making was described by Herbert Simon (an expert on decision-making processes who won a Nobel prize in economics in 1978 for his groundbreaking work), who proposes that our rationality is "bounded." **Bounded rationality** refers to the concept that individuals have the time and cognitive ability to process only limited amounts of information as they make decisions.[2] According to this concept, rather than an all-out search for the absolute best alternative, the decision maker will review feasible alternatives until he or she finds one that is good enough. In decision making, this is known as **satisficing**—seeking out alternatives that are satisfactory and sufficient. This concept can be explained by asking how you found the "significant other person" in your life. Did you review all possible alternatives or did you "accept" one that met your needs? While you may have a good laugh about this, the point is made that we don't have the capacity, ability, or time to analyze all possible alternatives. We can be rational up to a certain point—the point at which we begin to look at alternatives. Then, because of information processing limitations, we limit our search. This by no means suggests that entrepreneurs don't approach decision making seriously. They must and for the most part do. But, it does mean that individual differences in processing information and the resulting constraint of bounded rationality do influence how rational an entrepreneur can be in making decisions.

Individual Decision-Making Style. Another factor that influences the rationality of decision making is decision-making style. Entrepreneurs have different styles when it comes to making decisions and solving problems. One view of decision-making styles proposes that individuals approach problems in the workplace in three ways—they're problem avoiders, problem solvers, or problem seekers.[3] A **problem avoider** approaches problems by avoiding or ignoring information that points to a problem. Problem avoiders are inactive and do not want to confront problems. A **problem solver** is a person who addresses problems by trying to solve them as they come up. Solvers are reactive; they deal with problems after they occur. The **problem seeker** is proactive; he or she approaches problems by actively seeking out problems or new opportunities. Which of these tactics is the best? Actually, entrepreneurs should probably use all three approaches. There are times, for example, when ignoring a problem is the best response. At other times, being reactive may be the only option because the problem happens so quickly. Then, there are times, particularly when searching out opportunities and finding ways to do things better, that entrepreneurs need to be proactive; that is, they need to actively seek these situations out. Think back to our chapter-opening case. Would you classify John Healy as a problem avoider, problem solver, or problem seeker?

Entrepreneurs in Action ▶

Dave and Annette King's company, Triple Crown Sports, of Fort Collins, Colorado, puts on over 400 amateur sports events a year in softball, baseball, hockey, soccer, and basketball. In the early years of the business, Dave really didn't care whether he was financially successful; he just loved sports. However, he soon realized that he had to decide whether to make money or just have a lot of fun holding sporting events. Once he decided that he needed to get serious, he developed a model of how to make money running grassroot events and came up with a successful formula. The model King developed was a result of satisficing during the decision-making process. He didn't try to identify all possible alternatives, but instead hit upon an approach that was satisfactory to what he wanted to accomplish.

Source: R. Maynard, "Sliding into Home," *Nation's Business*, January 1998, p. 52.

Another perspective on decision-making styles proposes that people differ along two dimensions in the way they approach decision making.[4] One is their *way of thinking*. Some people tend to be rational and logical in how they think or process information. A rational type tends to look at information in order and makes sure that it's logical and consistent before making a decision. Other people tend to be creative and intuitive. These intuitive types don't have to process information in a certain order but are comfortable looking at it as a whole. The other dimension describes a person's *tolerance for ambiguity*. Again, some people have a low tolerance for ambiguity and must have consistency and order in the way information is structured so that ambiguity is minimized. Others can tolerate high levels of ambiguity and are able to process many thoughts at the same time. When these two dimensions are diagrammed, four different decision-making styles are formed. (See Figure 7-2.) Let's look briefly at each style.

The **directive style** is a decision-making style characterized by a low tolerance for ambiguity and a rational way of thinking. These types are efficient and logical. They make fast decisions and focus on the short run. Their efficiency and speed in making decisions often results in making decisions with minimal information and assessing few alternatives. The **analytic style** is a decision-making style that is characterized by a high tolerance for ambiguity and a rational way of thinking. These types have much greater tolerance for ambiguity than do directive types. They want more information before making a decision and they consider more alternatives. Analytic decision makers are best characterized as careful decision makers with the ability to adapt or cope with unique situations. The **conceptual style** is a decision-making style characterized by a high tolerance for ambiguity

Figure 7-2

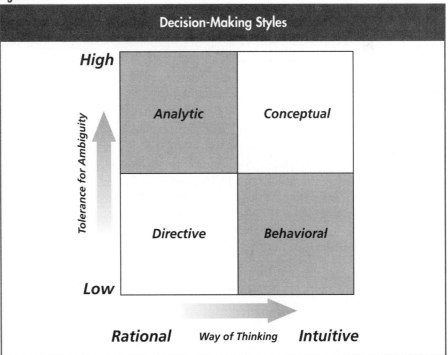

Source: *Supervision Today*, 2nd ed., by Robbins/DeCenzo. Reprinted by permission of Prentice Hall Inc., Upper Saddle River, NJ.

and an intuitive way of thinking. Individuals with this style tend to be very broad in their outlook and will look at many alternatives. They focus on the long run and are very good at finding creative solutions to problems. Finally, the **behavioral style** is a decision-making style characterized by a low tolerance for ambiguity and an intuitive way of thinking. These decision makers work well with others. They're concerned about the achievements of those around them and are receptive to suggestions from others. They often use meetings to communicate although they try to avoid conflict. Acceptance by others is important to the behavioral style decision maker. Which is the best style? There *is* no "best" style. What's important is that entrepreneurs recognize their unique style of making decisions, are aware of the characteristics of that style and how it influences their decision making, and acknowledge that others in the organization may approach decision making in their own unique way.

The Role of Intuition. How does intuition affect the rationality of decision making? Studies have shown that intuition is used regularly in decision making and may actually help improve decision making.[5] **Intuitive decision making** is a subconscious process of making decisions on the basis of experience and accumulated judgment. Making decisions on the basis of "gut feeling" doesn't necessarily happen independently of rational analysis; rather, the two complement each other. An entrepreneur who has had experience with a particular, or even similar, type of problem or opportunity often can act quickly with what appears to be limited information. Under these circumstances, the entrepreneur doesn't rely on a systematic and thorough analysis of the problem or opportunity and evaluation of alternatives, but instead uses his or her experience, knowledge, and judgment to make a decision.

Decision-Making Conditions. The last factor that can affect how rational the entrepreneur is in making decisions is the circumstances surrounding the decision to be made. Entrepreneurs face three potential conditions as they make decisions: certainty, risk, and uncertainty. **Certainty** is a situation in which an entrepreneur can make accurate assessments of which alternative is best because the outcome of every alternative is known. For instance, if the entrepreneur is trying to get the best rate of return from local financial institutions on excess funds, he or she can investigate how much interest each financial institution is offering. The outcome of each and every alternative is known, so the entrepreneur can approach the decision rationally and systematically. As you might expect, this decision-making condition isn't characteristic of most situations faced by most entrepreneurs! A far more common situation is one of **risk**, which describes those conditions in which the decision maker is able to estimate the likelihood of certain outcomes. The ability to assign probabilities to outcomes may be the result of personal experience or secondary information. Under the conditions of risk, the entrepreneur has historical data or personal experience that allows him or her to assign statistical probabilities to different alternatives. Under this decision-making condition, the entrepreneur can be partly rational because at least he or she can attempt to define reasonable probabilities of the likelihood of certain outcomes. However, keep in mind that these *are* just probabilities—they're not certain outcomes. But at least *some* guidelines can be developed to help make a rational decision, unlike our last type of decision-making situation. The final type of decision situation is one of **uncertainty**, which describes a situation in which the decision maker is neither certain about outcomes nor able to make reasonable probability estimates. Many decision-making situations that entrepreneurs face are ones of uncertainty. Under these conditions, the choice of alternatives is influenced by the limited amount of information available to the decision maker and by the entrepreneur's desire to maximize potential gains, satisfice with an acceptable gain, or minimize potential losses. Uncertainty often forces entrepreneurs to rely more on hunches, intuition, creativity, and "gut feel."

One area where entrepreneurs put their decision making to work in managing the processes of the up-and-running entrepreneurial venture is in measuring and evaluating organizational performance. That's the next major topic we want to look at.

MEASURING AND EVALUATING ORGANIZATIONAL PERFORMANCE

The entrepreneurial venture is launched! The entrepreneur and any other organizational members are performing their work. The floral bouquets are being designed and delivered, the Web pages are being created and posted, the motorcycle parts are being packaged and shipped, or the work is being done for whatever the venture's output may be. What now? Do we just assume that things are running smoothly and are going as planned? Well, maybe in another alternate realm that may be the case! But, the reality of managing the entrepreneurial venture isn't that simple. Things don't always go as planned and results don't always measure up, but the only way we're going to know this is to measure and evaluate performance. In this section, we want to discuss what performance results might be important to entrepreneurs and then look at some tools and techniques that entrepreneurs could use to measure and evaluate performance.

What Performance Results Are Important?

Working at something, anything, results in some level of performance—good, poor, fair, or whatever. This is just as true on the individual level (and we'll discuss the basics of individual performance appraisal in the next chapter as we look at managing people) as it is on the organizational level. What we're concerned with here is measuring and evaluating performance on the organizational level. **Organizational performance** is defined as the organization's success at achieving its goals effectively and efficiently. On the organizational level, what performance results might be important for the entrepreneur to know? Before we look at specific organizational performance measures, we need to recognize that these measures can be either quantitative or qualitative. **Quantitative measures** are stated as numbers. They're quantifiable and can be easily assembled, calculated, and compared. **Qualitative measures,** on the other hand, define organizational activities that are hard to quantify. Some activities that the entrepreneurial venture might be doing may not easily be reduced to quantitative terms, so qualitative assessments would be appropriate; for instance, evaluating whether the organization is being socially responsible and ethical if that's an important goal. Although quantitative data are easier to collect and compare, keep in mind that qualitative measures might be appropriate indicators of performance, as well. Now, with that said, there are a couple of different types of organizational performance results we want to describe that entrepreneurs might be interested in measuring and evaluating.

Organizational Efficiency and Effectiveness. First, entrepreneurs may want to assess organizational efficiency and effectiveness. **Efficiency** concerns the amount of resources that are being used to meet the stated goals. It refers to the relationship between inputs (resources) and outputs. If you can get more output from the given inputs, you have increased efficiency. Likewise, if you can get the same level of output from fewer inputs, you're also increasing efficiency. Because most entrepreneurial ventures have limited resources, using them efficiently is an important organizational performance concern. Efficiency is often referred to as "doing things right"—that is, not wasting resources. On the other hand, **effectiveness** concerns whether an organization is meeting its stated goals. Effectiveness is often described as "doing the right things" because the entrepreneur wants to concentrate on doing those things that will help the entrepreneurial venture reach its goals. Whereas efficiency is concerned with the means of getting things done, effectiveness is concerned with the ends or attainment of organizational goals.

Efficiency and effectiveness should go hand in hand. Yes, it's easier to be effective if you ignore efficiency. You could expend whatever resources needed to achieve the goals. Although you would be getting the job done, it would be at a high cost. Likewise, an organization can be efficient, but not effective. It can do the wrong things, but do them well. The goals might be achieved, but they would be the wrong goals. Entrepreneurs should strive for both high effectiveness (high goal attainment) *and* high efficiency (low waste of resources). Successful entrepreneurial ventures typically have achieved high levels of both efficiency and effectiveness.

Global Perspectives

Tim Bryant and Mark Wheeler's entrepreneurial courier service, Pony Express, has prospered in Russia by being both efficient and effective. The company has earned a reputation for finding fast, clever solutions to local problems. For instance, when a Russian airline abruptly quadrupled fares on a key delivery route, Bryant and Wheeler brokered a deal with the pilots' union to pay cockpit crews to deliver their courier pouches. This type of innovative, flexible response to problems has allowed the company to stay afloat. That, and the fact that to stay competitive, it has had to keep tight control over expenses. So, it's *both* effective *and* efficient.

Source: C. Matlack, "Russian Relay," *Business Week Enterprise,* December 7, 1998, p. ENT26.

Financial Performance. One of the primary purposes of business organizations is to earn a profit. Profit data and other types of financial data serve to describe and summarize in monetary terms what the entrepreneurial venture is doing and how well it is doing. Because of the importance of doing well financially, financial results serve as a critical measure of organizational performance. In addition, much of the financial data is used to calculate efficiency measures. For instance, total sales divided by number of employees (provides a measure of sales per employee) is one measure of efficiency as is gross profit margin (shows cost of goods sold and direct labor expenses as a percentage of sales). Other financial measures will be discussed in the next section as we look at the performance measurement tools and techniques that entrepreneurs might use.

What Performance Measurement Tools and Techniques Are Available?

Now that we know what performance results might be important for entrepreneurs to look at, how can these performance areas be measured and evaluated? We want to describe four important measurement tools: financial statement analysis, financial ratio analysis, cash flow analysis, and SWOT analysis.

Financial Statement Analysis. Keeping up-to-date and thorough financial records is important for entrepreneurs. Why? These records are crucial because they can provide accurate information regarding the health of the business. An organization's financial results are reflections of how efficiently and effectively it's been doing its work. In addition, information from financial records is needed to prepare federal and state tax returns and also may be needed by banks and other financial institutions if the entrepreneurial venture requires additional capital. Unless the entrepreneur is able—and willing—to put these important financial records together, professional accounting or bookkeeping help and advice may be necessary. No matter *who* puts them together, one thing that's important in the creation of the venture's financial records is following **generally accepted accounting principles (GAAP)**. These are standards developed by the Financial Accounting Standards Board (FASB) to ensure that all businesses create uniform financial statement formats. Even though these standards provide a measure of uniformity, some flexibility is allowable as long as consistency is maintained within the business's financial records.

Keeping financial records begins with the creation of journals and ledgers. (As we discuss the creation and use of the various financial records, keep in mind that any of these tools can be manual based or computer based.) Raw data from sources such as sales slips, check stubs, or purchase invoices are recorded in an **accounting journal**, which is simply a chronological record of a business's financial transactions. The entrepreneur may have several accounting journals such as a sales journal, a purchases journal, a cash receipts journal, and a cash disbursements journal. These journals are the backbone of the venture's financial records, and the entrepreneur needs to keep these journals accurate and timely. Depending on the frequency and complexity of financial transactions, the entrepreneur may need to do these daily, every other day, or maybe even weekly. Then, at some regular time interval—usually at the end of a month—the financial transactions are divided into separate accounts and posted into a **general ledger**. The ledger provides a summary record of financial transactions. At the end of an accounting

---

Entrepreneurs in Action ▶

Even though Joan B. Anderson, owner of JBA, Inc., was awarded her former husband's 55-employee company at their divorce, she didn't get much of a prize. The heating, ventilation, and air-conditioning company, located in Melrose Park, Illinois, had almost no financial controls and kept purchase orders on file cards in a recipe box. The accountant hired to straighten out the company's books described their condition as deplorable. However, Joan persevered. After the financial records had been organized, she established strict financial checks and balances. For instance, explanations of cost overruns that previously needed only a project manager's signature now required backup documentation. In addition, she invested heavily in technology to help employees be more efficient and accurate in their work. Now the firm's annual revenues have climbed to over $23 million, and Anderson has launched a second company, Advanced Cleanroom Technology, which will construct manufacturing facilities for high-tech firms across the United States.

Source: "Entrepreneurial Excellence," *Working Woman,* May 1999, p. 47.

---

period (month, quarter, year), each individual account in the ledger is closed and totaled. This information is compiled into commonly used financial statements that show an entrepreneur how the venture is doing financially. Let's look at some of these financial statements.

The **income statement** (also called the **profit and loss** or **P&L**) is a financial statement that shows the revenues and expenses of a business and the resulting profit or loss over a specific period of time. The income statement shows the financial condition of a business over time—that is, it provides a "moving picture" of the venture's financial performance. The main sections of the income statement that can be analyzed by the entrepreneur include sales (or revenues or income); cost of goods sold (the total costs of products or services sold during the time period); gross profit; operating, general, and other expenses of the entrepreneurial venture not associated with the cost of goods sold; and net income (or loss). How can the entrepreneur use this information to help measure performance? One thing you can do is calculate the percentage relationship of each item of expense to sales. This results in what is known as a **common-size income statement**, a valuable tool for checking the efficiency of the entrepreneurial venture. You're measuring the changes in the use of resources because resource usage is indicated by its cost or expense. Another way the entrepreneur can measure performance is by looking at the trends in sales, expenses, and income using both the regular income statement and the common-size income statement. If sales show a downward trend or if expenses (actual or percentage) show an upward trend without an accompanying upward trend in sales, the entrepreneur needs to evaluate what's happening. Is there a problem that needs to be addressed? By continually measuring and analyzing the financial information on the income statement, an entrepreneur is alerted to actual and potential problems in the actual working operations of the business.

The second primary financial statement is the **balance sheet**, a financial statement that shows the value of an organization's assets, liabilities, and owner's equity. This financial statement provides a snapshot of the entrepreneurial venture at any given point in time (usually at the end of a financial period —month, quarter, or year). The two main sections of the balance sheet show the value of the assets the venture owns and the claims against those assets in the form of liabilities (the value of what is owed to others) and owner's equity (the value of the owner's stake in the business). This information also can be shown in a **common-size balance sheet**, which takes each section separately (assets, and liabilities and equity), sets the total equal to 100 percent, and then shows each item in that section as a percentage of the total. As with the common-size income statement, these percentages can indicate areas of concern. Both actual numbers and trends can be measured and evaluated to see if there are any current or potential problems.

The third primary financial statement needed by entrepreneurs for measuring and evaluating performance is the **cash flow statement**, which is a financial statement that shows cash inflows and outflows of a business. You probably personally know the importance of keeping track of cash inflows and outflows if you've ever run out of money (cash) to pay your bills or to buy necessities. Keeping track of cash flow is critical to the survival of entrepreneurial ventures, maybe even more critical than profits. Many businesses show a profit, but have problems paying their bills on time because they have a cash flow problem. Negative cash flow (more cash going out than coming in) is common for new businesses. This situation isn't alarming *as long as* it happens infrequently and if the business is very young. But, if these situations aren't the case, then there's a problem of inadequate cash flow. Managing cash flow is such an important performance analysis and measurement tool for entrepreneurs that we've got a whole chapter section devoted to it. We'll get to it after we discuss financial ratio analysis.

Financial Ratio Analysis. With the information from the two primary financial statements— that is, the income statement and the balance sheet—the entrepreneur can measure and evaluate changes in financial performance through **financial**

Rapid Review

✓ How is organizational performance defined? Are quantitative performance measures or qualitative measures more important?

✓ What types of organizational performance results might entrepreneurs be interested in measuring and evaluating?

✓ What does it mean for an organization to be efficient? Effective?

✓ Why is it important to measure and evaluate financial performance?

✓ What are generally accepted accounting principles? Why are they important?

✓ What types of financial records should an entrepreneurial venture keep? How are an accounting journal and a general ledger related?

✓ Describe the common types of financial statements.

ratio analysis. What is financial ratio analysis? It's a way to express relationships between key accounting elements from the financial statements and a convenient and relatively easy technique for doing a financial analysis. By watching the trends in the financial ratios, an entrepreneur can spot red flags in performance and take appropriate action(s), if necessary, before they become critical.

There are four major categories of financial ratios. (See Table 7-1 for a description of these ratios and how they're calculated. We're not going to go into a detailed explanation of these ratios under the assumption that you've covered or will cover this information in an accounting or finance course.) The **liquidity ratios** measure the organization's ability to meet its current debt obligations with its current assets. The two main types of liquidity ratios are the

TABLE 7-1   Major Financial Ratios

Category	Ratio	Calculation	Objective
Liquidity	Current ratio	$\dfrac{\text{Current assets}}{\text{Current liabilities}}$	Tests the organization's ability to meet short-term obligations
	Quick or acid test	$\dfrac{\text{Current assets minus inventories}}{\text{Current liabilities}}$	Tests liquidity more accurately when inventories turn over slowly or are difficult to sell
Leverage	Debt-to-assets	$\dfrac{\text{Total debt}}{\text{Total assets}}$	Indicates the amount of the organization's assets being financed by debt; the higher the ratio, the more leveraged the organization
	Debt-to-equity	$\dfrac{\text{Total debt}}{\text{Total equity}}$	Shows the relationship of the organization's use of debt versus its use of equity
	Times interest earned	$\dfrac{\text{Profits before interest and taxes}}{\text{Total interest expenses}}$	Measures how many times the organization can cover its interest expenses
Operating	Inventory turnover	$\dfrac{\text{Sales}}{\text{Inventory}}$	Measures how many times the organization turns over (sells) its inventory
	Total asset turnover	$\dfrac{\text{Sales}}{\text{Total assets}}$	Shows how efficiently the organization is using its assets to generate sales
Profitability	Profit margin	$\dfrac{\text{Net income}}{\text{Sales}}$	Identifies how much is being made in profit for every dollar of sales
	Return on investment (ROI) or Return on assets (ROA)	$\dfrac{\text{Net income}}{\text{Total sales}}$	Identifies the profits per dollar of assets
	Return on stockholders' equity (ROE)	$\dfrac{\text{Net income}}{\text{Total stockholders' equity}}$	Identifies the profits per dollar of stockholders' equity
	Earnings per share (EPS)	$\dfrac{\text{Net income}}{\text{Number of shares of common stock outstanding}}$	Provides a measure of earnings available to the owners of common stock
	Price earnings ratio	$\dfrac{\text{Market price per share}}{\text{Earnings per share}}$	Provides an indicator of the attractiveness of the organization to equity markets

current and the quick (or acid test). **Leverage ratios** examine the organization's use of debt and the use of equity to finance its assets—in other words, they're measures of the firm's leverage. In addition, one other key leverage ratio examines whether the organization is able to meet interest payments on any debt. As you know from the balance sheet format, an organization's assets can be financed in only two ways—through debt or through equity. Remember the accounting equation: assets = liabilities + owner's equity. These ratios measure the organization's asset financing provided by the owners and that provided by creditors. The main leverage ratios include the debt-to-assets, debt-to-equity, and times interest earned. These ratios reflect important decisions about the type of financing used by the entrepreneur. The next major category of financial ratios is the **operating ratios**, which measure how efficiently the organization is using its assets—in other words, how efficiently is the venture operating? The key operating ratios are inventory turnover, total asset turnover, fixed asset turnover, average collection period, average payable period, and working capital turnover. For each of these operating ratios, you're calculating a measure of efficiency of asset usage. After all, the only reason an entrepreneurial venture has assets is to help it earn revenues (and, hopefully, profits). These operating ratios indicate how efficiently the organization is using its assets to do this. The final category of financial ratios is the **profitability ratios**, which measure how profitable the organization is. Very simply, the profitability ratios are a proxy of the venture's efficiency and effectiveness, and are critical indicators of performance. The main profitability ratios are the profit margin (both net and gross), return on investment (or return on assets), return on equity, earnings per share, and price earnings ratio.

Although it's important to calculate the financial ratios on a regular basis (usually quarterly and annually), the fact that the entrepreneur calculates financial ratios isn't enough! By themselves, the ratios are nothing more than a series of numbers and percentages reflecting an organization's financial performance for a certain period of time. He or she must understand how to interpret what the ratios are showing and apply this performance information to managing the venture's work processes more effectively and efficiently. Interpreting the ratios involves comparing them to industry ratios and to trends for both the organization and the industry. However, a cautionary note needs to be made regarding any comparison of organization ratios to industry ratios. The industry ratios are simply averages of financial information reported to the various data-gathering companies. Although knowing the industry average gives an entrepreneur some standard of comparison, the goal should be to manage the entrepreneurial venture so that work performance (and the resulting financial results) is better than the average. In addition, when a financial ratio is substantially out of line from the industry ratio, it's important for an entrepreneur carefully to assess why there's a discrepancy before making any drastic changes in what is being done and how. You must know what the ratios are showing and what they reflect.

Cash Flow Analysis. Cash. It's an absolutely vital economic unit of exchange. Unless you barter for your essentials of daily living, you know that cash is critical! Although bartering for goods and services may be something that entrepreneurs engage in occasionally, they also need cash to run their businesses. Without cash to purchase needed resources, to resolve unanticipated problems, or to invest in opportunities, the entrepreneur would be extremely limited in what could be done and how.

We're going to define **cash flow** as the actual amount of cash an organization brings in and the actual amount of cash it pays out in a given time period. Positive cash flow is when the amount of cash coming in is greater than the amount of cash going out, and likewise, negative cash flow is when the amount of cash going out is greater than the amount of cash coming in.

The major challenge in managing cash flow is timing. The goal of good cash flow management is making sure there's enough cash on hand when you need it. Having a positive cash balance three months from now doesn't matter if you have payroll, utility bills, and suppliers that need to be paid today. Although some cash inflows and outflows occur on a regular schedule, other cash flows do not. Fortunately, entrepreneurs can use certain cash flow management tools and techniques. In the process of managing cash flow, entrepreneurs do play different and important roles. (See Table 7-2.)

The cash flow management tools we're going to look at include the cash budget and ways to manage accounts receivable, accounts payable, and inventory. Let's discuss the cash budget.

TABLE 7-2 Key Cash Management Roles Played by Entrepreneurs

Role 1: CASH FINDER

- Most important role played by entrepreneur
- Making sure there's enough cash to pay present and future bills
- An ongoing job

Role 2: CASH PLANNER

- Making sure cash is used properly and efficiently
- Requires keeping track of cash and planning for its use
- Forecasting cash inflows and outflows

Role 3: CASH DISTRIBUTOR

- Controlling the cash used to pay bills and other obligations
- Keeping on top of priority and timing of these cash payments
- Making sure cash is available when needed

Role 4: CASH COLLECTOR

- Collecting the cash that's due
- Making sure it's collected on time

Role 5: CASH CONSERVER

- Getting maximum value for cash being spent
- Getting the most for your money
- Avoiding unnecessary expenditures

Source: Based on B. J. Blechman, "Quick Change Artist," *Entrepreneur*, January 1994, pp. 18–21.

The cash budget (or cash forecast) is a way for the entrepreneur to plan the venture's short-term cash needs. It shows the amount and timing of cash receipts and cash disbursements on a daily, weekly, or monthly basis. Keep in mind that a cash budget is just a forecast of cash inflows and outflows. It will never be completely accurate. However, it does give the entrepreneur a pretty good idea of cash balances for the time period. How often an entrepreneur does a cash budget would depend on the nature of the business. If the venture's cash flows are uncertain, it would be better to do more cash budgets in order to maintain some sense of control. Using monthly cash budgets is quite common, but some organizations may require daily cash budgets.

There are five steps to preparing a cash budget. (See Figure 7-3.) Step 1 is to *determine the desired cash balance to keep on hand.* The entrepreneur needs to decide what amount of cash he or she wishes to keep as a reserve. This amount should not be excessive because the cash may be put to better, more productive uses, but it also should not be so small that the entrepreneur worries every time period whether there's going to be cash to pay the bills. Probably the best way to determine this amount is based on experience. Step 2 is to *identify the beginning cash.* The entrepreneur must know what cash is on hand at the start of the time period. In step 3, you should *forecast cash receipts.* This forecast is an important element in the cash budget. Cash receipts includes cash sales, payment of any accounts receivables (amounts people owe you), interest payments, cash contributions by owner(s), and any other cash inflows. You want to have a good idea of what cash is

Figure 7-3

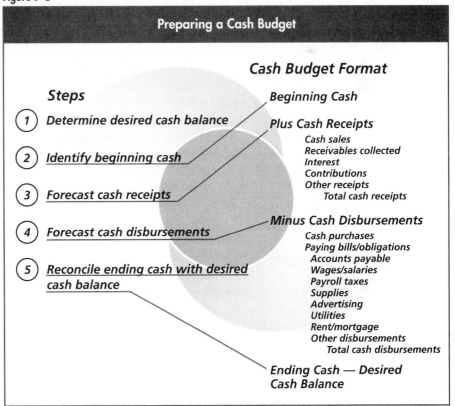

coming in, but it's not always easy to do this. Entrepreneurs in new entrepreneurial ventures and ones in highly uncertain industries may find it particularly challenging to forecast cash receipts. In step 4, you should *forecast cash disbursements.* This is relatively easy for an established business because the patterns of cash disbursements, for the most part, should be pretty similar. However, it's probably better to *over*estimate cash disbursements (within reasonable amounts) to ensure enough cash is on hand in case expenditures are higher than expected. Finally, in step 5, you should *reconcile ending cash with the desired cash balance.* If the ending cash figure is more than the desired cash balance, the entrepreneur has excess cash to invest or pay down loans. If there's a negative difference, the entrepreneur will have to arrange for financing or look for other sources of cash.

Other cash flow management techniques revolve around managing the "big three" of an organization's cash flow: accounts receivable, accounts payable, and inventory.[6] Accounts receivable are amounts owed to your business because customers have purchased on credit; that is, they get the product or service, but don't pay for it until a later time. Selling on credit is a common practice in business, but it's an expensive one. It's important for an entrepreneur to establish an effective and efficient collection approach. Remember that this is *your* cash. You want to get what's owed you. (The FYI box in this chapter section provides some practical advice for entrepreneurs in managing accounts receivable, accounts payable, and inventory.) Accounts payable are amounts that you owe to others. These amounts reflect what you have purchased on credit. The objective behind effectively and efficiently managing accounts payable is just the opposite from that of the accounts receivable. When you owe money, you want to take as long as possible to pay without damaging your venture's credit rating. Finally, how the entrepreneurial venture's inventory (both raw materials and finished goods) is managed can affect cash flow. You want to make sure you have the right type and amount of inventory to meet customers' needs. Carrying items in inventory can be expensive, especially if they sit there for a long time. The inventory needs to be turned into cash.

SWOT Analysis. SWOT. What an odd "word"! The letters actually are an acronym for **S**trengths, **W**eaknesses, **O**pportunities, and **T**hreats. More importantly, though, SWOT analysis is a tool that entrepreneurs can use in assessing the work being done in their entrepreneurial venture and how organizational performance is measuring up.

An analysis of the venture's internal work activities and processes identifies strengths and weaknesses. **Strengths** are activities that the organization is doing well. Organizational strengths should be reinforced and nurtured because they influence how well the organization ultimately performs its work. In addition, strengths can be important potential competitive weapons. **Weaknesses** are things that the organization does not do well. Organizational weaknesses need to be corrected if they're in critical areas that are affecting the venture's performance and its ability to be competitive. This internal analysis is typically done through an **internal audit**, which very simply is a thorough assessment of the venture's internal work areas. It usually includes an evaluation of the activities, processes, and strategies in production and operations, marketing, human resource management, research and development, information systems and technology, and financial. Obviously, however, the internal audit should cover a venture's own specific and

Tips for Managing the Big Three

The big three of cash flow management are accounts receivable, accounts payable, and inventory. There's bound to be significant cash flow in and through all of these areas. An entrepreneurial venture should always try to get cash as fast as possible from accounts receivable and to stretch out the payables. So, how can each of these areas be "managed" for the most efficient and effective use of your entrepreneurial venture's often scarce cash?

Accounts Receivable
Here are some tips to help get your cash in quicker. (1) Have a clear and well-thought-out credit and collection policy. (2) Speed up getting customer orders by offering fax services or on-line ordering. (3) Process customer orders as quickly as possible, but do so accurately. (4) Prepare the customer invoice the same day the order is received. Make sure it is clear and accurate. State payment terms exactly and clearly. (5) Mail the invoice the same day it is prepared. The sooner the bill is in the mail, the sooner you're going to see your cash. (6) Use aging schedules (a list of accounts receivables sorted by when they're due—also known as the "age" of the account). (7) Don't wait too long to start collection of a customer's unpaid bill.

Accounts Payable
Here are some tips for managing what you owe. (1) Set up a monthly payment calendar so you know what is due when and so you can take advantage of early payment discounts. It's usually to your benefit to take advantage of these cash discounts. (2) Keep all bill-paying paperwork organized. (3) Verify all invoices before paying. (4) If possible, stagger payments so you aren't paying several bills all at once. That can be a significant drain on cash flow. (5) Keep on the lookout for early warning signs that your cash flow is in trouble.

Inventory
Purchasing and holding inventory can be a significant drain on cash flow. You want to have enough inventory on hand to meet your operational and customer needs, but not too much that it's lying around not generating any return. In addition, unused inventory has to be stored, which can be another cash expense. Here are some tips for managing your inventory. (1) Make sure you have the right kind of inventory. (2) Keep inventory lean and turn it over frequently. (3) Use markdowns to get rid of inventory, if necessary. (4) Schedule inventory deliveries at the latest possible date to stretch out the time when the payment is due. (5) Other things being equal (that is, quality and price), order from the fastest supplier so you can keep inventory levels fairly low.

Sources: T. S. Hatten, *Small Business* (Upper Saddle River, NJ: Prentice Hall, 1997), pp. 468–69; T. W. Zimmerer and N. J. Scarborough, *Essentials of Entrepreneurship and Small Business Management*, 2nd ed. (Upper Saddle River, NJ: Prentice Hall, 1998), pp. 232–39; and "Steps for Improving Your Firm's Cash Flow," *Nation's Business*, November 1998, p. 12.)

unique work areas. An internal audit looks at what is being done in each area and assesses how efficiently (low waste of resources) and effectively (meeting goals) that particular area's work is being done. Depending on what results the internal analysis shows, the entrepreneur may need to make some decisions about correcting problems (weaknesses) or exploiting strengths. Although the internal analysis is a significant part of measuring and evaluating organizational performance, it's also important to look externally because there are things happening there that can impact a venture's current and future performance.

An analysis of the trends and changes happening outside the organization provides an indication of areas of potential opportunities and threats. *Opportunities* (as we defined earlier in this chapter and in other previous chapters) are positive and favorable external trends or changes that the entrepreneur might want to take advantage of. **Threats**, then, are negative and unfavorable external trends and changes that the entrepreneur will probably want to avoid or at least buffer against. The external analysis looks at what's happening in the world by examining trends and changes in the economic, technological, demographics, social–cultural, global, and political–legal arenas. By assessing these external factors, the entrepreneur attempts to pinpoint what changes may be necessary in the organization to exploit

Keeping Score

Do you keep track of your points earned in the various classes you're taking? Would basketball (or football, baseball, hockey, soccer) be as fun to follow if no scores were recorded? Keeping score provides a way to judge how you (or your favorite team) are doing. Entrepreneurs are discovering that keeping track of their company's performance can be as easy as keeping a scorecard.

Scorecards serve many purposes. They help entrepreneurs clarify strategic goals. You have to decide what's important and then identify the things you're going to track to ensure that performance in those areas is making a difference. In addition, scorecards help communicate those objectives to other people in the organization. Through the scorecards, there are no misunderstandings about the standards used in measuring nebulous organizational performance concepts such as customer satisfaction. Finally, because of their design, scorecards can provide rapid, easily understood feedback about how the entrepreneurial venture or any of its work areas are doing.

What should a scorecard include? The process starts with deciding organizational goals and then translating those goals into specific, concrete measures. Some experts recommend that a scorecard rates four areas: (1) financial scores, which cover such things as sales growth and profitability; (2) customer scores, which include rankings for market share, customer satisfaction, and so forth; (3) learning and growth scores, which measure such things as employee turnover, productivity, and other types of employee and organizational learning; and (4) an internal business process score, which measures product development, innovation, efficiency, and so forth. The choice of what to score should be determined by an organization's specific markets, strengths, and strategies. Once you've decided what the scorecard should keep track of, then it's just a matter of getting good information. You have to measure performance in the areas you've decided are important. Then, after a certain period of time (monthly, quarterly, semiannually, annually, or whatever), you'll need to show the performance results on a scorecard. The scorecard itself should be designed to present the "scores" as clearly and briefly as possible. The intent of the scorecard is not to be a long, involved performance measurement report, but a clear, succinct summary of the most critical performance measures.

Scorecards are tools that help entrepreneurs communicate the vision to all levels of an organization. As one proponent said, "It keeps you in tune with what's going on."

Sources: J. Case, "Keeping Score," *Inc.*, June 1998, pp. 80–86; and M. Henricks, "Who's Counting?" *Entrepreneur*, July 1998, pp. 70–73.

Rapid Review ◀◀◀

✓ Describe what the four categories of financial ratios measure and the major ratios in each of the four categories.

✓ Why isn't calculating financial ratios sufficient for measuring performance?

✓ What is cash flow? What cash management roles do entrepreneurs play?

✓ What is a cash budget? Outline the five steps to preparing one.

✓ How can entrepreneurs manage the big three for the most efficient cash flow?

✓ What does SWOT stand for? How is it a performance measurement tool?

✓ How can a performance scorecard be useful? What does a scorecard measure?

the opportunities and to keep away from the threats. These changes will affect what work is being done and how it's being performed.

All of the performance measurement tools and techniques that we've discussed in this section—financial statement analysis, financial ratio analysis, cash flow analysis, and SWOT analysis—provide a picture of how efficiently and effectively the entrepreneurial venture is performing. What happens next? Depending on organizational performance results, it may be necessary for the entrepreneur to make changes to what the venture is doing and how work is being done. That's the topic we want to look at next—stimulating and making changes.

STIMULATING AND MAKING CHANGES—BEING A CHANGE AGENT

Change—the only thing constant about it is the fact that it *is* constant. We know from earlier discussions that the context facing entrepreneurs is one of dynamic change. Both external and internal forces may bring about the need to make changes in the entrepreneurial venture. External forces for organizational change include changes in technology, global competition, economic trends, or in any other number of external factors. Internal forces for change may include any decisions and actions taken by organizational members in response to not meeting performance goals, developing and implementing a new strategy, or adapting to other changing organizational circumstances. Any of these changing external or internal forces may bring about the need to stimulate organizational change. What exactly is **organizational change**? We're going to define it as any alterations in what an organization does and how it does it. Entrepreneurs need to be alert to problems and opportunities that may create the need to change. In so doing, the entrepreneur may have to act as a **change agent**, a person who's a catalyst for change and who also manages the change process.

Of the many hats an entrepreneur wears, that of change agent may be one of the most important.[7] If changes are needed in the entrepreneurial venture, often it is the entrepreneur who first recognizes the need for change and acts as the catalyst, coach and cheerleader, and chief change consultant. Change isn't easy in any organization, but it can be particularly challenging for entrepreneurial organizations. Even if a person is comfortable with taking risks, as entrepreneurs usually are, change can be hard. That's why it's important for the entrepreneur to recognize the critical roles he or she plays in stimulating and implementing change.

As a change agent, the entrepreneur plays different roles. First and foremost, the entrepreneur is a catalyst for change. He or she should be alert to signals that change is needed—signs from external or internal circumstances and situations or signs from organizational performance results. Often, the entrepreneur is the first person who, while managing the organizational processes, recognizes the need for change and moves to take action. What kinds of organizational change efforts

---

Entrepreneurs in Action ▶

Terry Ehrich, publisher and editor in chief of *Hemmings Motor News* (**www.hemmings.com**), knows how important it is to be a change agent. He has built the magazine to its role as "the bible of the car-collector hobby market." It sells almost 265,000 copies a month and has gross annual revenues in the range of $20 million. Although Ehrich is quite modest about his accomplishments, the fact is that he's a savvy businessperson who has prospered by listening and responding to his customers and employees. He hasn't been afraid to take risks and make changes in guiding his entrepreneurial venture.

Source: R. Kiener, "Hitting on All Cylinders," *Nation's Business,* June 1999, pp. 57–58.

---

might the entrepreneur have to initiate? Organizational change may be necessary in any or all of the following organizational areas: strategy, technology, products, structure, or people and culture. Changes in strategy may range all the way from minor adjustments to major alterations in the way that organizational goals are pursued through the various strategies. Changes in technology usually involve the introduction of new equipment, tools, or methods; automation; or computerization. Product changes involve any innovations or creative developments in current or new products. (The process of managing creativity and innovation is a significant part of managing the venture's overall processes, and we'll look at it more in depth in the next section in this chapter.) Changes in structure involve any alteration in the way the venture is designed and structured. Remember from Chapter 5 that organizational design includes decisions about work specialization, chain of command, departmentalization, span of control, centralization–decentralization, and formalization. Any alterations in any of these aspects would involve structural change. Finally, changes in people include any changes in organizational members' values, attitudes, beliefs, norms, or behaviors—that is, a change in the culture. These types of "people" changes may be among the most difficult that entrepreneurs have to make because people are often reluctant and unwilling to change. However, resistance to organizational change efforts is to be expected. Managing resistance brings up the second role that entrepreneurs may have to play as change agents—that of being a coach and cheerleader.

During any organizational change, the entrepreneur may have to act as chief coach and cheerleader. Think about what coaches and cheerleaders do. They encourage, they support, they explain, they get you excited, they build you up, and they motivate you to put forth your best efforts. Organizational change of any type can be disruptive and scary. If there are other employees in the entrepreneurial venture, they may resist making changes. Thus, the entrepreneur must assume the role of explaining the change and encouraging change efforts by being a coach and cheerleader. Overcoming any resistance to change requires intense interpersonal efforts and support. If the entrepreneurial venture has a fairly open and flexible structure, the entrepreneur may find that being candid about the change, allowing organizational members to participate in the change, providing facilitation and support, and educating organizational members about the change may work best. If the entrepreneurial venture's structure isn't quite as open or flexible, the entrepreneur may need to rely more on telling people what to do. In either case, this role of being chief coach and cheerleader is an important one because it gets at the heart of making changes—getting people to accept and embrace the change.

Finally, the entrepreneur may have to act as the primary organizational change consultant if fees for hiring change consultants from outside the organization are beyond the venture's available financial resources. A change consultant guides the actual change process as changes in strategy, technology, products, structure, or people are being implemented. In this role, the entrepreneur answers questions, makes suggestions, gets needed resources, facilitates conflict, and does whatever else is necessary to get the change(s) implemented. In addition, in this role, the entrepreneur would evaluate the success of the change implementation—that is, would evaluate whether the change has been implemented efficiently and effectively—and then take any necessary action.

A predictable part of managing the ongoing processes of the entrepreneurial venture is stimulating and making changes. Whether the changes are in response to performance results that don't quite measure up or are made to exploit opportunities, the entrepreneur plays important roles as a change agent. In addition to the topics we've just covered that are part and parcel of managing the venture's processes, there are some contemporary issues that entrepreneurs face as they do manage processes.

Rapid Review ◀◀|

✓ What is organizational change?
✓ What brings about the need for organizational change?
✓ Why might the role of change agent be one of the most important an entrepreneur plays?
✓ Describe the different roles an entrepreneur might play in stimulating and implementing change.
✓ What types of organizational change might an entrepreneur have to initiate?

CONTEMPORARY ISSUES IN MANAGING PROCESSES

Throughout the ongoing and continual organizational processes of making decisions, measuring and evaluating organizational performance, and stimulating and making changes, the entrepreneur is focused on making sure the venture is operating as efficiently and effectively as possible. However, in today's intensely competitive climate, the entrepreneur also must be aware of the importance of managing creativity and innovation, managing quality, and becoming a world-class organization. We're going to discuss these important contemporary issues in this section.

Managing Creativity and Innovation

In today's dynamic, chaotic world of global competition, organizations must continually innovate new products and services if they want to compete successfully. We know from earlier chapters that innovation is a key cornerstone and characteristic of entrepreneurial organizations. Entrepreneurial organizations are continually innovating. In fact, you can say that innovation is what makes the entrepreneurial organization "entrepreneurial." In a sense, creativity and innovation involve change—change in *what* the organization makes or change in *how* it makes its products. We defined **creativity** in Chapter 2 as the ability to combine ideas in a unique way or to make unusual associations between ideas.[8] On the other hand, **innovation** was defined as the process of taking a creative idea and turning it into a useful (marketable) product, service, or method of operation. We're making a distinction between the two seemingly similar terms because creativity, by itself, isn't enough to make an entrepreneurial venture successful. That creativity has to be channeled into some product or process that the organization can benefit from. An innovative organization is characterized by its ability to turn creativity into valuable outcomes. How can innovation be cultivated in the entrepreneurial venture?

Cultivating Innovation. If an entrepreneur wants to encourage innovation in the organization, it's important to have creative individuals or groups planted in the right environment. Just as it takes the proper environment for a flower to grow beautiful blooms, it takes the right environment for innovation to take hold and prosper. What does this kind of environment look like? Three types of factors have been found to stimulate innovation in organizations: structural factors, cultural factors, and human resource factors.[9] (See Figure 7-4.)

An organization's structure can have a significant impact on whether or not innovation blooms. Extensive research into the effect of structural variables on innovation has shown three things.[10] First, organic-type structures have a positive effect on innovation. Remember from Chapter 5 that this type of organization is low in formalization, centralization, and work specialization. It's a highly open, free-flowing, and flexible type of structure. The organic design facilitates the flexibility, adaptability, and cross-fertilization among people and work units that are necessary for creativity and innovation to occur and thrive. The second structural factor that's been shown to impact innovation efforts positively is having sufficient resources to support the innovation process. Why are resources important?

Figure 7-4

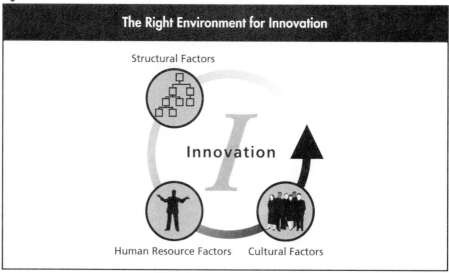

Resources—financial resources, in particular—allow the entrepreneur to purchase innovations, pay the expenses associated with implementing innovations, or absorb the costs of unsuccessful innovations. However, this may be the most difficult structural factor for the entrepreneur to control. Financial resources may be limited. However, even with the challenging constraint of limited resources, innovation processes are too important to ignore. Some investment in innovation is vital for the long-run survival and ultimate success of the entrepreneurial organization. The third structural factor that's important to the innovation process is encouraging frequent communication among the various organizational work units (departments, divisions, or whatever). Free-flowing and continual cross-communication has been shown to help break down barriers to innovation.[11] Sharing information and openly collaborating on ideas can create an environment that's conducive to high levels of creativity and innovation. Although the structural factors are important, they're just one aspect of nurturing innovation. Now let's look at the cultural factors.

Innovative organizations tend to have similar cultures.[12] They encourage experimentation, reward both successes and failures, and celebrate mistakes. An innovative culture is likely to have the following characteristics:

- *Acceptance of ambiguity.* Too much emphasis on objectivity and specificity constrains creativity.
- *Tolerance of the impractical.* Individuals who come up with impractical, even foolish, answers to what-if questions are not stifled. What at first seems impractical might lead to innovative solutions.
- *Low external controls.* Rules, regulations, policies, and similar organizational controls are kept to a minimum.
- *Tolerance of risk.* Employees are encouraged to experiment without fear of consequences if they should fail. Mistakes are treated as learning opportunities.
- *Tolerance of conflict.* Diversity of opinions is encouraged. Harmony and agreement between individuals or groups are not assumed to be evidence of high performance.
- *Focus on ends rather than means.* Goals are made clear, and individuals are encouraged to consider alternative routes toward meeting the goals. Focusing on ends suggests that there might be several right answers to any given problem or opportunity.
- *Open-system focus.* The entrepreneur closely monitors the environment and responds rapidly to changes as they occur.

Each of these cultural characteristics contributes to an atmosphere in which creativity and innovation can flourish. But culture is just a reflection of the people who comprise the entrepreneurial venture. What about the people factor? What role does it play in the innovative organization?

Innovative organizations understand the importance of the people who work there. Innovative organizations do many things to support the innovation efforts of their members such as actively training and developing people so that their knowledge remains current, offering their employees high levels of job security to reduce the fear of getting fired for making mistakes, and encouraging individuals to become champions of new ideas. These **idea champions** are individuals who actively and enthusiastically pursue new ideas, build support, overcome resistance, and ensure that an innovation is implemented. Having idea champions throughout the entrepreneurial organization goes a long way toward ensuring that creative and innovative thinking (and doing) will thrive. It's not only the entrepreneur who should play the role of idea champion. In a truly innovative organization, idea champions will be found in different areas. They'll be those individuals who are willing to take a stand, to try something different, and to passionately pursue different and unique ideas.

Managing creativity and innovation are important issues for entrepreneurs to recognize. Another contemporary issue entrepreneurs must understand is managing quality.

Managing Quality

Before we get into discussing how to manage quality, we need to define what **quality** is. First, from the customers' perspective, it means how well your product or service satisfies their needs. From the entrepreneurial venture's perspective, it's how closely your product or service conforms to the standards you have established. Both perspectives are important!

The 1980s and 1990s saw a veritable explosion in organizational quality programs. Many U.S. corporations saw quality improvement as a way to restore their global competitiveness. This quality revolution is better known by its more commonly used name, **total quality management (TQM)**. TQM is a philosophy of managing an organization in a way that emphasizes customer needs and expectations and uses any number of work actions and activities to improve quality. Few organizations, any size or type, can afford *not* to pay attention to quality.

Total Quality Organizations. Although there are no universal characteristics of a total quality organization, they tend to have 10 core values.[13] These are shown in Figure 7-5. Let's look briefly at each of these 10 values.

Customer driven means that all work methods, processes, and procedures are designed to meet the expectations of both external and internal customers. Leadership commitment refers to the fact that organizational leaders and decision makers fully understand the quality process and totally support organizational quality programs. Full participation means that every person in the organization is provided with quality training and participates in implementing the quality programs. A reward system refers to the fact that the organizational reward system should reward quality achievements and accomplishments. Reduced cycle time refers to efforts to reduce the time it takes to get work done (cycle time). Prevention, not detection, means that quality starts with the design of the product or service so that errors are prevented from occurring in the first place. Employees don't rely just on detecting and then correcting quality problems after they've already happened. Management by fact means that managers use actual data, not simply intuition, to measure progress toward quality goals. A long-range outlook means that employees are constantly and continually monitoring the external environment to help determine what levels of quality might be demanded by customers over the next couple of years. Partnership development describes the cooperative relationships the organization develops with vendors and customers to meet quality demands. Finally, corporate responsibility refers to

Figure 7-5

Ten Core Values of a Total Quality Organization

Source: Based on R. M. Hodgetts, F. Luthans, and S. M. Lee, "New Paradigm Organizations: From Total Quality to Learning to World Class," *Organizational Dynamics,* winter 1994, pp. 4–19.

the organization's commitment to sharing quality-related information with other organizations and working to reduce negative impacts on a community that occur because of product waste and product defects or recalls. These values reflect a serious and total commitment to quality as a way of doing business.

Tools for Managing Quality. Managing quality means measuring quality. TQM uses statistical techniques to measure critical variables in the organization's operations. These are compared against standards or benchmarks to identify problems, trace them to their roots, and eliminate their causes. Quality improvement can occur only if there is continual measurement of the organization's various work activities to determine whether quality standards are being achieved and making changes when they're not. Again, it takes a serious commitment to quality.

To publicly demonstrate their quality commitment, many organizations have pursued quality certification, such as **ISO 9000** (pronounced "ice-o 9000"). What is ISO 9000? It's a series of quality management standards that organizations work to meet. These standards cover everything from contract review to product design to product delivery. The ISO 9000 standards are established by the International Organization for Standardization and have become an internationally recognized criterion for evaluating and comparing organizations in the global marketplace. (By the way, ISO isn't an acronym for the international organization; it comes from the Greek word *iso*, which means "equal.") The goal of pursuing this type of certification should be having work processes in place that enable organizational members to perform their jobs in a consistently high-quality way. Gaining ISO 9000 certification provides proof that quality systems and processes are in place.

Getting to the point where strict quality standards, such as ISO 9000, are met isn't an easy task. As we've said, it takes a serious commitment to controlling quality day in and day out, in every single task included in the organization's work. How can this seemingly overwhelming goal be achieved? Many organizations do so through a program of **continuous improvement**, which is the implementation of numerous small, incremental improvements in all areas of the organization on an ongoing basis. In continuous improvement, there's a commitment to finding one small way to improve the quality of the work done today and then doing the same thing tomorrow and the day after. No quality improvement is too small. With this approach, work activities and tasks are fine-tuned all the time.

It's apparent that managing quality is an important consideration for today's entrepreneurs. But there's one more topic we want to look at in this chapter that's important for entrepreneurs to understand—the concept of world-class organizations.

Becoming a World-Class Organization

What is a **world-class organization**? It's an organization that is continually looking for ways through its decisions and actions to be the best in the world at what it does. Even if an organization operates in a single geographic location, it should still strive to be the best at what it does in its own little "world." As you can well imagine, becoming a world-class organization means excelling in many areas. What characteristics does a world-class organization have? The major ones are shown in Figure 7-6.

Entrepreneurs in Action

At Granite Rock Company of Watsonville, California, the quality management program is an important strategic tool. In fact, Granite Rock takes its quality program so seriously that it was awarded a Malcolm Baldridge National Quality Award. (The Baldridge Award is the United States' highest award for quality management and achievement.) What types of quality programs does Granite Rock use? The company found through numerous customer surveys that on-time delivery was its customers' highest priority. It then set about establishing standards (or benchmarks) for achieving on-time performance. It went to an unusual source for the standards: Domino's Pizza outlets, which guarantee fast, accurate delivery. From that study of Domino's, Granite Rock instituted a program in which customers simply drive up in their trucks, insert a card, and tell the machine how much of which material is needed—much as you do at a bank ATM. The truck is loaded automatically, and a bill is sent to the customer later. The company's Granite Xpress is open 24 hours a day, 7 days a week to meet customer needs. This quality innovation and several others have helped Granite Rock remain a successful competitor in the rough-and-tumble construction materials market.

Source: M. Barrier, "Learning the Meaning of Measurement," *Nation's Business*, June 1994, pp. 72–74.

A strong customer focus is by far the most important characteristic of a world-class organization. At the heart of what the world-class organization does and how it does it is what customers (external or internal) need now or in the future. After all, an entrepreneurial venture is not in business to please itself, but to delight its customers. If you don't do this, you won't be in business long. This strong customer focus guides everything the venture does and is critically important for being a world-class organization.

Another distinctive characteristic of world-class organizations is their emphasis on continual learning and improvement. Whether it's finding ways to be faster or more efficient and effective than their competitors, world-class organizations look for ways to continuously improve. As we know from our discussion of organizational change and total quality management, you can't stand still! You continually have to look for ways to improve what you do and how you do it.

Another characteristic of the world-class organization is that it has a fluid and flexible organizational structure that allows it to respond quickly, decisively, and intelligently to internal and external changes and trends. World-class organizations don't get hung up on rigid job classifications, duties, or relationships. Instead, their organizational structure facilitates open, responsive, and flexible approaches to resolving problems or pursuing opportunities.

Figure 7-6

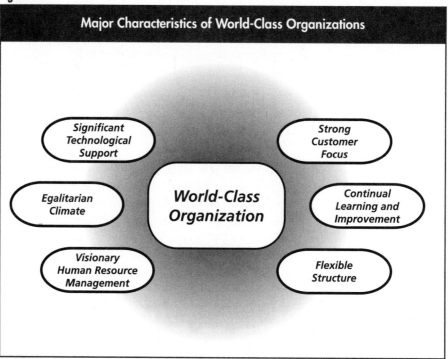

Major Characteristics of World-Class Organizations

Significant Technological Support

Strong Customer Focus

Egalitarian Climate

World-Class Organization

Continual Learning and Improvement

Visionary Human Resource Management

Flexible Structure

Source: Based on R. M. Hodgetts, F. Luthans, and S. M. Lee, "New Paradigm Organizations: From Total Quality to Learning to World Class," *Organizational Dynamics*, winter 1994, p. 15.

Speed Counts

Today's economic realities of being competitive are that it's not enough to be strong or shrewd, you also have to be swift. Speed and time compression have become considerably important currencies in the new economy. One of the most telling differentiators in business today is how close a company can come to operating in "real time"—that is, having the shortest possible lapse between idea and action, between implementation and result. What can world-class entrepreneurial organizations do to embrace speed? Here are some suggestions: (1) Seize the future. Don't wait until you feel the time is right. Someone else may just beat you to it. (2) Make speed the core of your business. Develop the capabilities to respond instantly—or at least rapidly—to customers' needs. (3) Accelerate your timetables. Make sure all work processes are being done in the best time possible without sacrificing quality. (4) Invest money to cut time. If it's important to move faster, spend the resources to do so. (5) Heed the caution signals. Recognize there are limits to how fast your speed can get. When work tasks become counterproductive, recognize it may be time to reconsider what you're doing and how you're doing it.

Source: D. D. Buss, "Embracing Speed," *Nation's Business*, June 1999, pp. 12–17.

The world-class organization also has visionary and creative human resource management policies, programs, and practices. Organizational members are valued and are treated in ways that they know their contributions are valued and appreciated. Most importantly, world-class organizations effectively energize their employees' creativity in decision making and in the ways they do their jobs. They're encouraged to be innovative and to continually look for ways to learn and improve.

Another attribute of the world-class organization is its egalitarian climate or culture. What does it mean to have this type of culture? It means that the organization and its members value and respect everyone both inside and outside the organization. Everyone and everything from customers, suppliers, fellow employees, and other stakeholders, to the community and the environment are treated with dignity and respect. World-class organizations recognize the interconnectedness of how they do business and their ultimate success.

The final characteristic of a world-class organization is significant technological support. In a world where speed and flexibility are critical to competitive success, technological support is crucial. But, understand that it's not the technology itself that's important. It's how the organization's people use the technology to serve customers more efficiently and effectively.

It's only fitting to end our discussion of world-class organizations by looking at a quote by Peter Drucker, one of the best-known and well-respected management thinkers and writers of today. In discussing the management challenges for the twenty-first century, he says, "No institution, whether a business, a university or a hospital, can hope to survive, let alone to succeed, unless it measures up to the standards set by the leaders in its field, anyplace in the world."[14] The challenge for you as an entrepreneur is to make sure that as you manage your venture's processes that you're doing just this.

Rapid Review

✓ Distinguish between creativity and innovation. Why are both important?

✓ What three types of factors have been found to stimulate innovation in organizations?

✓ Define idea champions. How important are they to innovation?

✓ What is quality? What is total quality management? List and describe the 10 core values of total quality organizations.

✓ What tools are available for managing quality?

✓ Define continuous improvement.

✓ What is a world-class organization? Describe the characteristics of a world-class organization.

CHAPTER SUMMARY

Once the entrepreneurial venture is launched, the entrepreneur must manage the various processes of the ongoing venture. This involves making decisions, measuring and evaluating organizational performance, stimulating and managing change, managing creativity and innovation, managing quality, and becoming a world-class organization.

A decision is a choice made between two or more alternatives. The process of making decisions involves six steps: (1) recognizing the need to make a decision, (2) identifying decision criteria, (3) weighting the criteria, (4) developing alternatives, (5) analyzing and evaluating each alternative, and (6) selecting an alternative. Once an alternative is selected, it would be implemented and after a period of time, evaluated. Although decision makers try to be as rational as possible in making decisions, certain factors limit how rational they can be. These include individual differences in information processing ability, individual decision-making style, the use of intuition, and different decision-making conditions.

One of the important tasks in managing processes is measuring and evaluating organizational performance. Organizational performance describes the organization's success at achieving its goals efficiently and effectively. The main types of organizational performance results entrepreneurs might be interested in measuring and evaluating are organizational efficiency and effectiveness and financial performance. Four important measurement tools include financial statement analysis, financial ratio analysis, cash flow analysis, and SWOT analysis. All of these tools provide a picture of how efficiently and effectively the entrepreneurial venture is performing. Depending on organizational performance results, it may be necessary for the entrepreneur to make changes.

Organizational change is defined as any alterations in what an organization does and how it does it. Stimulating and managing organizational change may require the entrepreneur to act as a change agent. In this capacity, the entrepreneur plays different roles. First, the entrepreneur is a catalyst for change. Organizational change may be necessary in any or all of the following organizational areas: strategy, technology, products, structure, or people and culture. Then, during any organizational change, the entrepreneur may have to act as chief coach and cheerleader. Finally, the entrepreneur may have to act as the primary organizational change consultant and guide the actual change process as changes in strategy, technology, products, structure, or people are being implemented.

In managing processes, entrepreneurs face some contemporary issues. One is managing creativity and innovation. Creativity is the ability to combine ideas in a unique way or to make unusual associations between ideas. Innovation, though, is the process of taking a creative idea and turning it into a marketable product, service, or method of operation. Innovation can be cultivated with the right type of organizational environment. Three types of factors have been found to stimulate innovation in organizations: structural, cultural, and human resource policies and practices. Another contemporary issue facing entrepreneurs is managing quality. The total quality management approach involves managing the organization in a way that emphasizes customer needs and expectations and uses any number of work actions and activities to improve quality. Total quality organizations tend to have 10 core values. In addition, many quality-minded organizations use tools including quality certification such as ISO 9000 and continuous improvement. Finally, an entrepreneur may wish to pursue becoming a world-class organization; that is, an organization that is continually looking for ways through its decisions and actions to be the best in the world at what it does. World-class organizations tend to have six characteristics: strong customer focus, emphasis on continual learning and improvement, fluid and flexible organization structure, visionary and creative human resource management, egalitarian climate, and technological support.

KEY TERMS

⟫ *Decision:* A choice made between two or more alternatives.
⟫ *Problem:* A situation where there's an inconsistency between actual and desired results.

➠ *Opportunity:* An optimistic possibility or positive trend.

➠ *Bounded rationality:* The concept that individuals have the time and cognitive ability to process only limited amounts of information as they make decisions.

➠ *Satisficing:* Seeking out alternatives that are satisfactory and sufficient.

➠ *Problem avoider:* A person who approaches problems by avoiding or ignoring information that points to a problem.

➠ *Problem solver:* A person who approaches problems by trying to solve them as they come up.

➠ *Problem seeker:* A person who proactively approaches problems by actively seeking out problems or new opportunities.

➠ *Directive style:* A decision-making style characterized by a low tolerance for ambiguity and a rational way of thinking.

➠ *Analytic style:* A decision-making style characterized by a high tolerance for ambiguity and a rational way of thinking.

➠ *Conceptual style:* A decision-making style characterized by a high tolerance for ambiguity and an intuitive way of thinking.

➠ *Behavioral style:* A decision-making style characterized by a low tolerance for ambiguity and an intuitive way of thinking.

➠ *Intuitive decision making:* A subconscious process of making decisions on the basis of experience and accumulated judgment.

➠ *Certainty:* A decision-making situation in which the decision maker can make accurate assessments of which alternative is best because the outcome of every alternative is known.

➠ *Risk:* A decision-making situation in which the decision maker is able to estimate the likelihood of certain outcomes.

➠ *Uncertainty:* A decision-making situation in which the decision maker is neither certain about outcomes nor able to make reasonable probability estimates.

➠ *Organizational performance:* The organization's success at achieving its goals effectively and efficiently.

➠ *Quantitative measures:* Performance measures that are quantifiable and easily assembled, calculated, and compared.

➠ *Qualitative measures:* Performance measures that describe organizational activities that are hard to quantify.

➠ *Efficiency:* A measure of the amount of resources being used to meet stated goals; described as doing things right.

➠ *Effectiveness:* A measure of whether an organization is meeting its stated goals; described as doing the right things.

➠ *Generally accepted accounting principles (GAAP):* Accounting standards developed by the Financial Accounting Standards Board (FASB) to ensure that all businesses create uniform financial statement formats.

➠ *Accounting journal:* A chronological record of a business's financial transactions.

➠ *General ledger:* A summary record of financial transactions.

➠ *Income statement (profit and loss or P&L):* A financial statement that shows the revenues and expenses of a business and the resulting profit or loss over a specific period of time.

➠ *Common-size income statement:* An income statement that shows the percentage of each item of expense to sales.

➠ *Balance sheet:* A financial statement that shows the value of an organization's assets, liabilities, and owner's equity.

➠ *Common-size balance sheet:* A balance sheet that takes each section separately, sets the total equal to 100 percent, and then shows each item in that section as a percentage of the total.

➠ *Cash flow statement:* A financial statement that shows cash inflows and outflows.

➠ *Financial ratio analysis:* A way to express relationships between key accounting elements from the financial statements.

➠ *Liquidity ratios:* Financial ratios that measure the organization's ability to meet its current debt obligations with its current assets.

➠ *Leverage ratios:* Financial ratios that examine the organization's use of debt and the use of equity to finance its assets.

➠ *Operating ratios:* Financial ratios that measure how efficiently the organization is using its assets.

➠ *Profitability ratios:* Financial ratios that measure how profitable the organization is.

➠ *Cash flow:* The actual amount of cash an organization brings in and the actual amount of cash it pays out in a given time period.

➠ *Strengths:* Activities and processes that the organization is doing well.

➠ *Weaknesses:* Activities and processes that the organization is not doing well.

➠ *Internal audit:* A thorough assessment of the venture's internal work areas.

➠ *Threats:* Negative and unfavorable external trends or changes.

➠ *Organizational change:* Any alterations in what an organization does and how it does it.

➠ *Change agent:* A person who's a catalyst for change and who also manages the change process.

➠ *Creativity:* The ability to combine ideas in a unique way or to make unusual associations between ideas.

➠ *Innovation:* The process of taking a creative idea and turning it into a useful (marketable) product, service, or method of operation.

➠ *Idea champions:* Individuals who actively and enthusiastically pursue new ideas, build support, overcome resistance, and ensure that an innovation is implemented.

➠ *Quality:* From the customer's perspective, it means how well your product or service satisfies their need. From the entrepreneurial venture's perspective, it's how closely your product or service conforms to the standards you have established.

⟫ *Total quality management (TQM):* A philosophy of managing an organization in a way that emphasizes customer needs and expectations and uses any number of work actions and activities to improve quality.

⟫ *ISO 9000:* A series of quality management standards that organizations work to meet.

⟫ *Continuous improvement:* The implementation of numerous small, incremental improvements in all areas of the organization on an ongoing basis.

⟫ *World-class organization:* An organization that is continually looking for ways through its decisions and actions to be the best in the world at what it does.

SWEAT EQUITY

1. Every year, *Nation's Business* magazine (**www.nbmag.com**) names the Blue Chip Enterprise winners from every state. These companies epitomize the best of the best and have sound business practices in place. The winners in 1999 ranged from Bankcard Service, a firm in Woodland Hills, California, which processes credit card sales for merchants, to CD Concept, a custom plastic-injection-molding company located in Elgin, Illinois. Despite the broad range of products and services offered by these award-winning companies, one thing that characterizes each and every one of them is that they understand the importance of not neglecting the fundamentals of business success. Choose one of the companies profiled on the *Nation's Business* Web site and write a paper describing what it does. Describe how this entrepreneurial organization managed its processes. In your conclusion, provide a bulleted list of ideas that you can share with other members of the class.

2. Surveys consistently point out that small companies create products faster (23 versus 30 months) and have more successful products (62 percent versus 58 percent) than do large companies. However, formal product development processes in small organizations are often quite haphazard. Yet there's help for entrepreneurs wanting to be more efficient and effective at this process. The Product Development and Management Association has provided some useful information on its Web site at **www.pdma.org**. Go to the Web site and check out all the information there. Make a bulleted list of important tips that you find on this site. Be prepared to share your tips with the class.

3. Dan Leever, chief executive of MacDermid Inc., a specialty chemical manufacturer based in Waterbury, Connecticut, says that his business helps its customers become more efficient. The company's more than 4,000 specialty chemicals are used mainly by circuit board makers. For example, a new chemical process developed by MacDermid allows companies to save 25 percent in the production of double-sided circuit boards. It recently created a chemical product for Boeing that strips the surface of an airplane before it's painted and is 15 percent faster than traditional hand sanding. CEO Leever has an interesting philosophy about customers as well. He says he will turn down any potential customer who demands big discounts. Because the company helps its customers save money, MacDermid doesn't have to slash prices like most of its competitors.

Check out the company's Web site at **www.macdermid.com**. Then answer the following questions.

a. What is MacDermid's philosophy? Do you agree or disagree with it? Explain your answer.

b. Do you think innovation would be important to this company? Why? How could it encourage innovation efforts?

c. What do you think of Leever's statement that he'll turn down any customer who demands big discounts? Do you think this would work for other entrepreneurial ventures? Explain. Why does it work for MacDermid Inc.?

(*Sources:* S. Sansoni, "Waste Makes My Guts Churn," *Forbes*, November 2, 1998, p. 228; and company Web site found at **www.macdermid.com**.)

4. Change is difficult and stressful. These 10 steps have been suggested for positive change:

- Develop a vision, mission, strategy, and operating plan that offers the greatest potential for success. Involve all organizational members in the planning process and communicate the results.
- Set high expectations with specific goals and objectives, but not unrealistic or unachievable ones. Communicate these along with the rationale. Embrace people who resist and carefully consider their reasons.
- Build trust by being totally honest, fair, and trustworthy. Regularly assess how things are going with people who are not key decision makers. Without trust, nothing else works.
- Define each person's roles and responsibilities. Clarify expectations.
- Establish agreed-upon measures so people can track how they and the business are doing. Post these openly and refer to them often.
- Provide frequent, balanced feedback and information about external conditions and how things are going. Provide opportunities for people to contribute ideas. Use collaborative problem solving. Make necessary resources and technology available.
- Continuously update employees on changes in the external environment—customers, markets, competition, and so on. Involve them in gathering this information. Inform them of any important news before they hear it from the media.
- Recognize and praise success but also identify and critique failure. Encourage action. Discourage inaction. Criticize methods or actions, not individuals. If some individuals aren't willing or able to perform, help them improve or let them go.
- Reward success and desired behaviors. Tie rewards to actions that employees can control.
- Celebrate success and grieve over setbacks together. Maintain an environment of enthusiasm, cooperation, collaboration, and sharing. Emphasize getting the job done together.

Write a paper discussing each of these points. Do you agree or disagree with them? Do you think they could actually be used by organizations? How would you improve upon them?

(*Source:* J. Mariotti, "10 Steps to Positive Change," *IW*, July 20, 1998, p. 82.)

5. No one likes to think that employees would intentionally steal, commit fraud, or embezzle funds from an organization. However, it can and does happen. Thus, an important part of managing processes might be protecting against these situations. Research the topic of employee theft, fraud, or embezzlement. Write a paper describing what it is, how often it happens, and what can be done to prevent it. Be prepared to share your findings with your class.

ENTREPRENEURSHIP IN ACTION CASES

CASE #1: Swatting the Bugs

Entrepreneurship in Action case #1 can be found at the beginning of Chapter 7.

Discussion Questions

1. What are some ways that Healy managed the processes in his company?
2. What approach to problems does Healy appear to exhibit? Explain.
3. Would innovation be important in this type of business? Why? In what areas might innovation be developed?
4. How might Healy use quality management in his business?

CASE #2: Success Is in the Bag

It's a job that few have the stamina or agility to do, especially in cities with lot of hills such as San Francisco. However, bicycle messengers perform an important service, hauling bulky loads swiftly from city location to city location. Their bags have to be tough, waterproof, lightweight, and functional—and it's nice if they look great, too! Rob Honeycutt knows well what bike knapsacks need to be—he was a messenger once himself. Today, his company, Timbuk2 Designs (**www.timbuk2.com**) manufactures bags that appeal to the "hip, young, wacky nuts on bikes."

From its early struggles as a one-man operation, Timbuk2 has become a successful entrepreneurial venture. Honeycutt and partner Brennan Mulligan describe their company as more than a bike bag maker. They say it's an ambitious experiment in manufacturing. Their goals are to make custom products more efficiently than mass manufacturers do and to become competitive with offshore manufacturing. Then, as if those ambitious goals aren't enough, they also hope to achieve efficiency and profitability while paying their workers among the highest wages and best benefits in the apparel industry. So far, the company has achieved several of its goals.

Many bike shops claim that Timbuk2 bags are the best and most popular bags. The company offers what none of its competitors do: a three-panel construction design that allows customers to custom choose from 13 colors for an astounding 2,197 possible color combinations. Timbuk2's bags cost no more than mass-produced ones. The company pays its employees more than other apparel makers and offers full medical benefits. The company is debt free and has financed growth through friends, family, and cash flow. How has it accomplished its goals?

Honeycutt and Mulligan wanted to do what Toyota Motor Corporation tried to do unsuccessfully with cars: mass customization or making cars to customers' orders. They thought it might work because manufacturing bags is much simpler than making cars. However, things didn't quite work out on the first try until Honeycutt began experimenting with something he had seen at a trade show demonstration. That something was the Toyota Sewing System, which calls for each sewing operator to move down a row of task-specific sewing machines instead of performing a single task and passing parts to the next sewing operator. This approach cuts labor costs because no floor assistants are needed to carry partially completed inventory from one machine to the next. In addition, Timbuk2 was able to keep its inventory costs low because it buys only a week's worth of materials and ships out completed bags daily. It has also discovered that the mass-customization approach has cut waste because mistakes are caught along the way.

Although there are many things that the company is doing right, Timbuk2 continues to refine its system, relying heavily on employee suggestions and ideas. In 1993, it took 144 minutes to make one bag. Using automated sewing machines and employees' suggestions, it has reduced that time to 16 minutes. The goal is getting that time down to 12 minutes. Labor costs are about 16 percent of total costs now and the goal is whittling that down to 12 percent. So, Timbuk2 continues its pursuit of success in a bag.

Discussion Questions

1. What types of performance measures might Timbuk2 want to use? Be as specific as possible.
2. Would you call this company efficient? Effective? Explain your answers.
3. Using information from the written case and from the company's Web site, would you describe Timbuk2 as a world-class organization? Support your answer.

(*Sources:* R. Furchgott, "Success Could Be in the Bag," *Business Week Enterprise*, December 16, 1996, pp. ENT8–ENT9; and information from company's Web site.)

CASE #3: A Little Slice of Nice

Lawyers running a pizza restaurant. Now that seems to be as unlikely a combination as tandoori chicken or barbecued chicken on pizza. Yet, Rick Rosenfield and Larry Flax have built a successful company called California Pizza Kitchen (**www.cpk.com**). The two former federal prosecutors decided to trade in the courtroom for the dining room and opened a unique restaurant that offers creative hearth-baked pizzas.

The pair opened their first CPK in Beverly Hills in 1985. Since that time, the company has grown to over 92 units in 20 states and 2 other countries outside the United States. As the leading premium pizza chain, Rosenfield and Flax have built a successful entrepreneurial venture by carefully managing processes. But things weren't always that way.

In 1992, PepsiCo Inc., bought 67 percent of the CPK chain for $94 million.

Rosenfield and Flax pocketed $34 million in cash and kept a 24 percent stake in their company. Both stayed on as co-CEOs and had the go-ahead from Pepsi to grow the company using corporate money for expansion. Pepsi's mandate: Open as many restaurants as possible. The only problem was that no one had a real plan about how to do that. The most restaurants the pair had ever opened in one year were seven locations. Pepsi sent in some corporate accountants to keep an eye on CPK's fairly loose organization. During the first 18 months under Pepsi's ownership, the company opened nearly 40 new restaurants. Although sales revenues doubled, occupancy costs were skyrocketing. Pepsi's accountants responded by cutting corners. Instead of grilled fresh vegetables on the pizzas, frozen vegetables were used. Instead of fresh mozzarella cheese, frozen was used. Customers noticed. Sales revenue growth crashed. Pepsi's decision makers were alarmed, needless to say. They tried several things, but to no avail. For the five years Pepsi owned CPK, the company lost money. Fortunately, Rosenfield and Flax had negotiated a buyout strategy. The cofounders got the company back through a unique buyback arrangement and took immediate steps to improve operations.

The first thing they did was hire an experienced chief executive, Frederick Hipp, who had run Houlihans, a successful chain of contemporary restaurants. Hipp brought logical planning to the operation. He first shut down the worst performing locations and revised the growth plans. He's not in any rush to open new stores and says, "I'll wait up to two years for the right site." He wants to fill in existing markets by opening sites in malls with strong anchors. In addition, Hipp is bringing back CPK's once notable quality. It made the switch back to fresh ingredients. In addition, the company decided to increase the size of the pizzas with no price increase. Once again, customers noticed. Same-store sales were up 8 percent.

Great food and service are crucial for any restaurant wanting to succeed. CPK has that and more. By continuing to manage the ongoing operations, the company hopes to maintain its position as the leading premium pizza chain.

Discussion Questions

1. What might have been some signs of problems or opportunities in CPK's operations?

2. Go to the company's Web site. Link to the employment section and check out the link called "environment." What's your reaction to this? How do these concepts contribute to CPK's success?

3. Obviously quality is an important goal of CPK. How would CPK define quality? How could it manage quality? (*Hint:* Think about all the areas in a restaurant.)

(*Sources:* K. Morris, "How to Have Your Pie and Eat It, Too," *Business Week*, November 16, 1998, pp. 100–2; A. Linsmayer, "Smothered by Money," *Forbes*, November 30, 1998, pp. 138–40; and information on company's Web site.)

At the Port of New Orleans, the largest coffee port in the United States, you'll find a company handling an old-fashioned product in a new-fashioned way. At Frederico Pacorini's SiloCaf, you'll find a fully computerized bulk coffee storage, handling, and processing facility. It's a place where tradition meets technology.

SiloCaf (**www.silocaf.com**) was founded in 1933 as a forwarding company; in other words, a company that takes any type of product and moves it from one location to any other location. Today, the company specializes in forwarding commodities, primarily coffee. The way it handles coffee is about as high-tech as it can get. Why has SiloCaf invested in technology for such a seemingly simple product? The main reason is that when customers buy a can of coffee, they want the same kind of taste each and every time they buy. Coffee, however, is a natural product with impurities and defects, and coffee crops are never the same, making blending consistency difficult. Without some way to control the coffee blend, it would be impossible to get that consistent taste. SiloCaf is addressing this challenge by using information systems technology and computer technology to achieve that taste consistency.

Mossimo Toma is SiloCaf's systems and resources manager. He is responsible for overseeing the process during which the coffee is blended. Coffee beans come into SiloCaf's warehouse from all over the world. Each week 10 million pounds of coffee are blended. (This translates to about 4 million bags per year.) The coffee never stays in SiloCaf's plant more than one week. Once it's processed and blended, it's loaded into bags or kept in bulk and shipped to a coffee roasting company. At any one time, SiloCaf has anywhere between 35 million and 40 million pounds of coffee in its facility for processing. If you consider the price of coffee per pound, SiloCaf has an extremely valuable resource in its possession. SiloCaf never actually "owns" the coffee. The coffee is owned by the roasting company or the dealer who delivers the coffee to the roasting company.

All the different mechanical parts in SiloCaf's New Orleans facility have been brought from Italy, which is where the company first developed the technology. Frederico Pacorini, the son of the founder and the manager of the New Orleans facility, says that technology in a business like theirs is important because it allows them to make all the blends they need for the customers (coffee roasters), to optimize the way they do blends, and to manage the organization's processes most efficiently and effectively. SiloCaf's employees receive continual statistical reports for each one of the scales used to blend the coffee. They are then able to check the consistency of the scale's performance, which is important for achieving the consistency of the product that the end user (customer) wants.

You would think that all this high-tech control would be expensive. However, the nice thing about SiloCaf's solution to the blend consistency challenge is that the technology it's using is relatively simple. In fact, the company's investment in technology was a mere 1 percent of all plant investment dollars spent.

Discussion Questions

1. What organizational performance measures might be needed by SiloCaf? What do you see them using?

2. Would quantitative measures or qualitative measures be more important? Explain.

3. Why is quality management important to SiloCaf's processes? How is quality managed? Check out the company's Web site for additional information.

(*Sources:* Based on *Small Business 2000, Show 109*; and information from company Web site.)

VIDEO CASE #2: Quality Is Our Name

Texas Nameplate has been in business for over 50 years and during that time has experienced both success and difficult times. Under its current owner, Dale Crownover (the son of founder Roy Crownover), the entrepreneurial company is experiencing financial success, organizational growth, and has received various awards for quality. Dale is sincerely proud of his company and is committed to the company, its employees, and its customers.

Under Dale's leadership, Texas Nameplate has turned its attention to quality and taking care of customers. Encouragement from Lockheed Corporation, one of its customers, to focus on quality improvements led Dale to implement a quality improvement program. However, he found that employees wanted more communication opportunities. At the company's monthly meetings, regular employees (not just managers) get involved. Crownover says it's really all about sharing and communicating; letting employees know the goals, the plans, why they're doing what they're doing, and how the company is

doing. Very simply, he found that employees want to be part of something.

All the emphasis on quality improvements has paid off. Texas Nameplate was the first small business to win the Texas Quality Award. The company has won other awards for its quality programs as well. Then, in November of 1998, Texas Nameplate Company was named the 1998 recipient of the Malcolm Baldridge National Quality Award for small businesses. It's the smallest company ever to receive the Baldridge Award.

Discussion Questions

1. What characteristics of a total quality organization do you see in this company?

2. How important are the employees to Texas Nameplate's quality quest? Explain.

3. Check out the company's Web site (**www.nameplate.com**) and the Malcolm Baldridge National Quality Award home page

(**www.quality.nist.gov**). Read all you can about Texas Nameplate's quality approach and other information provided on quality. Develop a bulleted list of the key points made about quality. Be prepared to share this information with the class.

(*Sources:* Based on *Small Business 2000, Show 313;* and materials from company Web site.)

ENDNOTES

1. L. Buchanan, "Uneasy Rider," *Inc. Technology*, No. 4, 1997, pp. 44–52.

2. J. G. March and H. A. Simon, *Organizations* (New York: John Wiley, 1958.)

3. J. R. Schermerhorn, Jr., *Management for Productivity*, 4th ed. (New York: John Wiley, 1993), p. 150.

4. A. J. Rowe, J. D. Boulgarides, and M. R. McGrath, *Managerial Decision Making*, Modules in Management Series (Chicago: SRA, 1984), pp. 18–22.

5. See K. R. Hammond, R. M. Hamm, J. Grassia, and T. Pearson, "Direct Comparison of the Efficacy of Intuitive and Analytical Cognition in Expert Judgment," *IEEE Transactions on Systems, Man, and Cybernetics* SMC-17 (1987), pp. 753–70; W. H. Agor (ed.), *Intuition in Organizations* (Newbury Park, CA: Sage Publications, 1989); and O. Behling and N. L. Eckel, "Making Sense Out of Intuition," *The Executive*, February 1991, pp. 46–47.

6. T. W. Zimmerer and N. M. Scarborough, *Essentials of Entrepreneurship and Small Business Management,* 2nd ed. (Upper Saddle River, NJ: Prentice Hall, 1998), p. 232.

7. Based on G. Fuchsberg, "Small Firms Struggle with Latest Management Trends," *Wall Street Journal*, August 26, 1993, p. B2; M. Barrier, "Re-engineering Your Company," *Nation's Business*, February 1994, pp. 16–22; J. Weiss, "Reengineering the Small Business," *Small Business Reports*, May 1994, pp. 37–43; and K. D. Godsey, "Back on Track," *Success*, May 1997, pp. 52–54.

8. These definitions are based on T. M. Amabile, "A Model of Creativity and Innovation in Organizations," in B. M. Staw and L. L. Cummings (eds.), *Research in Organizational Behavior*, Vol. 10 (Greenwich, CT: JAI Press, 1988), p. 126.

9. R. W. Goodman, J. E. Sawyer, and R. W. Griffin, "Toward a Theory of Organizational Creativity," *Academy of Management Review*, April 1993, pp. 293–321.

10. F. Damanpour, "Organizational Innovation: A Meta-Analysis of Effects of Determinants and Moderators," *Academy of Management Journal*, September 1991, pp. 555–90; S. D. Saleh and C. K. Wang, "The Management of Innovation: Strategy, Structure, and Organizational Climate," *IEEE Transactions on Engineering Management*, February 1993, pp. 14–22; J. F. Coates and J. Jarratt, "Workplace Creativity," *Employment Relations Today*, spring 1994, pp. 11–22; G. R. Oldham and A. Cummings, "Employee Creativity: Personal and Contextual Factors at Work," *Academy of Management Journal*, June 1996, pp. 607–34.

11. P. R. Monge, J. D. Cozzens, and N. S. Contractor, "Communication and Motivational Predictors of the Dynamics of Organizational Innovations," *Organization Science*, May 1992, pp. 250–74.

12. See, for instance, T. M. Amabile, "A Model of Creativity and Innovation in Organizations," p. 147; M. Tushman and D. Nadler, "Organizing for Innovation," *California Management Review*, spring 1986, pp. 74–92; R. M. Kanter, "When a Thousand Flowers Bloom: Structural, Collective, and Social Conditions for Innovation in Organization," in Staw and Cummings (eds.), *Research in Organizational Behavior*, Vol. 10, pp. 169–211; G. Morgan, "Endangered Species: New Ideas," *Business Month*, April 1989, pp. 75–77; S. G. Scott and R. A. Bruce, "Determinants of Innovative People: A Path Model of Individual Innovation in the Workplace," *Academy of Management Journal*, June 1994, pp. 580–607; T. M. Amabile, R. Conti, H. Coon, J. Lazenby, and M. Herron, "Assessing the Work Environment for Creativity," *Academy of Management*

Journal, October 1996, pp. 1154–84; and A. deGues, "The Living Company," *Harvard Business Review*, March–April 1997, pp. 51–59.

13. R. M. Hodgetts, F. Luthans, and S. M. Lee, "New Paradigm Organizations: From Total Quality to Learning to World Class," *Organizational Dynamics*, winter 1994, pp. 4–19.

14. P. Drucker, *Management Challenges for the 21st Century* (New York: HarperCollins Publishers, 1999), p. 61.

8

MANAGING PEOPLE

LEARNING OBJECTIVES

After reading this chapter, you should be able to:

1. Discuss the importance of people to organizational performance.
2. Describe the human resource management issues that entrepreneurs may have to deal with.
3. Explain why recruiting employees is important, yet one of the most challenging HRM tasks that entrepreneurs do.
4. Explain what employee stock ownership plans and stock option plans are.
5. Define motivation and explain why it's important.
6. Describe how entrepreneurs might motivate organizational members.
7. Describe the role of teams and leadership in entrepreneurial organizations.
8. Discuss the importance of managing conflict.
9. Explain why empowerment and delegating are important activities of entrepreneurs.

ENTREPRENEURSHIP IN ACTION CASE #1

Dream Team

Would you agree that an organization is nothing without its employees? If you do, then it would seem that the only sustainable competitive advantage an entrepreneurial organization would have for the future would be its employees, right? That human resource management philosophy has worked quite well for Rhino Foods Inc., a specialty dessert manufacturer located in Burlington, Vermont.[1]

Rhino Foods isn't a giant corporation, but it has developed a strong competitive advantage that has enabled it to succeed despite continuing intense competition and other types of external challenges. Although Rhino has had its share of ups and downs, its financial and organizational performance results have been above average. What is the source of Rhino's success? Rhino's founder, Ted Castle points to the company's workforce—its very own dream team! How does Rhino manage its employees? What does it do differently? What types of human resource management policies and practices has it implemented?

The company's purpose statement asserts:

The employees and families of Rhino Foods are its greatest assets. The company's relationship with its employees is founded on a climate of mutual trust and respect within an environment for listening and

As your entrepreneurial venture prospers and grows, eventually you're going to have to bring other people on board. Managing the people in an entrepreneurial organization can be challenging, yet rewarding. The quality of an organization is, to a large degree, merely the summation of the quality of people it hires and keeps. Just look at Ted Castle's approach to human resource management. He would readily agree that getting and keeping competent, talented, and motivated employees are critical to the success of an organization. In this chapter we want to look at the various aspects of managing people in the entrepreneurial venture. We'll examine some human resource management issues, look at motivation theories and how to motivate employees, discuss teams and leadership issues, and describe some other interpersonal issues that entrepreneurs may have to deal with.

HUMAN RESOURCE MANAGEMENT ISSUES

Until they get to a certain size, entrepreneurial organizations are unlikely to have a separate human resource management (HRM) specialist or department. That means as the organization grows the entrepreneur personally may have to handle human resource activities until the point at which it's necessary to hire a specialist in this area. An entrepreneur should be aware of a number of HRM issues. Let's discuss some of these issues.

Strategic Human Resource Management

How often have you heard or read about companies making the statement that "Our people are our *most* important asset"? Is it just a nice thing to say or is there some truth to the statement? How important *are* people to an organization's success? According to Jeffrey Pfeffer, a management professor who has spent his career studying people and organizations, they're *very* important![2] He asserts that what differentiates high-performing organizations from others is the way they treat their people. These high-performance organizations have people strategies that reward teamwork, commitment, excellence, integrity, and other crucial behaviors. The people philosophy of these high-performance organizations revolves around treating people appropriately by giving them the tools, training, and incentives they need to do their jobs. And guess what? They (both the individuals and the organization) excel! The common

personal expression. Rhino Foods declares that it is a vehicle for people to get what they want.

The words that make up the purpose statement were chosen very carefully as a reflection of Castle's philosophy about both the role of the organization and the role of the employee. Another human resource management practice that symbolizes Rhino's belief about its employees being the source of its success is the strong use of employee empowerment—

letting employees have significant control and say over what jobs they do and how they do them. Finally, Rhino uses an unusual approach to challenging its employees. The company's philosophy is that "employees who challenge themselves personally see a difference professionally too." Employees are encouraged to set and achieve goals no matter how intimidating those goals might be. The point is to challenge employees and show them that they can make things happen on their own.

thread in these **high-performance work practices**—that is, human resource policies and practices that lead to high levels of both individual and organizational performance—seems to be a commitment to improving the knowledge, skills, and abilities of the organization's current and potential employees; increasing their motivation; reducing loafing on the job; and enhancing the retention of quality employees while encouraging nonperformers to leave the organization. Pfeffer identifies seven people practices that he believes are key to a successful organization. (See Figure 8-1.) These seven practices include employment security, selective hiring, self-managed teams and decentralized decision making, training, high compensation linked to organizational performance, reduced status differences, and sharing information.

When all is said and done, however, what impact do such high-performance work practices have? Studies that have looked at the link between HRM policies and practices and organizational performance have found that these types of HRM policies and practices tend to have a positive impact on performance.[3] What type of positive impact? One study reported that if an average company implemented these high-performance work practices, it could potentially add annually (per employee) $27,044 more in sales, $3,814 in profits, and $18,641 in market value.[4] Now multiply these figures by 5 or 10 or 100 employees, and ask yourself if it might be worthwhile to take managing employees seriously. It would appear that a philosophy of managing employees in a way that encourages, sup-

Figure 8-1

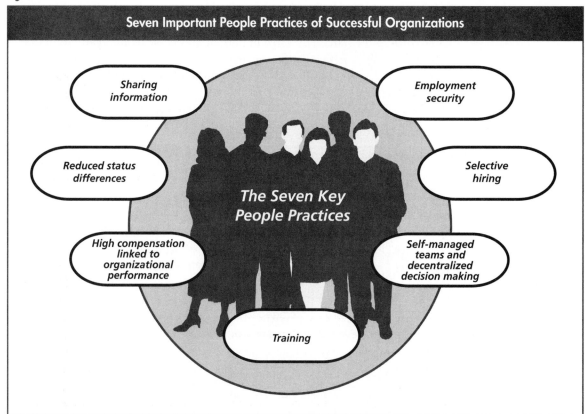

Source: Based on J. Pfeffer, *Competitive Advantage through People* (Boston: Harvard Business School Press, 1994).

> ### Entrepreneurs in Action
>
> Sabrina Horn, president of The Horn Group, based in San Francisco, knows the importance of having good people on board. Her public relations firm employs around 45 employees who create PR for technology firms. In this rough-and-tumble, intensely competitive industry, Sabrina knows that the loss of talented employees could cut into client services. To combat this, she offers employees a wide array of desirable benefits, such as raises of 6 percent or more each year, profit sharing, trust funds for employees' children, paid sabbaticals, personal development funds, and so forth. But, more importantly, Sabrina recognizes that employees have a life outside the office and treats them accordingly. This type of human resource approach has kept her employees loyal and productive.
>
> *Source:* "Best Employer," *Working Woman,* May 1999, p. 54.

ports, and recognizes their contributions might be a pretty good one! But, now that we know something about the important strategic role that an organization's human resources play, what types of other human resource management issues do entrepreneurs have to deal with? These issues include bringing people on board and managing them once they are on board.

Bringing People on Board

Look back at our chapter-opening case. Having a dream team of dedicated, hard-working employees didn't just happen by luck or chance. Not at all! There are things that Ted Castle did—things that any entrepreneur must do—to ensure that the venture has the people it needs to do the work that's required. These include human resource planning, recruiting and hiring, and having in place a process for dealing with situations when the same number of employees may no longer be needed or with employees who aren't working out. We're going to look at human resource planning first.

Human Resource Planning. The first step in bringing people on board is knowing something about the types of people needed (that is, what skills, abilities, experiences, education, and knowledge are needed) and how many people are needed. An entrepreneur should do some **human resource planning**—assessing current and future human resource needs—before even thinking about hiring. In this way, you can work toward ensuring that you have the right number and right kinds of people in the right places and at the right times. What's involved with human resource planning? Although some of the activities we're going to look at might seem overly cumbersome at times, keep in mind that managing the entrepreneurial venture's human resources effectively and efficiently takes more than a haphazard, halfhearted effort. Continually remind yourself of the importance of having on board exceptionally capable and motivated people. One of the first things an entrepreneur should do is inventory current employees by getting information on their education, training, prior employment, languages spoken, special abilities, and specialized skills. This inventory provides an important summary of peoples' talents and skills currently available in the organization. It supplies information on what current employees can do. If your entrepreneurial venture is just at the point where it's necessary to hire individuals, it would make sense to start and keep this inventory from the very beginning.

Another important part of human resource planning is the **job analysis**, which is an assessment that defines jobs and the behaviors necessary to perform them. Just as the human resource inventory provides fundamental information about the organization's people, the job analysis provides fundamental information about the organization's jobs—that is, the work that needs to be done. It defines the minimal knowledge, skills, and abilities necessary to perform each and every job adequately. Two important human resource documents are created with the information from the job analysis: the job description and the job specification. A **job description** is a written statement of the work a jobholder does, how it is done, and why it is done. It typically describes job content and focuses on the *job*. The **job specification** states the minimum acceptable qualifications that a jobholder or job seeker must possess to perform a given job successfully. It focuses on the *person*. These two documents are important to the efficient and effective functioning of the entire HRM process because they're focused on the key reason for having employees in the first place—having competent and motivated people performing job duties that are critical to the work of the organization.

The foundation for a successful human resources management program (one that brings and keeps on board capable and motivated employees) occurs during the human resource planning process. Without the information provided by the human resource inventory and the job analysis, bringing people on board will be more difficult and certainly less effective. Although these initial HR activities take time to perform, the effort and resources expended will be worth it. The payoff will be a core of competent, dedicated, and skilled individuals who will be able to initiate and drive the entrepreneurial venture's successful growth. However, the human resource inventory and the job analysis are just the first steps in making this happen. The next thing the entrepreneur must do is the actual recruiting and hiring.

Recruiting, Selecting, and Hiring. To bring people into the organization, you first have to find a pool of acceptable candidates. **Recruiting** is the process of locating, identifying, and attracting capable job applicants. It can be a frustrating process for entrepreneurs, particularly if the labor market is tight (that is, there are more jobs than qualified job seekers) and if the entrepreneurial venture can't offer the same types and amount of compensation and benefits that larger organizations can. However, the entrepreneur should approach recruiting with the perspective that what (in this case, *who*) comes into the organization affects what goes out of the organization (that is, its products

Rapid Review ◀◀|

✓ What are high-performance work practices?

✓ Explain the people practices that successful organizations tend to have.

✓ What type of impact have these high-performance work practices been shown to have?

✓ Why should an entrepreneur do some human resource planning, and what should be done during human resource planning?

✓ Differentiate among job analysis, job description, and job specification.

✓ Why are job descriptions and job specifications important documents?

and services). If your recruiting activities are done halfheartedly and with little thought or preparation, you're going to get below-average job applicants, and then the resulting work performance is going to be below average. (Computer types like to classify this phenomenon as GIGO—garbage in, garbage out.) The point is that an entrepreneur should take the recruiting process seriously because the organization's ultimate performance levels are a reflection of the quality of people brought in. We can't hire quality people if we don't locate, identify, and attract them. What types of recruiting sources might entrepreneurs use? (Figure 8-2 portrays eight sources.)

The first type of recruiting source is employee referrals—that is, asking your current employees for names of potential job candidates. One benefit of this approach is that the current employee knows the type of person who will be a good fit for the organizational culture and performance expectations. In addition, the current employee will want to refer someone who's going to reflect well on him or her. After all, a person isn't going to recommend someone who's likely to fail. That would make the person look bad, also. However, if you're just beginning to add employees to your entrepreneurial venture, this approach obviously won't work until you have current employees to ask for referrals. Another recruiting source is to use job advertisements in newspapers or other paper sources. Although this approach targets a wide audience, it's likely to generate many unqualified job applicants. A variation to advertisements in paper sources is advertising jobs on Web job posting boards. Again, these job postings will reach a vast global audience, but not everyone in that audience is going to be a quali-

Figure 8-2

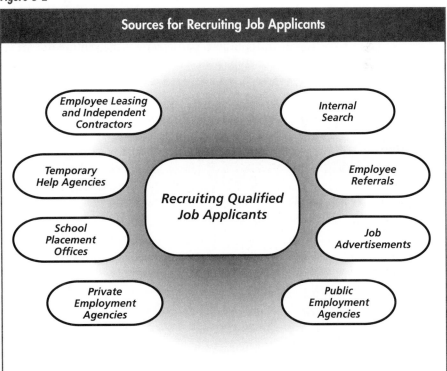

Sources for Recruiting Job Applicants

- Employee Leasing and Independent Contractors
- Internal Search
- Temporary Help Agencies
- Employee Referrals
- School Placement Offices
- Job Advertisements
- Private Employment Agencies
- Public Employment Agencies

Recruiting Qualified Job Applicants

fied applicant. Another source for recruiting is to use public or private employment agencies. Although public agencies (usually run by a state office) are free or may charge a nominal fee, they tend to attract unskilled or minimally trained job candidates. On the other hand, private employment agencies often attract higher-skilled individuals and will carefully screen job applicants for applicable skills, but there's typically a high cost for this type of service. School placement offices can be another source for job applicants. Although these sources can provide the entrepreneur with a large pool of potential candidates, the job applicants typically are new labor force participants who don't have a lot of relevant work experience. Another source for recruiting would be temporary help agencies. If the entrepreneurial venture has a need for temporary employees, these agencies can be a good choice. However, their services tend to be expensive. In addition, keep in mind that temporary employees generally will have a limited understanding of the organization's goals, activities, and culture. A variant of the temporary help services are employee leasing firms and independent contractors that typically deal with higher-skilled workers. These sources of job applicants often are used by organizations that have specific work projects that need to be completed. Rather than hiring permanent employees, the organization may look to lease employees or hire an independent contractor. Although this approach can help fill temporary needs, these employees typically will not have the commitment to the organization other than completing the current project. Finally, if the entrepreneurial venture is currently large enough to employ numerous employees, looking inside the organization for job applicants—an internal search—may be appropriate for filling positions as they open up. Obviously, the advantages of this type of recruitment are that it has relatively low cost, helps build employee morale because employees see that there are career opportunities within the organization, and results in candidates who are quite familiar with the organization. However, the main drawback of an internal search is the limited supply of applicants, particularly if the venture doesn't currently employ a large number of employees. However, as the venture grows and as more jobs open up, this approach can be a good one.

Global Perspectives

At Genesys Telecommunications Laboratories, Inc., a software design firm, recruiting skilled employees was an ongoing challenge. However, founders Greg Shenkman and Alec Miloslavsky have found recruiting engineers and technicians from Eastern Europe to be an answer to their talent shortage. Today, Genesys has around 500 employees, of which about 70 percent are foreign. One interesting aspect of this decidedly global company is that the programmers are referred to not by area of expertise, but by country origin. There's the St. Petersburg group, the Moscow team, the Kiev group, and so forth. Many of the company's talented Russian immigrants who were born and raised under communism are now millionaires after the company went public in 1997. Shenkman and Miloslavsky are each worth $100 million.

Source: S. McCormack, "The Russia House," *Forbes*, July 6, 1998, p. 146.

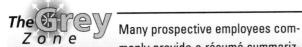

The Grey Zone Many prospective employees commonly provide a résumé summarizing background, education, work experiences, and other accomplishments. A number of these résumés are "creatively enhanced." For instance, people might indicate that they were making more money at their previous job than they really were. Or they might describe job responsibilities as more impressive than they really were. Are these types of "creative enhancements" wrong? What are the ethical implications for job applicants? For entrepreneurs wanting to hire the best employees?

Using the various recruitment sources, we've now assembled a pool of job applicants. What next? What comes next is selecting the best candidates. **Employee selection** is a process of screening job applicants to ensure that the best individuals are hired. Employee selection is an exercise in prediction. What you want to do is predict which job applicants will be successful performers if hired. How can you do this? By using any number of selection devices that can help pinpoint important, relevant information about the job applicants. The most commonly used ones include job applications, written tests, performance simulation tests, interviews, background and reference checks, and physical exams. Let's look at what each of these selection devices does.

The job application is used by almost all organizations. It may be a simple sheet of paper on which the job applicant gives his or her name, address, and telephone number. Or it might be a more comprehensive printed form where applicants provide relevant biographical information and details of their activities, skills, and accomplishments. Although the job application is a popular employee selection instrument, typically only a couple of items on the application form prove to be accurate predictors of job performance. Its use is probably best limited to information gathering because the process of determining which items on the application form are good predictors of job performance is difficult and expensive.

Written tests include tests of intelligence, aptitude, ability, and interest. These types of tests have been used for years although their popularity tends to run in cycles. Decision makers have become increasingly aware that poor hiring decisions are costly and that properly designed tests could reduce the likelihood of poor decisions occurring. In addition, the costs associated with developing and validating a set of written tests for a specific job also has decreased significantly. Yet, there are still some concerns about whether or not a test score can be a good indicator of how well an applicant will perform on a job. This criticism has led to an increased use of performance simulation tests.

What better way is there to find out whether a person applying for a technical writing position can write technical manuals than by having him or her do it? Performance simulation tests use actual job behaviors to assess a candidate's skills and abilities. The two most popular performance simulation tests are work sampling and assessment centers. **Work sampling** involves having job applicants perform tasks in a simulated model of a job. Applicants demonstrate they have the necessary skills and abilities by actually doing the simulated tasks. Work sampling is more appropriate for routine type jobs. **Assessment centers** are places where job applicants undergo more elaborate performance simulation tests as they perform exercises that simulate real problems they might encounter on the job. These

> ### Entrepreneurs in Action
>
> Many entrepreneurial ventures experience hiring problems, especially when they're going through a growth spurt. J. Mark Erler and his wife, Linda, did when their company, Erler Industries, was selected to fill a large contract with Dell Computer. They had to hire 175 people in a short period of time to do entry-level work. Because they were under a lot of pressure, they had to hire without checking references. Not surprisingly, some employees hired had significant work and personal problems. In addition, employee turnover was tremendous. Once the initial crunch was over, the Erlers eventually settled down with a stable, productive workforce. However, they say that if they had to do it over, they would be more systematic and careful in hiring, no matter what the time crunch. After all, there's too much at stake if bad hiring decisions are made.
>
> **Source:** M. Barrier, "Hiring the Right People," *Nation's Business*, June 1996, pp. 18–27.

tests are more appropriate for selecting people for managerial positions. Research on both work sampling and assessment centers has shown that both tend to be good predictors of future job performance.[5]

Have you ever gotten a job without one or more interviews? Probably not! The job interview, like the job application form, is an almost universal selection device, yet unless it's done effectively, the interview is questionable as a good predictor of job performance. How can interviews be done effectively? When interviews are structured and well organized, and when interviewers ask common questions, interviews have been shown to be effective predictors of future job performance.[6] Unfortunately, the typical interview—in which job applicants are asked a varying set of essentially random questions in an informal setting—usually provides little in the way of valuable information. A review of the research on interviews leads us to the following conclusions:

1. Prior knowledge about the applicant will bias the interviewer's evaluation.
2. The interviewer tends to hold a stereotype of what represents a "good" applicant.
3. The interviewer tends to favor applicants who share his or her own attitudes.
4. The order in which applicants are interviewed will influence evaluations.
5. The order in which information is elicited during the interview will influence evaluations.
6. Negative information is given unduly high weight.
7. The interviewer often makes a decision concerning the applicant's suitability within the first four or five minutes of the interview.
8. The interviewer forgets much of the interview's content within minutes after its conclusion.

TABLE 8-1   Suggestions for Effective Interviewing

1. Structure a *fixed set of questions* for all applicants.
2. Have *detailed information about the job* for which applicants are interviewing.
3. *Minimize any prior knowledge* of applicants' background, experience, interests, test scores, or other characteristics.
4. *Ask behavioral questions* that require applicants to give detailed accounts of actual job behaviors.
5. Use a *standardized evaluation form.*
6. *Take notes* during the interview.
7. *Avoid short interviews* that encourage premature decision making.

Source: Based on D. A. DeCenzo and S. P. Robbins, *Human Resource Management*, 4th ed. (New York: John Wiley, 1994), pp. 208–9.

9. The interview is most valid in determining an applicant's intelligence, level of motivation, and interpersonal skills.
10. A "cold" interviewer (one who's extremely formal and serious) can have a devastating effect on the verbal and nonverbal behaviors of applicants with low self-esteem.[7]

What do these research findings tell us? We can use what these studies have shown us to identify some ways to make employment interviews more effective. Table 8-1 lists some specific suggestions. However, even if you follow these suggestions, keep in mind that another important factor in interviewing job applicants is the legality of certain interview questions. Certain interview questions should *not* be asked because they could potentially open the organization up to lawsuits by job applicants. Table 8-2 lists some examples of "no-no" interview questions.

Background and reference checks usually include verifying data on the application form and references. Several studies indicate that going to the trouble of verifying facts given on the job application is worthwhile. A significant percentage

TABLE 8-2   "No-No" Interview Questions

- What is your date of birth?
- Have you ever filed a workers' compensation claim?
- What is your place of birth?
- Do you own a home?
- What is your native language?
- Do you have children? Plan to have children? Have child care?
- Do you have a physical or mental disability that would prevent you from doing this job?
- What religion do you practice?

Sources: Based on J. S. Pauliot, "Topics to Avoid with Applicants," *Nation's Business*, July 1992, pp. 57–58; and L. M. Litvan, "Thorny Issues in Hiring," *Nation's Business*, April 1996, pp. 34–36.

of job applicants—upwards of 33 percent—exaggerate or misrepresent dates of employment, job titles, past salaries, or reasons for leaving a prior position.[8] In addition, organizations must consider the liability that potential employees may create and get as much background information as possible.[9] Although background checks can be useful, reference checks are difficult to justify even though most organizations still ask for references. Whether work related or personal, references provide little valid information. Previous employers often are reluctant to give candid evaluations of a former employee's job performance for fear of legal action by the ex-employee. Personal references are no better because these people are likely to provide biased information. After all, who's going to put down as a reference someone who might give a bad report?

The last type of selection device we want to look at is the physical exam. Although there may be jobs that do have certain physical requirements, you have to be careful to ensure that these physical requirements are actually job related and do not discriminate. Some physical requirements may exclude disabled persons or individuals with physical limitations, when, in fact, such requirements do not affect job performance. Because of the legal questions, the physical exam today is used mostly for insurance purposes. Organizations want to be sure that new employees will not submit insurance claims for injuries or illnesses that they had before being hired.

Based on what we've just discussed, what *should* an entrepreneur do to select the best job applicants? Performance simulation tests, structured and well-organized interviews, and background verifications of biographical information are likely to provide the entrepreneur with the best information for making effective selection decisions. The job application should be used mainly for obtaining biographical information on the job applicant. Written tests are unlikely to provide effective information so the entrepreneur probably would not want to use these. In addition, asking for references (employment and personal) is unlikely to prove useful in selecting the best employee. Finally, physical exams should be used for insurance purposes only. What happens next?

At this point, the entrepreneur is ready to make the hiring decision(s). After looking at and carefully evaluating the information gathered and provided in the selection process, the entrepreneur should make a decision as to who would best fit the job criteria. But, even given this careful consideration, sometimes things just don't work out. Or, sometimes the entrepreneur may find that the level of business isn't enough to justify the number of employees already on board. What then? This is where the process of decruitment comes in to play.

Decruitment. **Decruitment** describes techniques for reducing the number of employees within an organization. Although asking employees to leave the organization isn't a pleasant task, doing so sometimes may be absolutely necessary for the best interests of the organization or even for its survival. Table 8-3 summarizes the major decruitment options.

Now that the entrepreneurial venture has on board the number and types of people it needs to

Rapid Review ◀◀|

✓ What is recruiting? Why is it an important process, even in entrepreneurial ventures?

✓ Describe each of the eight recruiting sources.

✓ What is employee selection? Why is it an exercise in prediction?

✓ Describe each of the six selection devices.

✓ What is decruitment?

✓ What options are there for decruitment?

TABLE 8-3 Decruitment Options	
Option	**Description**
Firing	Permanent involuntary termination
Layoffs	Temporary involuntary termination; may last only a few days or extend to years
Attrition	Not filling openings created by voluntary resignations or normal retirements
Transfers	Moving employees either laterally or downward; usually does not reduce costs but can reduce intraorganizational supply–demand imbalances
Reduced workweeks	Having employees work fewer hours per week, share jobs, or perform their jobs on a part-time basis
Early retirements	Providing incentives to older and more senior employees for retiring before their normal retirement date
Job sharing	Having employees share one full-time position

do the work, is that all there is to managing the organization's human resources? You probably know the answer to that question already! We want to look next at managing people on board.

Managing People on Board

Getting competent, qualified people into the organization is just the first step in effectively managing the human resources. Other HRM activities that an entrepreneur must be familiar with include orienting, performance appraisal, employee training, compensation, and benefits. We're going to discuss each of these important activities.

Orienting. A person starting a new job needs some introduction to that job. This introduction is called **orientation**. The major goals of employee orientation are to reduce the initial anxiety all new employees feel as they begin a new job; to familiarize new employees with the job, the work unit, and the organization; and to facilitate the transition from being an outsider to becoming an insider. Orientation expands on the information the employee received during the recruitment and selection processes. The three main areas that the orientation should cover are the job, the work unit, and the organization. In the job orientation, the new hire's specific duties and responsibilities are clarified, as are the performance expectations and performance evaluation techniques to be used. This is also the time to resolve any unrealistic expectations that new employees might have about the job. In the work unit orientation, the new employee is introduced to the goals of the work unit, to how his or her job contributes to the unit's goals, and to the co-workers.

The organization orientation should cover information about the organization's goals, history, philosophy, procedures, and rules. In addition, this is the time to cover relevant human resource policies and benefits such as work hours, pay procedures, overtime requirements, and fringe benefits. A tour of the entire organization might also be done. Each of these different orientations provides a unique perspective of the person's new work environment. However, if the entrepreneurial venture is still relatively small, all of these aspects may be covered (*should* be covered) in one generalized orientation. But, even in the smallest entrepreneurial ventures, the entrepreneur has an obligation to make the integration of new employees into the organization as smooth and as free from anxiety as possible. It is in the organization's and the new employee's best interests to get the person up and running in the job as soon as possible. A successful orientation, whether formal or informal, results in an outsider–insider transition that makes the new member feel comfortable and fairly well adjusted, lowers the likelihood of poor work performance, and reduces the probability of a surprise resignation by the new employee a short time after his or her starting the job.

Performance Appraisal. After orientation, the new employee starts performing the job duties he or she was hired to do. After a certain period of time, it's important to appraise the person's performance levels. Is the new employee's job performance up to expectations? Are there areas where the individual's performance is lacking and needs improvement? Are there areas where the individ-

FYI

Combating Sexual Harassment

You might think "It can't happen here," but that type of attitude about sexual harassment can bring a nasty legal surprise. What is **sexual harassment**? It's defined as any unwelcome sexual advance, behavior marked by sexually aggressive remarks, unwanted touching, requests for sexual favors, or other verbal or physical conduct of a sexual nature. Sexual harassment in the legal sense may be broader than you think. The Equal Employment Opportunity Commission has made it clear and courts have agreed, that sexual harassment can occur in either of two ways: "quid pro quo" sexuality—a supervisor tells an employee that a condition of continued employment is that he or she perform sexual acts; and hostile work environment—includes sexual comments, jokes, pictures, pornography, or derogatory comments about one gender. These definitions are fairly broad, and the potential for sexual harassment lawsuits should make any entrepreneur sit up and take notice, especially because legal judgments can be in the millions of dollars and the average judgment in a sexual harassment case is around $350,000. Yet, you can take certain steps to fight sexual harassment in your organization; these steps include education, company policy, and procedure. First off, training programs should educate employees as to what sexual harassment is and should raise employees' awareness of what might be sexually offensive to others. These training programs should also educate employees about what to do. In addition, your organization needs stated policies and procedures regarding sexual harassment. A policy should clearly state that sexual harassment will not be tolerated in the workplace, identify the responsibilities of employees in preventing harassment, specify the sanctions and penalties for violations, and spell out the procedures for reporting incidents of sexual harassment. Take sexual harassment seriously—it *is* a serious human resource management issue.

Sources: C. K. Goodman, "Sexual Harassment Cases Growing More Frequent," *Upstate Business,* November 24, 1996, pp. 4–5; K. Donovan, "Avoiding a Time Bomb: Sexual Harassment," *Business Week Enterprise,* October 13, 1997, pp. ENT20–ENT22; R. K. Robinson, et al., "U.S. Sexual Harassment Law: Implications for Small Businesses," *Journal of Small Business Management,* April 1998, pp. 1–13; R. McGarvey, "Hands Off!," *Entrepreneur,* September 1998, pp. 85–87; and K. Kelly, "Keeping Peace on the Floor," *Business Week Enterprise,* October 12, 1998, p. ENT20.

ual's job performance exceeds expectations and has the new employee been recognized for his or her accomplishments? **Performance appraisal** is the process of evaluating an individual's work performance. How is employee performance appraised?

An entrepreneur might use different performance appraisal methods. (See Figure 8-3.) The **graphic rating scale** is a popular method of appraisal in which an evaluator uses an incremental numerical scale to rate an employee on a set of performance factors. This appraisal approach is widely used because the numerical scales are relatively easy to create and use, but unfortunately it doesn't provide the depth of information that other methods do. **Written essays** are a performance appraisal technique whereby an evaluator writes a description of an employee's strengths, weaknesses, past performance, and potential, and then makes suggestions for improvement. This is probably the simplest method of appraisal because it requires no complex forms to fill out or extensive training to complete. However, a drawback is that a good or bad appraisal may be determined as much by the evaluator's writing skill as by the employee's actual performance. The **critical incidents** approach is one in which an evaluator lists specific key behaviors that separate effective from ineffective job performance. A list of critical incidents for a given employee provides a rich set of examples that can be used to point out desirable and undesirable behaviors. Although listing specific examples of an employee's work performance provides good information, keeping a record of these critical incidents can be quite time-consuming. Another performance appraisal approach that's received a lot of attention in recent years involves **behaviorally anchored rating scales (BARS)**. This is a technique in which an evaluator rates employees using a numerical scale, just like a graphic rating scale. But the difference is that the BARS focus on specific and measurable job *behaviors*, as opposed to general descriptions or traits. Key elements of jobs are broken down into performance dimensions and then specific illustrations of effective and ineffective behaviors are identified for each performance dimension. The result is

Figure 8-3

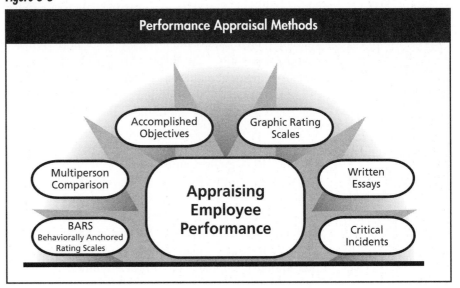

behavioral descriptions that capture the essence of what doing that particular job is all about. By appraising an individual using these behaviorally anchored dimensions, you get a good feel for how well the person is performing. This approach is quite effective, but the biggest drawback is the amount of time it takes to create the behaviorally anchored rating scales. The **multiperson comparison** approach is a performance appraisal technique in which individuals are compared to other individuals in the work group. Although this approach would provide a good indicator of an individual's performance in relation to relevant others, it can be quite cumbersome to complete. Finally, there's a performance appraisal technique that evaluates a person's performance on the basis of how well he or she met established goals. Because this approach puts the emphasis on goal accomplishment by simply assessing whether or not goals had been met, other important job performance factors may be overlooked.

The results of an employee's performance appraisal are used for different things. For instance, if the individual's work performance isn't up to expectations, the performance appraisal will pinpoint areas where improvement is needed. It may simply be a matter of the individual needing additional direction or more serious prodding. Or it may be that the individual needs further training or development. (We'll discuss the whole area of training and development in the next section.) The performance appraisal is also used to highlight performance accomplishments that may be used for recognition purposes, for promotion purposes, or for compensation and reward purposes. Keep in mind that regardless of whether the performance appraisal process is relatively formal or informal and what type of appraisal instrument is used, *some* form of performance appraisal needs to be done, particularly as the entrepreneurial venture grows and adds employees. The performance appraisal acts as a scorecard. If employees aren't performing at or above expected levels, you want to know it and take the necessary actions. Otherwise, the organization will find it difficult to be competitive and to achieve the kinds of performance results that will ensure the venture's continuing success.

Employee Training. An important HR activity that ensures the continued skills and capabilities of an organization's human resources is employee training. During 1999, U.S. businesses spent $62.5 billion on formal training—that is, instruction that is deliberately planned and structured.[10] Obviously, employee training is big business and is big *for* business. Although entrepreneurs may feel that they can't afford the dollars or time to have an ongoing formal program of employee training, the real question is can they afford *not* to have such a program? Given today's dynamic and intensely competitive environment, it's important to keep employees well trained, like finely tuned machines or racehorses—ready to put their skills and abilities to the test at a moment's notice. What types of employee training might entrepreneurs want to implement? Employee skills training can be grouped into three categories: technical, interpersonal, and problem solving. Most employee training activities seek to modify an employee's skills in one or more of these categories.

Technical training involves upgrading and improving an employee's fundamental technical skills such as math, reading or writing, and job-specific competencies. For instance, many jobs require an individual to be able to use computerized equipment, digitally controlled machines, or other types of sophisticated technology, and they need basic math, reading, and computer skills to be able to do so. Technical training can provide the necessary tools and skills in these areas. Interpersonal training involves helping employees develop their skills and abilities at interacting effectively with co-workers—otherwise known as people skills. Interpersonal training might include such things as learning how to be a better listener, how to communicate ideas more clearly, or how to reduce conflict. Finally, training in problem solving helps employees be better problem solvers. This might include developing the ability to define problems, assess causes, develop alternatives, be creative, analyze alternatives, and select appropriate solutions. Think back to our chapter-opening case and how Rhino's employees set goals and come up with alternatives.

Each of these training categories addresses an important employee skill, ability, or competency. Organization-provided training opportunities can be a significant benefit for employees, particularly in entrepreneurial organizations where other types of benefits may not be as available. Employee compensation and benefits are the next HRM topics we need to look at.

Compensation and Benefits. The purpose of designing an effective and appropriate compensation system is to attract and retain competent and talented individuals who can help the organization accomplish its mission and goals. In addition, an organization's compensation system has been shown to have an impact on its strategic performance.[11] Entrepreneurs must develop compensation systems that reflect the changing nature of work and the workplace in order to keep employees motivated, committed, and excited. Compensation can include many different types of rewards and benefits. Figure 8-4 outlines the typical compensation components an organization may provide.

Figure 8-4

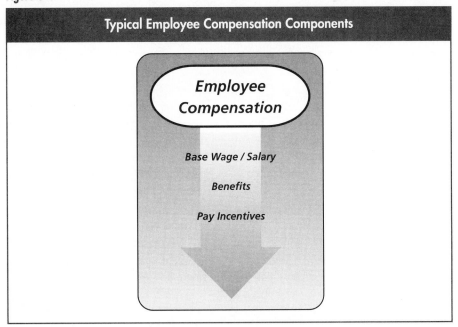

Typical Employee Compensation Components

Employee Compensation

Base Wage / Salary

Benefits

Pay Incentives

Source: Based on L. R. Gómez-Mejía, D. B. Balkin, and R. L. Cardy, *Human Resource Management* (Upper Saddle River, NJ: Prentice Hall, 1995), p. 357.

The base wage–salary is the fixed dollar amount that an individual receives on a regular basis for performing a job. This wage or salary is usually paid weekly, biweekly, or monthly. Pay incentives are compensation programs designed to encourage and reward good work performance. These incentives may be in the form of merit pay, bonuses, profit sharing, or some other type. Benefits consist of a wide variety of compensation programs such as insurance (health, life, or other), vacations, unemployment benefits, stock options, and so forth. Deciding which forms of compensation to use to attract and keep talented employees is an important decision for entrepreneurs because scarce resources may preclude offering

FYI

Taking Stock

We've all heard the news stories of employees making millions off their stock options, particularly at dot.com companies. Although not every stock option plan put in place makes millionaires of employees, these plans can be an excellent way to attract and retain talented employees, particularly if other compensation alternatives tend to be less than competitive. Stock option plans give employees the right to purchase a certain number of their company's shares at a fixed price for a certain period of time. Most options usually begin partially vesting after one year and vesting fully after four years. Once an option is vested, the employee can exercise it, which means purchasing from the company the allotted number of shares at the price that's been set (the strike price) and then either holding the stock or selling it on the open market. The difference between the strike price and the market price of the shares at the time the option is exercised is the employee's gain in the value of the shares. When an employee exercises an option, the company must issue a new share of stock that can be publicly traded. The intent behind stock options is that employees will be motivated to continue performing at high levels, thus increasing the company's performance and the value of its stock. However, even though they're touted as being an effective incentive to keep employees motivated to achieve the long-term goals of an

organization, often they bring about the opposite result. Employees may cash in (exercise) their stock options at the earliest possible point rather than waiting for the desired long-term increase in value and other talented employees may still job hop looking for the best payoff.

Another way to compensate and motivate employees is through an **employee stock ownership plan (ESOP)**, which is a program in which employees become part owners of an organization by receiving stock as a performance incentive. According to the National Center for Employee Ownership (**www.nceo.org**), about 10,000 companies have ESOPs. The research on ESOPs indicates that they can increase employee satisfaction and frequently result in higher performance. However, that potential will be realized only if employees are treated as owners by keeping them regularly informed about the status of the business and giving them opportunities to influence business decisions.

Whether you decide that a stock option plan or an ESOP will work best for you, it's extremely important to get good legal and accounting advice. A number of tax and legal issues would need to be addressed before setting up either a stock option plan or an ESOP.

Sources: P. Weaver, "An ESOP Can Improve a Firm's Performance," *Nation's Business*, September 1996, p. 63; S. Kaufman, "ESOPs' Appeal on the Increase," *Nation's Business*, June 1997, pp. 43–44; E. O. Welles, "Motherhood, Apple Pie, and Stock Options," *Inc.*, February 1998, pp. 84–97; and S. Gruner, "Stock Options & Equity," *Inc.*, February 1998, pp. 110–13.

Rapid Review ◀◀|

✓ What is orientation and why is it important? What should be covered in each of the three main areas of orientation?

✓ Why is performance appraisal important?

✓ Describe the different performance appraisal methods an entrepreneur might use.

✓ What might the results of a performance appraisal be used for?

✓ Why is employee training important even in entrepreneurial organizations?

✓ What are the typical compensation components an organization might provide?

high salaries or a wide variety of typical benefits. Many entrepreneurial organizations will offer other incentives such as stock options to attract skilled and competent employees. Although granting employees stock options may seem like a wonderful solution to a complicated and complex dilemma, entrepreneurs need to think about some issues before jumping in and doing so. The FYI box in this section provides basic information about stock option plans and ESOPs (employee stock ownership plans).

The decisions on compensation and benefits play an important role in attracting and keeping talented employees. It's also crucial to keep talented employees motivated to perform their jobs. Although motivating employees is not considered a specific HRM activity, it is an extremely important consideration in managing people.

MOTIVATING EMPLOYEES

When you're motivated to do something, don't you find yourself energized and willing to work hard at doing whatever it is you're excited about? Wouldn't it be great if all of a venture's employees were energized, excited, and willing to work hard at their jobs? That's what we want to look at in this section—getting employees energized and excited about performing their jobs at or above expected levels. As an entrepreneur, you'll need to understand what motivation is and how to motivate employees.

What Is Motivation?

Motivation is the willingness of an individual to exert high levels of effort in doing a job in order to help the organization reach its goals. Although motivation can also refer to a person's efforts toward reaching personal goals, we're primarily interested in motivation as it relates to the workplace. If an entrepreneurial venture is going to achieve its goals, it's going to need motivated employees—that is, employees who are willing to exert high levels of effort.

Motivation is one of the most thoroughly researched and studied topics in management and organizational behavior. Although we're not going to examine all the various motivation theories in depth, we do want to describe briefly some of the more important ones. If you want to know more about any of these motivation theories, you can pick up any introductory management or organizational behavior textbook for additional information.[12]

Early motivation theories focused on trying to describe *what* it was that motivated individuals. The best known of these content theories is probably **Maslow's hierarchy of needs**, which states that there is a hierarchy of five human needs (physical needs on the bottom of the hierarchy and moving up through safety, social, esteem, and at the top of the hierarchy, self-actualization) that serve to motivate a person to exert effort.[13] According to Maslow's theory, as each need is substantially satisfied, the next need becomes dominant. In addition, a need that has been substantially satisfied will no longer motivate an individual. Using Maslow's hierarchy, if you wanted to motivate someone, you would have to understand what need level that person was on and focus on satisfying needs at or above that level.

Another of these well-known content motivation theories (that is, motivation theories that attempted to explain the content of what motivated individuals) is **Herzberg's motivation-hygiene theory**, or the **two-factor theory of motivation**.[14] This motivation theory proposed that the job factors contributing to *job satisfaction* (or being motivated to perform) were not the same as those job factors contributing to *job dissatisfaction*. Herzberg called those job factors that caused people to feel satisfied with their jobs and thus more motivated to perform, the *motivators*. These motivators encompassed job content (the job itself) and included such things as the opportunity to achieve, recognition for work, taking on additional responsibility, opportunity for advancement, and so forth. The job factors that caused people to feel dissatisfied with their jobs were called *hygiene* factors and encompassed job context—things surrounding the job such as the type and quality of supervision, relationship with supervisor, salary, organizational policies and administration, working conditions, relationships with co-workers, and so forth. According to Herzberg's theory, providing for the hygiene factors would do nothing to motivate employees; it simply would keep them from being dissatisfied with their jobs. In order to motivate employees, you had to look at creating opportunities for them to achieve by focusing on job content.

Although these content theories of motivation got managers and entrepreneurs thinking about motivation, researchers began to recognize that the emphasis on what motivates individuals was misdirected because what motivates each of us is different. What motivates you is different from what motivates the person sitting next to you in class and is different from what motivates your close friends. Rather than trying to understand and describe motivation from the perspective of *what*, the emphasis

Improving Worker Performance

An entrepreneurial venture that wants to grow (and survive) has to get continually improving performance from its employees. Because the work performance of a venture's human resources is the only resource that competitors cannot duplicate, you've got to understand how to improve your employees' performance. But what can you do to motivate employees to do their best? Here are some questions that you might ask to see if you're creating an environment in which employee performance is enhanced: (1) Do you try to make sure there's the right fit between employee and job? (2) Do you search for ways to put your employees in direct contact with your customers? (3) Does your company's culture encourage employees to strive for high performance levels? (4) Do you seize opportunities to offer informal rewards and recognition to your employees? (5) Do you try to tailor rewards and recognition to individual employees? (6) Do you recognize that many employees may find their greatest reward in the work itself and allow them to do their jobs the way they think is best?

Source: M. Barrier, "Improving Worker Performance," *Nation's Business,* September 1996, pp. 28–31.

switched to understanding *how* motivation takes place. These process theories focused on understanding the process of motivation and proposed that by understanding how motivation takes place, motivation efforts could then be individually tailored to each person. We'll look briefly at three of the major process motivation theories: goal-setting theory, reinforcement theory, and expectancy theory.

We know that an individual's intention to work toward a goal is a major source of job motivation.[15] The **goal-setting theory** of motivation proposes that specific goals increase performance and that difficult goals, when accepted by an individual, result in higher performance than do easy goals. Studies on goal setting have demonstrated the superiority of specific and challenging goals in motivating individuals. When people are given specific challenging goals, they produce a higher level of output than when they're simply told, "Do your best." Another important element of goal-setting theory is understanding employee participation in setting goals. Will employees try harder if they've had the opportunity to participate? We can't say that having employees participate in the goal-setting process is *always* desirable. In some cases, research showed that participatively set goals elicited superior performance, although in other cases, individuals performed best when goals were assigned by someone else. However, the fact that individuals may better accept goals when they've had a chance to participate in setting them, would seem to indicate that allowing employees to participate in goal setting might be a desirable approach. What can we conclude about goal-setting theory and the role it plays in understanding how individuals are motivated? An overall conclusion from goal-setting theory is that a person's intentions to work toward a goal are powerful motivators. Channeled and used properly, they can lead to higher performance.

The next process motivation theory we need to look at is **reinforcement theory**, which proposes that an individual's behavior is a function of its consequences. According to reinforcement theory, what controls an individual's behavior are the consequences (or reinforcers) that follow that behavior. Reinforcement theory was first proposed by B. F. Skinner, who said that people will most likely engage in desired behavior if they are rewarded for doing so. These rewards are most effective if they immediately follow a desired behavior, and behavior that isn't rewarded, or is punished, is less likely to be repeated.[16] As a motivation theory, reinforcement theory proposes that you can influence an employee's behavior by reinforcing work actions that you see as favorable (that is, actions that contribute to the accomplishment of the venture's goals). Although research indicates that external reinforcement is undoubtedly an important influence on how motivated an employee is, do understand that it isn't the only explanation for differences in employee motivation.

The most comprehensive explanation of how motivation takes place is **expectancy theory**.[17] This theory proposes that an individual tends to act in a certain way based on the expectation that the behavior will be followed by a given outcome and on the attractiveness of that outcome to the individual. It includes three variables or relationships (see Figure 8-5):

1. *Expectancy* or *effort–performance linkage*, which is the probability perceived by the individual that exerting a given level of effort will lead to a certain level of performance.

Figure 8-5

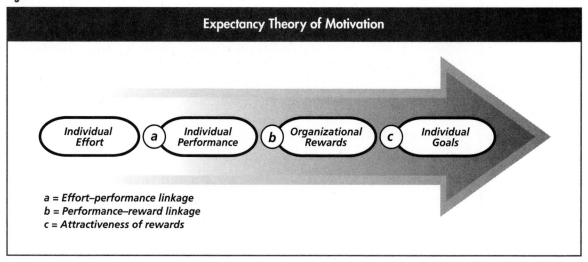

2. *Instrumentality* or *performance–reward linkage*, which is the degree to which the individual believes that performing at a certain level is instrumental in leading to the attainment of a desired outcome.

3. *Valence* or *attractiveness of reward*, which is the importance that the individual places on the potential outcome or reward that can be achieved. Valence considers both the goals and the needs of the individual.

Although this theory of motivation might sound complex, it really isn't that difficult to visualize. It can be summed up in the following questions: How hard do I have to work to achieve a certain level of performance, and can I actually achieve that level? What reward will performing at that level get me? How attractive is that reward to me, and does it help me achieve my goals? Whether you are motivated to put forth effort (that is, to produce) at any given time depends on your particular goals and your perception of whether a certain level of performance is necessary to attain those goals. Think of how hard you work in a particular class for a grade. Isn't it based on your beliefs about what type of effort (studying, doing homework, coming to class, etc.) it takes to achieve a certain level of performance, the "reward" or grade for achieving that level of performance, and how important that reward or grade is to you? If getting an A is important to you, you'll put forth whatever effort it takes to achieve the level of performance (maybe 90 percent or above) it takes to get that A. The key to expectancy theory as an explanation of motivation is understanding an individual's goals and the linkages between effort and performance, between performance and rewards, and between rewards and individual goal satisfaction. Individuals will be motivated if they see a link between the amount of effort exerted, the resulting performance level, and the rewards received because of that level of performance.

Each of the motivation theories just described—both content and process—provides clues to understanding the motivation process. But, practically speaking, how can an entrepreneur utilize what is known from the motivation theories and apply it in real life to actually motivating employees?

Entrepreneurs in Action ▶

Sapient Corporation builds Internet and software systems for e-commerce and for automating back-office tasks such as billing and inventory. It's a people-intensive business, and cofounders Jerry Greenberg and J. Stuart Moore recognized that employee motivation was critically important to their company's ultimate success. They designed their organization so that individual employees are part of an industry-specific team that works on an entire project rather than on one small piece of it. Their rationale was that people often feel frustrated when they are doing a small part of a job and never get to see the whole job from start to finish. They figured people would be more productive if they got the opportunity to participate in all phases of a project. Their approach seems to be working so far, as revenues and profits have continued to climb.

Source: S. Herrera, "People Power," *Forbes*, November 2, 1998, p. 212.

How to Motivate Employees

Although there's no simple, easy answer to the question of how best to motivate employees, we do know some things about increasing the likelihood of successfully motivating employees. First of all, *recognize individual differences*. Almost every contemporary motivation theory recognizes that employees aren't homogeneous. They have different needs. They also differ in terms of attitudes, personality, and other important variables. Try to understand what's important to individual employees. This also means that you should *individualize rewards*. Because employees have different needs, what acts as a reinforcer for one may not be so for another. Use your knowledge of employees' differences to individualize the rewards they can get. Another suggestion is to *match people to jobs*. A great deal of evidence shows the motivational benefits of carefully matching people to jobs. For instance, high achievers will do best in jobs that provide opportunities to participate in setting challenging goals and that involve autonomy and feedback. However, others will not be motivated by those kinds of jobs or job responsibilities. The fourth suggestion is to *use goals*. The research on goal-setting theory suggests that employees should have challenging, specific goals and feedback on how well they're doing in accomplishing those goals. If you expect resistance to the goals, use participation to increase acceptance. Next, *ensure that goals are perceived as attainable*. Regardless of whether goals are actually attainable, employees who see goals as unattainable will reduce their effort. Their attitude is "why bother, it won't do any good to work hard." Be sure, therefore, that employees feel confident that increased efforts *can* lead to achieving work goals. Another suggestion is to *link rewards to performance*. Entrepreneurs should attempt to make rewards contingent on performance. Rewarding factors other than performance will reinforce only those other factors. Entrepreneurs should also look for ways to increase the visibility of rewards. If employees can see what types of behaviors and performance levels are being rewarded, this can serve to motivate others. Next, *check the system for fairness.* Employees should perceive that rewards or outcomes are fair and equitable and relate to the amount of effort expended in doing the work. Finally, *don't ignore money.* It's so easy to get caught up in setting goals, creating interesting jobs, and providing opportunities for participation that you overlook the fact that money is a major reason why most people work. Thus, the allocation of performance-based wage increases, bonuses, and other pay incentives is important in determining employee motivation. We're not saying that your motivation techniques should focus solely on money. Rather, we're simply stating the obvious—that is, if money is removed as an incentive, people aren't going to show up at work. You can't say the same for removing goals, enriched work, or participation.

Having motivated employees is an important goal for any entrepreneurial venture. Another important aspect of managing people, however, is dealing with employee teams and leadership issues. Those are the topics we're going to look at next.

Rapid Review ◀◀|

✓ What is motivation? Why is it important?

✓ Describe and differentiate between the two content theories of motivation presented.

✓ How does goal-setting theory approach motivation?

✓ What does reinforcement theory say about motivation?

✓ Describe expectancy theory and how it relates to motivation.

✓ Explain how entrepreneurs can motivate employees.

EMPLOYEE TEAMS AND LEADERSHIP

Many organizations, entrepreneurial and otherwise, are using teams to perform organizational tasks, create new ideas, and resolve problems. Teams are popular and likely to continue being used. In this section, we want to discuss what a work team is, the different types of teams an organization might use, how to develop and manage effective work teams, and how to lead a team.

What Is a Work Team?

Most of us are probably pretty familiar with the idea of a team, especially if we have ever participated in or watched any type of organized sports activity. Although an athletic team has many of the same characteristics as a work team, work teams are different and have their own unique traits. Just what are **work teams**? They're formal work groups made up of interdependent, interacting individuals who are responsible for the attainment of work goals.

Types of Work Teams

Although there are many possible ways to categorize work teams, we're going to describe them in terms of four characteristics: purpose, duration, membership, and structure.[18] Let's look at each of these characteristics in more detail.

Work teams can vary in their purpose or goal. Examples abound of the variety of work activities teams have tackled in entrepreneurial organizations. For instance, a team might be involved in product development, problem solving, or any other work-related activity. So, one way work teams can be described is in terms of what they're set up to do. In addition, teams can also be classified in terms of duration as either permanent or temporary. Teams that are formal ongoing components of an organization's structure would be classified as permanent. Many entrepreneurial organizations that have adopted the work team concept have an organizational structure designed around these permanent teams. On the other hand, temporary teams would include ad hoc task forces, project teams, or any other type of short-term team created for a specific purpose that will disband once that purpose or goal is accomplished. The next characteristic that can be used to classify teams is that either the team's membership can be functional based—that is, composed of people from a particular organizational functional area or department—or it could be a **cross-functional team**, which has team members from various organizational functional areas or departments. Finally, teams can be classified as either supervised or self-managed. A supervised team is under the direction of some person who is responsible for guiding the team in setting goals, in performing the necessary work activities, and in evaluating performance. A self-managed team, as its title suggests, assumes these responsibilities as it manages itself.

Although knowing how to describe work teams in terms of their characteristics is important, what we're really interested in is how to make sure that these work teams perform their work at the highest levels of efficiency and effectiveness. What's involved with that?

Developing and Managing Effective Teams

One thing you need to realize is that teams are not automatic productivity improvers. If the team isn't effective, its performance accomplishments are likely to be disappointing as well. However, an entrepreneur's goal should be to have the venture's work teams achieving more than individuals working separately (even if their work is coordinated) can achieve. An effective team can do this! Research on teams provides insights as to the characteristics of an effective team.[19] (See Figure 8-6.)

Figure 8-6

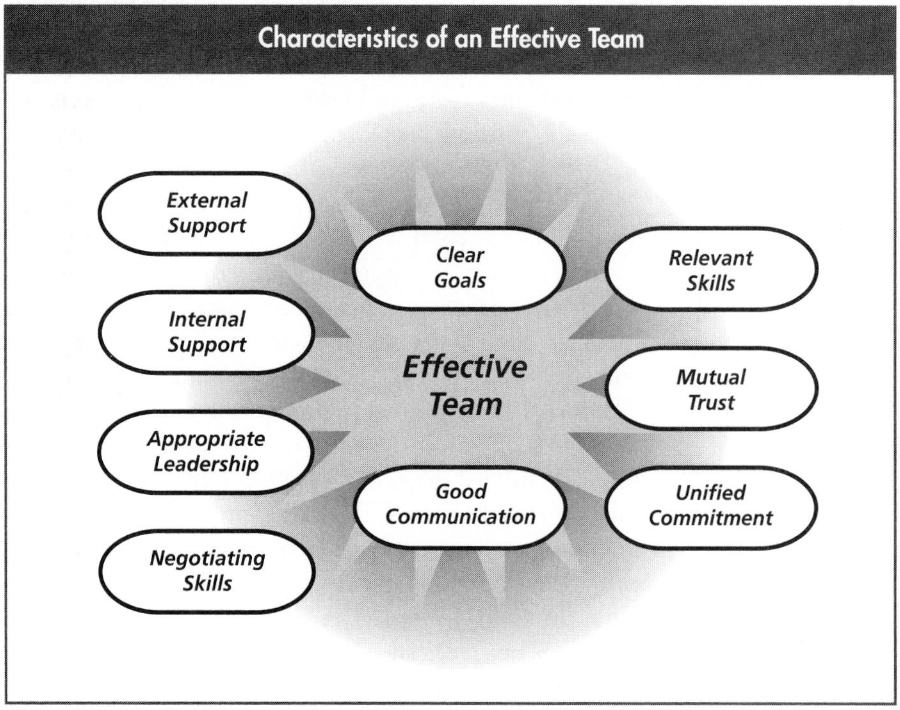

Characteristics of an Effective Team

- External Support
- Clear Goals
- Relevant Skills
- Internal Support
- Effective Team
- Mutual Trust
- Appropriate Leadership
- Good Communication
- Unified Commitment
- Negotiating Skills

First, an effective team will have *clear goals*. High-performance teams have both a clear understanding of the goal to be achieved and a belief that the goal embodies a worthwhile or important result. In effective teams, members are committed to the team's goals, know what they're expected to accomplish, and understand how they will work together to achieve those goals. The next characteristic of effective teams is *relevant skills*. Effective teams are composed of competent and talented individuals. They have the necessary technical skills and abilities to achieve the desired goals, and the interpersonal skills required to achieve excellence while working well with others. High-performing teams have members who possess *both* technical and interpersonal skills. Next, effective teams exhibit *mutual trust*. Team members must believe in one another's integrity, character, and ability. However, this trust is fragile. It takes a long time to build and can be easily destroyed. But ultimately, to be effective, the team members must have this mutual trust.

Another characteristic of effective teams is *unified commitment*. Members of an effective team exhibit intense loyalty and dedication to the team. They're willing to do whatever it takes to help the team succeed. We call this loyalty and dedication unified commitment. Next, effective teams exhibit *good communication*. It shouldn't surprise you that effective teams are characterized by good communication. Team members are able to convey messages between each other in ways that are readily and clearly understood. This includes nonverbal as well as spoken messages. Good communication also means the team engages in relevant and continual feedback among team members and between the team and any other individuals or teams. The next characteristic of an effective team is *negotiating skills*. When a team has negotiating skills, it means that the team is flexible and continually making adjustments. Team members are able to negotiate among themselves and with others outside the team. Since problems and relationships are regularly changing in a team, members must be able to confront and reconcile differences.

Next, effective teams will have *appropriate leadership*. Effective teams need effective leaders. Effective leaders can motivate a team to follow them through the most difficult situations. How? They help clarify goals. They demonstrate that change is possible. They increase the self-confidence of team members, helping members to realize their potential more fully. Increasingly, effective team leaders are taking on the role of coach and facilitator. They help guide and support the team, but don't control it. Finally, effective teams are going to have *internal and external support*. An effective team needs a supportive climate. Internally, the team should have proper training, an understandable measurement system that team members can use to evaluate their overall performance, an incentive program that recognizes and rewards team activities, and a supportive human resource system. The internal climate should support members and reinforce behaviors that lead to high levels of performance. Externally, the team needs to be provided with the resources needed to get the job done. External support is an important requirement of effective teams. Think back to our chapter-opening case. At Rhino Foods, the organization provided extraordinary support to employee teams, particularly as they faced the difficult decision about how to handle employee layoffs.

Knowing what characteristics make a team effective isn't enough, though. As entrepreneurs, we need to understand how effective teams are developed and managed so that our entrepreneurial venture can capitalize on the positive gains

> ## Entrepreneurs in Action ▶
>
> Steve Rifkind, founder of a marketing company that bears his name, has found that giving employee teams the opportunities to make decisions and not always to be told what to do has worked well. He says, "Give smart employees an opportunity to soar and they will always make it happen." Rifkind expects energy and commitment, but in turn allows employees to be entrepreneurial.
>
> *Source:* S. Greco, "Share the Power," *Inc.*, February 1999, p. 52.

that can come from work teams. What's involved in developing and managing a team? It's probably most logical to think in terms of the planning, organizing, leading, and controlling activities that must occur.[20]

Planning for and by the team is an important activity. The team must take the time to determine goals and establish plans. As we pointed out previously, effective teams have clear goals. Team members must also understand and accept the team's goals.[21] Whether the goals are provided for the team or whether the team develops its own goals, every team member needs to know and accept the goals.

Once the team's goals have been agreed on, organizing tasks involve clarifying authority and structural issues. One of the key questions for the team is "How much authority do we have?" If the team is a self-directed or self-managed team, it's already been empowered with the authority to make certain decisions and perform specific work activities. However, even if a team isn't self-managed, questions will come up regarding what it can and cannot do. It's important that these authority issues be addressed early so that a team knows its parameters and constraints. Structural issues also need to be resolved within the team itself. Has a leader been appointed or will the team designate one? What tasks should be done in order to accomplish the team's goals? What are the most effective and efficient ways to do the work? Who's going to do what tasks? How will work assignments be made? These types of organizing questions must be answered.

Important leading issues that a team must address include, among others, what role the team's leader will play, how conflict will be handled, and what communication processes will be used. Although the team leader often plays an important role in directing the efforts of the team, team leaders are increasingly assuming the roles of facilitator and coach rather than of "person in charge." If the entrepreneur is the person leading the team, he or she wants to make sure not to dictate what the team is doing and how it should do its work. Sometimes it's hard to let go and let others make decisions, yet an effective leader should know when to step in and when to step back. If the team leader is not the entrepreneur, the person who *is* put in charge of the team must have the "right stuff" to help the team achieve its maximum potential. This means having (1) sufficient technical knowledge to understand the team's duties and (2) strong interpersonal skills to be able to deal with encouraging individual participation, motivating outstanding performance, resolving conflicts, and gaining consensus on key issues. Table 8-4 lists some key people skills that have been found to be important in leading a team.

Finally, these are two of the most important controlling issues in managing teams. How will the team's performance be evaluated, and what type of reward system will be used? As entrepreneurial organizations make greater use of teams, they're going to have to address these issues and make changes in their performance appraisal and reward systems. Performance criteria may need to be modified to incorporate teamwork behaviors in employee evaluations. Not only should individual performance be evaluated, but factors that indicate how well the individual works in the team context also should be considered. In addition, entrepreneurs may have to look at how teams are rewarded for their efforts and performance levels. Group incentive plans may be an answer. Under these systems, group rewards are directly related to performance. If the team succeeds, team members will be rewarded. In addition, teams may be rewarded with one-time bonuses, team incentives, or informal team recognition. Whatever approach is used, the entrepreneur needs to look to the work teams for direction in deciding what types of rewards and recognition are important.

Developing and managing effective work teams is an important "people" issue that entrepreneurs may have to deal with as the venture grows. There are two final interpersonal (people) issues that we need to discuss in this chapter.

Rapid Review

✓ What is a work team?
✓ How can work teams be categorized?
✓ What is unique about a cross-functional team?
✓ Describe the characteristics of an effective team.
✓ What's involved with developing and managing an effective team?
✓ How do planning, organizing, leading, and controlling issues play a role in developing and managing an effective team?

TABLE 8-4   Key People Skills in Leading a Team

- Ask appropriate questions to bring out ideas and stimulate discussion.
- Listen closely and intently to members' ideas and concerns.
- Manage group discussions to encourage shy team members to participate.
- Establish an informal and nonthreatening climate so members feel free to speak their thoughts candidly.
- Use the consensus method to reach decisions on key team issues.
- Involve team members in setting goals.
- Implement meeting guidelines to minimize wasted time in group meetings.
- Encourage respect for each other so each member knows that his or her contributions are valued.
- Identify and deal with dysfunctional behaviors immediately.
- Celebrate the achievement of milestones and other team accomplishments.
- Use recognition, task assignments, and other techniques to motivate team members.

Source: Based on G. M. Parker, *Cross-Functional Teams* (San Francisco: Jossey-Bass, 1994), pp. 57–58.

OTHER INTERPERSONAL ISSUES

Although managing the entrepreneurial venture's people may be one of the most challenging things an entrepreneur does, it can also be one of the most rewarding. In addition to the human resource management issues, motivation issues, and teams and leadership issues, you need to understand two other people issues. One is managing conflict and the other is empowering employees and delegating duties.

Managing Conflict

When you have people working together, conflict is inevitable. **Conflict** refers to any perceived disagreements or differences that result in interference or opposition. Whether the disagreements or differences are real or not is irrelevant. If people perceive that disagreements and differences exist, then a conflict exists.

Our perception of conflict has evolved from a view that all conflict is bad and must be avoided to a view that some conflict is necessary for a work team to perform effectively. However, we're not so naïve to think that all conflicts within a group are good. Some conflicts support a group's goals whereas other conflicts prevent a group from achieving its goals. Unfortunately, the difference between whether a conflict is functional (good) or dysfunctional (bad) isn't clear or precise. No one level of conflict can be assumed good or bad under all conditions. The type and level of conflict that will promote a healthy and positive interchange of ideas and involvement toward the team's goals may, in another group or in the same group at another time, be highly dysfunctional. As an entrepreneur, you want to create an environment in which team conflict is healthy but not allowed to run to extremes. If the work team is apathetic, unresponsive to change, lacking new ideas, or stagnant, you may need to stimulate conflict. However, if conflict

---

Entrepreneurs in Action

Conflict is managed well at Higher Octave, a New Age record label based in Malibu, California. Lunchtime involves recreation at the beach, and a massage therapist pays a weekly visit. The relaxed environment makes the staff of 25 want to stay. And they do stay—employee turnover is almost zero. Cofounders Matthew Marshall and Daniel Selene have created an organization where popular songs aren't referred to as "hits" and the word *deadline* is banned because both conjure up images of destruction and death. But even with the company's laid-back, mellow approach, employees bring out 16 to 20 albums a year, and Higher Octave has reached the number-one spot on *Billboard* magazine's New Age chart five of the past eight years. That's not a bad record for an organization that epitomizes calm and serenity.

Source: A. Marsh, "Malibu Mellow," *Forbes,* August 10, 1998, pp. 62–64.

has caused the team to become disruptive, chaotic, and uncooperative, you need to minimize the amount of conflict because at this point, it's a disruptive force.[22] If conflict levels have become too high (performance is being negatively impacted), then you may need to take steps to manage the conflict.

Empowering Employees and Delegating Duties

Entrepreneurs are strongly self-reliant, and letting others take over decisions and tasks doesn't come easily to them. However, if you truly want to grow your entrepreneurial venture, you're going to have to learn how to let go. Letting go entails a whole new, often radical, managerial philosophy of empowering employees—that is, giving them the power and freedom to do things. It means trusting employees to make good decisions and to work competently and in the best interests of the organization. We introduced the concept of **empowerment** back in Chapter 5 as we were discussing the organizational chain of command. If you recall, we defined it as increasing the decision-making discretion of individuals. In an empowered organization, individual employees are free to resolve problems as they arise, are encouraged to approach their work the way they feel is best because they do have more detailed knowledge about it, and are encouraged to think for themselves rather than being told what to do. Empowerment really is a philosophical concept you have to "buy into" as you accept and embrace giving employees more control over what they do and how they do it. This doesn't come easily. In fact, it's hard to do. Your life is tied up in this business. You've built it from the ground up. But, continuing to grow your entrepreneurial venture is eventually going to require handing over more responsibilities to your employees. It will mean accepting and embracing a philosophy of employee empowerment. What's involved? Let's take a closer look.

Entrepreneurs can begin empowering employees in a couple of ways. One way to start is through participative decision making where you get employee input into decisions. Although getting employees to participate in decisions isn't quite taking the full plunge into employee empowerment, it, at least, is a way to begin tapping into the amazing array of employees' talents, skills, knowledge, and abilities. What if your use of participative decision making is successful? What else can you do? Another way to empower employees is through delegation. **Delegation** is the process of assigning certain decisions or specific job duties to individual employees. By delegating these decisions and duties, you're turning over to someone the responsibility for carrying them out. You're entrusting the accomplishment of these work activities to this person. Delegating effectively means following some simple guidelines. See the FYI box for some advice on effective delegation.

When you're finally comfortable with the idea of empowerment, fully empowering employees means redesigning their jobs so they have discretion over the way they do their work. It's allowing employees to do their work effectively and efficiently by using their creativity, imagination, knowledge, and skills. If the entrepreneur implements employee empowerment properly—that is, with complete and total commitment to the program and with appropriate employee training—results can be impressive for the entrepreneurial venture and for the empowered employees. The business can enjoy significant productivity gains, quality improvements, more satisfied customers, increased employee motivation, and

Delegate Like a Pro

If your entrepreneurial venture succeeds and grows (which is, of course, what you want it to do), eventually you're going to have to delegate some decisions and duties to other employees. How can you do so effectively? The first thing is to *approach delegation carefully and with thought.* Although you may finally have accepted that you're going to have to delegate, don't cast off your responsibilities in a rush. Think about what, how, and who. Next, be sure to *choose individuals carefully.* You need to trust the skills and abilities of the person(s) to whom you're going to be delegating. Once you've decided on those individuals who will be taking over certain decisions and duties, *be specific about what you're delegating* to them. Be direct about

expectations. Clarify what decisions and duties are being assigned. Next, *communicate.* Let those affected by the delegation of certain decisions and duties know that another person is now handling these. Also establish feedback procedures. This way you can find out what's happening and take care of any problems that might arise. Finally, *make good use of your freed-up time.* An entrepreneur has a lot of things to do. When you've delegated some of your decisions and tasks, use the time to attend to other important aspects of growing your business.

Sources: "Do You Delegate as Much as You Can?" *Nation's Business,* July 1996, p. 9; B. Bernard, "Delegating Duties the Right Way," *Nation's Business,* April 1998, p. 10; and R. McGarvey, "Ready, Set, Delegate!" *Entrepreneur,* July 1998, pp. 77–79.

improved morale. Employees can enjoy the opportunities to do a greater variety of work that is more interesting and challenging. In addition, employees are encouraged to take the initiative in identifying and solving problems and doing their work. Do be aware, however, that not every employee wants to be empowered. Some will not want the responsibility and others may be afraid of the responsibility. Yet, the dynamic, often chaotic, nature of a growing and successful entrepreneurial venture is going to require at some point that the venture's employees take an active role in what work gets done and how. If employees resist empowerment attempts, you may need to recognize that these are not the kind of employees that are going to contribute to the long-term and continued success of your entrepreneurial venture.

Rapid Review

✓ What is conflict? Is all conflict bad? Explain.
✓ What is empowerment?
✓ How can an entrepreneur design an empowered organization?
✓ What is delegation?
✓ What are the advantages and drawbacks of empowering employees?

CHAPTER SUMMARY

Managing the people in an entrepreneurial organization is challenging yet rewarding. The quality of an organization is, to a large degree, the summation of the quality of people it hires and keeps. This chapter described some human resource management issues, motivation issues, team and leadership issues, and other interpersonal issues that entrepreneurs may have to deal with.

It's important for an entrepreneur to recognize the strategic importance of the venture's human resources. High-performance organizations give their employees the tools, training, and incentive they need to do their jobs. The high-performance work practices of these organizations reflect a strong commitment to improving the knowledge, skills, and abilities of their employees. Other human resource management issues involve bringing people on board and managing them once they're on board. Bringing people on board involves human resource planning, recruiting, selecting, and hiring. Different methods and tools are available to help entrepreneurs do these important HR tasks. Although it seems contradictory, part of bringing people on board is having in place techniques for decruiting, or reducing the number of employees in the organization. Once employees have been brought on board, what next? An entrepreneur has additional HRM tasks including orienting, appraising performance, training, and deciding on compensation and benefits. Again, different methods and tools are available to help entrepreneurs do these HR tasks.

Motivating employees is an important people issue. Entrepreneurs need to understand what motivation is and how to motivate employees. Motivation is defined as the willingness of an individual to exert high levels of effort in doing a job in order to help the organization reach its goals. If an entrepreneurial venture is going to reach its goals, it needs motivated employees. There are two approaches to explaining motivation. One approach is the focus on *what* motivates employees and includes Maslow's hierarchy of needs theory and Herzberg's two-factor theory. The other approach focuses on *how* motivation takes place and includes goal-setting theory, reinforcement theory, and expectancy theory. Although these theories do a good job of explaining motivation, what entrepreneurs really need to know is how to motivate employees, and there are a number of suggestions for motivating employees.

Many entrepreneurial organizations are using work teams to perform organizational tasks, create new ideas, and resolve problems. Work teams can be categorized according to their purpose, duration, membership, and structure. But having work teams isn't enough. These work teams need to be effective. Effective teams exhibit certain characteristics. Developing and managing effective teams involves understanding the planning, organizing, leading, and controlling activities that need to take place.

Finally, entrepreneurs may have to deal with two other important "people" issues: managing conflict and empowering employees. Conflict is inevitable and may even be desirable. However, too much conflict is dysfunctional and will have to be managed. Even though entrepreneurs tend to be self-reliant, growing their entrepreneurial ventures is going to require letting go and empowering employees with the power and freedom to do things the best way they know how. Entrepreneurs can begin empowering employees in a couple of ways. One way is to use participative decision making. Another approach is through delegating certain decisions or specific job duties to individual employees. However, fully empowering employees means redesigning their jobs so they have discretion over the way they do their work. If the entrepreneur implements employee empowerment properly, results can be impressive for the entrepreneurial venture and for the empowered employees.

KEY TERMS

⮕ *High-performance work practices:* Human resource policies and practices that lead to high levels of both individual and organizational performance.

⮕ *Human resource planning:* Assessing current and future human resource needs.

⮕ *Job analysis:* An assessment that defines jobs and the behaviors necessary to perform them.

⮕ *Job description:* A written statement of the work a jobholder does, how it is done, and why it is done.

⮕ *Job specification:* A written statement of the minimum acceptable qualifications that a jobholder or job seeker must possess in order to perform a given job successfully.

⮕ *Recruiting:* The process of locating, identifying, and attracting capable job applicants.

⮕ *Employee selection:* The process of screening job applicants to ensure that the best individuals are hired.

⮕ *Work sampling:* A performance simulation test in which job applicants perform tasks in a simulated model of a job.

⮕ *Assessment centers:* Places where job applicants undergo more elaborate performance simulation tests as they perform exercises that simulate real problems they might encounter on the job.

⮕ *Decruitment:* Reducing the number of employees in an organization.

⮕ *Orientation:* The introduction of a new person to a new job.

⮕ *Sexual harassment:* Any unwelcome sexual advance, behavior marked by sexually aggressive remarks, unwanted touching, requests for sexual favors, or other verbal or physical conduct of a sexual nature.

⮕ *Performance appraisal:* The process of evaluating an individual's work performance.

⮕ *Graphic rating scale:* A popular method of appraisal in which an evaluator uses an incremental numerical scale to rate an employee on a set of performance factors.

⮕ *Written essays:* A performance appraisal technique whereby an evaluator writes a description of an employee's strengths, weaknesses, past performance, and potential, and then makes suggestions for improvement.

⮕ *Critical incidents:* An approach to performance appraisal whereby an evaluator lists behaviors from specific incidents of employee's effective and ineffective job performance.

⮕ *Behaviorally anchored rating scales (BARS):* A technique in which an evaluator rates employees using a numerical scale that focuses on specific and measurable job behaviors.

⮕ *Multiperson comparison:* A performance appraisal technique in which individuals are compared to other individuals in the work group.

⮕ *Employee stock ownership plan (ESOP):* A program in which employees become part owners of an organization by receiving stock as a performance incentive.

- ➡ *Motivation:* The willingness of an individual to exert high levels of effort in doing a job in order to help the organization reach its goals.
- ➡ *Maslow's hierarchy of needs:* A content theory of motivation that states there is a hierarchy of five human needs that serve to motivate a person to exert effort.
- ➡ *Herzberg's motivation-hygiene theory (two-factor theory of motivation):* A content theory of motivation that proposed that the job factors contributing to job satisfaction (or being motivated to perform) are not the same as the job factors contributing to job dissatisfaction.
- ➡ *Goal-setting theory:* A process theory of motivation that proposes that specific goals increase performance and that difficult goals, when accepted by an individual, result in higher performance than do easy goals.
- ➡ *Reinforcement theory:* A process theory of motivation that proposes that an individual's behavior is a function of its consequences.
- ➡ *Expectancy theory:* A process theory of motivation that proposes that an individual tends to act in a certain way based on the expectation that the behavior will be followed by a given outcome and on the attractiveness of that outcome to the individual.
- ➡ *Work teams:* Formal work groups made up of interdependent, interacting individuals who are responsible for the attainment of work goals.
- ➡ *Cross-functional team:* A work team that has team members from various organizational functional areas or departments.
- ➡ *Conflict:* Any perceived disagreements or differences that result in interference or opposition.
- ➡ *Empowerment:* Increasing the decision-making discretion of individuals.
- ➡ *Delegation:* The process of assigning certain decisions or duties to individual employees.

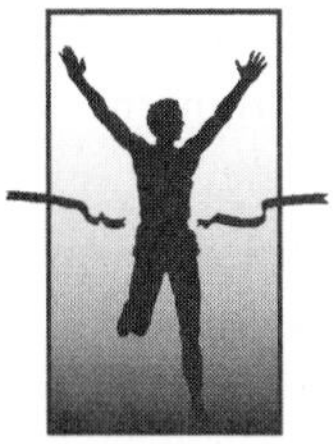

SWEAT EQUITY

1. When the labor market is tight, companies compete as fiercely for employees as they do for customers. Here are some tips for successfully keeping employees on board: Make it a long-term commitment; hire the right people; offer a competitive salary and benefits package; provide an economic stake in the company; be flexible with work schedules; communicate; encourage creativity and innovation; build a sense of camaraderie; reward individual and group performance; invest in training; and remember that your employees have lives outside the company.

   Take each tip and write an explanation of what you think it means and what you think it would require for an entrepreneur to practice it successfully.
2. At Click Interactive Inc., a Chicago-based software design firm, founder Michael Ferro Jr. says he has found a way to bring out the best in his workers: punish them. How? Ferro has what he calls the "penalty box," which simply is a temporary stint in the company's sales department offices. Programmers who are burned out or acting overly arrogant get sent to the

penalty box. Part of the punishment is that the person is required to wear professional business attire instead of the usual jeans and T-shirt. (That usually results in some good-natured teasing of the person.) Instead of writing software, the person is sent out to call on customers—after a few hours' coaching by the sales staff.

Explain Ferro's approach to motivation using the following theories: expectancy theory, reinforcement theory, and goal-setting theory. What do you think the positive motivational aspects of such an approach might be? Negative motivational aspects? Do you think Ferro's approach is good or bad? Explain.

(*Source:* Brown, "Spare the Rod. . . ," *Forbes*, May 18, 1998, pp. 76–78.)

3. "Good economic conditions are a double-edged sword for restaurant operators." So says Hudson Riehle, senior director of research for the National Restaurant Association. A booming economy means more people have more spending money to eat out and are doing so more frequently. However, that same economy shrinks the available labor pool.

Form small teams in class. Your team is getting ready to open its first restaurant. Getting and keeping talented people is going to be crucial to your venture's success. Given the realities of the economy as described above, explain how you will successfully manage the HRM issues (getting people on board and keeping them on board) and the motivational issues. Come up with a bulleted list of specific suggestions for each of these important people issues.

(*Source:* R. Balu, "Eateries Say Good Help Is Hard to Find," *Wall Street Journal*, May 27, 1999, p. A2.)

4. Workforce diversity is a fact of life for organizations. Research the topic of workforce diversity (using the Internet–World Wide Web or the library). Compile a bulleted list of important points about diversity. Then, write a paper explaining the implications of these for the entrepreneur. Be sure to focus on the "people" implications.

5. Interviewing is one of the employee selection techniques that most entrepreneurs think is easy and that they can do without much preparation. However, preparation is the key to successful interviews. In this assignment you're going to interview entrepreneurs about their interviewing processes. Interview three to five entrepreneurs. Ask them to describe their interviewing processes. What types of questions do they typically ask? Do they have job applicants do any special assignments? Have they found anything to be particularly effective while interviewing? When you have completed your interviews, write a report of your findings. Be prepared to share them with your class.

ENTREPRENEURSHIP IN ACTION CASES

CASE #1: Dream Team

Entrepreneurship in Action case #1 can be found at the beginning of Chapter 8.

Discussion Questions

1. What do you think Rhino's philosophy might be regarding the role of strategic human resource management? Explain.
2. On the basis of information included in the case, create a recruitment advertise-

ment for a production line position that Rhino Foods might use.

3. How do you think Rhino Foods motivates its employees? Give specific examples and explain them in terms of the motivation theories described in the chapter.

CASE #2: Dream Team II

Who would have ever thought that an aging hippie could build a successful food empire? Well, not just any food empire, but one built by selling, of all things, natural foods. John Mackey founded and runs an efficiently operated and brilliantly marketed health-food empire that has tapped into society's yearning for healthy living and eating. His Austin, Texas–based Whole Foods Market Inc. (**www.wholefoods.com**) boasts 87 supermarkets nationwide and is the market leader in the natural foods retailing industry. Its sales are four times greater than its largest competitor. Industry sources estimate that Whole Foods now has about 12 percent market share of the total natural foods retailing industry. With these kind of results, they must be doing something right.

The company's motto—Whole Foods, Whole People, Whole Planet—emphasizes that its vision reaches beyond being just a food retailer. The company believes that its success in fulfilling that vision is measured by customer satisfaction, team member excellence and happiness, return on capital investment, improvement in the state of the natural environ-

ment, and local and larger community support. The key to Whole Foods' ultimate success is its team members—the collective energy and intelligence of its own dream team!

The Whole Foods culture is based on teamwork. Each store is made up of an average of 10 self-directed teams—teams in grocery, produce, and so forth. These teams, and only the teams, have the power to approve new hires for full-time jobs. Store leaders screen applicants and recommend them for a job on a specific team, but there has to be a two-thirds approval vote by the team before the individual is hired. Needless to say, with this much responsibility placed on work teams, building and sustaining employee trust is an important goal of Whole Foods Market. The company does this in many ways such as recognizing how important leisure time, family, and community involvement outside of work are for a rich, meaningful, and balanced life; by encouraging participation and involvement by employees at all levels of the organization; and by recognizing and honoring diversity and individual differences.

Discussion Questions

1. What would be the advantages and drawbacks of letting employee work teams have sole decision-making power over who gets hired?

2. Log onto Whole Foods Web site (**www.wholefoods.com**). Click on "The Company" and check out the sections on Mission, Quality, and Values. How would you describe Whole Foods' philosophy for managing people? Do you agree with its philosophy? Why or why not? What could entrepreneurs learn from Whole Foods approach?

3. How would you explain Whole Foods' approach to employee motivation? Do you think it would work in other types of entrepreneurial organizations? Explain.

(*Sources:* W. Zellner, "Peace, Love, and the Bottom Line," *Business Week*, December 7, 1998, pp. 79–85; and information from company's Web site.)

CASE #3: The Bizarre Bean Counters

It's not quite what you would expect at the offices of a certified public accounting firm. But at Lipschult, Levin, & Gray, Certified Public Accountants, in Northbrook, Illinois, they aren't your typical "bean counters." Instead, Steve Siegel, LLG's managing member, has implemented a number of changes that are strikingly entrepreneurial and also a little bit bizarre!

Every telltale sign of what most people consider boring, dull CPA work has been eliminated. Although the firm still delivers traditional accounting, tax, and audit services, it also has launched four new business consulting services that have been quite successful. However, Siegel has paid most attention to developing the creativity, talent, and diversity of its staff so that new knowledge could be acquired and shared without getting hung up on traditional organizational relationships or having employees shut away in corner offices. They've truly done some unusual things at LLG.

None of the firm's 26 employees (called team members) or 5 partners (called members) has an office or a desk to call his or her own. Instead, everyone who works at LLG is part of a nomadic group who hauls their work stuff (files, phones, laptops) to a new spot every day. This isn't as difficult as it sounds because each piece of furniture is mounted on casters and rolls around easily. Everywhere you look in the company's office, you see evidence of versatility, comfort, and eccentricity. A miniature golf course is located right in the middle of everything. Because Siegel had long felt that the managing members ought to be accessible to every other team member and his goal was to get people out of their imposed solitude, the golf course serves its purpose nicely. In addition, Siegel was convinced that people do their best intellectual work in nontraditional, perhaps even idiosyncratic, settings. That's the motivation behind the "open" office design where professionals could gather—on purpose or by accident—without walls, cubicles, or offices to get in the way. To support this open concept, every space is wired with data ports and telephone jacks. There's even some fun stuff, too! There's a giant wall-mounted abacus (remember, the image of bean counters) made from steel tubes and bright plastic balls. In addition, when clients and visitors first come in, they're greeted by a "Welcome Wall" with a big-screen television that flashes a continuous slide show of one-liners about business, life, and innovation.

Although part of the reason behind LLG's radical open office design was to save money, a bigger strategic objective was to leverage and showcase the company's intellectual capital. Siegel wanted a place where people who were always in contact with each other actually got smarter. It's an unusual, perhaps even somewhat wacky, approach. But, for these bean counters, it seems to have worked well.

Discussion Questions

1. What people philosophy do you think Steve Siegel and LLG have? Explain.
2. Do you think LLG's open office concept would be motivating to professional accountants? Explain.
3. What implications does LLG's approach have for bringing people on board and managing people on board? Be as specific as possible.

(*Source:* N. K. Austin, "Tear Down the Walls," *Inc.*, April 1999, pp. 66–76.)

VIDEO CASE #1: The Fine Art of Managing People

Every business has three basic components: the *product* or service being provided; the *process* or the way the product or service is being delivered; and the *people*. Out of these three components, the most critical issue that entrepreneurs deal with is the people. A successful entrepreneur is more likely to say that the single most important factor in a business's success is the people. Although there's some science behind managing people, there's a lot of art as well. What do some successful entrepreneurs have to say about the fine art of managing people? Let's take a look!

Jeff Gordon, owner of an advertising agency in Washington, DC, says that selection is the single most important task of any business leader. He selects full time, and he's found that he may have to sift through 150 to 300 people to get that one outstanding person. However, in his business, he's found that he's got to put that kind of effort into selecting to identify the "gems" that are so critical to his company's success.

Jill and Doug Smith approached people management somewhat differently than what experts advise. They developed their business, Buckeye Beans and Herbs of Spokane, Washington, using friends and family. As Jill

says, this can be either a tremendous negative or a tremendous positive. It's been a tremendous positive for their business because they all share similar values. In fact, she describes her business as a values-added people company.

Dale Crownover, owner of Texas NamePlate of Dallas, found that as part of a quality improvement program, his employees wanted more communication opportunities. At the company's monthly meetings, regular employees (not just managers) get involved. Dale says it's really all about sharing and communicating; letting employees know the goals, the plans, why we're doing what we're doing, and how we're doing. Very simply, he's found that employees want to be part of something.

Finally, Greg Thurman of Hartford Communication in Priest River, Idaho, says he doesn't tell people what to do but asks them what they think they should do to solve a problem. His goal was to create an environment in which people didn't feel stifled. As Greg says, "I don't know every job as well as the people doing the job." Therefore, instead of him telling them how to do their job, he encourages employees to look for answers and then together they'll "polish" a solution.

Discussion Questions

1. What "people" advice do each of these entrepreneurs profiled give?
2. What's your opinion of this advice?
3. How might what these entrepreneurs have said affect the design of HRM activities and processes and affect the design of a motivational approach? Explain.

(*Source:* Based on *Small Business 2000, Show 413.*)

VIDEO CASE #2: Tires Plus

Tom Gegax is not the president of Tires Plus—he's the "head coach." Tires Plus does not have employees—it has "team members." The team members do not serve customers—they serve "guests." The company's operations manual is known as the "playbook." The simple act of using a special management vocabulary speaks volumes about Tom's business philosophy, which he sums up this way: "Take something that you believe is not being done well, and then go for it and make it better." It's an approach that has served Tom well.

He spent the early years of his career at Shell Oil Company and went from there to owning a few gas stations. Tom recalls, "I didn't feel that I had the know-how to make a big impact in, say, the computer industry." But he did recognize that, with the right management formula, selling tires could be a lot more profitable than selling gasoline. Tom and partner Don Gullit started with a mission that could be shared with others, found a niche, and relied on self-coaching. Tom explains, "Everybody wants to go out and manage others. But until you learn how to manage yourself, it's pretty hard to manage others." With that in mind, the partners have built Tires Plus (**www.tiresplus.com**) into a company with over $150 million in annual sales and 130 stores located in the upper Midwest.

Tires Plus competes with some very well-known companies. For example, Goodyear Tire & Rubber has a national network of more than 2,500 independent dealers. Sears is also an important competitor with its auto centers. Still, Tires Plus has carved out a prosperous niche for itself by offering a wide selection of brands, speedy service, and clean, modern stores. Moreover, Tom and Don have succeeded by creating a business environment that allows employees to gain the satisfaction that comes from providing products and services that people need while getting the chance to reap financial rewards.

Tom and Don try to hire people who buy into their philosophy. "We start by finding people who are trainable and can be motivated. Then we compensate them right—a 'pay for productivity' situation. Third, you have to take care of them." Don continues, "We're looking for people who care about others. A good team member is one who is willing to sit back and explain something to a customer, who comes across as sincere." Team members who attend training sessions at Tires Plus University are treated to healthy doses of business philosophy from their head coach. With his intense gaze, piercing blue eyes, and fervent demeanor, Tom resembles a preacher. He reminds trainees, "If money is your focus, it doesn't work. What does work is taking care of our guests, and helping our teammates. When that occurs, the by-product of that is you'll make money. But don't try to make money." Tom admits that selling has gotten a tarnished reputation in some circles. But, in his view, "Selling is communicating. It's the ability to communicate with guests about what their needs are and whether we can fill those needs in a proper way." Tom believes that, "People sense your purpose and if your purpose really is a greater good. If teammates feel you're serving them and caring about them, then they'll perform better. If guests perceive you care about them, sales will go up."

A period of personal growth following a divorce and a brush with cancer helped Tom fine-tune his business philosophy. He says, "As long as our lives seem to be going OK, we don't get on the path for personal growth. It often takes a wake-up call. I encourage my teammates to not wait for a wake-up call." In his search for personal growth, Tom found emotional teachers who could supplement what he had learned from spiritual and intellectual teachers. The world of sports was also an important inspiration for Tom's business model. Tom recalls, "I saw college basketball coaches on the sideline. I said to myself, 'I like the way they're giving constant feedback.' " Tom recognized that language could

play a big role in helping him motivate his employees by verbalizing what is expected of them. "People don't want to be managed," Tom says. "If you call them 'manager' every day, then they're going to manage. But if we call them 'coach,' then that gets in their mind as what we want them doing."

Discussion Questions

1. What is Tom's approach to managing people?

2. Tom does not believe that money should be the most important motivator for Tires Plus team members. What other types of motivators are important at Tires Plus?

3. Tom believes that language can play a special role in motivating employees. What are some of the specific things he does to communicate effectively with employees?

(*Sources:* Based on *Small Business 2000, Show 103*; and materials from company Web site.)

ENDNOTES

1. T. H. Naylor and R. Osterberg, "The Search for Community in the Workplace," *Business and Society Review*, spring 1995, pp. 42–47; G. Flynn, "Why Rhino Won't Wait 'Til Tomorrow," *Personnel Journal*, July 1996, pp. 36–43; and T. Castle, "A Creative Way to Avoid Layoffs," *Nation's Business*, August 1997, p. 6.

2. J. Pfeffer, *Competitive Advantage Through People* (Boston: Harvard Business School Press, 1994); J. Pfeffer, "Producing Sustainable Competitive Advantage Through the Effective Management of People," *Academy of Management Executive*, Vol. 9, No. 1, 1995, pp. 55–69; and J. Pfeffer, *The Human Equation: Building Profits by Putting People First* (Boston: Harvard Business School Press, 1998).

3. J. B. Arthur, "Effects of Human Resource Systems on Manufacturing Performance and Turnover," *Academy of Management Journal*, June 1994, pp. 670–87; M. A. Huselid, "The Impact of Human Resource Management Practices on Turnover, Productivity, and Financial Performance," *Academy of Management Journal*, June 1995, pp. 635–72; M. J. Koch and R. G. McGrath, "Improving Labor Productivity: Human Resource Management Policies Do Matter," *Strategic Management Journal*, May 1996, pp. 335–54; B. Becker and B. Gerhart, "The Impact of Human Resource Management on Organizational Performance: Progress and Prospects," *Academy of Management Journal*, August 1996, pp. 779–801; M. A. Youndt, S. A. Snell, J. W. Dean, Jr., and D. P. Lepak, "Human Resource Management, Manufacturing Strategy, and Firm Performance," *Academy of Management Journal*, August 1996, pp. 836–66; J. T. Delaney and M. A. Huselid, "The Impact of Human Resource Management Practices on Perceptions of Organizational Performance," *Academy of Management Journal*, August 1996, pp. 949–69; and M. A. Huselid, S. E. Jackson, and R. S. Schuler, "Technical and Strategic Human Resource Management Effectiveness as Determinants of Firm Performance," *Academy of Management Journal*, January 1997, pp. 171–88.

4. Huselid, "The Impact of Human Resource Management Practices on Turnover, Productivity, and Corporate Financial Performance."

5. I. T. Robertson and R. S. Kandola, "Work Sample Tests: Validity, Adverse Impact, and Application Reaction," *Journal of Occupational Psychology*, Vol. 55, No. 3, 1982, pp. 171–83; and G. C. Thornton, *Assessment Centers in Human Resource Management* (Reading, MA: Addison-Wesley, 1992).

6. R. L. Dipboye, *Selection Interviews: Process Perspectives* (Cincinnati: South-Western Publishing, 1992), p. 180.

7. See R. D. Arveny and J. E. Campion, "The Employment Interview: A Summary and Review of Recent Research," *Personnel Psychology*, summer 1982, pp. 281–322; M. D. Hakel, "Employment Interview," in K. M. Rowland and G. R. Ferris (eds.), *Personnel Management: New Perspectives* (Boston: Allyn & Bacon, 1982), pp. 192–255; E. C. Webster, *The Employment Interview: A Social Judgment Process* (Schomberg, ON: S.I.P. Publications, 1982); M. M. Harris, "Reconsidering the Employment Interview: A Review of Recent Literature and Suggestions for Future Research," *Personnel Psychology*, winter 1989, pp. 691–726; A. P. Phillips and R. L. Dipboye, "Correlational Tests of Predictions from a Process Model of the Interview," *Journal of Applied Psychology*, February 1989, pp. 41–52; H. G. Baker and M. S. Spier, "The Employment Interview: Guaranteed Improvement in Reliability," *Public Personnel Management*, spring 1990, pp. 85–87; and R. C. Liden, C. L. Martin, and C. K. Parsons, "Interviewer and Applicant Behavior in Employment Interviews," *Academy of Management Journal*, April 1993, pp. 372–86.

8. *Human Resource Management: Ideas and Trends* (Commerce Clearing House, May 17, 1992), p. 85.

9. N. D. Bates, "Understanding the Liability of Negligent Hiring," *Security Management Supplement*, July 1990, p. 7A.

10. "Industry Report 1999," *Training Magazine* Web site (**www.trainingmag.com**), November 1, 1999.

11. L. R. Gomez-Mejia, "Structure and Process of Diversification, Compensation Strategy, and Firm Performance," *Strategic Management Journal*, Vol. 13, 1992, pp. 381–97; and E. Montemayor, "Congruence Between Pay Policy and Competitive Strategy in High-Performing Firms," *Journal of Management*, Vol. 22, No. 6, 1996, pp. 889–908.

12. See, for example, S. P. Robbins and M. Coulter, *Management*, 6th ed. (Upper Saddle River, NJ: Prentice Hall), 1999; and S. P. Robbins, *Organizational Behavior*, 9th ed. (Upper Saddle River, NJ: Prentice Hall, 2001).

13. A. Maslow, *Motivation and Personality* (New York: McGraw-Hill, 1954).

14. F. Herzberg, B. Mausner, and B. Snyderman, *The Motivation to Work* (New York: John Wiley, 1959); and F. Herzberg, *The Managerial Choice: To Be Effective or to Be Human*, rev. ed. (Salt Lake City: Olympus, 1982).

15. J. C. Naylor and D. R. Ilgen, "Goal Setting: A Theoretical Analysis of Motivational Technique," in B. M. Staw and L. L. Cummings (eds.), *Research on Organizational Behavior*, Vol. 6 (Greenwich, CT: JAI Press, 1984), pp. 95–140; M. E. Tubbs, D. M. Boehne, and J. S. Dahl, "Expectancy, Valence, and Motivational Force Functions in Goal-Setting Research: An Empirical Test," *Journal of Applied Psychology*, June 1993, pp. 361–73.

16. B. F. Skinner, *Science and Human Behavior* (New York: Free Press, 1953); and B. F. Skinner, *Beyond Freedom and Dignity* (New York: Alfred A. Knopf, 1972).

17. V. H. Vroom, *Work and Motivation* (New York: John Wiley, 1964).

18. Based on C. E. Larson and F. M. J. LaFasto, *TeamWork* (Newbury Park, CA: Sage Publications, 1989); and E. Sundstrom, K. P. DeMeuse, and D. Futrell, "Work Teams," *American Psychologist*, February 1990, p. 120.

19. See Sundstrom, DeMeuse, and Futrell, "Work Teams"; Larson and LaFasto, *TeamWork;* J. R. Hackman (ed.), *Groups That Work (and Those That Don't)* (San Francisco: CA: Jossey-Bass, 1990); and D. W. Tjosvold and M. M. Tjosvold, *Leading the Team Organization* (New York: Lexington Books, 1991).

20. P. E. Brauchle and D. W. Wright, "Fourteen Team Building Tips," *Training & Development*, January 1992, pp. 32–34; R. S. Wellins, "Building a Self-Directed Work Team," *Training & Development*, December 1992, pp. 24–28; S. T. Johnson, "Work Teams: What's Ahead in Work Design and Rewards Management," *Compensation and Benefits Review*, March–April 1993, pp. 35–41; V. A. Hoevemeyer, "How Effective Is Your Team?" *Training & Development*, September 1993, pp. 67–71; S. G. Cohen and G. E. Ledford Jr., "The Effectiveness of Self-Managing Teams: A Quasi-Experiment," *Human Relations*, January 1994, pp. 13–43; and J. Panepinto, "Maximize Teamwork," *Computerworld*, March 21, 1994, p. 119.

21. D. M. Enlen, "Team Goals: Aligning Groups and Management," *Canadian Manager*, winter 1993, pp. 17–18; and A. M. O'Leary, J. J. Martocchio, and D. D. Frink, "A Review of the Influence of Group Goals on Group Performance," *Academy of Management Journal*, October 1994, pp. 1285–1301.

22. K. M. Eisenhardt, J. L. Kahwajy, and L. J. Bourgeois III, "How Management Teams Can Have a Good Fight," *Harvard Business Review*, July–August 1997, pp. 77–85.

9

MANAGING GROWTH AND OTHER ENTREPRENEURIAL CHALLENGES

LEARNING OBJECTIVES

After reading this chapter, you should be able to:

1. Describe the various ways organizational growth can be measured.
2. Discuss the various strategies for growing an entrepreneurial venture.
3. Explain the key challenges in pursuing growth.
4. Describe what issues an entrepreneurial venture might face in restrained and rapid growth.
5. Tell how entrepreneurs might recognize organizational downturn situations and describe some of the contributing factors to organizational decline.
6. Discuss the strategies an entrepreneur might use in dealing with downturns.
7. Describe the reasons an entrepreneur might wish to exit an entrepreneurial venture.
8. Explain what's involved with exiting an entrepreneurial venture.
9. Discuss the various business valuation methods.
10. Describe the problems faced by minority and women-owned entrepreneurial ventures and how these entrepreneurs can deal with them.
11. Discuss the special challenges of family businesses and how these entrepreneurs can deal with them.
12. Explain how entrepreneurs can successfully manage their personal lives.

ENTREPRENEURSHIP IN ACTION CASE #1

Recipe for Success

William Williams, cofounder of Glory Foods (**www.gloryfoods.com**) has concocted a sweet deal and followed his own recipe for success.[1] Glory Foods, Inc. a company based in Columbus, Ohio, sells "down-home tasting" southern cuisine specialties that are quick and easy to prepare, a delicious alternative to the traditional southern cooking that takes hours. The company has successfully cornered a market niche by following a conservative path to growth.

Williams formed the company after he saw all the ethnic foods being sold while walking down a grocery store aisle. As the owner of a soul food restaurant in Columbus, Williams "smelled" opportunity. He felt there had to be a market for already-prepared African American food and he decided to pursue his entrepreneurial idea.

Williams brought together three partners, all with food industry experience. From the beginning the founders followed a conservative path. They all kept their day jobs until the business

Growth is what distinguishes an entrepreneurial venture. However, as our chapter-opening case illustrates, growth doesn't have to be frantic and chaotic. Growing slowly can be just as successful. Yet even slow-growing ventures have challenges and issues to deal with in order to be effective and efficient. In this final chapter we're going to discuss managing growth and other entrepreneurial challenges. These "other" challenges include the issues faced during organizational performance downturns, harvest and exit decisions, problems encountered by minority and women entrepreneurs, and issues faced by family businesses. In addition, we're going to look at some of the personal life choices and issues that entrepreneurs must deal with.

MANAGING GROWTH

Growth. It's a natural and desirable outcome for entrepreneurial ventures. In fact, it's part of our definition of entrepreneurship. Remember how we defined entrepreneurship—the process whereby an individual or group of individuals uses organized efforts and means to pursue opportunities to create value *and grow* by fulfilling wants and needs through innovation and uniqueness, no matter what resources are currently controlled. Entrepreneurial ventures pursue growth.[2] An organization that isn't growing but instead is staying the same isn't entrepreneurial. Growing successfully doesn't necessarily occur just randomly or by luck. Successfully pursuing growth typically requires an entrepreneur to manage all the challenges associated with growing. That's what we're going to look at in this section—managing growth. We first need to look at how growth is defined and measured.

Introduction

What is growth? When an organization is growing, what does it mean? As it relates to entrepreneurial ventures, **organizational growth** is any increase in the level, amount, or type of the organization's work and outputs. It involves expanding, enlarging, or extending what the venture does. In our chapter-opening case, for example, Glory Foods was growing, albeit slowly, by expanding its market base and extending its product lines. This idea of growth as increases in size or coverage is a common and important one. But another dimension to growth encompasses a spirit of vitality and energy.[3] An organization that's growing is vibrant and flourishing. It's striving and pushing to be excellent. There's

was financially stable. The foursome worked two years to develop their recipes. They wanted food that tasted delicious and authentic but would be healthier. The partners deliberately chose not to go to market with their products until they had all 17 specialties ready.

Even with its calculated, careful growth, the time was fast approaching when the company would need more capital to continue in business. The four partners agreed to invest additional

money and to sell 17 percent of the company to 40 investors, mainly friends and a few relatives.

Williams's decision to move slowly was based mostly on the fact that he didn't want to dilute the founders' equity portions down to minority levels. Although the slow growth approach may have taken more time, Glory Foods' partners felt it was worth it because they still have total control over what happens to the company.

> ### Entrepreneurs in Action
>
> Ellen Wessel, founder of Moving Comfort Inc., and Missy Park, founder of Title Nine Sports, are just two of a number of women entrepreneurs who have successfully grown their businesses by focusing on the fast-growing women's sports equipment and apparel market. They grew their businesses by listening to their customers, hiring women athletes as advisers, and paying attention to female physiology. Their products are women friendly and include things such as sleeping bags with extra insulation, sports bras for all different shapes and sizes, and bicycle seats that don't chafe. To continue their growth, each is looking at expanding its market base and extending its product lines.
>
> *Source:* B. Wolverton, "Our Sports Gear, Ourselves," *Business Week*, September 1, 1997, pp. ENT 12–ENT14.

a level of excitement about what is being accomplished in the organization and a strong desire on the part of organizational members to be part of it. So although growth does involve increases and expansions in what the organization does, it also involves a feeling of and a commitment to being all that we can be and being the best that we can. Now that we have a better understanding of what growth is, how is growth measured?

A number of variables have been used in measuring organizational growth.[4] The most common measures are financial—increases in sales or revenues, increases in venture capital, increases in profitability, or other financial measures. But growth has also been defined by things such as number of customers, products, locations, employees, or any other characteristic that could be quantified. As you can see, it's easier to measure growth if you can quantify the factor. It doesn't matter what the factor is. In fact, it should be one that's important to your specific type of entrepreneurial venture. So look closely at your entrepreneurial venture. Decide how you are going to measure whether your business is growing. Will it be by number of clients served, number of outlets opened, types of products offered, or what? Also, define what financial measures you will use to evaluate whether the growth strategies are working. Will it be sales (revenues), profit, or some combination or variation of these? It doesn't matter which measure(s) you use, but it *does* matter that you use some factors to measure growth that are appropriate for your type of business. Now that we know something about what growth is and how to measure it, we need to look at how to pursue organizational growth—that is, the various growth strategies.

Pursuing Growth

The best growth strategy is a well-planned one.[5] Ideally, the decision to grow doesn't come about spontaneously, but instead is part of the venture's overall business plan. Rapid growth without planning can be disastrous. Do make growth part of your business planning, but don't be overly rigid in your planning. Your plans should be flexible enough to exploit unexpected opportunities that arise. You *want* your entrepreneurial venture to grow. But how? What are some ways that you can grow your business?

One approach to pursuing growth identifies four possible strategies based on combinations of current and new products and customers.[6] Figure 9-1 illustrates these various combinations. Let's briefly discuss each option.

The **product–customer exploitation strategy** describes attempts to increase sales of current products to current customers. Under this strategy, the entrepreneur might use incentives to get current customers to buy more of the venture's product(s) or might advertise other uses for the product(s). There are a variety of ways to try to get current customers to buy and use more of the current product(s). In fact, that's the primary job of the venture's advertising and marketing function.

The **product development strategy** involves creating new products for use by current customers. A new product may include improved or modified versions of existing products. In addition, new features, options, sizes, and ingredients are often used in developing new products for current customers. For example, in our chapter-opening case, Glory Foods added a new line of frozen foods to its existing products. These were new products created for current customers.

The **customer development strategy** describes attempts to sell current products to new customers. New customers might come from additional geographic areas or market segments not currently served. For instance, Day Runner, the retail leader in the personal organizer market, developed a line of organizers aimed at 6- to 12-year-olds, a market segment that it had not sold to previously. This is an example of market development—a current product aimed at new customers. The decision to sell globally would be another example of market development because the venture is moving into additional geographic areas with its current products.

Figure 9-1

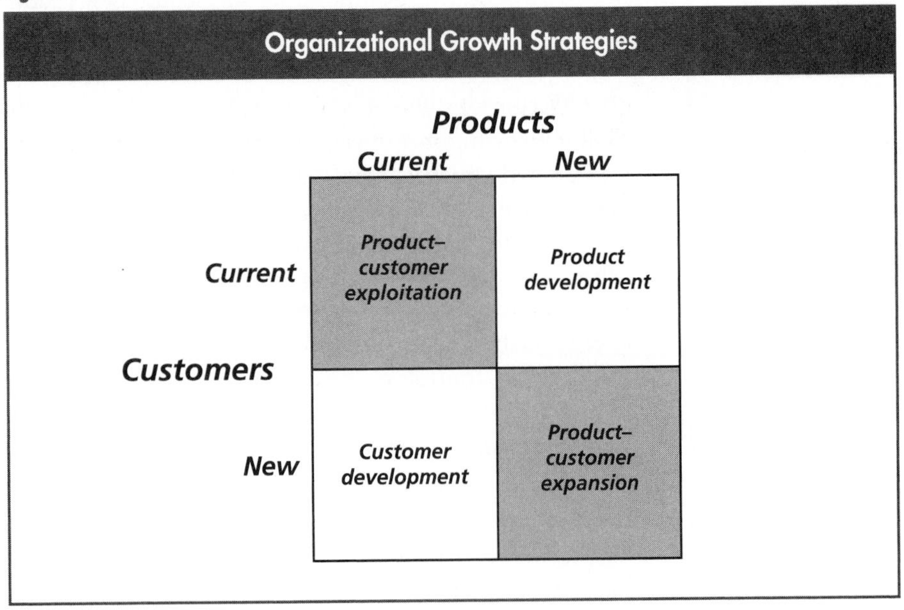

Organizational Growth Strategies		
	Products	
	Current	**New**
Customers — **Current**	Product–customer exploitation	Product development
New	Customer development	Product–customer expansion

The final growth strategy is termed **product–customer expansion**. Under this approach, the venture attempts to expand both into new products and new customers. This approach tends to be one of the riskiest growth strategies because you're dealing with both new products and new customers. However, it can be a way to continue growing.

These strategies are the ones typically used by entrepreneurial ventures pursuing growth. Actually, they're pretty descriptive of what an entrepreneurial venture has to do in order to grow. If you want to increase sales revenues, you must develop new products, pursue new customers, or both. If you "do it right"—that is, effectively and efficiently—revenues and profits should grow also! What's involved with "doing it right"? The key challenges for an entrepreneur in organizing for growth include finding capital, finding people, reinforcing organizational controls, and strengthening the organizational culture.

Organizing for Growth

Having enough capital is a major challenge facing growing entrepreneurial ventures. The money issue never seems to go away, does it? It does take capital to expand. If you want to open new locations or markets or if you want to continue innovating new products, it's going to take capital. You have to decide how much capital is necessary and where the capital is going to come from. Is this the time you'll attempt an initial public offering of stock? Do you have the cash reserves on hand to support your growth? Will you have to go through traditional—or even nontraditional—financing channels? The processes of finding capital for pursuing growth are much like going through the initial financing of the venture. However, at this time, hopefully you have a successful track record to back up your request. If you don't, it may be extremely difficult to acquire the necessary capital. That's why we said earlier that the best growth strategy is a planned one. Part of that planning should be how growth will be financed.

Another important issue that a growing entrepreneurial venture needs to address is finding people. If you're opening additional locations, increasing sales of current products, or innovating and selling new products, you're going to need additional employees to do the work. We know from Chapter 8 that finding talented, competent, and capable people is a challenge in itself. When the venture is growing quickly, the challenge may be intensified because of the time constraints you're often dealing with. It's important to plan, as much as possible, the numbers and types of employees you're going to need to support the increasing workload as your entrepreneurial venture grows. Also, it may be necessary to provide additional training and support to employees to help them handle the increased pressures associated with a growing organization.

Another challenge that growing entrepreneurial ventures face is reinforcing already established organizational controls. Maintaining good financial records and financial controls over cash flow, inventory, customer data, sales orders, receivables, payables, and costs should be a priority of every entrepreneur—whether pursuing growth or not. However, it's particularly important to reinforce these controls when the entrepreneurial venture is expanding. It's all too easy to let things "get away" from you or to put off doing them when there's an unrelenting urgency to get things done—such as, for instance, when sales orders are coming in so quickly that they're not checked for accuracy. Here's a personal example of why controls are so important during periods of organizational growth. During the 1999 holiday season, I ordered some merchandise from a well-known online e-commerce retailer. When I received my merchandise, someone else's order was there in my shipment. Fortunately, that person's packing slip was wrapped around the merchandise so I went ahead and sent it on to that individual. However, what if that packing slip hadn't been there? Or what if I hadn't wanted to take the time and money to ship it on to that person? There would have been additional expense on the part of the organization to resend the merchandise, and there would have probably been one dissatisfied customer because of all the hassle to get the merchandise she had ordered. Rapid growth—or even slow growth—does not excuse the need to have effective controls in place. In fact, it's particularly important to have established procedures, protocols, and processes and to use them. Even though you'll never entirely eliminate mistakes and inefficiencies, at least you can ensure that every effort is being made to do business effectively and efficiently. Part of this emphasis on controls and accountability arises from the venture's culture, which is the last challenge we need to discuss associated with managing organizational growth.

When a venture is growing, it's important to create a positive, growth-oriented culture that enhances the opportunities to achieve success, both organizationally and individually. This sometimes can be difficult to do, particularly when changes are happening rapidly. However, employees' values, attitudes, and beliefs—that is, the organizational culture—that are established and reinforced during these times are critical to the entrepreneurial venture's continued and future success. Table 9-1 lists some suggestions that entrepreneurs might use to ensure that their venture's culture is one that embraces and supports a climate in which organizational growth is viewed as desirable and important. Keeping

FYI

When Success Is Failure

How can success ever be failure? You're probably thinking to yourself that success was supposed to be something entrepreneurs strived to achieve. Yet, a history of success can actually make you a failure. How? When you're focused on past successes, you can miss new opportunities or changing conditions. Here are some suggestions for not allowing past successes to lead to failure. *Reward contrary opinions.* Encourage honest criticism of ideas, plans, and strategies. This doesn't mean criticizing a person but does mean honestly evaluating a person's ideas and work product. *Reduce the risk of all-or-nothing outcomes.* If the future of your venture rests on more than one product, strategy, or plan, you'll be better able to get rid of those that are not worthwhile. *Keep in mind that change is a continual reality.* Even though predicting the future is impossible, prepare for changes by monitoring the external environment and by having plans in place to deal with change. *Don't assume that when some idea fails that you're a failure, too.* People often define themselves by their successes. If one of your ideas doesn't work out, it doesn't automatically make you a loser. What it should do is make you better the next time.

Source: S. Berglas, "Know When to Fold," *Inc.*, March 1998, pp. 31–32.

TABLE 9-1   Suggestions for Achieving a Supportive Growth-Oriented Culture

- *Keep the lines of communication open.* Employees need to be informed about major issues.
- *Establish trust* by being honest, open, and forthright about the challenges and rewards of being a growing organization.
- *Be a good listener.* Find out what employees are thinking and facing.
- *Be willing to delegate duties.* You cannot continue to make every decision.
- *Be flexible.* Although planned growth is desirable, be flexible enough to change your plans.
- *Provide consistent and regular feedback.* Let employees know the outcomes—good and bad.
- *Reinforce the contributions of each person* to the venture's ultimate success. People like to be recognized for the efforts they're putting forth.
- *Continually train employees.* It's important to enhance employees' capabilities and skills.
- *Maintain the focus on the venture's vision and mission.* The organizational vision and mission are the reasons the venture is in business.
- *Establish and reinforce a "we" spirit.* A successful growing entrepreneurial venture takes the coordinated efforts of all the employees.

employees focused and committed to what the organization is doing is crucial to the ultimate success of the venture's growth strategies. If employees don't "buy into" the direction the entrepreneurial venture is headed, it's unlikely the venture's growth strategies will be successful. For instance, the four cofounders of the business (Glory Foods) profiled in the chapter-opening case shared the same beliefs, values, and attitudes about how their organization was going to grow. This shared acceptance of what the organization was doing and how it was doing it was important to the company's performance. Having a culture that upholds and supports the venture's growth activities is an ongoing challenge in effectively managing that growth. However, even if an entrepreneur successfully manages the challenges associated with growing the venture—that is, finding capital, finding people, reinforcing organizational controls, and strengthening the organizational culture—some special issues are associated with strategies of both restrained and rapid growth.

At the two extremes of growth—restrained versus rapid—the entrepreneur must be prepared to deal with some unique challenges. Restrained growth means making tricky choices about what to do, when to do it, and how much to do. Do you pass up some opportunities because you're not prepared to exploit them or are you potentially forfeiting a financial gold mine? Do you deliberately choose to limit your venture's financial gains now so that you can better position it for the future? These are tough decisions. There are no easy answers. Our chapter-opening case illustrated how the entrepreneurs behind Glory Foods chose to approach growth carefully and in a more cautious and restrained manner. Their choice was based on the fact that they wanted to "get it right" and also wanted to maintain control of their company. Although their decisions appeared to be good ones, there are some drawbacks to restraining growth.[7] One is that it might be more difficult to hold on to talented people. Employees who are drawn to the excitement of a rapidly growing entrepreneurial venture might get bored or frustrated if there's not that impassioned level of innovative energy and a continual challenge of their skills and abilities. A venture following the path of restrained growth may also find itself quickly getting out of touch with changing technology and customer trends. This could lead to a deterioration of capabilities in product innovation, customer service, marketing, or in any of the other organizational functional areas. If not managed appropriately, this could lead to the venture's eventual demise. The key to successfully pursuing a path of restrained growth is planning for it. Growing slowly doesn't have to mean no passionate energy, no excitement, or no future. Instead, restrained growth can help an entrepreneur establish a solid foundation for the continued and future success of the venture.

The other extreme growth situation where there are challenges for entrepreneurs is rapid growth. When an entrepreneurial organization is growing at exponential rates, the entrepreneur has some unique issues to deal with. Finding capital and people can be particularly difficult and frustrating. Efficiently managing cash flow, inventory, and other organizational areas becomes exceptionally important. Expanding a company rapidly doesn't mean just coping with problems on a larger scale.[8] It entails understanding, adjusting to, and managing a whole new set of challenges. Rapid growth can produce an organization that's much more complex than before. More sophisticated management, processes, and procedures may be needed. The venture's infrastructure will have to change to support the demands of a rapidly growing business. It can be chaotic. It can be frustrating. It can, at times, be overwhelming. But the rewards, and not just the financial ones, can be exhilarating. The key to successfully managing explosive growth, just like restrained growth, is also planning for it. Although some unexpected opportunities may arise that could not be foreseen or predicted, the best way to exploit the explosive growth without the organization falling victim to chaotic out-of-control frenzy is to prepare for it. Have plans in place for securing financing, hiring employees, reinforcing organizational controls, and reinforcing a growth-oriented organizational culture. Even though it's not possible to eliminate every problem associated with rapid growth, you can effectively manage the problems so that you're maximizing the gains and minimizing the risks.

Organizational growth. It's a desirable and important goal for entrepreneurial ventures. What happens, though, when things turn sour—when the growth strategies don't result in the intended outcomes and, in fact, result in a decline in performance? What challenges are there in managing business downturns? That's what we're going to look at in the next section.

Rapid Review ◀◀|

- ✓ Define organizational growth.
- ✓ What does the concept of growth include other than increases in size or coverage?
- ✓ What variables have been used to measure organizational growth?
- ✓ Why is it important to be able to quantify a measure of organizational growth?
- ✓ Describe the best growth strategy.
- ✓ What are the four possible growth strategies?
- ✓ What does an entrepreneur have to do to organize for growth?
- ✓ Describe the challenges in restrained growth and in rapid growth situations.

MANAGING DOWNTURNS

Nobody likes to fail. Although some might choose to do so for whatever reasons, most entrepreneurs would not deliberately choose to fail. But organizational performance declines—downturns—happen. The entrepreneurial venture is in trouble and something needs to be done or it won't be able to achieve high levels of success or, even in the worst-case scenario, may not survive. How can these downturns be successfully managed? The first step is recognizing that a crisis is brewing and the next step is dealing with the situation. Let's look first at recognizing crises.

Recognizing Crisis Situations

An entrepreneur should be alert to the warning signs of a business in trouble. Figure 9-2 illustrates some signals of potential performance decline.[9] One of these signals is inadequate or negative cash flow. Although an occasional cash flow crisis can be triggered by a variety of factors, such as seasonal business fluctuations, customers that pay late or not at all, or major equipment breakdowns, what we're concerned about here is the continual cash flow shortage. When an organization's cash flow position is chronically inadequate or negative, it's an indication that performance is heading downhill. Another signal of potential performance decline is an excessive number of employees. How do you know if there is an excessive number of employees? Some entrepreneurs track trends in performance measures such as sales revenue/employee or profits/employee. If these trends worsen, it can be a sign that organizational performance is declining. Another sign that perfor-

Figure 9-2

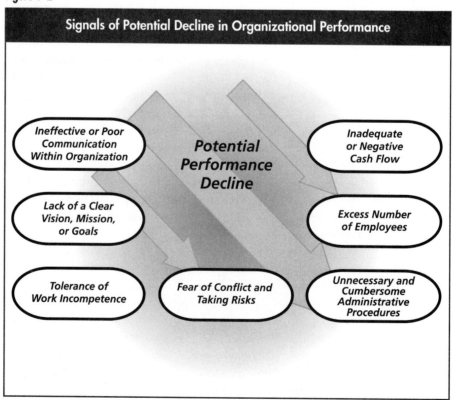

Signals of Potential Decline in Organizational Performance

Ineffective or Poor Communication Within Organization

Inadequate or Negative Cash Flow

Potential Performance Decline

Lack of a Clear Vision, Mission, or Goals

Excess Number of Employees

Tolerance of Work Incompetence

Fear of Conflict and Taking Risks

Unnecessary and Cumbersome Administrative Procedures

mance may be declining is unnecessary and cumbersome administrative procedures. Processes and procedures are supposed to help the flow of work go smoother, not make it more difficult. Fear of conflict or taking risks could be particularly critical signs of potential performance decline in entrepreneurial ventures. Why? Conflict (that is, *productive* conflict, not destructive conflict) and risk-taking are cornerstones of entrepreneurial vitality. Continual experimentation and questioning the status quo are particularly important in an entrepreneurial venture that's going to be successful. When a venture's employees fear conflicts and disagreements or when they become too cautious in trying new and different things, it can be a signal that performance may soon deteriorate. Another signal of potential performance decline is tolerance of work incompetence. It's absolutely foolish to allow incompetent employees to remain in an organization. They're not contributing to and, in fact, in the worst-case scenario, may actually be detracting from, the organization's work. If this type of work incompetence is accepted, organizational performance will soon suffer. Another sign that organizational performance may decline is lack of a clear vision, mission, or goals. We discussed in earlier chapters the importance of having a clear, specific, and accepted organizational vision, mission, and goals. Without these guiding statements, there will be no coherent direction or coordination to what employees are working on. Then, how can employees know what they're supposed to be doing and whether what they're doing is what's expected? With no clear direction, organizational performance will suffer. The last signal of potential performance decline that's shown in Figure 9-2 is ineffective or poor communication within the organization. When employees aren't sharing information, good *and* bad, their attempts to coordinate work efforts will suffer because no one knows what anyone else is doing and no one is trying to learn from someone else's experiences. This communication breakdown ultimately will lead to individual and organizational performance declines.

Another perspective on recognizing performance declines revolves around what is known as the **"boiled frog" phenomenon**.[10] The "boiled frog" is a classic psychological response experiment. In one case, a live frog that's dropped into a boiling pan of water, reacts instantaneously and jumps out of the pan. But, in the second case, a live frog that's dropped into a pan of mild water that is gradually heated to the boiling point, fails to react and dies. A small firm may be particularly vulnerable to the boiled frog phenomenon because the entrepreneur may not recognize the "water heating up"—that is, the subtly declining situation. When changes in performance are gradual, a serious response may never be triggered or may be done too late to do anything about the situation. So what does the boiled frog phenomenon teach us? That we need to be alert to the signals that our venture's performance may be worsening. Don't wait until the water has reached the boiling point to react.

Now that we've discussed the signs of organizational performance decline, we need to look at some of the factors that may be contributing to the declining performance. Figure 9-3 illustrates some of these possible causes. Each of these possible causes is an indicator that someone—ultimately, the entrepreneur—isn't paying attention. For example, decisions to overexpand or expand too rapidly indicate poor judgment. If the organization has inadequate financial controls or if costs are out of control or too high, the entrepreneur isn't being an effective deci-

Figure 9-3

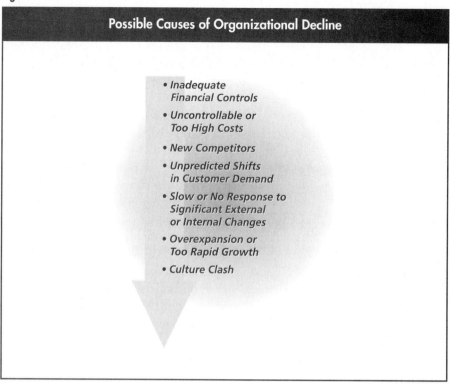

Possible Causes of Organizational Decline

- *Inadequate Financial Controls*
- *Uncontrollable or Too High Costs*
- *New Competitors*
- *Unpredicted Shifts in Customer Demand*
- *Slow or No Response to Significant External or Internal Changes*
- *Overexpansion or Too Rapid Growth*
- *Culture Clash*

sion maker. Likewise, there's no excuse for not anticipating new competitors or shifts in customer demand. Although entrepreneurs don't have crystal balls that give them all the answers, they should—as we discussed in Chapters 2 and 3—systematically scan and evaluate the external environment for significant trends and changes. There's simply no excuse for an entrepreneur not to be aware of what's happening in the external environment. That's being a poor manager. In addition, entrepreneurs who are slow to respond or who never respond to significant changes in their external and internal situations are doing a poor job of managing the venture. Inertia can be a kiss of death in the dynamic and complex competitive environment that most entrepreneurial organizations face. Finally, when an organization's culture is in turmoil and has turned hostile, employee productivity suffers. Employees stop putting out any effort on behalf of the organization as a whole and do just what's required to get by in their jobs—an attitude that's lethal to the company's performance.

What the entrepreneur does after recognizing the problems is crucial to the venture's future. The decisions made and the actions taken by the entrepreneur at this point can help solidify or doom the business. It's obvious that *something* needs to happen. But what? That's what we're going to look at next.

Dealing with Downturns, Declines, and Crises

Although an entrepreneur hopes never to have to deal with organizational downturns, declines, and crises, there may come a time when he or she must do just that. After all, nobody likes to think about things going bad or taking a turn for the worse. But that's exactly what you should do—think about it before it hap-

Preparing for the Worst

As an intelligent entrepreneur, you read news periodicals and you listen to news reports to keep up on what's happening. What if the economists begin predicting an economic downturn? What would you do? What *could* you do? Are there steps you can take to protect your entrepreneurial venture? Financial experts say, "Yes, there are!" The first thing they recommend is *not to overworry.* Instead, review your venture's financing structure and business plan. Make sure that you've covered important details. If you have a bank line of credit, check for any clauses that might permit cancellation in an economic downturn and consider renegotiating the loan. The next suggestion is to *think conservatively.* Make cash flow a priority. Build up a cash reserve. Look at your bal-

ance sheet, and if you are carrying too much debt, use some cash to pay it down. Experts' next recommendation is *don't wait to lock in financing.* If you had been planning new financing, finish it up now while the loan terms are still fairly flexible and borrowing rates low. You might also want to think about refinancing old debt to take advantage of the current rates. Finally, *stretch out the time.* Look at your current debt structure. If you have shorter-term debt, replace it with longer maturities. Consider borrowing against any real estate owned to get a 20- to 25-year loan. When economic conditions improve, you can always pay down these long-term loans.

Source: H. Rosenberg, "Shoring Up Your Finances Is a Capital Idea," *Business Week Enterprise*, November 9, 1998, pp. ENT4–ENT6.

pens.[11] It's important to have an up-to-date plan for covering bad times. It's just like mapping out exit routes from your home in case of a fire. You want to be prepared before an emergency hits. What should this plan focus on? It should provide specific details for controlling the most critical and fundamental aspects of running the venture—cash flow, accounts receivable, costs, and debt. Beyond having a plan for controlling the venture's critical inflows and outflows, what specific actions might entrepreneurs take in dealing with downturns, declines, and crises? We can look to the strategic management literature for some guidance in dealing with these situations.

Entrepreneurs can use two main types of strategies to halt the organization's declining performance in an attempt to return it to more desirable and positive performance levels. The first type is a **retrenchment strategy**, which is a common short-run strategy designed to address organizational weaknesses that are leading to performance declines. In a retrenchment situation, the venture may not necessarily have negative financial returns. Although it may have had some time periods when revenues didn't cover expenses, this isn't the typical sign that an organization needs to retrench. Instead, the usual situation in retrenchment is that the business hasn't been able to meet its goals in whatever performance areas are being measured. Revenues and profits may be declining but aren't necessarily negative. However, the entrepreneur needs to take some actions to reverse the slide or the venture may soon face significant performance declines. *Retrenchment* is a military term that describes situations in which a military unit "goes back to the trenches" in order to stabilize, revitalize, and prepare for entering battle again. That's pretty descriptive of what entrepreneurial organizations must do, as well, in retrenching.

The organization's decision makers must stabilize operations, replenish or revitalize organizational resources and capabilities, and prepare to compete once again in the marketplace battlefield.

The second type of strategy an entrepreneur might use is a **turnaround strategy**, which is a strategy designed for situations in which the organization's performance problems are much more serious, as reflected by its performance measures. Financial results are negative and other measures of performance are usually seriously declining as well. In a turnaround situation, the organization is facing severe external and internal pressures. In this type of situation, something must be done or the organization may well find itself forced out of business.

Implementing both retrenchment and turnaround strategies is dependent primarily on two actions: cutting costs and restructuring. Retrenchment typically will not involve as extensive a use of these actions as a turnaround strategy will. The retrenchment strategy may, in fact, require only selected cost cutting to get organizational performance back on track. Let's look at each of these actions more closely.

Cutting costs is an action to bring the venture's financial performance results back in line with expectations. You want to avoid cutting costs in those critical

---

Entrepreneurs in Action ▶

A restaurant owner in Portland, Oregon (who will remain nameless), needed money fast. Bills had to be paid. Getting a bank loan or other financing would take too much time and would involve a bunch of paperwork. So, he decided to use his credit cards to get through the crunch. He used one, then another, and then another. Pretty soon, he had accumulated $95,000 in charges on 15 different personal credit cards. Paying them off is impossible, so he faces personal bankruptcy.

Now, for another story. Josephine and Joseph Brashear opened The One-Off CD Shop, a CD publishing and information service in Minneapolis, in the mid-1990s. Because they had had no salaried income for almost two years and no track record for bank financing, their only resort for financing was maxing out the credit limit on five different credit cards. However, through careful control of costs and faithfully paying down their debt over a period of four years, the company paid off its cards. Same story—different ending.

What can you learn from these examples? Credit cards can be a financial lifesaver to an entrepreneur, but you should carefully control their use so you don't end up unable to pay back what you've borrowed. Using plastic (credit cards) carelessly and thoughtlessly can lead to a financial disaster that will be hard to erase.

Source: D. Kurschner, "The Pitfalls of Plastic," *Business Week Enterprise*, April 28, 1997, p. ENT18.

areas that contribute to the venture's competitive advantage, however weak that advantage may be. Instead, the intent in cutting costs is to revitalize the organization's performance (retrenchment) or to save the organization (turnaround).

Cost cutting can be approached from the angle of across-the-board cuts (that are implemented in all areas of the venture) or selective cuts (that are implemented in selected areas of the venture). Obviously, in a turnaround situation, the cost cuts need to be more extensive and comprehensive.

What are some ways to cut costs? Entrepreneurs should look closely at work tasks and activities to see if there are any wastes, redundancies, or inefficiencies that could be eliminated. They should also determine if there are resources that could be eliminated or used more efficiently. One study of small firms facing downturns proposed that effective cost cutting should focus on carefully managing the costs in the research and development and product development functions.[12] But, the tendency for most entrepreneurs is to start slashing advertising and marketing costs because you can usually see immediate results from these actions. However, this same study of how businesses dealt with downturns also found that it can be counterproductive to overemphasize cost cutting in advertising and sales-related areas.[13] Generally, if additional cuts are needed to keep performance from declining further, the entrepreneur may have to look at reducing or eliminating certain work tasks and activities or even entire departments, which is part of what the restructuring option is all about.

Restructuring is the other option an entrepreneur might use in retrenching or turning around the venture. One restructuring action might be **reengineering**, which is a radical redesign of the organization's business processes.[14] Reengineering forces decision makers to question traditional assumptions and approaches. You throw out everything you know and believe about the way your business operates and start from scratch. Can the work processes be designed better—that is, to be more efficient and effective? Although this type of radical and drastic change may be necessary to get the venture back on track, it's not an easy thing to do and may not have the desired effect.

Downsizing is another restructuring action that involves laying off employees from their jobs. Downsizing can be a quick way to cut costs, but simply cutting the number of employees without some type of analysis of where employee cuts might be most beneficial is dangerous.[15] Downsizing is a serious decision. Numerous issues are associated with a decision to downsize an organization, both for the individuals who will be laid off as well as for those who will remain with the organization. Any downsizing actions should be approached carefully and with some thought.

Another restructuring action is **bankruptcy**, which involves dissolving or reorganizing a business under the protection of bankruptcy legislation. It's typically the result of significant performance declines where other restructuring or cost-cutting actions have had little effect. What happens when an organization "goes bankrupt"? With the passage of the Bankruptcy Reform Act, business firms were encouraged to reorganize (Chapter 11 bankruptcy) rather than liquidate their assets (Chapter 7 bankruptcy).[16] Therefore, the aftermath of filing for bankruptcy depends on which type is used. An organization in Chapter 11 bankruptcy reorganizes its debts and is protected from creditors collecting on their debts until such time the business can emerge from bankruptcy. An organization in Chapter

Rapid Review ◀◀|

✓ What are some signals of potential performance decline? What factors might be contributing to a performance decline?

✓ Explain the boiled-frog phenomenon and how it relates to recognizing performance declines.

✓ How is a retrenchment strategy different from a turnaround strategy? What two actions are used to implement these strategies?

✓ How can costs be cut?

✓ What is reengineering? What is downsizing?

✓ Explain the bankruptcy option.

7 bankruptcy will have its assets liquidated by a bankruptcy court with the proceeds used to pay off all outstanding debts. Although bankruptcy may not be a preferred option, if a venture's turnaround strategy hasn't worked, it may be the *only* option open to the entrepreneur.

The final action an entrepreneur might use in restructuring is exiting the business. However, exiting the business isn't used only in situations when performance is declining. Therefore, next we're going to discuss the exit decision and all its aspects.

EXITING THE VENTURE

Getting out of an entrepreneurial venture might seem a strange thing to discuss in a book devoted to explaining and championing the development and management of a thriving, growing business. However, there may come a point when the entrepreneur decides it's time to move on. That decision may be based on the fact that the entrepreneur hopes to capitalize financially on the investment in the venture—called **harvesting**—or that the entrepreneur is facing serious organizational performance problems and wants to get out, or even on the entrepreneur's desire to focus on other pursuits (personal or business). The issues involved with making the exit decision effective and successful are choosing a proper business valuation method and knowing what's involved in the process of selling a business. We need to look at each of these topics next.

Business Valuation Methods

"If you value your business . . . value your business."[17] Knowing what your entrepreneurial venture is worth is important. All sorts of events could trigger the need for a valuation. (See Figure 9-4.) For instance, it's particularly important when exiting the business to get an accurate and fair valuation of its worth. However, setting a value on a business can be a little tricky. In many cases, the entrepreneur has sacrificed much for the business and sees it as his or her "baby." Calculating the value of the baby based on objective standards such as cash flow or some multiple of net profits can sometimes be a shock. For a true and accurate value of your entrepreneurial venture, you'll want to get a comprehensive business valuation prepared by professionals. What are some of the approaches that might be used to place a value on a business?

Because there are many approaches to valuing a business, the approach used usually depends on what's accepted practice in the industry. Valuation techniques generally fall into three categories: (1) asset valuations, (2) earnings valuations, and (3) cash flow valuations.[18]

Asset valuations are also known as book value because they're based on the value of the assets as listed in the books or financial statements. The argument for asset valuations is based on the fact that it's the assets of a business that allow it to generate income so the assets reflect the organization's true value. However, many experts contend that asset valuations aren't appropriate because a business with

Figure 9-4

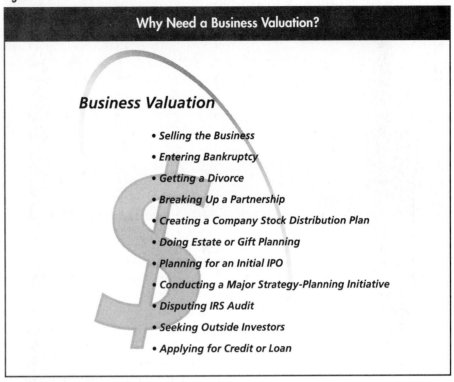

Source: Based on J. A. Fraser, "What's Your Company Worth?," *Inc.*, November 1997, p. 111.

high earnings and low asset value is worth more than a business with low earnings and high asset value. That brings us to an approach that uses earnings as a base for the valuations. These are based on the belief that an organization's value derives from the earnings stream generated. However, the decision here is what earnings measure is most appropriate—gross sales, projected earnings, some multiple of net profit, or some derivation of these? Although earnings valuations do focus on the ability of the business to generate earnings, the challenge is choosing which earnings measure is most appropriate and fairly represents the business's value. The last method of business valuation is based on the cash flow of the business. In this approach, you're focusing on the amount and timing of cash returns to establish a value of the business. Although this approach provides an indication of the actual cash return provided to the owner—as opposed to valuing the assets of the business or the earnings potential—determining which cash flow measure is most appropriate (net cash flow, cash flow multiple, timing of cash flow) can be a problem. The key to business valuation is knowing your options and getting good professional advice.[19]

Although establishing a venture's value can be a challenge, this is just the first consideration in the process of exiting a business. Let's take a closer look at the other factors in the process.

Important Considerations in Exiting the Venture

We've already looked at what is typically the hardest part of preparing to exit a business—valuing it. However, some other factors should be considered.[20] First

Questions to Ask When Selling

When the time comes to sell your business, you should ask yourself certain questions. Asking these questions forces you to think about important issues associated with both the process of selling and the aftermath of the sale. Here are the questions:

- Why am I selling?
- Is this the best time to sell?

- What type of adviser should I hire?
- What valuation method would be best?
- Who's the best buyer?
- What should the terms of sale specify?
- What should I do with the sale proceeds?
- How involved will I be with the business after the sale?

Source: T. Gutner, "Putting Your Company on the Block," *Business Week,* January 26, 1998, pp. 96–97.

of all, you want to *be prepared.* Because you never know when you might be approached by someone interested in buying your business or when circumstances might dictate your exiting the business, you should have on hand a good business plan and at least three to four years of audited financial statements. Next, decide *who will sell the business.* Although you may feel like you know the ins and outs of your business better than anybody else, stop and consider if selling the business is really your area of expertise. It makes more sense to use someone whose specialty is in selling a business. Like a successful real estate agent, a good business broker knows where buyers are, what they're looking for, and how to make your venture stand out from others. Another factor to take into account is the *tax considerations.* Your choice of legal business organization decided back when you organized the venture (sole proprietorship, partnership, LLC, or whatever) will have an impact on the tax consequences of selling the venture. Look at these consequences carefully before deciding how to sell your business. Another factor to consider is *screening potential buyers.* Even if you use a professional business broker to screen out unqualified buyers, you also should carefully screen the prospective purchasers to make sure you're not disclosing any business secrets to potential competitors. Finally, you must decide whether to *tell employees.* The drawback of telling is that employees might be uncertain about their future and either look for another job or be distracted from their work, making them less productive and affecting both individual and organizational performance. On the other hand, the drawback of not telling is that employees may find out anyway and be upset over the lack of communication with them about such an important issue.

The process of exiting the entrepreneurial venture should be approached as carefully as the process of launching it. If you're selling the venture on a positive note, you want to realize the value you have built in the business. If you're selling the venture because of declining performance, you want to maximize the potential return. The next topic we

Rapid Review ◀◀▌

✓ Why might an entrepreneur decide to exit a business?
✓ What is harvesting?
✓ What events could trigger the need for a business valuation?
✓ Describe each of the three categories of business valuation techniques.
✓ What factors should be considered when preparing to exit a business?

want to look at involves some of the challenges facing minority and women-owned businesses.

MINORITY AND WOMEN-OWNED BUSINESSES

Minority and women-owned businesses are playing a significant role in the surge of entrepreneurial activity in the United States. Minority-owned businesses are a rapidly growing segment of the U.S. economy. By 1997 (the most current information available), an estimated 3.25 million minority-owned businesses were in the United States.[21] This number was up 168 percent from 1987. These businesses generated $495 million in revenues (an increase from 1987 of 343 percent) and employed nearly 4 million workers (an increase from 1987 of 362 percent). Women-owned businesses also increased, although not as dramatically. The number of women-owned businesses increased 42 percent to 9.1 million in 1999 from 6.4 million in 1992.[22] These businesses employed over 27.5 million people and generated over $3.6 trillion in sales. The contributions of these entrepreneurs to the economic prosperity of the United States cannot be ignored. Yet, minority and women entrepreneurs face significant challenges as they attempt to manage their ventures successfully. Let's look at some of these challenges.

Challenges Faced by Minority and Women Entrepreneurs

Being an entrepreneur—let's add being a *successful* entrepreneur—is hard. Face it. It's not easy to research, plan, organize, launch, and manage an entrepreneurial venture successfully. With all the challenges to being a successful entrepreneur, facing additional obstacles because of your race or your gender seems unbelievable. Yet, minority and women entrepreneurs do face all sorts of challenges.

The main challenge these entrepreneurs encounter is getting the funding they need to start and continue their businesses.[23] Access to capital is a serious issue for minority and women entrepreneurs. A study by the Federal Reserve

---

Entrepreneurs in Action

Although we don't want to believe that it happens, black entrepreneurs often find it difficult to overcome the racial obstacles of trying to operate a successful business. Black women entrepreneurs face a double whammy—being black *and* being female. However, the anonymity of the Internet is proving to be a boon for black entrepreneurs. Betty A. Ford, a black female entrepreneur, launched City Boxers, an online retailer of hand-tailored boxer shorts (**www.cityboxers.com**), partly to overcome some of the obstacles she faced as an owner of another entrepreneurial business. She's hoping to sell that business (Mailbox Haven—a package delivery business) and concentrate solely on her Internet-based business.

Source: R. O. Crockett, "Invisible—And Loving It," *Business Week,* October 5, 1998, pp. 124–28.

System of small business financing patterns found that minority small business owners have an extremely hard time getting credit.[24] Figure 9-5 shows the disparity in credit denial rates for small business owners. The statistics are quite telling! Women also have problems getting credit lines for starting and growing their businesses. Studies have shown that they have lower levels of available credit than do their male counterparts.[25] Minority women business owners face credit obstacles that white female business owners do not. So, the capital problem is definitely real and very serious. Access to capital to start and grow their entrepreneurial ventures is an extremely difficult barrier for minority and women entrepreneurs.

Another challenge that women entrepreneurs, particularly, face is the conflict between work and family. Although this issue can, and does, arise for male entrepreneurs also, it's especially acute for women because many child-rearing and family responsibilities fall on them. Being an entrepreneur can be a 24-7 (24 hours a day, 7 days a week) commitment. Running a successful business often means finding a healthy balance between work and family lives. (We'll discuss this issue again when we get to the section on being an entrepreneur and managing your personal life.)

Finally, minority and women entrepreneurs face the challenges of managing business growth successfully, finding and keeping qualified employees, and keeping up with technology and other marketplace changes. These are challenges that *all* entrepreneurs face. However, because of society's slowly changing attitudes toward minority and women entrepreneurs, they often face additional hurdles in dealing with these issues. Some people may question whether minorities or women have what it takes to succeed and be reluctant to go to work for them, or these entrepreneurs may have to prove themselves before some people will do

Figure 9-5

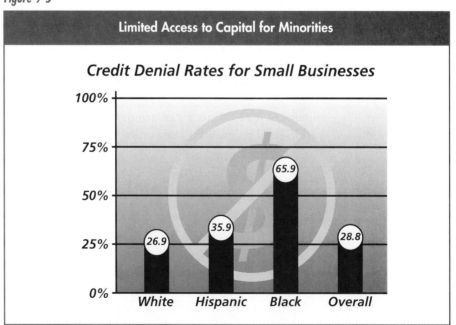

Source: Republished with permission of *The Wall Street Journal,* from "Small-Business Lenders Rebuff Blacks," by J. Tannenbaum, *Wall Street Journal,* July 7, 1999.

business with them. Although these attitudes may seem out-of-place in today's multicultural and increasingly tolerant society, these issues are real for minority and women entrepreneurs. However, even with the additional challenges they face, minority and women entrepreneurs are "making it." Let's take a look at some of the government programs and other help available to minority and women entrepreneurs.

Making It as a Minority or Woman Entrepreneur

Assistance is available for minority and woman entrepreneurs who want to make their ventures successful. One of the best sources for free advice and assistance is **SCORE—Service Corps of Retired Executives**. SCORE, a nonprofit organization and resource partner with the U.S. Small Business Administration, is dedicated to helping entrepreneurs in the formation, growth, and success of small businesses nationwide.[26] These retired business executives (just a note that some SCORE counselors are still employed) consult with and advise business owners on any and all issues faced in running a business. These people have "been there and done that," and their years of business experience and exposure to all sorts of problems are invaluable to entrepreneurs who need this advice and assistance. It's a wonderful program that can help guide minority and women entrepreneurs as they launch and manage their businesses. SCORE can be contacted through its Web site (**www.score.org**) or at its toll-free number (1-800-634-0245).

Another government program that minority and women entrepreneurs may tap into is the Small Disadvantaged Business (SDB) program, run under the direction of the U.S. Small Business Administration. The SDB program was created in the 1980s to help businesses owned by socially and economically disadvantaged individuals get a bigger share of federal contracts. Because of ongoing issues with fraud in determining who fit the guidelines of being socially and economically disadvantaged, the program has implemented stricter guidelines on race- and gender-conscious federal contracting goals. These new regulations make the application more complex. Yet, the Small Business Administration says these changes will ensure that federal contracts go to the business owners who really need SDB help. This might be a program worth checking into, especially if you're interested in selling to the government.

The U.S. Small Business Administration has also committed itself to promoting business ownership by minority groups by increasing the share of SBA-backed business lending to them. This includes the SBA's 504 program, which provides long-term fixed-rate financing for major fixed assets. This type of assistance is welcomed by minority entrepreneurs who may have trouble getting capital from traditional sources to start or grow their businesses.

Another government agency providing assistance to minority businesses is the Minority Business Development Agency (MBDA), which is part of the U.S. Department of Commerce. (Check out its Web site at **www.mbda.gov**.) This agency was created specifically to foster the creation, growth, and expansion of minority-owned businesses in the United States. Assistance in business plans, marketing, management, technical areas, and financial planning are provided in centers located in areas with large concentrations of minority populations and large numbers of minority businesses.

The **Grey** *Zone*

Judy Y. Wiles, founder and owner of First Impressions, Inc., a restaurant and food-service employment agency based in Detroit, has dealt with the prejudices of being a minority in her own way. When she sends someone to close a deal with a suburban client, she sends one of her employees who is white even though one of her minority workers did the client research, helped develop the sales strategy, and made the initial contact. Judy herself is a minority female. What do you think about this? Do you agree with her approach? What are the advantages and drawbacks to her approach?

Source: A. B. Henderson, "Black Entrepreneurs Face a Perplexing Issue: How to Pitch to Whites," *Wall Street Journal,* January 26, 1999, p. A1.

Women entrepreneurs can tap into the Women's Business Center (WBC) program, an offshoot of the U.S. Small Business Administration program. The WBC program helps female entrepreneurs focus their business plans through courses, workshops, and mentoring services, and provides access to capital and financing sources. (Check out its Web site at **www.onlinewbc.org**, which provides free information, interactive tools, personalized counseling, topic forums and newsgroups, an extensive data resource guide, market research, and much more.)

Another thing that successful minority and women entrepreneurs are doing that's not part of any government-sponsored program, is creating their own reliable network of business advisers.[27] Although entrepreneurship may seem to be a solitary pursuit, it's not. Having a network of people whose advice you trust can be a definite asset. It's valuable to be able to tap into the collective knowledge and wisdom of individuals who can get you to question, to shake things up, or to think differently.

As you can see, there are many sources of help and assistance for minority and women entrepreneurs wanting to make it. Although we've described just a few here, there are numerous others. Several Internet sites devoted to successful entrepreneurship are described in the Killer Apps Appendix. Many of these also are good sources of advice and assistance.

Another group of entrepreneurs that faces unique challenges are family businesses. That's what we want to look at next.

FAMILY BUSINESSES

In some respects, every entrepreneurial venture is a family business, started and managed by an entrepreneur who's a member of some "family." But that's not really what is meant by a family business. What *is* a family business? Entrepreneurship researchers have noted some problems with defining a family business—such as how many members of the family have to be involved, what roles family members have to play, how many generations it has to cover, and so on.[28] We're going to define a **family business** as one that includes two or more members of the same family who control, are directly involved in, and own a majority of the business.

As one person said, "When it works right, nothing succeeds like a family firm. The roots are deep, embedded in family values. The flash of the fast buck is replaced with long-term plans. Tradition counts."[29] A family business can be an exceptionally successful and satisfying experience for all involved. However, family businesses face serious challenges in the pursuit of being successful entrepreneurial ventures.

Challenges Faced by Family Businesses

Although family businesses are an integral part of our economy, they face two major challenges. The first challenge is the complex interrelationships that arise, and the second challenge is management succession.

In a family business, the boundaries between work and family are quite complex and multifaceted. Entrepreneurship researchers have proposed that three overlapping perspectives influence the decisions and actions of family business owners.[30] One perspective is from that of the family and wanting to take care of family members. Another perspective is from that of ownership where the concern is doing what's in the best interests of the business. Then there's the perspective of management where the concern is doing what's in the best interests of other organizational employees. How can these three overlapping perspectives create challenges? For example, let's take a fairly common business situation—a family member needs a job. From the family perspective, you probably would see this as a chance to help out someone in the family. From the ownership perspective, you might be concerned about the impact of an additional employee on organizational expenses and profits. From the management perspective, you might be concerned about the effect of the hiring on other nonfamily employees. Each of these perspectives is valid, but which takes precedence? Keep in mind that we're not trying to imply that these three perspectives have to be mutually exclusive all the time. But, there will be situations when the decision or action is going to be influenced more strongly by one of the perspectives. The entrepreneur behind a successful family business needs to be able to balance all three perspectives simultaneously in managing the complex interrelationships.

The second major challenge facing family businesses is management succession. Studies of family firms have shown that, on average, only 30 percent of family businesses survive to the second generation, and only 10 percent make it to the third generation.[31] Those are pretty alarming statistics, aren't they? Many entrepreneurs dream of passing on the family business to their children or other family members. Unfortunately, human traits such as jealousy, lack of interest, or incompetence may get in the way.

Even though complex interrelationships and management succession pose challenges to the family business entrepreneur, there are ways to make it. Let's look at some of the things that family businesses can do to be successful.

Making It as a Family Business

One study of successful family firms discovered some "best practices" characteristics that these businesses shared.[32] One of these characteristics was a *focus on business, not family, needs.* Although a family business entrepreneur may feel an obligation to take care of all family problems, the business shouldn't be used as a family employment agency or loan center. Another best practices characteristic was *reinvestment in the business.* Profits should be plowed back into building and sustaining the business. The company's revenues shouldn't be "sucked dry" just to support family wants and desires. Next, *use caution with family.* Think about and discuss relevant issues of employment and money before hiring family members or giving out generous severance packages to family members. Try to forestall potential conflicts by being cautious. Another characteristic of these successful family businesses was *delegation of decisions.* A family business entrepreneur who makes all decisions and never delegates will be viewed as a control freak. Decisions should be delegated to those who are capable of making them. The final best practices characteristic identified was a *big-picture view*. In making decisions, successful family business entrepreneurs considered all stakeholders—from nonfamily employees to local community to family. This supports what we were discussing earlier about balancing the three perspectives—family, ownership, and management—when making decisions and taking action.

The other important thing for family businesses is having a good management succession plan, which will consider six important factors.[33] (See Table 9-2.) These six factors include the role of the owner during the transition; family dynamics, relationships, and new roles; income for family members employed in the business and other shareholders; business conditions during transition; treatment of loyal long-term employees; and tax consequences. Each of these factors affects the choices made during the transition and can influence whether the outcome is smooth, functional, and effective. If no family member wishes to be involved with the business and the decision is made to transfer the business to a nonfamily member, the key question to be answered is ownership—what type and how much (if any) will be retained by the family. These issues do need to be addressed. The main thing in either circumstance—transferring the business to family members or transferring it to nonfamily—is planning ahead. You don't want to wait until something happens and then be forced to make rash and ill-advised decisions.

A successful and satisfying family business can be a thing of joy for a family. One subject that all entrepreneurs and their families have to deal with, however, is managing the personal demands of being an entrepreneur. We're going to look at that important topic next.

MANAGING YOUR PERSONAL LIFE

Being an entrepreneur is extremely exciting and demanding. There are long hours, difficult demands, and high stress. But, as we've discussed in earlier chap-

---

Global Perspectives

The east coast of South Africa has long been known for its spice trade. Chimanlal K. Haribhai of Durban has created a major company in the spice business. His Spice Emporium occupies a full block in downtown Durban and offers an impressive assortment of condiments, nuts, fruits, juices, grains, and sweetmeats. Oh, and it also sells spices. But the retail store is only the most visible part of the family business. The company wholesales spices and rice to customers all over Africa and Europe and is becoming a bigger force in the United States. In order to assure the business he has worked hard to build continues (Mr. Haribhai is in his middle seventies), his daughter Chandrika and her husband, Vinod Harie, have joined the business. They're helping run the retail side of the operation but will continue to take on more responsibility.

Source: P. Gupte, "The Spice King," *Forbes*, July 27, 1998, pp. 52–53.

TABLE 9-2 What Effective Management Succession Plans Should Consider
■ The role of the owner during the transition stage ■ Family dynamics ■ Income for family members employed in the business and shareholders ■ Business conditions during the transition ■ Treatment of loyal long-term employees ■ Tax consequences

ters, being an entrepreneur has many rewards as well. In this last section of the textbook, we want to take a look at how to manage your personal life. How can you make it work—that is, how can you be a successful entrepreneur and effectively balance the demands of your work and your personal life?

Making It Work

Entrepreneurs are a special group. They are focused and persistent, hardworking and intelligent. Because they put so much of themselves into launching and growing their entrepreneurial ventures, many may neglect their personal lives. You will have to make certain sacrifices to pursue your entrepreneurial dreams. However, you can make it work. You can balance your work and personal life. Some suggestions for doing just that follows.

One of the most important things you can do as an entrepreneur to balance your work and personal life is to *become a good time manager.* Prioritize what needs to be done. Use a planner (daily, weekly, monthly) to help you schedule your priorities. Some entrepreneurs don't like taking the time to plan or prioritize or think it's a ridiculous waste of time. Yet, identifying the important duties and distinguishing them from those that aren't so important actually makes you a more efficient and effective manager. In addition, part of being a good time manager is delegating to trusted employees those decisions and duties that you don't need to be personally involved in. It may be hard to let go of some of the things you've always done, but if you delegate effectively (look back at our discussion in Chapter 8), your personal productivity level will probably rise. Another suggestion for finding that balance is to *seek professional advice* in those areas of business where you may need it. Although you may be reluctant to spend scarce cash, the time, energy, and potential problems you save in the long run are well worth the investment. Competent professional advisers can provide you with information to make more intelligent decisions. Use these professionals' expertise. To achieve that work life–personal life balance, it's also important to *deal with conflicts* as they arise. This includes both workplace and family conflicts. If you don't deal with conflicts, negative feelings are likely to crop up and lead to communication breakdowns. When communication breaks down, vital information may get lost and people (employees *and* family members) may start assuming the worst. It can turn into a nightmare situation that feeds upon itself. So, the best strategy is to deal with conflicts as they come up. Talk, discuss, argue (if you must), but don't avoid the conflict or pretend it doesn't exist. Another suggestion for achieving that bal-

Rapid Review ◀◀|

✓ What type of economic impact are minority and women entrepreneurs having?

✓ Describe the main challenges that minority and women entrepreneurs face.

✓ What types of programs are available to help minority and women entrepreneurs succeed?

✓ What is a family business?

✓ Describe the two main challenges that family businesses face.

✓ What are the best practices characteristics that successful family businesses share?

✓ How should an effective management succession plan be developed?

✓ What are some suggestions for balancing your work as an entrepreneur and your personal life?

ance is to *develop a network of trusted friends and peers*. Having a group of people you can talk to is a good way to think through problems and issues. You might want to develop both a professional network of entrepreneurs and business people and a personal network of friends. The support and encouragement from these groups of people can be an invaluable source of strength for an entrepreneur. The final suggestion for achieving work life–personal life balance is to *recognize when your stress levels are too high*. Entrepreneurs *are* achievers. They like to make things happen. They thrive on working hard. Yet, too much stress can lead to significant physical and emotional problems. You have to learn to recognize when the stress is overwhelming you and do something about it. After all, what's the point of growing and building a thriving entrepreneurial venture if you're not around to enjoy it?

Hopefully, you're just as excited now about entrepreneurship as when you first started reading this book. Keep in mind that being an entrepreneur isn't easy, yet it's one of the most exciting and rewarding paths you can take. Good luck in your pursuit! May your entrepreneurial experiences be all that you dreamed!

CHAPTER SUMMARY

Growth is what distinguishes an entrepreneurial venture. Managing that growth can be a significant challenge for entrepreneurs. In addition, other entrepreneurial challenges must be faced. These challenges include the issues encountered during organizational performance downturns, harvest and exit decisions, problems encountered by minority and women entrepreneurs, issues faced by family businesses, and personal life issues faced by entrepreneurs.

Growth is a natural and desirable outcome for entrepreneurial ventures. Organizational growth is any increase in the level, amount, or type of the organization's work and outputs. It involves expanding, enlarging, or extending what the venture does. But, growth also means a spirit of vitality and energy. An organization that's growing is vibrant and flourishing. How is organizational growth measured? Although a number of variables could be used, the most common measures are financial. It's much easier to measure growth if you quantify the factor. It doesn't matter what the factor is. In fact, it should be something that's important to your specific type of entrepreneurial venture. How is organizational growth pursued? The best growth strategy is a well-planned one. One approach to pursuing growth identifies four possible strategies: product–customer exploitation, product development, customer development, and product–customer expansion. The key challenges for an entrepreneur in organizing for growth include finding capital, finding people, reinforcing organizational controls, and strengthening the organizational culture. Entrepreneurs also need to be aware of some special challenges in restrained and rapid growth situations.

When an organization's growth strategies don't result in the intended outcomes and when performance results are declining, entrepreneurs need to look at managing the downturns. The first step is recognizing that a crisis is brewing and then dealing with the situation. Some signals of potential performance decline include inadequate or negative cash flow, excessive number of employees, unnecessary and cumbersome administrative procedures, fear of conflict or taking risks, tolerance of work incompetence, lack of a clear vision, mission, or goals, and ineffective or poor communication in the organization. The boiled-frog phenomenon is another perspective on recognizing performance declines. It proposes that entrepreneurs should be alert to gradual changes in performance. The factors that may be contributing to performance declines include decisions to overexpand or expand too rapidly, inadequate financial controls, out-of-control costs, not anticipating new competitors or shifts in customer demand, being slow to respond to significant external or internal trends and changes, and an organizational culture in turmoil. To deal with downturns, declines, and crises, an entrepreneur should have an up-to-date plan for dealing with bad times. In addition, the entrepreneur may have to implement a retrenchment strategy if the situation isn't too serious yet or a turnaround strategy if the situation is critical. Cost cutting and restructuring are ways that these strategies are implemented. Restructuring actions include reengineering, downsizing, bankruptcy, and exiting the business.

An entrepreneur may, at some point, decide it's time to exit the business, whether for reasons of declining performance or just wanting to harvest the investment. An important task in exiting is valuing the business. Valuation techniques generally fall into three categories: asset valuations, earnings valuations, and cash flow valuations. Besides the valuation issue, the entrepreneur needs to consider other factors in exiting the business.

Minority and women entrepreneurs and family businesses face some special entrepreneurial issues. Each of these groups plays a significant role in our economy. The main challenge for minority and women entrepreneurs is getting the funding they need to start and grow their businesses. The main challenges for family businesses are the complex interrelationships between work and family and the issue of management succession. Although they face serious obstacles, each of these groups is finding ways to make it successfully as entrepreneurs.

Finally, entrepreneurs carefully need to consider balancing the demands of their work and personal lives. Being an entrepreneur is demanding and often requires significant sacrifices for the family, yet it is possible to balance work and personal life.

KEY TERMS

➠ *Organizational growth:* Any increase in the level, amount, or type of the organization's work and outputs.

➠ *Product–customer exploitation strategy:* An organizational growth strategy that describes attempts to increase sales of current products to current customers.

➠ *Product development strategy:* An organizational growth strategy that involves creating new products for use by current customers.

▣➤ *Customer development strategy:* An organizational growth strategy that describes attempts to sell current products to new customers.

▣➤ *Product–customer expansion strategy:* An organizational growth strategy that involves expanding into both new products and new customers.

▣➤ *"Boiled frog" phenomenon:* A description of a situation when negative changes in organizational performance are so gradual that the entrepreneur may miss the signs.

▣➤ *Retrenchment strategy:* A short-run strategy designed to address organizational weaknesses that are leading to performance declines.

▣➤ *Turnaround strategy:* A strategy designed for situations in which the organization's performance problems are more serious, as reflected by its performance measures.

▣➤ *Reengineering:* A restructuring option in which an organization's business processes are radically redesigned.

▣➤ *Downsizing:* A restructuring option that involves laying off employees from their jobs.

▣➤ *Bankruptcy:* A restructuring option that involves dissolving or reorganizing a business under the protection of bankruptcy legislation.

▣➤ *Harvesting:* A decision to exit a business based on the fact that an entrepreneur hopes to capitalize financially on the investment in the venture.

▣➤ *SCORE—Service Corps of Retired Executives:* A nonprofit organization and partner with the U.S. Small Business Administration composed of retired business executives who consult with entrepreneurs in the formation, growth, and success of their businesses nationwide.

▣➤ *Family business:* A business that includes two or more members of the same family who control, are directly involved in, and own a majority of the business.

SWEAT EQUITY

1. *Nanomanagement* is a term used to describe micromanagement in a small organization. It's a problem that should be addressed before it stifles organizational growth. Why do you think entrepreneurs nanomanage? What suggestions would you suggest to entrepreneurs for controlling the tendency to nanomanage?

(***Source:*** L. Formichelli, "Letting Go of the Details," *Nation's Business*, November 1997, pp. 50–52.)

2. A study of family businesses showed that parents' actions have a direct influence on their kids' becoming entrepreneurs. The findings showed that 32 percent of the sons with entrepreneurial fathers started a business, compared with 12 percent of sons without self-employed fathers. The study also showed that 24 percent of daughters with entrepreneurial mothers also became entrepreneurs whereas 13 percent of daughters whose mothers weren't self-employed did so. The study also showed that children of entrepreneurs don't start more businesses because they get money from their parents. A more likely explanation is the attitudes that entrepreneurial parents

instill in their children, such as the value of being your own boss, and specific talents they pass on.

Your assignment is to find a father–son or mother–daughter duo where both are entrepreneurs. Talk to them about their experiences. Are they in the same line of business? Did the son or daughter always want to be an entrepreneur? What made each (father and son or mother and daughter) want to be an entrepreneur? Do they learn from each other's experiences? Write a paper describing your findings and be prepared to present it to your class.

Alternate Assignment

Because your access to father–son or mother–daughter entrepreneurs may be limited, here's an alternate assignment that your professor may have you complete. Co-preneurs are a special subset of family businesses. Do some research on co-preneurs and the challenges they face. Write a paper that describes these challenges and how co-preneurs are dealing with them.

3. The Gooseberry Patch Company catalog is one of thousands of catalogs mailed annually in the United States. The catalog industry is a cutthroat one, and the cofounders behind Gooseberry Patch, Jo Ann Martin and Vickie L. Hutchins, are trying to make good decisions to keep their company growing. Check out their Web site at **www.gooseberrypatch.com**. Do some research on the direct-marketing industry by going to the Direct Marketing Association Web site (**www.the-dma.org**). Come up with a bulleted list of recommendations you would make to Martin and Hutchins to continue growing their company. Try to be as specific as possible.

4. "Turning down business can help your company grow." What? How can turning away customers help your business grow? A new business performance measure called *return on management*, or ROM, explains it all. Read the article "How High Is Your Return on Management?" by Robert Simons and Antonio Davila in the January–February 1998 issue of *Harvard Business Review*. Then write a paper (your professor will tell you the expected length of your written paper) explaining the concept of ROM and how it relates to entrepreneurship. Be sure to indicate what *you* see as the advantages and drawbacks of this concept.

5. Stress and burnout are serious problems for entrepreneurs. Research the topic of stress and burnout. Focus on finding out what causes stress and burnout for entrepreneurs and how to deal with them. Create a presentation that provides the key points you uncover. (Make the presentation with PowerPoint, other software-based transparencies, or posters.) Be prepared to give your presentation in class.

ENTREPRENEURSHIP IN ACTION CASES

CASE #1: Recipe for Success

Entrepreneurship in Action case #1 can be found at the beginning of Chapter 9.

Discussion Questions

1. If you were William Williams and his co-owners, how would you measure growth in your business? Why would these measures be important?

2. Is slow, cautious growth a good strategy in the food industry? Explain.

3. As a minority business, Glory Foods has faced obstacles that nonminority businesses do not. If the owners came to you for advice, what suggestions might you make to them?

CASE #2: Not Just a Pretty Face

Claudia Schiffer has one of the world's most beautiful and most recognized faces and bodies. Yet, she's not just a pretty face. She's also a very smart entrepreneur. She has built a business venture with revenues believed to be between $8 million and $14 million a year. Her business is herself. She also is looking continually at ways to grow her business investment.

Schiffer isn't the first supermodel to recognize the importance of maintaining her "brand." Cindy Crawford, another supermodel, combined good looks with marketing savvy to become a successful entrepreneur. Crawford founded her own company, humorously called Crawdaddy, to oversee her interests, which included a series of successful exercise videos, calendars and other items that carried her photo, and the launch of her own line of makeup. Crawford also teamed up with companies such as Blockbuster Video, Kay Jewelers, and Pepsi to become their spokeswoman. These choices have kept her face and name in the public eye. Schiffer also recognized the importance of marketing herself in various ways commercially. She, too,

has diversified the selling of her image. Like Crawford, she has used calendars, movies, books, television shows, exercise videos, spokesperson contracts, and other means to keep her image out there in the public eye.

However, don't think that building a minibeauty conglomerate is easy. There are no guarantees that just because you have a famous face and name that your products will sell. For instance, one of Schiffer's partners in the Fashion Cafe international chain of theme restaurants, Naomi Campbell, tried to market a music CD and a novel she had written. Both flopped. Industry experts attribute this to the fact that the CD and novel weren't really Campbell's strong areas of expertise. So, even supermodels have to make good decisions about how to grow their businesses.

So what can Schiffer's success be attributed to? Schiffer herself says it's because she's "interested." She's very hands-on and likes to know what's happening both within and outside the business. She's very focused and has a strong competitive desire to remain at the top. In addition, Schiffer is a hardworking individual and a dedicated CEO. She puts in seven day weeks if needed and expects those who work for her to do the same if there are pressing issues and tasks. She also believes that fun is the key to getting herself and her staff to produce the most. But one other thing that characterizes Schiffer's business approach is her caution in her business dealings. She does a lot of research, preparation, and reading the fine print. She also is highly involved in decisions and is almost obsessed with controlling all aspects of her business. Schiffer says, "If I put my own money in, I make sure that I will never lose it."

Discussion Questions

1. What type of growth strategy would you say Schiffer is pursuing? Explain your choice.

2. How would you value a business such as Schiffer's that's based primarily on name and image?

3. What are the advantages and drawbacks of being "obsessed" with controlling all aspects of your business?

(*Source:* D. Carnoy, "Claudia Schiffer," *Success*, August 1998, pp. 52–55.)

CASE #3: Letting Go

One of the biggest problems for a family business is when the older family member turns over the reins to the business to one of the children but finds it hard to let go of the business that he or she has built. This problem is being played out at the Colony Beach & Tennis Resort in Longboat Key, Florida. Murray Klauber, the Colony's founder and patriarch, may have retired from the presidency and day-to-day operating responsibilities, but he has found it difficult to really let go. Klauber turned over the management of the business to his daughter, Katie Moulton, over 10 years ago. But, his strong and close presence sometimes gets a little *too* close for her comfort. For instance, one morning Mr. Klauber sought out his daughter at breakfast in one of the resort's restaurants to tell her that he thought the maintenance director was doing just a fantastic job. Mrs. Moulton, who had been addressing some unresolved issues with the maintenance director, told her father that she hoped he hadn't told the maintenance director his thoughts. That could have made it extremely difficult for her to address the problems she was having with the person.

Another issue is that Mr. Klauber also lives in a suite near the resort's lobby and finds it convenient for "patrolling" the property. But, it's not only Mrs. Moulton who endures the continued attentions of her father. He constantly makes suggestions to Colony employees with his ideas for improving the place. Often, he'll put his thoughts into memos with a red-ink stamp that reads, "Do It Now." Klauber doesn't apologize for his actions, but says that, "It's my life's work."

The generational succession issue is getting more difficult for family businesses particularly because so many founders are living longer and leading more vigorous lives. Says one expert on family businesses, "When they're that energetic, it's hard for them to completely let go of the reins even after they hand them over." The Klauber family is making it work by informally negotiating an understanding that transcends titles, organizational charts, and egos. Mrs. Moulton listens to his ideas, but isn't afraid to tell him that they're too off-the-wall. She never intends to have a "showdown" with her father because she understands that he only wants what's best for the business.

Discussion Questions

1. What are the advantages and drawbacks of having the retired founder of a family business stay involved with the business?

2. Based on what this case illustrates, what suggestions might you make to other owners of family businesses?

(*Source:* R. Johnson, "Turning It Over," *Wall Street Journal*, May 24, 1999, p. A1.)

VIDEO CASE #1: Grace Under Fire

With a name like Pyro Media, you would probably not know quite what to expect, but you would figure it was going to be something pretty unusual. Grace Tsjuikawa Boyd's business, Pyro Media, has pursued a pretty unusual direction. But the decision to do something different wasn't made randomly.

Grace's Pyro Media started off as a manufacturer of huge ceramic glazed pots such as the ones you might see holding trees or plants in the lobbies of large hotels. Using her degree in art, Grace herself initially made the high-quality glazed pots that sold for about $1,500 each. But as her business grew to the point where it had back orders of 8 to 12 weeks, Grace decided it was time to move to a bigger facility and invest in equipment and employees. She says, "We were in business making money and assumed that business was going to grow at the same rate it had been." Grace soon found, however, that Pyro Media's revenues didn't keep increasing by 30 percent as they had been, but instead were dropping off. Upon investigating the situation, Grace found out that huge corporations had begun importing and distributing terra cotta planters, essentially stealing away her business.

Grace knew she had to do something. She had this equipment, this 56,000-square-foot facility, and employees who knew ceramics. She called in some consultants to see what other markets her business might pursue. Their study, which took about six months, rec-

ommended that Pyro Media look into high-tech ceramic applications using the same technology that Grace had developed and used in making ceramic pots and applying it to a new area. Based on this information, Grace hired a ceramics engineer and went after the ceramics "castables" market. The company's decision to move into this new market has been so successful the one engineer has since been joined by seven others!

Recognizing that business was falling off and analyzing the reason behind the loss of revenue was instrumental in Pyro Media's continued success. Grace says that being able to recognize a problem is critical, especially for small businesses. Why? Because small businesses have no money or time to waste. If problems are ignored and not analyzed, the business might face quick failure.

Discussion Questions

1. Do you agree with Grace's assertion that being able to recognize a problem is especially critical for small businesses? Why or why not?

2. If you were in Grace's shoes, what signals would you have looked for that performance might be declining?

3. How would you describe Pyro Media's move into ceramic castables? Explain your choice of growth strategy.

(*Source:* Based on *Small Business 2000*, Show 108.)

VIDEO CASE #2: On Target Supplies and Logistics

Albert Black is a man with a mission. Even though he grew up in a government housing project in south Dallas, his parents gave him careful guidance and instilled in him a sense of confidence that helped prepare him for success in the business world. As a boy, Albert learned the value of hard work by mowing lawns. Albert's mother expected the best from her children. Albert credits his grandmother with teaching him to "treat people with Christian passion and to look out for others." His father worked for many years as a doorman at a Dallas hotel and became acquainted with many prominent Dallas businesspersons. Albert's father encouraged him to set his sights on becoming a businessman, and Albert listened to that advice.

After attending college on a football scholarship, Albert borrowed money from friends and started On Target Supplies and Logistics. The company supplies printing and photocopy paper to Dallas-area businesses. While running On Target Supplies was Albert's "day job," he also worked nights in the information systems department at Lone Star Gas. Over the course of 10 years, this second job provided much-needed funding for On Target Supplies. It also made Albert familiar with the technology needs of large businesses that he hoped would one day be his customers. Albert recalls, "I had a goal. I would pick up a skill set, a management ability, a competency that I could take into my company and make it work. I managed information systems. I managed technology development. I managed customer satisfaction."

Today, Albert has 30 people on the payroll and On Target generates around $10 million in annual sales. Customers include some big business names—EDS (Electronic Data

Services), Texas Instruments, Southwestern Bell, and Texas Utilities. High visibility in the community is one reason Albert has attracted such an impressive roster of customers. Early on, Albert recognized the benefits of active participation with not-for-profit organizations in the Dallas area. "We decided to get involved with communities, and provide leadership around town. By volunteering, we would get exposure and a chance to network while doing real good for the city of Dallas. Our goal was to make business friends that we could eventually call on and do business with."

Another reason for Albert's success is that he knows how to listen. For example, On Target is a supplier to Lone Star Gas, where Albert once worked nights. At first, On Target's paper products moved from its loading dock to Lone Star's loading dock. Albert devised a strategy of just-in-time desktop distribution that added value to the supply chain by delivering boxes of paper directly to the persons who needed them. Albert's solution saved Lone Star time, money, and inventory expense. Albert explains, "I have the ability to listen, to plan, to present, to perform, to adjust. The flexibility of the supplier must be demonstrated so that it's continuously changing, and continuously adding value, and continuously redefining value for our customers."

In keeping with his desire to learn, Albert earned an MBA from Southern Methodist University. Albert also understands that he needs ongoing input from others if he is to take his company to the next level. On Target's board of advisers is comprised of representatives from client companies. Albert has also formed a board of directors, made up of professionals from the Dallas business community. John Castle, a senior executive at EDS, serves as chairman of the board of directors. "Our role is to serve as a sounding board. Albert brings his ideas and strategies, and we give him our perspective." Albert says, "John Castle felt that once On Target reached the $10 million mark, we needed more challenge and balance in our strategic direction." Albert acknowledges that initially he felt intimidated at the prospect of approaching Castle. He says, however, "Business leaders must have courage. We must get beyond that emotional feeling of being intimidated. We have to find common interests and build on those things to build a partnership."

Having tasted success for himself, Albert is driven to create jobs and make the American dream available to his employees. His purpose in building a business, he says, was to "hire people, improve the infrastructure of the inner city where we do business, pay taxes, provide leadership, and get rich along the way." He relishes the opportunity to dispel some myths about business, and in doing so, come to the attention of the broader business community. For example, On Target's success contradicts the myth that a small business cannot capitalize itself sufficiently to finance growth. Albert has also proven that a minority business can indeed put together the type of management team necessary to take advantage of market opportunities. Albert does not hesitate to become involved in the private lives of his employees. For example, On Target has a 401k plan, and Albert encourages employees to maximize their tax-deferred retirement savings. He also encourages—even insists—that employees continue their educations.

Albert's promise to employees involves three things. First, they will earn an "educational" income. Albert believes in open-book management. Employees at On Target know about the company's expense and revenue streams, as well as its cost of sales. At many companies, such information is not shared with employees. Albert wants his employees to learn enough so that they can eventually start their own businesses if they so desire. Second, On Target employees earn "psychological" incomes. As Albert explains, "I want you to feel good about what you do. You'll get a good sense of esprit de corps, that together we can climb mountains and make a contribution every day." Finally, there is "financial" income. Albert's goal is to pay his employees salaries that exceed the industry average. He takes great personal pride in noting that, despite the fact that many of his employees come from impoverished backgrounds like his own, the average annual salary of On Target's employees is about $30,000. "I've taken tax users and helped them become tax producers," he says.

Discussion Questions

1. Managing a business as it grows presents special challenges. As On Target reached $10 million in sales, what did Albert Black do to assure proper guidance as the company grew?

2. How did Albert Black overcome the challenges that minority entrepreneurs often have to deal with?

3. What can you learn from Albert Black regarding being a successful entrepreneur?

(*Source:* Based on *Small Business 2000, Show 212.*)

ENDNOTES

1. C. Shook, "Making Haste Slowly," *Forbes*, September 22, 1997, pp. 220–22; and information from company's Web site (**www.gloryfoods.com**).

2. G. R. Merz, P. B. Weber, and V. B. Laetz, "Linking Small Business Management with Entrepreneurial Growth," *Journal of Small Business Management*, October 1994, pp. 48–60.

3. T. Stevens, "And One to Grow On," *IW*, July 3, 1995, pp. 27–34.

4. Merz, Weber, and Laetz, "Linking Small Business Management with Entrepreneurial Growth."

5. L. Beresford, "Growing Up," *Entrepreneur*, July 1996, pp. 124–28.

6. The discussion of these strategy options has been slightly modified from information found in P. Kotler, *Marketing Management*, 8th ed. (Upper Saddle River, NJ: Prentice Hall, 1994).

7. M. Barrier, "Can You Stay Small Forever?" *Nation's Business*, October 1996, pp. 34R–35R.

8. S. Nelton, "Coming to Grips with Growth," *Nation's Business*, February 1998, pp. 26–32.

9. P. Lorange and R. T. Nelson, "How to Recognize—and Avoid—Organizational Decline," *Sloan Management Review*, spring 1987, pp. 41–48.

10. S. D. Chowdhury and J. R. Lang, "Crisis, Decline, and Turnaround: A Test of Competing Hypotheses for Short-Term Performance Improvement in Small Firms," *Journal of Small Business Management*, October 1993, pp. 8–17.

11. C. Farrell, "How to Survive a Downturn," *Business Week*, April 28, 1997, pp. ENT4–ENT6.

12. J. K. DeDee and D. W. Vorhies, "Retrenchment Activities of Small Firms During Economic Downturn: An Empirical Investigation," *Journal of Small Business Management*, July 1998, pp. 46–61.

13. Ibid.

14. M. Hammer and J. Champy, *Reengineering the Corporation* (New York: HarperCollins, 1995).

15. W. McKinley, C. M. Sanchez, and A. G. Schick, "Organizational Downsizing: Constraining, Cloning, and Learning," *Academy of Management Executive*, August 1995, pp. 32–44; and G. D. Bruton, J. K. Keels, and C. L. Shook, "Downsizing the Firm: Answering the Strategic Questions," *Academy of Management Executive*, May 1996, pp. 38–45.

16. C. M. Daily, "Bankruptcy in Strategic Studies: Past and Promise," *Journal of Management*, Vol. 20, No. 2, 1994, pp. 263–95; J. P. Sheppard, "Strategy and Bankruptcy: An Exploration into Organizational Death," *Journal of Management*, Vol. 20, No. 4, 1994, pp. 795–833; and Y. Chen, J. F. Weston, and E. I. Altman, "Financial Distress and Restructuring Models," *Financial Management*, summer 1995, pp. 57–75.

17. J. Burton, "Making Sure the Price Is Right," *Business Week Enterprise*, March 29, 1999, pp. ENT10–ENT14.

18. R. W. Pricer and A. C. Johnson, "The Accuracy of Valuation Methods in Predicting the Selling Price of Small Firms," *Journal of Small Business Management*, October 1997, pp. 24–35.

19. For a concise summary of 12 different business valuation methods, see ibid., p. 28.

20. D. Rodkin, "For Sale by Owner," *Entrepreneur*, January 1998, pp. 148–53; A. Livingston, "Avoiding Pitfalls When Selling a Business," *Nation's Business*, July 1998, pp. 25–26; and G. Gibbs Marullo, "Selling Your Business: A Preview of the Process," *Nation's Business*, August 1998, pp. 25–26.

21. "Minorities in Business," *Office of Advocacy, Small Business Administration* (Washington, DC: Small Business Administration, 1999).

22. "Women Launch Businesses for Freedom and Flexibility, Not Money," *Wall Street Journal*, June 8, 1999, p. A1; and "Key Facts," *National Foundation for Women Business Owners* Web page (**www.nfwbo.org/key.html**), December 6, 1999.

23. S. Leibs, "Against the Odds," *IW*, May 1998, pp. 36–40; "Capital Harder to Obtain for Women," *Springfield News Leader*, May 4, 1998, p. 7A; G. Koretz, "Wanted: Black Entrepreneurs," *Business Week*, December 14, 1998, p. 26; and J. A. Tannenbaum, "Small-Business Lenders Rebuff Blacks," *Wall Street Journal*, July 7, 1999, p. A2.

24. Tannenbaum, "Small-Business Lenders Rebuff Blacks."

25. "Key Facts," *National Foundation for Women Business Owners* Web page.

26. Check out SCORE's Web site at **www.score.org**.

27. D. Fenn, "A League of Your Own," *Inc. State of Small Business*, 1998, pp. 102–209.

28. R. H. Brockhaus Sr., "Entrepreneurship and Family Business Research: Comparisons, Critique, and Lessons," *Entrepreneurship Theory and Practice*, fall 1994, pp. 25–38.

29. E. Calonius, "Blood and Money," *Newsweek*, special issue 1995, pp. 82–84.

30. F. Hoy and T. G. Verser, "Emerging Business, Emerging Field: Entrepreneurship and the Family Firm," *Entrepreneurship Theory and Practice*, fall 1994, pp. 9–23.

31. T. W. Zimmerer and N. M. Scarborough, *Essentials of Entrepreneurship and Small Business Management*, 2nd ed. (Upper Saddle River, NJ: Prentice Hall, 1998), p. 17.

32. "How to Avoid a Dysfunctional Family Business," *Business Week Enterprise*, March 2, 1998, p. ENT3.

33. P. Brothers, "Succession Plan Vital for Family Businesses," *Cincinnati Enquirer*, December 19, 1996, p. S11.

KILLER APPS APPENDIX

Killer apps. Now that's a pretty strange name for a book appendix, and it may be one that evokes images that you're thinking have nothing to do with entrepreneurship. However, the term "**killer apps**," coined during the latter part of the 1990s, has nothing to do with gangs and guns and killing. It is a phrase being used by entrepreneurial organizations obsessed with success to refer to new goods or services that are completely rewriting the rules of an industry and that ultimately serve as the driving force behind a company's strategy.[1] These entrepreneurial organizations are continually innovating, creating, and growing in order to be the best. They're focused on creating and innovating killer apps and not accepting being second best. In this Appendix, we want to look at additional information that will help you in your journey to being a successful entrepreneur. We would like to equip you with support and content unlike anything you would find in other entrepreneurship books—and in the process, rewrite the "rules." Ultimately, we hope that the information included in this Appendix spurs you in your search to develop your own killer apps.

Four major parts are included in the Killer Apps Appendix. First, some additional information about business plans is provided. Then, there's a section devoted to explaining the essentials of the evolution of e-business and the implications of e-business design for entrepreneurial organizations. Next, a section provides an annotated list of entrepreneurship Web sites. Finally, additional cases describe entrepreneurs in action, which you can read for your own enjoyment and learning or which your professor may assign you to read and analyze.

BUSINESS PLANS

As you know from reading earlier chapters in this book, the business plan is a critical piece of the puzzle for successful entrepreneurial ventures. Often, the process of preparing an initial business plan for a new start-up venture—or even a business plan for a venture that's already up and running—takes the entrepreneur on a voyage through unknown territory. However, this process of creating a useful and effective business plan helps an entrepreneur focus on producing results, which is what the pursuit of entrepreneurship boils down to. "A business plan is worth the results it creates."[2]

One thing that may help you in your process of creating a useful and effective business plan is studying sample business plans for ideas that might work for you. Rather than including a finite number (and extremely limited number because of space considerations) of sample business plans here in the book, we're going to steer you to a Web site that's a treasure trove of business plans. The Web site address is **www.bplans.com**. When you get to the home page, you'll find several options. You can simply browse through dozens of sample business plans for ideas, or you can actually use some of the simple interactive tools there. (Please note that other Web sites have business plan information, and we'll describe these in the third section of the Killer Apps Appendix. We highlight this particular Web site because we've found it to be a good one for sample business plans.)

Once you've browsed through the sample plans, it's time to develop your own business plan. If your textbook has been packaged with the Business Plan Pro software, you can use this step-by-step guide to write a winning business plan. The software follows the sequence of a business plan as shown next.[3]

1.0　Executive Summary
 1.1　Objectives
 1.2　Mission
 1.3　Keys to Success
2.0　Company Summary
 2.1　Company Ownership
 2.2　Company History or Start-Up Plan
 2.3　Company Locations and Facilities
3.0　Products (or services, or both)
 3.1　Product (or service, or both) Description
 3.2　Competitive Description
 3.3　Sales Literature
 3.4　Sourcing
 3.5　Technology
 3.6　Future Products
4.0　Market Analysis Summary
 4.1　Market Segmentation
 4.2　Target Market Segment Strategy
  4.2.1　Market Needs
  4.2.2　Market Trends
  4.2.3　Market Growth
 4.3　Industry Analysis
  4.3.1　Industry Participants
  4.3.2　Distribution Patterns
  4.3.3　Factors of Competition
  4.3.4　Main Competitors

Keep in mind that this is just one approach for a business plan. If certain sections don't meet the needs of your particular entrepreneurial venture, then don't use those. If there is other information that you think is critical to the description of your business, then include that. The sample outline is intended simply to provide a general approach to creating a business plan.

Remember that the business plan is an essential tool for the entrepreneur. Yes, you can probably launch an entrepreneurial venture without one. But, why would you want to?

E-BUSINESS

The business environment entrepreneurs find themselves in today is so exciting *and* challenging. This changed (and changing) business environment has been characterized as the "digital economy," which simply refers to the availability of digitized information anywhere and at any time. This availability of information and a person's ability to interact easily with this information is changing the way business is conducted, both inside and outside organizations. For instance, just look at the way the online (digital) world has changed the way you are receiving an education. You can log on to the Web any time of the day or night to research topics of interest, buy your textbooks, e-mail your professor with questions, study for a test using an interactive study guide (see, for example, **www.prenhall.com/coulter**), or chat with other students thousands of miles away. In fact, some of you may have taken online classes, which never met within the physical and temporal confines of a classroom. The most obvious (and well-publicized) evidence we see of this changed business environment is in e-commerce applications. Practically every advertisement (both print and broadcast media) provides a Web site address. You never used to see this. Now it seems every company has a Web site address. Some of those Web sites are incredibly effective at strengthening the connection with customers. Others leave much to be desired. However effective or ineffective their Web sites may be, few companies or industries are immune to the push of **e-commerce (electronic commerce)**, which we defined in Chapter 2 as business transactions that take place online. In fact, many entrepreneurial ventures have been launched to seize emerging opportunities in e-commerce. (Remember the story of Amazon.com described in the chapter-opening case in Chapter 2?) However, e-commerce is just the beginning of the changed environment entrepreneurs are going to experience. What we're seeing now is a whole evolution—maybe even revolution—in the way an organization does business. This metamorphosis is called **e-business**, which is defined as a complex fusion of business processes, enterprise applications, and organizational structure necessary to create a high-performance business.[4] Successful entrepreneurial organizations of the twenty-first century are going to have to understand e-business and all its aspects. In this section of the Killer Apps Appendix, we're going to provide a bulleted list of the key points about e-business and a list of information sources you might want to look at. This is by no means intended to be a comprehensive overview of this area. In fact, what we know about e-business is evolving and changing even as this material is being written. One thing is for certain, though: The environment entrepreneurs do business in will never be the same. Keep finding out all you can about how it's changing. Study the examples of successful entrepreneurial organizations. Learn from their successes *and* their mistakes. In fact, one day maybe your entrepreneurial venture will become one of those businesses that everyone looks to as a shining example of success in this e-business world.

E-Business Essentials

e·biz

- The old rules for being a successful organization in business (economies of scale, scope or depth of products offered, efficiency of operations, market share, and vertical integration) are no longer sufficient.
- The new rules of e-business will require a new business design and new organizational capabilities.
- The challenge for entrepreneurs is bridging the gap between the "physical" and the "digital" worlds.
- In order to be successful, these new business designs must efficiently and effectively integrate the business's functions, technologies, and processes.
- Customer needs and the ability to satisfy those needs are at the core of a successful e-business model.
- Building customer relationships and connections is an important capability known as customer relationship management.

- Becoming customer focused doesn't simply mean improving customer service. It means having consistent, dependable, and convenient interactions with customers in every single encounter—physical and virtual.

- Successful e-business companies have focused on only one of three possible e-business designs. They choose service excellence, operational excellence, or continuous innovation excellence.

- The choice of e-business design is dictated by the customers: what they value and what they care about.

- Technology must be embedded in an effective e-business design. Technology is not the end, but the means to an end.

- Software applications used by successful e-businesses must be cross-functional and integrated.

- Creating this "applications architecture" is an ongoing process of integration encompassing the business's entire operating base.

- Pulling off this e-business design (or redesign) isn't easy. It's been described as changing the tires on a car that's going 70 mph.

- Formulating an e-business strategy involves the following: *knowledge building*, which helps an organization understand what the customer is looking for and where the industry is going; *capability evaluation*, which defines the existing business and identifies what capabilities it has today and what capabilities it needs for tomorrow; and *e-business design*, which asks what products, services, or experiences a business needs to provide to take advantage of digital capabilities.

- The e-business strategy must be turned into action by creating an overview (blueprint) of your overall goals, establishing priorities, planning and executing projects, and communicating with all relevant constituencies.

For More Information on E-Business and the Changing Business Environment

Amor, Daniel, *The E-business (R)evolution* (Upper Saddle River, NJ: Prentice Hall PTR, 2000).

Cortada, James W., and Thomas S. Hargraves, *Into the Networked Age* (New York: Oxford University Press, 1999).

Kalakota, Ravi, and Marcia Robinson, *e-Business: Roadmap for Success* (Reading, MA: Addison-Wesley, 1999).

Kelly, Kevin, *New Rules for the New Economy* (New York: Penguin Putnam, 1998).

Siebel, Thomas M., and Pat House, *Cyber Rules: Strategies for Excelling at E-Business* (New York: Doubleday, 1999).

Tapscott, Don, Alex Lowy, and David Ticoll, *Blueprint to the Digital Economy: Creating Wealth in the Era of E-Business* (New York: McGraw-Hill, 1998).

WEB SITES FOR ENTREPRENEURS

AllBusiness.com—Solutions for Growing Businesses
www.allbusiness.com/homepage/index.asp

AllBusiness.com leverages the power of the Internet to be your single source for critical business solutions and expertise. AllBusiness.com features a business, finance, and entrepreneur center as well as a marketplace section. The business center offers tools and services to solve real-world business problems. The finance center offers innovative solutions and advice for your financial needs. The entrepreneur center gives insights, expertise, and resources for building your business. Finally, you can find great deals on the business products you need most.

American Express Small Business Exchange
americanexpress.com/smallbusiness

The Small Business Exchange is a community for entrepreneurs. It offers information and resources on buying or selling a business, expanding internationally, finding more customers, government contracting, law and insurance, managing clients and customers, and online marketing. The site provides travel services, savings and discounts, and a business-to-business directory. Finally, the Small Business Exchange provides news, expert advice, and interactive tools.

The Benchmarking Exchange and Best Practices Homepage
www.benchnet.com/

The Benchmarking Exchange (TBE) is a very comprehensive and user-friendly electronic communication and information system designed specifically for use by individuals and organizations involved in Benchmarking and Process Improvement. TBE provides users with a comprehensive, centralized and specialized forum for all phases of benchmarking. The site also provides best practice surveys in progress relating to topics such as contract labor, supplier and material management, team-based improvement, organizational chance, facility management, and order fulfillment.

Bloomberg Financial Markets—Entrepreneur Network
www.bloomberg.com

Bloomberg.com provides resources for small businesses including small-cap news, a small business feature story, a calendar of events, interview archives, e-commerce resources, products and services, and feedback. The site provides up-to-date interest rates and mortgage rates as well as a tip of the month. Finally, Bloomberg.com provides stock quotes and an audio commentary that allows users to hear from experts.

Bottom Up: The magazine for the high-tech start-up—Home Page
www.bottom-up.com/

Bottom-up.com provides links to a compensation center, a business plan center, research updates, a public relations resource center, and news and views from the business of high tech (called Short Circuits). In addition, Bottom Up gives new technology entrepreneurs a chance to meet investors through a program called The Pitch.

Bplans.com—The Business Planning Resource Center
www.bplans.com/

Bplans.com offers resources on creating business plans, such as the Plan Wizard, which helps users find business-relevant sample plans. The site also provides features such as the business planning resource center and advice for preparing to submit a final business plan. Finally, Bplans.com gives information on international business and helps users find local small business development centers and planning consultants.

The Business Forum Online®
www.businessforum.com/

The Business Forum Online is an independent informational and professional resource center for the owners–managers of the emerging business and entrepreneurs. An Internal Index offers a compendium of two years of weekly columns addressing a broad range of issues and opportunities of immediate and practical interest to the owner–manager of the emerging business and entrepreneurs. An External Index offers wide-ranging links to approximately 100 important informational and professional resources throughout the world to meet the needs of the emerging business and entrepreneurs.

Business Resource Center—Business Plans, Marketing, Financing, News, and Sample Contracts for Small Business
www.morebusiness.com/

The Business Resource Center provides information regarding start-up, running your business, news, and business plans. It provides featured articles and templates as well as a marketplace. Users can register to receive a free e-mail newsletter that provides business and product news, tips, articles, and other information to help manage a business.

Business Week Frontier Online: The Small Business Resource
www.businessweek.com/smallbiz/

Business Week Frontier Online keeps entrepreneurs up-to-date with recent stories and a news center. The site provides financial, technological, market research, and personal business resources. Business Week also provides services for travel, free e-mail, and a job bank. Finally, the site has a toolbox of free expert help, a contact search, and free archives.

CACI Free Samples ZIP Code Data
demographics.caci.com/Free/data.html

CACI Marketing Systems gives users the opportunity to find demographic data for any zip code. This site also provides the national averages for the statistics requested. Finally, CACI includes graphs of the data and provides information about regional marketing segmentation.

CEO Express: The Executive's Internet
www.ceoexpress.com/

CEO Express provides links to sites regarding daily news and information, business research, Internet information, office tools, travel, and leisure activities. The site also provides a bookshop, a career center, and feedback. Members can customize CEO Express and suggest additional links. Finally, CEO Express provides information on the *Fortune* 500, the Global 500, and the Web 100 companies.

CIA—The World Factbook 1999
www.odci.gov/cia/publications/factbook/

The *CIA World Factbook* provides country-specific information that is useful for international business owners. Information about geography, people, government, economy, communications, transportation, military, and transnational issues is provided for each country. The *Factbook* also provides a reference map as well as notes and definitions.

ClickCity—2,000,000+ links to city and state resources!
clickcity.com/index2.htm

ClickCity allows users to find information about cities with Web sites and state resources. This site provides topical information about each city and state. It also provides a search engine for the International Chamber of Commerce. Finally, ClickCity provides over 2,000 news sites covering a comprehensive list of topics.

County Business Patterns
www.census.gov/epcd/cbp/view/cbpview.html

County Business Patterns is an annual series that provides subnational economic data by industry. The series is useful for studying the economic activity of small areas; for analyzing economic changes over time; and as a benchmark for statistical series, surveys, and databases between economic censuses. The series serves various business uses such as analyzing market potential, measuring the effectiveness of sales and advertising programs, setting sales quotas, and developing budgets. The data are also used by government agencies for administration and planning.

Cross Cultural Communication for Business and Industry
www.bena.com/ewinters/xculture.html

Cross Cultural Communication for Business and Industry provides practical tips for those who develop material, services, or products for translation or export. This site is produced as a service for the international Internet community and covers topics such as culture and information, document design, technology, and infrastructure in target cultures, writing for translation, and internationalization of documentation and Internet communication.

Current Industrial Reports
www.census.gov/ftp/pub/cir/www/

The U.S. Census Bureau presents Current Industrial Reports concerning topics such as apparel, lumber production and mill stocks, paint and allied products, pharmaceutical preparations, internal combustion engines, computers and office, major household appliances, consumer electronics, and the aerospace industry as well as many others. The reports cover surveys, industry information, and related findings.

Current Population Survey
www.bls.census.gov/cps/datamain.htm

The Current Population Survey provides data related to topics such as displaced workers, job tenure and occupational mobility, school enrollment, race and ethnicity, voting and registration, food security, work schedules, computer ownership, and fertility and marital history. CPS also provides a basic monthly survey and an annual demographic survey.

Dow Jones Business Directory
bd.dowjones.com/

The Dow Jones Business Directory provides a guide to high-quality business Web sites. The Business Directory reviews business Web sites each week according to content, speed, navigation, and design. This site also provides links to resources on careers, companies in the Dow, financial markets, industries, law, personal finance, public records, and small businesses.

Employee Stock Ownership Plan (ESOP), Stock Options, the NCEO
www.nceo.org/

The National Center for Employee Ownership (NCEO) is a private, not-for-profit membership and research organization that serves as the leading source of accurate, unbiased information on employee stock ownership plans (ESOPs), broadly granted employee stock options, and employee participation programs. Users can read articles in the library and the columns by leading experts, sample NCEO publications, and become involved in workshops, conferences, and other events. Finally, NCEO provides interactive services.

Entrepreneur *Magazine—The Online Small Business Authority*
www.entrepreneurmag.com/

Entrepreneur magazine provides recent feature articles about small business topics. The site also provides small business tools such as an Internet print shop, trade show information, a software library, and free business forms. *Entrepreneur* magazine also links to entrepreneur's databases such as the Franchise 500, Business Opportunity 500, and Top International Franchises. Finally, this site has a small business search engine and a marketplace.

Entrepreneurial Edge Online—Information for Small Business Owners and Emerging Growth Entrepreneurs
www.edgeonline.com/

Entrepreneurial Edge resources include tutorials, a bookstore, electronic documents, researched Internet sites, and an e-mail subscription newsletter. Finally, this site provides an interactive forum for users to compare processes and interact with financial management models. Entrepreneurial Edge is associated with the Edward Lowe Foundation (**www.lowe.org/**), which creates peer-learning environments for entrepreneurs and provides access to information, solutions, and resources to grow a company.

The Entrepreneur's Mind
www.benlore.com/index2.html

The Entrepreneur's Mind (EM) is a Web resource that presents an array of real-life stories and advice from successful entrepreneurs and industry experts on the many different facets of entrepreneurship and emerging business. Each story in the EM presents in-depth profiles of entrepreneurs and how they grew their successful companies, as well as interviews with industry professionals discussing an aspect of starting and growing a new business venture.

Entrepreneurship Resources
www.prenhall.com/scarbzim/html/resource.html

Small Business and Entrepreneurship Resources offers information on topics such as advertising, cash flow, ethics and social responsibility, global business and exporting, human resources management, market research, purchasing and inventory control, strategic management, and technology. This site also provides a business plan evaluation scale, case solutions, and a small business management audit.

EntreWorld: Resources for Entrepreneurs
www.EntreWorld.org/

EntreWorld is an online information resource for entrepreneurs and supporters of entrepreneurship. EntreWorld provides a solution to information overload on the Web by providing highly filtered information coded by stage of business development. This site provides resources for each stage of a small business: start-up, growth, and entrepreneurship support.

EPI DataZone
www.epinet.org/datazone/

The Economic Policy Institute has a Quarterly Wage and Employment Series, which is a current analysis of wage and employment trends in the Current Population Survey. The site also provides national, state, and regional data on historical employment and earnings. DataZone spreadsheet tables can be downloaded and online supplemental tables are provided.

eWeb
www.slu.edu/eweb/

eWeb's mission is to provide support to students and faculty interested in starting, running, and growing businesses—whether you call them entrepreneurial firms, SMEs, small businesses, family businesses, home-based businesses, or new businesses. Its target markets are entrepreneurs, potential entrepreneurs (including students), and those who consult to or train or educate entrepreneurs. eWeb offers book recommendations, business plan help, how-to guides, a list of entrepreneurial centers, a list of core journals of entrepreneurship, and Ph.D. education resources.

fambiz.com
www.fambiz.com/

fambiz.com, formerly known as the NetMarquee Family Business NetCenter, is the Internet's leading Web site for executives and owners of family-controlled companies. fambiz specializes in creating content-driven Internet marketing campaigns for major companies. It crafts custom Internet content programs that enable our clients to reach targeted audiences with Web-based and e-mail initiatives.

Federation of International Trade Associations
www.fita.org/

The Federation of International Trade Associations (FITA), founded in 1984, fosters international trade by strengthening the role of local, regional, and national associations throughout North America that have an international mission. This site has an index of

Web resources, a global bookstore and publications center, a trade leads hub, a job bank, an international marketing research library, and a directory of export management companies.

FedWorld Information Network Home Page
www.fedworld.gov/

In 1992, FedWorld was established by the National Technical Information Service (NTIS), an agency of the U.S. Department of Commerce, to serve as the online locator service for a comprehensive inventory of information disseminated by the federal government. FedWorld offers a comprehensive central access point for searching, locating, ordering and acquiring government and business information.

Forbes Small Business Center
www.forbes.com/tool/smallbus/

The Forbes Small Business Center provides information on entrepreneurship topics such as venture capital, start-ups, growing pains, and current articles. The site also provides a database of the *Forbes* 200 best small companies and forums where users can go one-on-one with Forbes's editors. Finally, the Small Business Center has a search engine and stock quotes.

Forum for Women Entrepreneurs
www.fwe.org

The Forum for Women Entrepreneurs (FWE) is the leading entrepreneurial forum for women in technology and life science start-ups. FWE offers programs and services that accelerate women entrepreneurs' ability to launch and build world-class companies. Founded in 1993, FWE has offices in the Bay Area and Seattle, and membership numbers over 650. FWE provides women-founded businesses with timely information through a strong online community; access to top-tier funding sources; and connections to a high-caliber community of entrepreneurs, investors, and service providers—resources they need to bridge the venture capital funding gap.

The Foundation for Enterprise Development
www.fed.org/

The Foundation for Enterprise Development is a not-for-profit organization that provides leading-edge equity compensation and employee ownership strategies to thousands of entrepreneurs and key executives worldwide who are making critical decisions to improve their companies' bottom lines. This site provides a Virtual Interactive Consultant, an Interactive Dilution Model, and an Employee Ownership Quiz. Finally, the Foundation for Enterprise Development has a selection of publications in an Employee Ownership Bookstore and a listing of job opportunities.

FRED®—Economic Research
www.stls.frb.org/fred/index.html

FRED® (Federal Reserve Economic Data) provides historical U.S. economic and financial data, including daily U.S. interest rates, monetary and business indicators, exchange rates, balance-of-payments and regional economic data for Arkansas, Illinois, Indiana, Kentucky, Mississippi, Missouri, and Tennessee. Database categories include business–

fiscal data, monthly commercial banking data, monthly monetary data, gross domestic product and components, monthly interest rates, and monthly reserves data.

Garage.com—we start up start-ups
www.garage.com/

Garage.com helps entrepreneurs and investors build great businesses. The site gives entrepreneurs assistance in obtaining seed level financing so that the entrepreneur can focus more time building his or her business. Garage.com also provides members with expert advice, research and reference materials, and topical forums. Finally, Garage.com works with investors to identify and provide prescreened investment opportunities that match the investor's identified interests.

GovCon
www.govcon.com/

GovCon is an online community for government contractors. The site provides current business opportunities and profiled contractors of the week. GovCon has a small business resource center and a consultant procurement service. Finally, the site provides free services such as teaming opportunities, SIC codes, and per diem rates as well as a subscription service.

IBM e-business
www.ibm.com/e-business/

IBM focuses on business intelligence and offers ways to learn more about business intelligence, order a free CD-ROM, and contact a business intelligence specialist. IBM also provides information on supply chain management and customer relationship management. Finally, users can look at case studies and browse for products and services on this site.

IBM Intellectual Property Network
www.patents.ibm.com/

The Intellectual Property Network (IPN) lets you search and view patent documents from the United States, Europe, and Japan as well as patent applications published by the World Intellectual Property Organization (WIPO). This site offers a comprehensive search for patents and provides a gallery of obscure patents for a taste of the strange and wonderful.

Idea Café: The Small Business Channel
www.ideacafe.com/

The Idea Café provides a fun approach to serious business. The site provides tech review for small business, a financial focus of the day, a bookstore, a venture capital forum, and a Biz Idea of the Day. The Idea Café serves critical information fast, fresh, friendly, and for real.

Inc. Online—The Web Site for Growing Companies
www.inc.com/

Inc. Online is the Web Site for Growing Companies. A full-service electronic consultant to people starting and running businesses, Inc. Online goes beyond *Inc.* to present resources and interactive networking opportunities available only on the Web. Full contents of the 14 annual issues of *Inc.* and 4 annual issues of *Inc. Technology* are posted at

Inc. Online when the magazines go on newsstands. *Inc.* also provides a broad array of books, videos, software, conferences, seminars, consulting services, and awards programs.

International Business Guide: Worldclass Supersite
web.idirect.com/~tiger/supersit.htm
The Worldclass Supersite provides instant free access and step-by-step commentary for 1,025 top business sites from 95 countries, chosen based on usefulness to world commerce, timeliness, ease of use, and presentation. The Supersite has seven sections: reference, news, learning, money, trade, networking, and world beaters. The world beaters section examines how globally active companies of various sizes, sectors, and countries of origin are using the Internet to promote themselves internationally.

International Entrepreneur Association: Business Resource Center
www.theiea.com/
International Entrepreneur Association is an organization that provides useful tools and promotes the creativity necessary to start and operate any successful organization or venture. Membership benefits include business plans, free business software, business resources, assistance programs, e-mail publications, and a business chat room.

A Global World—Exclusive Travel and Holiday Information
www.aglobalworld.com
A Global World provides international information concerning global weather, time zones, global distances, dialing codes, power voltage, global holidays, and a global traveler report. The Global Reporter covers topics such as how to dial between foreign countries, driving abroad and what to expect, clearing customs, and how to send a letter overseas.

Krislyn's Strictly Business Sites
www.krislyn.com/sites.html
Krislyn's Strictly Business Sites came on the Web in December 1995. Its aim is to provide a broad list of business sources in a wide variety of areas. Many sites link to Krislyn's Strictly Business Sites, including a number of educational institutions that include it in a list of sources for business and other courses. The majority of listed sites are noncommercial and have a high degree of intrinsic content. The commercial sites listed are assessed to have a particular benefit to visitors. Site subjects including accounting, banking, business schools, multilevel marketing, philanthropy, public relations, retail, small business–entrepreneurial, and much more.

Larry Chase's Web Digest for Marketers
wdfm.com/
Think of WDFM as a biweekly bulletin or executive summary that reports on the latest marketing sites to come onto the Web. Its editors in the United States and Europe spend many hours each week combing the newsletters, and trade journals for new or substantially improved marketing sites in categories such as financial, retail, travel, direct response, *Fortune* 500 companies, Internet marketing tools, to name a few. When you view WDFM online, you can point and click to each site mentioned.

Microsoft Business Advantage
www.microsoft.com/

Microsoft Smallbiz (now part of Microsoft Business Advantage) offers technology guides to getting work done, taking business online, and networking PCs. It offers a buyer's guide to Microsoft software, hardware smart buys, finding a tech consultant, and finding a custom-built PC. This site also provides smallbiz talk with links to success stories, smallbiz resources, and expert advice.

Mind Tools—Planning
www.mindtools.com/planpage.html

Mind Tools Bookstores offers articles about planning skills and how to plan complex tasks. Subjects include reasons to plan, the planning cycle, managing change, overcoming resistance to change, completing a plan, and a summary of planning. The site offers two planning templates: a military–expedition planning template and a business–marketing plan template.

The National Association for Female Executives (NAFE)
www.nafe.com/

The National Association for Female Executives (NAFE), the largest women's professional association and the largest women business owners organization in the country, provides resources and services—through education, networking, and public advocacy—to empower its members to achieve career success and financial security. Member benefits include information about insurance, lifestyle, money, online services, travel, and books.

National Women's Business Council
www.nwbc.gov

The members of the National Women's Business Council are prominent women business owners and leaders of women's business organizations. The mission of the council is to promote bold initiatives, policies, and programs designed to support women's business enterprises at all stages of development in the public and private sector marketplaces. Projects and reports include Expanding Business Opportunities, Changing the Face of the Economy, Women Succeed in Business: Success Guide for Women Entrepreneurs, and Growing Women's Businesses.

New Venture Café
www.mgt.smsu.edu/nvcafe

Where entrepreneurs spend their nights discussing their dreams. A site designed by Professor Charles Boyd of Southwest Missouri State University for his entrepreneurship class. It includes Appetizers (entrepreneurship sites, funding sources, leasing services, Hitchhiker's Guide to Capital), Salads (soup—hot topic—of the day, ethics booth, legal corner, your online business, and funding articles), Entrées (chapter notes, outlines, and PowerPoint presentations), Desserts (music clips, software downloads, Jack Stack's booth), Live Start-up (follows the launch of a new coffee house chain), and Café Radio (audio clips of entrepreneurial issues from NPR and other sources).

Online Women's Business Center
www.onlinewbc.org/entry.html

By combining the expertise and resources of the U.S. Small Business Administration with several major corporate sponsors, this Web site will provide you with the very best information for running your business. A "one-stop shopping" site, where you can find information about everything from how to start your business to how to operate in the global market place. Information from more than 60 SBA-affiliated Women's Business Centers across the country to bring you the most current information on business principles and practices, management techniques, mentoring, networking, and business resources.

Patent and Trademark Office Home Page
www.uspto.gov/

The Patent and Trademark Office (PTO) provides information on patents and trademarks as well as databases, inventor resources, kids' pages, download forms, PTO fees, FTP data, public affairs, statistics, acquisitions, jobs at PTO, and document formats. The site is constantly updated to provide "New on the PTO Site" items and related current events.

SBA Office of Advocacy—Economic Statistics and Research on Small Business
www.sba.gov/ADVO/stats/

The Office of Advocacy works to reduce the burdens that federal policies impose on small firms and to maximize the benefits small businesses receive from the government. This site provides links to the Office of Economic Research, the Office of Interagency Affairs, the Office of Public Liaison, and regional advocates. General small business reports and data include the small business answer card, state small business economic profiles, small business economic indicators, and SBA-sponsored research.

SBA Small Business Administration Home Page
www.sbaonline.sba.gov/

The U.S. Small Business Administration, established in 1953, provides financial, technical, and management assistance to help Americans start, run, and grow their businesses. With a portfolio of business loans, loan guarantees, and disaster loans worth more than $45 billion, SBA is the nation's largest single financial backer of small businesses. Last year, the SBA offered management and technical assistance to more than 1 million small business owners. The SBA also plays a major role in the government's disaster relief efforts by making low-interest recovery loans to both homeowners and businesses.

SBDC Business Information Resources
www.pasbdc.org/Pages/busindex.html

The Internet Business Resources section contains links that connect to Web sites useful for small businesses. Included are sites about running a small business and those useful for conducting business research. This site contains links for reference, entrepreneurship and management, company directories, commercial database vendors, federal government, organizations and associations, and international business.

SBFocus.com—The Small Business Focused Search Engine
www.smallbizplanet.com/index.html

The SmallBiz Planet.com site has the best sources on the Internet for the entrepreneur. The in-depth search engine indexes magazines, business basics, and award winners on a variety of topics. Topics include accounting, computers, finance, franchising, home business, human resources, information systems, international, Internet, insurance, legal, management, marketing, sales, start-up, and technology.

Small & Home Based Business Links
www.bizoffice.com/

Small & Home Based Business Links offers links to topics such as reference, financing, services, news, opportunities, marketing, franchises, and multilevel marketing. Additional links include a library, a business forum, a bookstore, and business forms. This site offers advice on growing a business along with services to market your site, take credit cards, send press releases, and get credit by applying online.

Small Business 2000
www.sb2000.com/

There are more than 250 public television stations in the United States. You can find *Small Business 2000* on more than 200 stations and in all the major population markets. The show profiles a successful business owner each week. This site provides television show schedules, events and speakers, a money exchange index, and an opportunity to register as a member. Finally, *Small Business 2000* outlines the eight steps it takes to start, run, and grow a business.

Small Business Advancement National Center
www.sbaer.uca.edu/

Instant, up-to-the-moment electronic small business information is provided to small business clients through the Small Business Advancement Electronic Resource. This connection electronically links small business owners; entrepreneurs; foundations; educational institutions; associations; international partners; and local, state, and federal governments. The World Wide Web site offers information geared toward helping already established businesses as well as those just beginning. At the present time, the electronic resource is servicing the United States and its protectorates as well as over 70 nations worldwide. Examples of information provided include industry profiles, business plans, research articles, international and domestic contact databases, and loan information.

Small Business Innovation Research Awards
fundedresearch.cos.com/SBIR

Many U.S. government agencies award Small Business Innovation Research Awards (SBIR) to small U.S. companies in an effort to promote their growth and development. In effect, the SBIR program is the federal government's venture capital investment program. The SBIR program is administered by the U.S. Small Business Administration (SBA), which was created by Congress in 1953 to help America's entrepreneurs form successful small enterprises. Today, SBA's program offices in every state offer financing, training, and advocacy for small firms. These programs are delivered by SBA offices in every state, the

District of Columbia, the Virgin Islands, and Puerto Rico. In addition, the SBA works with thousands of lending, educational, and training institutions nationwide.

SmallOffice.com
www.smalloffice.com/

SmallOffice.com offers articles, surveys, entrepreneurial quizzes, and information on topics such as telecommuting, finance and taxes, hardware, software, communications, and business services. Minisites include telephony, tax, home networking, office design, credit, and a link to small business associations. In addition, SmallOffice.com provides a free newsletter.

Smart Business Supersite
www.smartbiz.com/

SBS was designed with one clear mission: to be the single most important source of high-quality, "how-to" business information on the Internet. Its name, Smart Business Supersite, contains three words, each denoting a cornerstone of its philosophy: (1) *Smart*. The how-to information and resources will help you make the best possible business decisions and save you time and money. They will help you run your business smart. (2) *Business*. Whether your business is a start-up or has been around for 50 years, SBS has information of value to you. You'll find articles, checklists, reports, profiles of books, software, newsletters, magazines, and much more, all neatly categorized. (3) *Supersite*. In the same way that Staples and Home Depot have the largest possible selections under one roof, SBS strives to have the largest possible collection of business information under one cyberroof: thousands of articles, hundreds of detailed profiles, special services, ongoing events, and vendors for every possible business service.

State and Metropolitan Area Data Book—5th Edition
www.census.gov/statab/www/smadb.html

The Data Book contains a collection of statistics on social and economic conditions in the United States at the state and metropolitan area levels. Selected data for component counties and central cities of metropolitan areas are also included. The Data Book is also your guide to sources of other data from the Census Bureau, other federal agencies, and private organizations.

Strategic Business Planning, Co.
www.bizplan.com/bplan.html

The mission of the Strategic Business Planning Company is to help companies become more efficient and effective by carefully planning their business and to systematically (re)evaluate the environment in which they operate. The Strategic Business Planning Company offers U.S. domestic plans and studies and international plans and studies. The site provides information about business plans, plan types, international services, and financing.

Surveys of Minority-Owned and Women-Owned Business Enterprises
www.census.gov/csd/mwb/

The U.S. Census Bureau devotes this page to surveys of minority-owned and women-owned business enterprises. These surveys are now underway at the U.S. Census Bureau.

Every five years, these surveys collect information on business owners' race, ethnicity, and gender. The site provides the latest results, related surveys such as characteristics of business owners, and press releases.

TSCentral
www.tscentral.com/
The TSCentral Web site represents the next generation of trade and professional event resources. Each month, thousands of visitors come to find new ways to add value to their trade or professional event participation. With over millions of page-views per month, tscentral.com is one of the most popular events-related sites on the Internet. In addition to free, comprehensive event data, detailed venue information, and an event industry suppliers database, visitors benefit from our value-added products and services such as our event webcasting and online travel centers. TSCentral also specializes in delivering a wide range of management products and services for event organizers, sponsors, and exhibitors including: Web advertising and promotion, online event registration, floor-plan management, event representation, direct marketing, webcast production, premium incentives, and Web site development.

U.S. Business Advisor
www.business.gov/
The U.S. Business Advisor exists to provide business with one-stop access to federal government information, services, and transactions. Their goal is to make the relationship between business and government more productive. Links on this site include business development, financial assistance, taxes, laws and regulations, international trade, workplace issues, buying and selling, and agencies and gateways.

U.S. Census Bureau
www.census.gov/
The U.S. Census Bureau is part of the U.S. Department of Commerce, and it provides timely information about people, business, geography, news, and other special topics. Other links on this site include a search engine, a catalog, access tools, job opportunities, related sites, and publications.

U.S. Economic Indicators
www.census.gov/ftp/pub/indicator/www/indicat.html
The U.S. Census Bureau provides highlights from the latest economic indicators including U.S. International trade in goods and services, advance monthly retail sales, housing starts, manufacturing and trade inventories and sales, and monthly wholesale trade. Other links on this site provide information about the advance report on durable goods, manufacturers' shipments and orders, and indicators such as manufacturers' shipments, inventories, and orders.

U.S. Treasury Department
www.treas.gov
The U.S. Treasury site provides general information and latest news regarding the Treasury Department. The main menu links to a business services page that offers infor-

mation about the office of business and public liaison, the office of procurement, registering a business, a simplified tax and wage reporting system, and small business assistance.

Working For A Loser!!!!
www.myboss.com/

Working For A Loser!!!! is a book compiled from three years of crazy submissions and endless reader requests. This site lets users read book excerpts and view the table of contents. In addition, this site provides links to online bookstores that carry the book. Finally, it has a weekly compilation of crazy quotes and insane anecdotes submitted by working people from around the world.

YEO—Young Entrepreneurs' Organization
www.yeo.org/

As a global, not-for-profit educational organization for young entrepreneurs, the Young Entrepreneurs' Organization (YEO) strives to help its members build upon their successes through an array of educational and networking opportunities. With more than 3,000 members in chapters around the world, YEO provides its members access to a dynamic network of peers on an international level. Links include the YEO strategic alliance, YEO graduate organizations, and entrepreneur resources.

ENTREPRENEURSHIP IN ACTION CASES

CASE #1: Stringing Together Success

For over a century and a half, the Martin Guitar Company (**www.cfmartin.com**) of Nazareth, Pennsylvania, has been producing acoustic instruments considered to be among the finest in the world. Like a Steinway grand piano, a Buffet clarinet, or a Baccarat crystal vase, a Martin guitar—which can cost more than $10,000—is among the best that money can buy. Annual company revenues for 1999 were close to $58 million. This family business has managed to defy the odds and survive six generations of family members even through to the current CEO, Chris Martin, who continues to be committed to the guitar maker's craft. Few companies, much less a family business, have had the staying power of Martin Guitars.

What's the key to the company's success? It boils down to one word—quality.

Even through changes in product design, distribution systems, and manufacturing methods, Martin Guitars has remained committed to making quality products. The company's steadfast adherence to high standards of musical excellence has led to a loyal customer base who demands, and expects, quality. Part of that quality approach encompasses a long-standing ecological policy. The company has embraced the judicious and responsible use of traditional natural materials and encouraged the introduction of sustainable-yield, alternative wood species for manufacturing its guitars. Through customer research, Martin introduced guitars that utilized structurally sound woods with natural cosmetic characteristics that were once considered unacceptable. In addition, Martin follows the directives of CITES (**www.cites.org**), the Convention on International Trade in Endangered Species of Wild Fauna and Flora. The company has also begun exploring the viability of using Forest Stewardship Council (FSC) certifiable wood sources and supports the introduction of FSC guitar models as soon as it's commercially feasible. Although it has a long and colorful history, the company also is firmly committed to the future. It's an interesting combination of old and new.

Speaking of new, Christian Martin IV, the great-great-great-grandson of the company's founder and the current CEO, is taking Martin Guitars in a new direction. He made a difficult decision to start selling guitars in the under-$800 market segment. This segment accounts for 65 percent of the acoustic guitar industry's sales. Martin's DXM model was introduced in 1998. Although it doesn't look, smell, or feel like the company's pricier models, customers claim it has a better sound than most other instruments in that price range. But, what kind of risk is it to take a company that's dependent on a revered luxury item and to start selling a low-end product? Will those longtime customers be alienated? Martin justifies his decision by saying that, "If Martin just worships its past without trying anything new, there won't be a Martin left to worship." Chris knows that he's going to have to fight to keep his loyal customers playing the expensive models. He's doing this by introducing a series of replicas of the company's flagship product, the Dreadnought guitar, produced before World War II. He's also collaborating on a series of special-edition guitars with Roger McGuinn of the Byrds and Dave Matthews. Chris has also started a custom shop for the guitarist who wants custom features such as his or her name inlaid in mother-of-pearl on the fingerboard.

So although the company is spreading its wings in new directions, there's still the commitment to making the finest products. The main challenge appears to be a succession one. Chris and his wife have no children, which makes it likely that Martin Guitars will eventually be managed by an outsider for the first time in its history.

Discussion Questions

1. What do you think has contributed to the success of this family business? (Check out the company's Web site for additional information.)

2. What do you think of CEO Chris Martin's direction for the company? What are the advantages? The drawbacks?

3. Do you think the succession issue at Martin is as big as it's being made out to be? Explain your position.

(*Sources:* S. Fitch, "Stringing Them Along," *Forbes,* July 26, 1999, pp. 90–91; information from company's Web site, **www.cfmartin.com**, January 16, 2000.)

CASE #2: S-U-C-C-E-S-S—That's the Way You Spell Success

The cheerleading industry is big business and getting bigger every year. With more than a million active participants, tens of millions of dollars in revenues, and nationwide television coverage, the spirit industry has evolved into a growth industry. Cheerleading is becoming more athletic, more competitive, and more expensive. The industry doesn't include just cheerleading squads. It now encompasses school dance teams, pom-pom squads, dance studio participants, and all-star cheerleading squads (called all-stars), who do not actually cheer for a team but exist only to compete. It's an extremely interesting market segment.

Cheerleading isn't just a sideline activity during fall and spring anymore. Many cheerleaders practice and attend camps and competitions year-round. Of course, you must have uniforms to look like a cheerleading squad. The camps, the apparel, the competitions—it all adds up to serious money for participants *and* for the companies supplying the participants.

The two biggest players in the cheer industry are Varsity Spirit Corporation (**www.varsity.com**) and National Spirit Group (**www.nationalspirit.com**). Both companies have capitalized on the cross-marketing opportunities. First, the cheerleaders come to summer camps. While at camp, the company's special events—that is, the regional and national competitions—are promoted. Then there's the clothing—camp shirts, shorts, hair ribbons, and so forth—and the other merchandise. We can't leave out the all-important uniform business. Although uniforms aren't actually sold at the camps, the company's sales representatives are there meeting with customers, making presentations, and taking orders.

Just like any good cheerleaders cheering for their teams, the two industry leaders claim to be the best, the leader, number one. There's no love lost between the two. Jeffrey G. Webb, the CEO of Varsity Spirit Corporation, based in Memphis, used to work for the National Spirit Group. He left National Spirit after two years' working there and formed Varsity Spirit in 1974, setting up summer camps in direct competition with his old employer. Then, in 1979, Webb started man-

ufacturing uniforms, the most lucrative segment of the cheer business because it accounts for about 60 percent of revenues. In 1981, Varsity began national competitions that continue to be televised on ESPN. National Spirit soon followed suit and developed national competitions that are shown on CBS, the USA Network, and Fox. Both Varsity and National Spirit are looking at moving into uniforms for other women's and some men's sports. Varsity took the first step when it signed a U.S. licensing agreement with Umbro Corporation, the British manufacturer of soccer uniforms. Under this agreement, for the next five years Varsity will manufacture and sell male and female soccer uniforms under the Umbro name to American school and league markets. Webb said he hoped to eventually use the same cross-marketing model of camps, competitions, and uniform sales in the soccer market as they had in the cheerleading market.

Discussion Questions

1. Of the two companies described, which do you think is the industry innovator? Explain your choice.

2. Now, check out the Web sites of both Varsity Spirit Corporation and National Spirit Group. Would your answer to #1 be the same? Explain.

3. A big fear of entrepreneurs is bringing someone into the business who learns the ins and outs, leaves, and starts his or her own venture in the same line of business. What might entrepreneurs do to lessen the likelihood of this occurring?

(*Sources:* E. Yellin, "School Spirit Inc.," *New York Times*, July 17, 1999, p. B1; and information from Web sites of Varsity Spirit Corporation, **www.varsity.com**, and National Spirit Group, **www. nationalspirit.com**, January 16, 2000.)

CASE #3: Internet Fever

Charly Alberti may seem an unlikely Internet entrepreneur. He's best known as the drummer of the Argentine rock band Soda Stereo. However, with the band's breakup in 1997, Alberti's new gig is the Internet. His entertainment-oriented Web site Cybrel Argentina (**www.cybrel.com**) is playing to a much larger potential audience than his former band could ever have packed into a stadium. At Cybrel, you can explore a variety of information from a well-designed, impressive, and energetic Web site.

As have others around the world, Latin Americans have taken to the Internet in droves. The lure of readily available information and communication have attracted millions online. However, getting to that information and communication isn't always easy. Poor dial-up connections and limited access are some of the challenges that Latin American Internet entrepreneurs are dealing with. Shopping online is another area where

Latin American consumers have been cautious. Analysts explain that credit cards (the most frequently used form of payment) are relatively new in this region. However, that isn't stopping people like Alberti. He feels it's just a matter of time before the electronic revolution firmly takes hold, and he wants to be positioned to take advantage of it.

Discussion Questions

1. What things would Charly Alberti have needed to do to get his new venture launched? Be as specific as possible.
2. What does Alberti need to do to be positioned to take advantage of the growth in the use of the Internet in Latin America? Be as specific as possible.
3. Log on to Cybrel's Web site. Describe and evaluate what's there.

(*Sources:* D. Stinson, "Internet Fever," *Latin Trade*, August 1998, pp. 61–64; and information from Cybrel's Web site, **www.cybrel.com**, January 16, 2000.)

CASE #4: Flying High?

Amy Nye Wolf's first "takeoff" could best be described as a crash landing. When she quit her job as a financial analyst for Goldman, Sachs, she started planning a new business—using freestanding kiosks to sell music CDs in airport terminals. She intended the business to be a music and portable entertainment retail outlet for customers on the fly. There were no competitors, relatively low overhead, and a captive audience. What more could an entrepreneur ask for? She convinced officials at New York's LaGuardia Airport to let her open a 150-square-foot kiosk. However, Wolf hadn't done her homework. Airport officials rejected her initial construction plan. It took

her a month to answer all their questions. Another mistake she made was not inquiring about regulations governing construction. Airport security had to inspect and approve all building materials, and as a result, her construction costs doubled and the project completion time was three months behind schedule. However, even after this first turbulent takeoff, the company's problems still continued. A construction problem at New York's Kennedy Airport delayed that location's opening by a month, resulting in more than $45,000 in lost revenues and adding $20,000 in costs to satisfy a design concern. Then, at Ronald Reagan National Airport in

Washington, DC, officials objected to her construction design. Although she protested the objections, she lost the protest and ended up having to spend an additional $60,000. But, Wolf continues on as she tries to make AltiTunes a successful business. AltiTunes (**www.altitunes.com**) currently operates 25 airport locations and has opened an outlet at its first train station, located in New York City's Grand Central Terminal.

Each AltiTunes location stocks over 1,000 different music titles. The typical inventory includes a variety of music ranging from pop to jazz, rap to gospel, country to classical. All major music categories are stocked with enough products to meet customer demand. In addition to music titles, AltiTunes also sells portable electronics (Walkman, Discman, Palm Pilot), music product accessories, books-on-tape, and Gameboy bases and cartridges. The electronic products are offered in a variety of price ranges to meet customers' needs. At each location, customers can select their music by using one of the EARports™, an interactive listening station. These individual stations are each sponsored by a record label or distributor, and equipped with headphones for listening. In addition, each location has a MUZE Station, an interactive computer database containing detailed information on over 350,000 pieces of published music that's updated monthly. It helps both customers and AltiTunes staff to identify a specific title or artist.

AltiTunes' five-year mission is to become the leading brand for small format, extraordinary-location, music and electronics retailing with an expanding network of domestic and international locations. Wolf plans on taking her company outside of airports and train stations to hospitals, hotels, and travel plazas. She definitely wants her businesses to fly high.

Discussion Questions

1. Evaluate Wolf's launching of her business, AltiTunes. What would you suggest that she might have done differently?

2. What growth challenges is AltiTunes going to face? How might it deal with these challenges?

3. Go to AltiTunes Web site and click on Press Releases. Read the press releases there. What impression do you get from reading these?

(*Sources:* C. Mastony, "Turbulent Takeoff," *Forbes,* May 3, 1999, p. 94; and information from AltiTunes Web site, **www.altitunes.com**, January 16, 2000.)

CASE #5: Worn to Be Wild

Langlitz Leathers (**www.langlitz.com**) is well known by motorcycling enthusiasts. However, the company's famed leather garments are also worn by rock stars and investment bankers who may ride motorcycles or who just want to look like they do. For more than 50 years, Langlitz jackets have given motorcycle riders a nice fit and a sensation of invulnerability mixed with danger. The jackets aren't cheap. Prices begin at $650 and go on up from there. Yet, even at those prices, the company's products are considered good buys. The jackets are so popular among thieves that they now bear a serial number for easier tracing.

Langlitz Leathers was started by Ross Langlitz in 1947. Unhappy with the motorcycle jacket he had purchased, Langlitz decided to make his own. His first jacket was so well done that many of his friends wanted one like it. After a couple of years of sewing jackets in his basement after work, Langlitz decided to go into business. His reputation for high-quality custom leathers was born and spread quickly. The basic styles that Ross designed in the 1940s are still the mainstay products today. The Columbia style is the flagship jacket and still the company's most popular one. It reflects the traditional look of motorcycling with its classically handsome and extremely practical design. Other products include the Cascade style, which is a sport-touring jacket; leather pants called Westerns, competition breeches, and rangers; and other leather-related motorcycle products.

The company not only sticks with tradition in its marketing, it also sticks with tradition in its production area. The shop is small (less than 3,000 square feet) and crowded. A total of 15 people work there with hundreds of leather garments hanging around. They cut and sew only about 6 garments a day. Half are custom created to a customer's measurements. The other half are built to stock pattern sizes for walk-in customers. High demand has caused the production time for custom work to fluctuate from less than half a year to more than a year and a half.

The current president of Langlitz Leathers, Dave Hansen (founder Ross Langlitz's son-in-law), says that although the company specializes in custom work, "it is not our desire to build fashion wear. We are a small family business and intend to remain that way for a long time. We currently have a long backlog of work orders. So, please don't ask us to build something we don't normally do. What we do, we do very well . . . and we want to keep it that way."

Discussion Questions

1. Does Langlitz Leathers fit the definition of an entrepreneurial organization? Explain.
2. How can a business with a backlog of orders of up to a year and a half stay in business?
3. What do you think are the keys to Langlitz Leathers' success?

(*Sources:* P. Fish, "Western Wanderings," *Sunset*, November 1999, p. 20; and information from company's Web site, **www.langlitz.com**, January 16, 2000.)

ENDNOTES

1. L. Buchanan, "Killer Apps," *Inc.*, May 1998, pp. 92–96.
2. T. Berry, *Business Plan Pro Version 3.0* (Palo Alto Software, 1998), p. 1.
3. Ibid., pp. 16–17.
4. R. Kalakota and M. Robinson, *e-Business: Roadmap for Success* (Reading, MA: Addison-Wesley, 1999, p. xvi).

Index

Notes

Notes

Notes

Notes